ABOUT THE AUTHORS

David M. Zesmer is currently Professor of English at the Illinois Institute of Technology. He has taught also at Marietta College, Hunter, Queens College, and City College (New York). He received his B.A., M.A., and Ph.D. degrees from Columbia University. Dr. Zesmer is the author of *Guide to Shakespeare* (in preparation), the editor of *Poems, Plays, and Essays of John Dryden,* and Coordinating Editor of the *Shakespeare Newsletter.*

Stanley B. Greenfield is Professor of English at the University of Oregon, and has taught at the University of Wisconsin and Queens College. He is the annual bibliographer for the Old English section of the Modern Language Association. During 1965–66 he was a John Simon Guggenheim Fellow in England. A number of articles by Dr. Greenfield on Old English poetry, notably the elegies, have appeared in English reviews and scholarly publications.

THE CANTERBURY PILGRIMS

COLLEGE OUTLINE SERIES

Guide to English Literature

From Beowulf through Chaucer and Medieval Drama

BY DAVID M. ZESMER

WITH BIBLIOGRAPHIES
BY STANLEY B. GREENFIELD

 BARNES & NOBLE, INC. NEW YORK

PUBLISHERS · BOOKSELLERS · SINCE 1873

Manufactured in the United States of America

TO MY FATHER

PREFACE

This book aims to provide a comparatively brief survey of Old and Middle English literature and to indicate some of the directions of recent scholarship and criticism. As the title implies, the book is a "guide." It is designed for students, both graduate and undergraduate, as well as for those readers outside the classroom who may wish to explore a rich literature with greater appreciation and understanding. One of its principal objectives is to be accurate and up-to-date in its information. At the same time, I have not found it possible—or even desirable—to conceal my own opinions and enthusiasms.

An important feature of this book is its carefully annotated bibliographies. The bibliographies and the text may be used independently, but both have been prepared in such a way as to complement and reinforce each other. It is hoped that they will help readers at all levels by synthesizing and evaluating the results of modern research, and the specialist may also find in them suggestive avenues for independent investigation. Occasionally there are cross references in the text to relevant items in the bibliographies. In such cases the abbreviation OEB refers to the Old English Bibliographical Guide and MEB to the Middle English Bibliographical Guide.

In order to sustain and illustrate points made in the text, I have quoted generously from Old and Middle English literary works. Apart from an early decision that *Beowulf* had to be quoted in translation and that Chaucer had to be quoted in the original Middle English, I made it a general rule to cite a passage in the original if, in my judgment, the twentieth-century reader could follow it with the aid of an occasional gloss. Thus, for example, quotations from *Pearl* and *The Owl and the Nightingale* have been modernized, while those from *Sir Orfeo* and the *Second Shepherds' Play* have not. One possible exception to the rule is *Piers Plowman*, which I have chosen to leave in the original—despite its difficulty—because I do not think its distinctive qualities can be adequately suggested in modernized versions.

I cannot hope to do justice to the "sondry folk" who have contributed to the shaping of this book; they must number "Wel nyne and twenty" and then some. I feel fortunate that my formal introduction to Old and Middle English literature took place under the tutelage of Roger Sherman Loomis and E. Talbot Donaldson, both of whom are reflected in these pages in ways almost impossible to specify. Many friends and colleagues have read portions of the manuscript and made helpful suggestions: Robert H. Ball, Charles A. Dahlberg, Joseph Raben, Robert A. Colby, Vineta Colby, Julian Franklin, Thelma Greenfield, and William Kinter. I have profited from the editorial and academic experience of Roger Walterhouse, Laurence Hawkins, Samuel Smith, Nancy Cone, and Françoise Bartlett—all of Barnes & Noble. Walter Clyde Curry read the entire manuscript of the text and the bibliographies, and his encouragement —to say nothing of his valuable criticisms—has meant a great deal to me. Dorothy Spector and John M. Clayton assisted diligently with the proofreading.

There are three faithful scholars and friends whom I must single out for a special word of thanks. James R. Kreuzer, of Queens College, read the entire manuscript in an earlier draft and offered incisive criticism that made the finished book—I hope—more respectable. James E. Tobin, also of Queens College, painstakingly read and criticized the final draft in the light of his vast knowledge of medieval life and thought; he also gave me the benefit of his impeccable sense of style. Stanley B. Greenfield, in addition to performing his official labors as bibliographer, read the whole manuscript, listened patiently as I aired an assortment of problems, and made countless suggestions—large and small—for the strengthening of the book.

I should like, finally, to express deep gratitude to my wife, Suzanne, and to my daughters, Jennie and Sarah. All three maintained over the years an indestructible cheerfulness that made the writing of this book a particular delight.

D. M. Z.

TABLE OF CONTENTS

Part One: The Old English Period

PART ONE
THE OLD ENGLISH PERIOD
(449–1066)

I: HISTORICAL AND LINGUISTIC BACKGROUND OF THE OLD ENGLISH PERIOD

In August, 1939, just before the outbreak of World War II, a private estate in southeastern Suffolk, Sutton Hoo by name, was making its own kind of history. Unearthed at Sutton Hoo were the remains of a magnificent ship-burial that took place sometime between A.D. 650 and 670. The wood of the ship had almost entirely rotted away, but the outline of the hull, more than eighty feet long, was still clearly imprinted in the sand. This "burial ship," while not the first to have been discovered by archaeologists, was certainly among the richest. It reflected the ancient Scandinavian practice (based on the concept that the dead were setting forth on a long journey) of surrounding the corpse of a king or hero with treasures and setting it afloat.

The Sutton Hoo "burial ship" had perhaps never been launched at sea, and it did not contain a body. In all probability it had served as a cenotaph, or memorial, to an Anglo-Saxon king whose body had been buried elsewhere or lost. Most scholars now believe that the man so honored was either the East Anglian King Anna, who died in 654, or his successor Æthelhere, who died one year later. Not only did the discovery command the attention of scholars, but its effects were felt in books for the general reader and in popular magazines throughout the world. Full-page color reproductions of the ship and some of the objects it contained were published in *Life* twelve years later, after the British Museum had completed its restoration of the treasure.*

Because the Sutton Hoo "ship-burial" was roughly contemporaneous with the great period of Old English literature and was perhaps less than a century earlier than the composition of *Beowulf* (which begins and ends with an account of funeral ceremonies per-

---

* *Life*, XXXII (July 16, 1951), 82–85. For an authoritative survey of the "burial ship," see R. S. Bruce-Mitford's Appendix to the third edition of Robert H. Hodgkin, *A History of the Anglo-Saxons* (3rd ed.; London: Oxford University Press, 1953), II, 696–734.

Silver Plate from Sutton Hoo burial ship.

formed over Scandinavian heroes), it inevitably stirred up fresh interest in the daily life of the Anglo-Saxons and substantially modified a long-standing conception of what these early invaders of England were like. It has been too easy to regard the Anglo-Saxons as barbarians, crude warriors out of the "Dark Ages" for whom life was a cheerless succession of murder and pillage. According to the popular image—and scholars, too, contributed to the image—these grim warriors brought to England an equally grim religion in which the major gods, like Woden and Thor, represented tremendous and fearful forces of nature that had to be dreaded, appeased, and cajoled. The dark of the night was dramatically infested with witches, trolls, and goblins who toyed cruelly with the lives of men. To combat these evil spirits, the "simple-minded" and "superstitious" pagans armed themselves with a battery of magical herbs and charms, but beyond the control of men and gods alike was Wyrd—relentless, implacable Fate. In such a romanticized context even *Beowulf,* the greatest monument to Anglo-Saxon literary culture, becomes distorted as a semibarbaric expression of meaningless ferocity in what is taken to have been a bleak and menacing world.

There may be a certain kernel of truth lurking in the foregoing notion of *earlier* Germanic life; but one need look no farther than Sutton Hoo to realize that the Anglo-Saxons, at least by the middle of the seventh century, had developed a many-sided culture. (Northumbria, in northern England, was in fact one of the greatest intellectual centers of the Western world during the seventh and eighth centuries.) In material wealth alone, these ancestors of modern England had reached a high level—witness, for example, the huge sword encrusted with garnets found in the cenotaph; the golden harness containing forty-one individual items of solid gold; the sixteen pieces of late classical silver of eastern Mediterranean origin; and the purse containing thirty-seven gold coins (which helped date the burial with reasonable exactitude). But there is also evidence of cultural wealth. The artistic workmanship of the gold is extremely fine. The small six-stringed harp implies that music and poetry occupied a prominent place in Anglo-Saxon court life. Moreover, the absence of any human remains in the grave, together with the placement of many unmistakably Christian objects where the body would ordinarily have been located, suggests that the cenotaph was built for a Christian king who presumably had been buried on holy grounds and who was being honored with this reminder of a pagan ritual that was rapidly becoming obsolete. A pair of spoons, inlaid with the names *Saulos* and *Paulos* (Saul and Paul) to recall Damascus, further emphasizes that the conversion of the Anglo-Saxons to Christianity had begun relatively early after their arrival in England.

Sutton Hoo, in short, confirmed the direction in which Anglo-Saxon studies had been steadily moving since about 1930 or earlier and have continued to move in recent years. The myth of Anglo-Saxon benightedness is giving way to an appreciation of the greatness and variety of Anglo-Saxon civilization.*

HISTORICAL BACKGROUND

In the middle of the fifth century several Germanic tribes invaded the British Isles and established permanent settlements there. They brought with them a language, a religion, and a poetic tradition. In time, their culture was transformed by natural processes from within and by invasions and other influences from without, the most im-

---

* See Dorothy Whitelock, *Changing Currents in Anglo-Saxon Studies: An Inaugural Lecture* (Cambridge: Cambridge University Press, 1958). (OEB 18.)

portant single force being the conversion of the island to Christianity early in the seventh century. Their society may seem remote from twentieth-century life, but from these Teutonic settlers date many of the basic social and political institutions of modern England.

The Anglo-Saxon Invasion (A.D. 449)

When Julius Caesar invaded Britain in 55 B.C., he found the island inhabited by a branch of the Celts, a people that included the Gauls. Caesar had to withdraw in the face of stiff resistance from the Celts. In A.D. 43, under Emperor Claudius, the Romans again invaded Britain, and their conquest of the island (south of the Clyde) was concluded by the year 85. Although England retains to this day some impressive remnants of the Roman occupation, that distant land was never regarded by the Romans as a very important stronghold. Consequently, when barbarians began to make attacks upon the heart of the Roman Empire (attacks which were to culminate in the collapse of the Empire), the occupation forces were recalled to Rome. Early in the fifth century the evacuation had been completed.

Shorn of virtually all military protection, Britain was an alluring prey to the restless Germanic tribes of the Continent. Our most reliable source for the details of the new invasion is the great scholar and historian Bede (673–735). According to Bede, the Anglo-Saxons came originally at the invitation of Vortigern, a fifth-century king of the Britons, who was fighting a war with the Picts and Scots. With Anglo-Saxon aid, Vortigern defeated the Picts, but he made the alarming discovery that his invited "guests" had no intention of being dislodged from the pleasant new home. Bede records that the Anglo-Saxons completed their betrayal of the Britons: they plundered, violated, and burned the native temples, and they murdered many native priests.*

The invaders, according to Bede, consisted of three Germanic tribes—the Angles, the Saxons, and the Jutes. The origins of all three, especially of the Jutes, are clouded in obscurity and controversy. It is almost certain that distinctions between Angles and Saxons had been blurred even before their migration to England. The term *Anglo-Saxon* originally differentiated the English from the Continental Saxons, but it came to include *all* the Germanic invaders,

---

* Bede, *The Ecclesiastical History of the English Nation,* translated by J. Stevenson, revised by L. C. Jane (Everyman's Library; London: J. M. Dent & Sons, Ltd.; New York: E. P. Dutton & Co., Inc., 1954), Book I, chap. 15.

England in the late sixth century. (Reprinted by permission from *History of England* by George M. Trevelyan. Copyright 1945, by Longmans, Green and Co., London.)

possibly because of the overwhelming prominence of the Saxons. Yet, surprisingly enough, *England* and *English* are derived from the word *Angle*. At any rate, by the end of the sixth century the Jutes occupied Kent (in the southeast); the Saxons held Sussex and Wessex (in the south); the Angles had settled in East Anglia (north of Kent), Mercia (in central England), and Northumbria (in the north, bordering on Scotland). Tribal affiliations soon gave way to somewhat loose political units, small kingdoms based upon new geographic ties.

To the Roman historian Tacitus we are indebted for a picturesque account of the early Germanic tribes. It should be remembered, however, that his *Germania* (the full English title is *On the Origin, Geography, Institutions, and Tribes of the Germans*) was written in A.D. 98, three and a half centuries before the Anglo-Saxon invasion, and therefore cannot be accepted as an authoritative guide to English life in the fifth and sixth centuries. Moreover, when Tacitus wishes to moralize upon the degeneracy of his fellow Romans, he tends to idealize the simplicity, independence, and fierce bravery of the Germans; on other occasions he can be quite critical—as in his statement that the Germanic mind, when not occupied with war, was "sunk in sloth." Still and all, Tacitus' comments are of considerable interest.

The social unit of the Germans, says Tacitus, was the family or clan. Each member bore responsibility for any wrongs inflicted or suffered by his kinsmen; included among his duties was the obligation to execute revenge or to arrive at a peaceful settlement through the payment of a predetermined value in money or property (*wergyld*). Tacitus also explains what he calls the *comitatus*, a quasi-feudal arrangement whereby a youth would attach himself to a strong leader. In exchange for economic and legal protection, the young man (*gesith* or *thegn*) offered military service. The chief, writes Tacitus, fought for victory, and the followers fought for their chief. If the *gesith* retreated from the field after his leader had been killed, he suffered reproach and infamy for the rest of his life.*

Whatever his limitations, Tacitus sheds a good deal of light upon the social organization of the Germanic tribes as reflected in *Beowulf* (for example, the *comitatus* relationship and the duty of revenge) and in other Old English poems. Moreover, the structure of Anglo-Saxon society at least partially conforms to his detailed and colorful description.

* See Tacitus, *Germania,* secs. XIV, XV, XXI.

The Coming of Christianity (A.D. 597)

Many Celts had been Christianized during the Roman occupation, and in the middle of the fifth century St. Patrick, himself a newly converted Christian, converted Ireland. The conversion of the English began in 597, when Pope Gregory I ("the Great") sent a mission across the Channel.

To account for Gregory's desire to bring Christianity to Britain, Bede tells an attractive story. One day, in the market place in Rome, Gregory chanced to meet some handsome captives being sold as slaves. When he found out that they were pagans, he sighed deeply. "Alas! what pity," he is quoted as saying, "that the author of darkness is possessed of men of such fair countenances; and that being remarkable for such graceful aspects, their minds should be void of inward grace." When told, further, that they were called "Angles," Gregory replied with a kindly play on words: " 'Right,' said he, 'for they have an Angelic face, and it becomes such to be coheirs with the Angels in heaven.' " * Gregory then sent a mission to England led by St. Augustine, who became the first Archbishop of Canterbury (not to be confused with the greater St. Augustine, author of the *City of God*). He instructed Augustine to proceed slowly with the conversion. Pagan customs were not to be immediately stamped out but were, instead, to be gradually remolded. This policy of moderation may explain the sometimes awkward mixture of pagan and Christian elements such as one finds commingled in the Sutton Hoo burial as well as in other expressions of Anglo-Saxon culture.

Augustine converted Kent and made Canterbury the seat of the Roman Church in England, and in 627 Paulinus converted King Edwin of Northumbria. The latter event is unforgettably re-created by Bede: In order to decide whether to accept the Christian religion, Edwin calls a solemn council. The characters as portrayed by Bede emerge with skillfully differentiated personalities and opinions. The chief priest, Coifi, wearily confesses to the king that the old religion does not seem to be of much material use. "For none of your people has applied himself more diligently to the worship of our gods than I; and yet there are many who receive greater favors from you, and obtain greater dignity than I, and are more prosperous in all

---

* Bede, *The Ecclesiastical History of the English Nation*, Book II, chap. 1. (Everyman's Library; London: J. M. Dent & Sons, Ltd.; New York: E. P. Dutton & Co., Inc., 1954.) Reprinted by permission of the publishers.

their undertakings." In his disillusionment he is willing to try any new doctrine. Another priest confirms Coifi's opinion, then urges, in an arresting figure of speech that is one of the highlights of Anglo-Saxon literature, that the Christian religion may offer a more satisfying haven for man during his all-too-brief life on earth:

> O king, the present life of man on earth seems to me, in comparison with the time of which we are ignorant, as if you were sitting at a feast with your chief men and thanes in the winter time, and a fire were kindled in the midst and the hall warmed, while everywhere outside there were raging whirlwinds of wintry rain and snow; and as if then there came a stray sparrow, and swiftly flew through the house, entering at one door and passing out through another. As long as he is inside, he is not buffeted by the winter's storm; but in the twinkling of an eye the lull for him is over, and he speeds from winter back to winter again, and is gone from your sight.*

"So this life of man," he goes on, "appeareth for a little time; but what cometh after, or what went before, we know not." The decision is made to accept Christianity, and Coifi himself publicly profanes the old idols and temples which he had at one time consecrated.

There were, indeed, several differences between the church under Irish leadership, centered on the island of Iona, and the church in the rest of the islands, where leaders followed the liturgical practice determined at Rome. The North, generally, followed Irish leadership; the South, that of Rome. The Synod of Whitby (664) resolved the differences—at least, officially.

It is virtually impossible to overestimate the importance of the coming of Christianity to England. The new religion brought Mediterranean civilization to the island and imbued that civilization with fresh life. Theodore of Tarsus, Archbishop of Canterbury from 668 to 690, came with parchment and books, together with a genuine reverence for learning. Monasteries at Canterbury, York, and Jarrow (Bede's monastery in Northumbria) emerged as internationally esteemed citadels of Latin and Greek scholarship. Literature had been transmitted orally before the middle of the seventh century, but now the clerics in monasteries committed works to writing in order to preserve an accurate and unbroken literary and scholarly tradition. Besides copying Latin manuscripts, clerics began to create

---

* Bede, *The Ecclesiastical History of the English Nation*, Book II, chap. 13. Translation is from *Select Translations from Old English Prose*, ed. by Albert S. Cook and C. B. Tinker (Boston: Ginn and Company, 1908), p. 32. Reprinted by permission of the publisher.

original compositions both in Latin and in the English vernacular. Thus, the English Christians, while remembering an older culture, looked ahead toward new and exciting growth.*

The Danish Invasion

Near the end of the eighth century the vikings, bands of Danish and Norwegian adventurers (mostly Danish), started to make periodic raids on the English coast. These raids grew in number and intensity. Not long after the middle of the ninth century, the invaders, having ravaged Northumbria, turned southward in an attempt to finish the subjugation of Wessex.

But Wessex was blessed with one of the great political and military leaders of the Western world—Alfred the Great (849–899). Alfred organized a strong and unified defense against these marauders who were threatening the complete overthrow of Anglo-Christian civilization. He stopped the enemy at the Battle of Edington (878); many of the Danes, under the terms of the Treaty of Wedmore, accepted Christianity and retired peacefully to the Danelaw, the territory which they occupied in northeastern England. Alfred then established Wessex as a new center of English culture by encouraging literary production, by improving educational standards throughout the country, and by attracting scholars to his court from other parts of England and from the Continent.

For some time after the death of Alfred, Wessex continued to flourish. But toward the end of the tenth century, during the reign of Ethelred the Unready, the Danes renewed their assaults. In 1017 a Danish military leader, Cnut, or Canute, occupied the English throne (this able man became King of Denmark, too). Nevertheless, Anglo-Christian culture, which had been guarded and reinforced by Alfred, the first truly English national champion, proved healthy enough to survive the Danish invasion.

THE DEVELOPMENT OF THE ENGLISH LANGUAGE

In Sir Lawrence Olivier's motion-picture version of *Hamlet*, the hero, breaking away from Horatio and Marcellus, who would restrain him from following the ghost of his father, is heard to utter an angry

---

* On the conversion, see George O. Sayles, *The Medieval Foundations of England* (Philadelphia: University of Pennsylvania Press, 1950), pp. 35–56; and Hodgkin, *op. cit.*, I, 245 ff. The impact of Christianity on England is described by George M. Trevelyan, *History of England* (3rd ed.; New York: Longmans Green & Co., 1945), p. 49.

threat: "By heaven, I'll make a ghost of him that hinders me!" A glance at Shakespeare's text, however, reveals that Hamlet really says, "By heaven, I'll make a ghost of him that *lets* me!" Now this Elizabethan meaning for *let* still survives, although faintly, in the legal formula, "without let or hindrance." But the producers of the film, for better or for worse, made the change in Shakespeare's text on the assumption that a mass audience in the twentieth century would not understand what Hamlet meant if the word *lets* were retained.

The reader of Shakespeare, or even of Chaucer (who wrote some two centuries earlier), need make only minor readjustments in order to understand and appreciate the language of these poets. But if one opens *Beowulf* in the original Old English, he faces what is, in effect, a foreign language:

> Hwaet, wē Gār-Dena   in gēardagum,
> þeodcyninga   þrym gefrūnon,
> hū ðā aeþelingas   ellen fremedon! *

These examples bear out the fact that English, like other languages, has continually changed and continues to change in response to fresh influences. New habits slowly develop among those who use the language, and drastic modifications take place as a result of contacts with foreign cultures through trade, migration, and war. Sometimes a new field of learning catapults into public recognition—nuclear physics or rocket science, for instance—with the eventual result that portions of a highly specialized vocabulary filter down into popular usage.

Our present-day English language is the product of several thousand years of such evolution. In 1786 Sir William Jones, an orientalist with the East India Company, hypothesized a common linguistic origin for ancient Sanskrit, Greek, Latin, and their modern descendants, including English. Consider, for example, the English word *father:* its affinity with the German *Vater*, the Dutch *vader*, and even with the Latin *pater* had long been recognized. But *father*, Sir William emphasized, is also linked with the Gothic *fadar*, the Old Norse *faðir*, the Greek *patēr*, the Old Irish *athir*, and—this was the newest and most crucial part of his theory—the Sanskrit *pitar*. It was on the basis of such evidence that Sir William formulated his "Indo-European

* Fr. Klaeber (ed.), *Beowulf and the Fight at Finnsburg* (3rd ed.; Boston: D. C. Heath and Company, 1936, with Supplements, 1941, 1950). Reprinted by permission of the publisher.

Hypothesis," now generally accepted in its broad outline. Elaborations of the hypothesis were made by classical philologists and, later, by those interested in the Germanic languages. Jacob Grimm (better known for his collaboration with his brother on a collection of fairy tales) is one of the latter group and is remembered among linguists for his formulation of the systematic consonant changes which distinguish the Germanic languages, of which English is one, from other members of the Indo-European family.

The problems posed by the Indo-European language are enormously difficult, and scholars can at best offer only conjectures as to what may have happened historically. Inasmuch as there is no universal agreement as to details of origin, terminology, and classification, it will be convenient here simply to present one view that has won a substantial body of adherents.

The ancestral Indo European language (sometimes called Indo-Germanic) was presumably spoken, perhaps in the neighborhood of Lithuania and southern Russia, long before written history. As early as 2500 B.C. it split into nine main branches: Indian, Iranian, Armenian, Hellenic, Albanian, Italic, Balto-Slavic, Teutonic (Germanic), and Celtic. The Hittite language, discovered in relatively recent years, is often regarded as a tenth branch; but some scholars have postulated an older language, "Indo-Hittite," from which Indo-European and Hittite both evolved. In any case, these branches of Indo-European became, in time, subdivided. The Hellenic branch, for example, gave rise to Ancient Greek and, subsequently, Modern Greek; the Italic branch produced Latin and the Romance languages, Balto-Slavic numbers among its descendants Lettic, Lithuanian, Polish, and Russian. Teutonic, with which students of English literature are mainly concerned, branched into North Teutonic, East Teutonic, and West Teutonic. North Teutonic is the parent language of Icelandic and of the modern Scandinavian tongues; East Teutonic produced Gothic, now extinct; and from West Teutonic have emerged, among others, English, German, Flemish, and Dutch. English, then, is a member of a large and ancient family of languages.*

English itself falls into three major periods: Old English or "Anglo-

* For a readable account of the origin and development of Indo-European, one written by a distinguished comparative philologist, see Paul Thieme, "The Indo-European Language," *Scientific American,* CXCIX (October, 1958), 63–74. See also Albert C. Baugh, *A History of the English Language* (2nd ed.; New York: Appleton-Century-Crofts, 1957), chap. 2; and Otto Jespersen, *Growth and Structure of the English Language* (9th ed.; New York: The Macmillan Company, 1955).

Saxon" (449 to 1066), Middle English (1066 to 1485), and Modern English (1485 to the present day). The development has, of course, been gradual, and the dates suggested are at best only convenient landmarks. The year 449 is the date traditionally taken as marking the beginning of the Anglo-Saxon invasion; 1066 is the date of the Norman Conquest; 1485 marks the accession of Henry VII, first of the Tudors, to the English throne. The linguistic distance traveled can be gauged if a reader examines the Lord's Prayer in Old English (the characters ð and þ corresponding to our *th*):

> Faeder ūre, Þū þe eart on heofonum, sī þīn nama gehālgod. To-becume þīn rīce. Gewurþe ðīn willa on eorðan swā swā on heofonum. Ūrne gedaeghwāmlīcan hlāf syle ūs tō daeg. And forgyf ūs ūre gyltas, swā swā wē forgyfað ūrum gyltendum. And ne gelǣd þū ūs on costnunge, ac ālȳs ūs of yfele. Sōþlīce.

> Our Father which art in heaven, hallowed be thy name. Thy kingdom come. Thy will be done in earth, as it is in heaven. Give us this day our daily bread. And forgive us our debts, as we forgive our debtors. And lead us not into temptation, but deliver us from evil. . . . Amen.*

The foregoing quotation suggests how Old English differs from Modern English in spelling and pronunciation. To cite just an example or two, *faeder* (pronounced "fadder") is now *father*, and *tō daeg* (pronounced roughly "toe-die") is our single word *today*. Equally striking are differences in grammar. Notice, for instance, the initial *ge* in *gehālgod*, which has disappeared entirely from the present-day participle *hallowed*. Old English, like Latin and Modern German, is inflectional: verbs have person, number, and tense; nouns, pronouns, and adjectives have case, number, and gender—all indicated by endings added to a root or by internal change. *Forgyf* is an imperative, but *wē forgyfað* is first-person plural, present indicative; *um* is added to *heofon* (heaven) to make *heofonum*, object of the preposition *on* (in). An example of internal change (one that is not found in the Lord's Prayer) appears in the formation of the plural *menn* from the singular *mann*—a practice retained in this instance down to the present time. Unlike the almost inflectionless Modern English, in which clarity requires a virtually inflexible word order, Old English permitted the writer considerable freedom in arranging his words. The word order of "faeder ūre" or "gewurþe ðīn willa" would not ordinarily be possible in Modern English.

* Matthew 6:9–13 (King James Version).

Perhaps the most formidable difference between Old English and Modern English is in vocabulary. Old English was essentially unilingual: instead of borrowing from other languages it formed new words out of its own native resources. Take the word *mōd*, "heart" or "spirit" (*mood* in Modern English). Add *ig* and you have *mōdig* (spirited); add *lic* to that and you have *mōdiglic* (magnanimous). Combine *mōd* and *craeft* (craft, skill), and the result is *mōdcraeft* (intelligence). Place *guþ* (war) in front of *mōd* and you have formed *guþmōd* (warlike). And *unmōd* means "despondency." Old English also uses "self-explaining compounds." *Daegred*, "day red," means "dawn." *Eorþcraeft*, "earth craft," becomes the Old English word for "geometry."

The Old English vocabulary shows only the faintest connections with that of the Romance languages. Some Latin words, to be sure, had been absorbed while the Germanic tribes were still on the European continent; and although surprisingly few Latin words remained from the Roman occupation of Britain (probably because the English had little cultural contact with the Romanized Celts), others came to England with Christianity. But the English language was yet to be enriched by French importations—"temptation," for example, to replace Old English *costnunge* (the dative case of *costnung*) in the Lord's Prayer. These French additions arrived with the Normans, and they comprise more than half of our present-day vocabulary.*

Old English, which resembled the Old Frisian and Old Saxon employed in northern and southern Germany, survives in manuscripts and relics in four major dialects: Northumbrian, Mercian, Kentish, and West Saxon. But most of the extant literature in Old English, whatever the place and date of its original composition, is found in West Saxon (Wessex) manuscripts of about the year 1000. With Northumbrian culture virtually obliterated by the Danes, the Wessex of King Alfred for a long time set the pattern for literary English. But the Norman Conquest was to shift the social and political center of England from Wessex to London, a predominantly Mercian area. Modern English, as we usually speak of it, proceeded to evolve largely from London English.

It has been the purpose of this chapter to explore the nature of the culture which the Anglo-Saxons brought to England and to indicate the qualities of the West Germanic language which they spoke. Subsequent chapters will reveal that the Anglo-Saxons have bequeathed

* On Old English vocabulary, see Baugh, *op. cit.*, secs. 48–50.

an important literary legacy. The Old English writings that have
come down to us, especially the epic *Beowulf*, live not merely as documents in social and linguistic history but as literature of undeniable
artistic and emotional power.

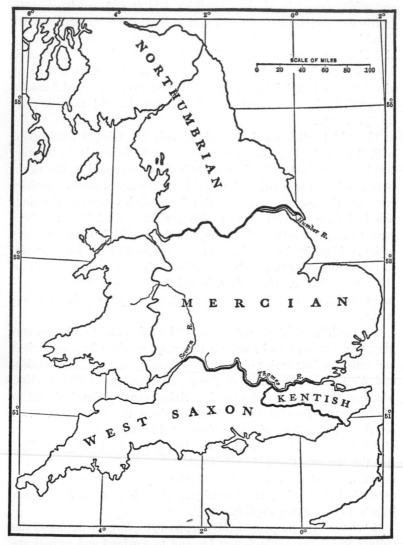

The dialects of Old English. (Reprinted by permission from *A History of the
English Language*, Second Edition, by Albert C. Baugh. Copyright © 1957,
Appleton-Century-Crofts, Inc.)

II: ANGLO–SAXON LITERARY CULTURE

Behind the literary products of the Anglo-Saxons, especially the poetry, lies a long oral tradition developed during the time when the Germanic tribes still inhabited the European continent. Early Germanic poetry was composed and recited by the *scop* ("shaper"), a professional bard who may have often wandered from court to court hoping to acquire the patronage of some generous lord. At court feasts the *scop* would celebrate in song the deeds of real or legendary heroes out of the remote past—Sigemund the Volsung, for example, whose triumph over a dragon is the theme of one of the lays sung by the bard at Hrothgar's court in *Beowulf*. Audiences must have delighted in hearing these glorious exploits recited over and over because many of the warriors immortalized by the *scop* had achieved the status of ancestral heroes. These illustrious figures were part of the legacy which the Anglo-Saxon invaders brought with them to England.

Harp from Sutton Hoo burial ship.

But with the conversion of England to Christianity, the subject matter of poetry underwent a crucial change. Poetry and prose were committed to writing, and, with the Church virtually monopolizing the art of copying old works and creating new ones, the clerics generally preserved only such material as was considered serviceable to Christianity. The distinction which literary scholars used to make between "pagan" and "Christian" literature does not help much in classifying Old English poetry (and prose), for mere survival in writing almost guarantees that a work is more or less Christian. The Old English poets either used Christian material from Scripture or the liturgy, or they tried, with varying degrees of success, to fit subjects of pagan derivation into the framework of the Christian universe. In the Anglo-Saxon mind Christ and His disciples could be visualized in a *comitatus* relationship; God absorbed the functions of Wyrd (Fate), whom He for the most part superseded; Beowulf could be comprehended as an ideal Christian king who had not been entirely divested of the thirst for worldly glory that motivated the Germanic warrior.

The verse patterns utilized by Old English poets also represented an accumulation of centuries of oral tradition. The poetic line, which was really two half-lines separated by a distinct pause, contained four accented syllables and a varying number of unaccented syllables. It was once thought that each of the four stressed syllables was accompanied by chords struck by the *scop* on a small harp, like the one unearthed at Sutton Hoo; but a newer and more plausible theory emphasizes the rests that often occur before unaccented initial syllables and suggests that the *scop* may have struck his harp during these rests.*

Old English poets rarely used end rhyme, but they regularly used a system of alliteration. This alliteration involved the initial sounds, whether vowels or consonants, of the four stressed syllables. As a rule, three of the stressed syllables were alliterated, and it was the initial sound of the *third* accented syllable that normally determined the alliteration. The pattern can be readily seen in the fourth and fifth lines of *Beowulf*:

> Oft *Sc*yld *Sc*ēfing   *sc*eaþena þrēatum,
> *m*onegum *m*ǣgþum   *m*eodosetla oftēah.

* See John C. Pope, *The Rhythm of Beowulf* (New Haven: Yale University Press, 1942). (OEB 52.)

Observe the following more extended sample describing the monster Grendel's approach to the Danish hall—a passage quoted both in the original Old English and in the verse translation by Charles W. Kennedy, who attempts to re-create some of the alliterative effect in Modern English: *

> Đā cōm of mōre   under misthleoþum
> Grendel gongan,   Godes yrre baer;
> mynte se mānscaða   manna cynnes
> sumne besyrwan   in sele þām hēan.
> Wōd under wolcnum   tō þaes þe hē wīnreced,
> goldsele gumena   gearwost wisse
> faēttum fāhne.

> From the stretching moors,   from the misty hollows,
> Grendel came creeping,   accursed of God,
> A murderous ravager   minded to snare
> Spoil of heroes   in high-built hall.
> Under clouded heavens   he held his way
> Till there rose before him   the high-roofed house,
> Wine-hall of warriors   gleaming with gold.

(ll. 710–16)

The pounding rhythm, in conjunction with the alliteration, conveys an impression of unrelenting strength. Although alliteration is no longer the chief basis of our prosody, it remains an indispensable tool of English rhetoric and is commonly used by writers of both poetry and prose. †

Rhythm and alliteration were not the only poetic devices. In order to achieve variety, as well as to suggest important attributes of his subject, the *scop* would frequently introduce a kind of metaphor called the *kenning*, a compound of two terms used in place of a common word. The sun, for example, could be referred to as "world-candle"; the prince, as "ring-giver"; the ocean, as "sea-monster's home" or "gannet's bath." To be sure, the kenning sometimes degenerated into a cliché; the uninspired poet found "life's house" a ready-made circumlocution for *body,* and a prince in Old English po-

---

* From *Beowulf* by Charles W. Kennedy. Copyright 1940 by Oxford University Press, Inc. Reprinted by permission of the publisher.

† The alliterative tradition was to decline during the years following the Norman Conquest, but its "revival" in the fourteenth century produced two of the most gifted poets of the Middle Ages—the *Pearl* (or *Gawain*) poet and William Langland. (See Chapter X.)

etry is almost automatically called "ring-giver." Still, the kenning in the hands of a talented poet could provide a fresh appeal to the imagination of the audience.

Two other rhetorical techniques of Old English verse deserve mention here—*variation* and *litotes*. Variation has been defined as "the use of equivalents for poetic purposes." * The poem *Widsith*, for example, begins (in modern English) as follows:

> Widsith spoke,   his word-hoard unlocked.

The second half of the line furnishes no additional information: its intention is purely decorative. Variation is employed as the messenger in *Beowulf* announces that the hero is dead:

> "Our leader lies low,   the lord of the Weders,
> The king of the Geats,   on the couch of death.
> He sleeps his last sleep   by the deeds of the worm."

The technique of variation, it should be observed, is not restricted to Old English poetry, but it seems to be a prominent stylistic feature of a good deal of poetry intended for recitation. *Litotes* may be defined as ironic negative statement or understatement. The *Exodus* poet (see p. 54), exulting over the spectacle of the Egyptians drowning in the Red Sea, tersely observes that they were not very happy: "Less blithe was their boasting." In *Beowulf*, when Grendel, who for twelve years has nightly gorged himself on the flesh of Danish warriors whom he has slain, is at last caught in the deadly handgrip of the hero, the poet comments,

> Far different his fate
> From that which befell him   in former days!

"Sorry the venture," the poet continues, "The raid that the ravager made on the hall." Here understatement is most effective, coming as it does after the poet's gory description of the fight.

A tremendous amount of Old English literature has perished, and much of that which has survived is in fragmentary form. Regarding the poems and fragments we *do* have, moreover, there are staggering problems of authorship and dates of composition.

Most of the extant Old English poetry is in four manuscripts, all somewhat damaged, compiled around the year 1000 in the West

---

* See Kemp Malone, in *A Literary History of England,* ed. Albert C. Baugh (New York: Appleton-Century-Crofts, 1948), pp. 28–29.

Saxon dialect: (1) the *Beowulf* MS (in the Cotton collection of the British Museum), which contains *Beowulf* and *Judith;* (2) the Junius MS (in the Bodleian Library at Oxford), which has the "Caedmonian" poems (but not Caedmon's *Hymn,* which is quoted in Latin by Bede); (3) the Exeter Book (in Exeter Cathedral), which includes *Widsith,* riddles, elegies, and some "Cynewulfian" poems; and (4) the Vercelli MS (at Vercelli, in northern Italy), which includes *Andreas* and the *Dream of the Rood.*

The manuscripts may date from around 1000, but in all probability most of the poems and fragments mentioned in the foregoing paragraph were composed at a much earlier date. Linguistic scholars have found in these predominantly Wessex manuscripts numerous traces of earlier Anglian dialectal forms, evidence that the poems may have been originally written in a Mercian or Northumbrian dialect and later translated into West Saxon by scribes who simply left many of the Anglian words undisturbed. Mercian or Northumbrian origin would suggest the "Age of Bede," that period around the first quarter of the eighth century when Anglian culture was at its peak. Some scholars, however, believe that a standard artificial poetic diction may have been adopted for use throughout England some time before the year 1000.* As regards dates, then, linguistic tests are significant but by no means conclusive.

What are we in a position to decide? Not very much. The authorship and dates of composition of particular Old English poems remain unsolved mysteries. There is one partial exception to the preceding statement: the poet Cynewulf, who lived in the late eighth or early ninth century, was obliging enough to leave his signature embedded in runic characters in four poems (see p. 56). But although Cynewulf is the only Old English poet with whom we can safely identify a definite body of extant verse, we know practically nothing about him as a person.

With prose, however, we are on much surer ground. Most of the significant English prose of the period may be linked with specific writers of the late ninth, tenth, and eleventh centuries. The man most responsible for the development of literary prose during the Old English period was Alfred the Great (849–899), who, as part of his systematic efforts to make Wessex a center of English culture, translated or caused to be translated into English certain important

---

* Jespersen, *op. cit.,* sec. 53; Kenneth Sisam, *Studies in the History of Old English Literature* (Oxford: Oxford University Press, 1953), pp. 119–39.

Latin texts. Other English prose writers include the Abbott Ælfric (*c.* 955–*c.* 1020) and Bishop Wulfstan (d. 1023), both of whom are mainly remembered for their homilies (though Ælfric also translated the first seven books of the Bible into English).

As might be expected, many of the earliest works written by English churchmen were in Latin; and throughout the Old English period, as well as during the Middle Ages and thereafter, a number of English writers—John Milton, to cite a distinguished example—continued to produce sizable quantities of Latin verse and prose. Anglo-Latin literature in the Old English period, at least the fragments that remain, was often didactic, its principal functions being to provide religious instruction or inspiration; but Anglo-Latin literature boasts a few writings which combine charm with piety and still others which can almost be called secular. Alcuin (735–804) composed, in addition to doctrinal tracts, an important commentary on the Book of Genesis. Aldhelm (640?–709) was a skillful writer of Latin verse (and of songs in English, which have been lost) and a pioneer in various kinds of religious prose. The historians Gildas (516?–570?) and Nennius (fl. 796) left us, together with some valuable facts, a good deal of wonderful fantasy about semilegendary figures from British history. Asser (d. 909?) wrote an illuminating biography of Alfred the Great.

The outstanding representative of Anglo-Latin culture was, of course, Bede (673–735). In his monastery at Jarrow, in Northumbria, an institution that for Christian scholarship ranked with the finest on the European continent, Bede encompassed many areas of intellectual accomplishment. He wrote Latin treatises on medicine, astronomy, mathematics, and philosophy; he was also a biographer. His immortal achievement, however, was in the field of history.

Bede's monumental *Historia Ecclesiastica Gentis Anglorum* (*Ecclesiastical History of the English People*) traces the history of England from Caesar's invasion, in 55 B.C., to 731, the year in which the *Historia* was completed. The first writer to conceive of the English as one people with a single destiny, Bede would have his readers become more familiar "with the actions and sayings of former men of renown, especially of our own nation." * To make his narrative still more attractive, he introduces anecdotes, dramatic speeches, miracles

* Bede, *The Ecclesiastical History of the English Nation,* Book I, Preface. (Everyman's Library; London: J. M. Dent & Sons, Ltd.; New York: E. P. Dutton & Co., Inc., 1954). Reprinted by permission of the publishers.

—all designed to show the Christian ideal as the most compelling force in the universe. Bede distinguishes to the best of his abilities fact from hearsay; he always mentions his sources and assesses their reliability, and he often reproduces authentic documents of inestimable value to present-day historians. Modern readers may experience difficulty in reconciling his integrity as a historian with his acceptance of miracles and his frequent mention of fantastic events—a river that dries up in order that a holy man may travel more quickly to his place of martyrdom, prophetic visions, journeys to and from the other world, extraordinary cures effected by the relics of holy men. For Bede, as well as for the rest of his age, miracles were considered real occurrences, dramatic evidence of God's direct intervention in the affairs of men. On the other hand, he and the preachers of his day often employed imaginary stories, recognized as fictional, to illustrate a point of doctrine. To Bede, for example, it was much more important that a holy man have power to stem an actual tide of evil than that he stop a rushing river in a story.

For a long time after the Norman Conquest, Latin held its own in many important areas of discourse. It was the language of law, the language of international relations, the language of treaties, and the language of scholarship (religious and secular). Latin, moreover, was the language used in the schools as late as Milton's time, in the first half of the seventeenth century; even after its eventual surrender to English, it was to remain an integral part of England's intellectual life for several centuries. Judged merely as literature, the Latin writings of the Anglo-Saxons, with the exception of the works of Bede, may not rank very high. But as a measure of the level of culture achieved and sustained in Anglo-Saxon England they are extremely valuable.*

* On Anglo-Latin literature, see Kemp Malone, in *A Literary History of England,* ed. Albert C. Baugh, pp. 12–19; and George K. Anderson, *The Literature of the Anglo-Saxons* (Princeton: Princeton University Press, 1949), pp. 212–41.

III: BEOWULF AND THE HEROIC TRADITION

The principal focus of this chapter is upon one major work that could have been created only in a rich and diversified culture. *Beowulf* is not an isolated literary phenomenon, for perhaps the most striking element in the mature art of the poem is the way in which its author took historical and legendary materials from the Germanic past, materials pagan in origin and outlook, and, using the poetic form and style inherited from this past, transmuted them into a unified epic that gave effective expression to a Christian view of the universe.

We shall first consider the heroic tradition as it is reflected in Old English poetry that is perhaps earlier than *Beowulf;* then explore some of the facets of this exciting poem which infused Christianity into the fabric of the heroic tradition; and, finally, observe how the heroic spirit was introduced into works, like *Andreas* and *Judith,* dealing with religious subjects.

EARLY POEMS OF GERMANIC LEGEND *

An *epic* may be defined as a long narrative poem which concentrates upon the exploits of a single hero, usually someone prominent in the history or folklore of a particular tribe or nation. Although no complete Old English epic survives from the earlier "heroic" age, we fortunately possess a few poems or poetic fragments—among them *Widsith, Waldere,* and *The Fight at Finnsburg*—which are interesting in themselves and which shed light upon the Continental backgrounds of the Germanic invaders, thereby helping to place the epic *Beowulf* in proper historical, intellectual, and artistic perspective.

Widsith (650–700?)

In *Widsith,* a "digest" of heroic history and myth, parts of which may be the earliest extant poetry in the English language, Widsith

* Quotations from *Widsith, Waldere,* and *The Fight at Finnsburg* are from *The Earliest English Poetry* by Charles W. Kennedy. Copyright 1943. Reprinted by permission of Oxford University Press, Inc.

("Far Traveler"), an idealized *scop,* unlocks his "word-hoard" and
boasts of the faraway places he has seen and the mighty princes he
has allegedly served. It does not matter that some of the masters
Widsith claims to have entertained during the course of his prodigious globe-trotting were separated historically by nearly two centuries. (Eormanric, for example, ruled the Goths around 375, and
Ælfwine flourished around the year 568.) Nor does it even matter that
Widsith is negligible as poetry, much of it little more than a catalogue of famous names. What really counts is that through a wealth
of allusion that must have enkindled the imagination of his hearers
or readers, the poet has left a splendid "who's who" of kings and
kingdoms of the heroic age. *Widsith* is also interesting because of
the immense pride the *scop* displays in his craft; when Widsith
lifted his harp and sang, his more discriminating patrons avowed that
they had never heard better music. But patronage is never certain,
and the future is vague in its prospects. The minstrel wanders wearily wherever Fate takes his steps, always searching for a generous
lord who will protect him "until light and life fall in ruin together."

Waldere and The Fight at Finnsburg (c. 750?)

Fragments of two heroic tales survive in Old English, both, oddly
enough, as flyleaves for manuscripts of sermons. Full versions of the
Waldere story exist in other languages, including a tenth-century
Latin poem *Waltharius.* And while no complete account of the *Finn*
story is extant, we do have the "Lay of Finnsburg" sung by Hrothgar's *scop* in *Beowulf,* a tale that deals with some later consequences
of the fight described in the Old English *Finnsburg* fragment.

In the complete *Waltharius* the hero, Walther of Aquitaine, and
his bride-to-be, Hildegund, who are hostages of Attila the Hun, escape together and proceed toward Aquitaine. They are intercepted
by Gunther, king of the Franks, and by Hagen, Walther's former
comrade, now in league with Gunther to despoil him of the treasure
he has carried away from the Huns. After a furious battle, Walther
and Hagen are reconciled, and the hero takes Hildegund to reign as
his queen in Aquitaine. Meanwhile, Gunther and Hagen return to
their Frankish land.

The Old English *Waldere* fragment consists of two spirited
speeches. In the first, Hildeguth (Hildegund) encourages Waldere
before combat and assures her beloved that God will preserve his
heart from fear. In the second speech, a typical prebattle boast,

Waldere, wearing a coat of mail, dares the haughty Guthhere (Gunther) to remove it from his shoulders:

> Try and take, if you dare,
> Battle-worn though I be,   my good gray byrny.
> Here it lies on my shoulders,   shining with gold.
>
> .   .   .   .
>
> It fails me not   when the false and unfriendly
> Renew their tricks,   and attack me with swords
> As ye have done.

Judged by the two samples, *Waldere* in its entirety must have been a vigorous poem.

On the basis of the *Finnsburg* fragment and the "Lay of Finnsburg," it is possible to piece together a more or less continuous story of a bitter feud between the Danes and the Frisians. The reason for the feud is nowhere explained, but the events related in the fragment occur during an interval of so-called peace. One night, while the Danes under King Hnaef are visiting King Finn and his Frisians at Finnsburg, the Frisians treacherously attack their guests and kill Hnaef and his men. Hengest, Hnaef's successor, concludes a truce with the Frisians; but after many months of inner conflict, during which time he is torn between keeping the peace and avenging the earlier attack, he resumes the feud. In an ensuing battle Finn is killed and the Frisians are defeated. Hengest enjoys the satisfaction of knowing that he has not let his countrymen go unmourned and unavenged.

The *Finnsburg* fragment, however, includes only the initial clash at Finnsburg. We hear the ill-fated Hnaef rousing his sleeping followers to resolute action. The glimmer of light the Danes have seen is neither the dawn, nor a flying dragon, nor a burning fire—but Frisian men armed for attack:

> Awake, my warriors!   Grasp your shields!
> Fight like men   in the front of battle!
> Be bold of mood;   be mindful of glory!

For five days the Danes hold fast while the swords flash amid a deafening clamor. At this point the *Finnsburg* fragment ends abruptly. From *Waldere* and *The Fight at Finnsburg* the reader may gain a vivid insight into some of the ideals of Germanic life as described by Tacitus—a life that demanded fervent loyalty to the tribe and expected wholehearted revenge in behalf of a wronged kinsman.

BEOWULF *
(650–750?)

It will be remembered that when Pope Gregory the Great sent Augustine to England, he instructed him to work gradually at the sensitive task of converting the Anglo-Saxons to Christianity. Augustine followed Gregory's advice, and it was precisely this flexible attitude toward pagan culture that established the religious and intellectual climate in which a poem like *Beowulf* could flourish. Without sacrificing any of the rugged power inherent in the verse of the heroic age, the anonymous *Beowulf* poet has managed, with uncommon artistry, to create from pagan materials an epic that is fundamentally Christian in design and spirit. *Beowulf* is the greatest literary product of Anglo-Saxon civilization, a poem of incontestable beauty and strength.

Commentary on the Action: Beowulf's Youth

The basic narrative is in two sections: Beowulf's Youth and Beowulf's Old Age. As a prelude to the two main adventures of the hero's youth, the slaying of the monster Grendel and Grendel's mother, we are given an account of the mythical founder of the Danish royal line, Scyld Sceafing ("Shield, son of Sheaf"). Starting his life as a wretched castaway, Scyld grew in power and goodness until he was feared and loved throughout a vast empire. "That was a good king," the poet says, in one of his characteristic moral judgments. Then Scyld's son Beowulf—not the Geatish Beowulf who is the hero of the poem—won renown throughout Scandinavia; it is proper, the poet moralizes, for a son to merit the respect of his father's comrades. Because the poet enjoys dramatic contrast, he follows with accounts of Scyld's death and funeral. The dead Scyld, in life the bestower of rings, is honored with gifts from a grateful people. He is laid amid splendid treasures in a lordly ship (the reader will recall

* Through a series of accidents the *Beowulf* manuscript (*Cotton Vitellius,* A. XV, from the library of the seventeenth-century antiquarian Sir Robert Cotton) has almost miraculously survived invasion, fire, bombardment, and progressive deterioration. Late in the tenth century it was produced by two West Saxon scribes (the handwriting changes at a point about two-thirds through) working from an earlier manuscript, now lost. The poet himself, perhaps a chaplain in a royal household, probably flourished either in Northumbria during the "Age of Bede" (700–725) or in Mercia very late in the eighth century. See Dorothy Whitelock, *The Audience of Beowulf* (Oxford: Oxford University Press, 1951), especially pp. 5 and 21–33. (OEB 129.)

Sutton Hoo) and is launched on the lonely sea that had originally borne him to Denmark. Thus the poem, which is to celebrate the "coming of age" and the death of its hero Beowulf, and which has a constant background motif (as will be shown) of the flourishing and fall of nations, appropriately opens with the mysterious arrival and departure of the eponymous ancestor of the Scyldings.

Although Scyld and his son Beowulf were mythical figures, the later Scyldings ("Sons of Scyld") seem to have been a dynasty that ruled Denmark from around the middle of the fifth century to the middle of the sixth century. All were worthy of their illustrious forebear: Scyld's son Beowulf, his grandson Healfdene, and finally Healfdene's son Hrothgar, a major character in the poem. The grandeur of the Scyldings is manifested in Hrothgar's palace, Heorot ("Hart," the hart being a symbol of royalty), "A mightier mead-hall than men had known." Here the king apportions to his loyal retainers "All goodly treasure that God had given." The scenes at Heorot throw vivid light upon the lord-thane relationship that was so prominent in early Germanic society: Hrothgar, the chieftain and "ring-giver," distributes gold bracelets and rings, either intact or broken into pieces, and it is in the nature of the *comitatus* relationship that his faithful retainers should expect such gifts; the warriors spend their peaceful hours feasting and drinking mead; the *scop* is there to entertain with songs chanted to the accompaniment of the harp. While describing the splendor of Heorot, however, the poet hints at the future destruction of the hall by fire.

The revelry at Heorot angers Grendel, a troll-like monster out of Scandinavian folklore who, at the same time, is said to be one of the demons descended from Cain, the first murderer. The name Grendel has been derived from Old English *grindan,* meaning "grind" or "destroy," as well as from *grund,* meaning "bottom of a body of water." Roused from his watery abode, Grendel invades Heorot, finds the Danish warriors asleep, and snatches up and devours thirty men. Grendel repeats the attack on the following night; it was easy, the poet says in ironic understatement, to find men who preferred to sleep in a place remote from the hall. Night after night, for twelve long years, Grendel maintains his unflagging feud with the Danish race. In vain the Danes call upon their heathen deities to succor them; they know not the Lord of Hosts, the poet comments.*

---

* The apparent contradiction between the reference here to the Danes as heathens and the presentation throughout the poem of Hrothgar as a Christian

When news of Grendel's ravages spreads to the Geats (also called Weders, a tribe that probably lived in southern Sweden), Beowulf, nephew of the Geatish King Hygelac, decides to sail to the rescue of Hrothgar. (We later learn that there is a long-standing bond of friendship between the Danes and the Geats as well as a special tie between Hrothgar and Ecgtheow, Beowulf's father.) The sea normally brings out the best in Old English poets, and the voyage of Beowulf and his fourteen companions is brilliantly depicted:

> Over breaking billows,   with bellying sail
> And foamy beak,   like a flying bird
> The ship sped on,   till the next day's sun
> Showed sea-cliffs shining,   towering hills
> And stretching headlands.   The sea was crossed,
> The voyage ended,   the vessel moored.
> And the Weder people   waded ashore
> With clatter of trappings   and coats of mail;
> Gave thanks to God   that His grace had granted
> Sea-paths safe   for their ocean-journey.*
>
> (ll. 219–28)

When Beowulf arrives, he and his men are challenged by a vigilant Danish coast guard—stern and polite, but undeniably impressed by the bearing and speech of the remarkable stranger. Upon announcing his identity and his errand of mercy, the hero is conducted to Hrothgar, who receives him warmly and invites him to the nightly feast at Heorot. During the feast, Hrothgar's *thyle* (orator, spokesman), Unferth, taunts Beowulf with the story of a swimming contest in which, says Unferth, he was bested by Breca, chief of the Brondingas. Beowulf angrily answers Unferth with a version of the story that redounds to his own credit, concluding his reply with the traditional Germanic *bēot* (boast) that he will do battle with Grendel and either save the Danes or die. The Danes are well pleased, Hrothgar's richly bedecked Queen Wealhtheow passes the goblet of mead among the warriors with dignity and grace, and Hrothgar promises Beowulf ample rewards if he destroys Grendel. The feast completed, the Danes retire for the night, leaving Beowulf and his

---

or at least a monotheist is one of many unsolved cruces in *Beowulf*. For the latest "solution" to this crux, see the chapter on "Pagan and Christian" in Arthur Brodeur's *The Art of Beowulf* (Berkeley, Calif.: University of California Press, 1959). (OEB 99.)

* Translations in this section are from *Beowulf* by Charles W. Kennedy. Copyright 1940 by Oxford University Press, Inc. Reprinted by permission of the publisher.

companions to keep vigil for Grendel. The hero, perhaps out of
sportsmanship, decides that he will not use his sword against Grendel,
who may not know how to fight with weapons and who, in any case,
cannot be harmed by a sword. All the Geats, with the exception of
Beowulf, fall asleep in the mead-hall.

Into the hall storms the monster. Quickly clutching one of the
sleeping warriors, Grendel tears him to pieces, gulps down his blood,
and devours his flesh. Fearsome though he may be, Grendel is seized
by Beowulf, who has the power of thirty men in his grip. During the
fight Beowulf grasps Grendel's arm and, as the fiend struggles to
get away, rips it out of its socket. The monster, mortally wounded,
escapes to his home.

The next day Hrothgar and the Danes are overjoyed at their deliverance. Some of the thanes ride out, following the trail left by
Grendel's blood, a trail which leads to the pool in which he has lived.
On the return journey, a *scop* improvises a song in honor of Beowulf;
then he sings the "Lay of Sigemund" celebrating the Volsung hero
of old and follows, somewhat abruptly, with a song about the proud
King Heremod, apparently a member of the dynasty that preceded
the Scyldings. Grendel's huge arm and claw are hung in Heorot as a
trophy, and a feast is prepared. After Hrothgar, as he has promised,
rewards Beowulf, we hear once again from the *scop,* this time the
"Lay of Finn," which has already been discussed (see pp. 25–26).
Queen Wealhtheow, preparing to present Beowulf with additional
gifts, requests him to safeguard the interests of her sons, Hrethric
and Hrothmund. The banqueting ended, the Geats leave the hall,
which has apparently been cleansed of evil, and the Danes remain
there to sleep peacefully as they had done in the years preceding
Grendel's attacks.

One of the Danes, the poet remarks in an ironic understatement,
paid a high price for his evening's rest; for without warning, Grendel's mother invades the hall to avenge the death of her son. She
seizes Æschere, one of Hrothgar's favorite thanes, and makes off for
her underwater home at the edge of the sea, carrying Grendel's arm
along with her captive. Again Heorot is enveloped in gloom. There is
nice contrast as Beowulf, summoned to the hall, asks in all innocence
whether Hrothgar has passed a restful night. When he learns of the
new threat, however, he prepares to set out after the female monster
who, while she may be less powerful than her son, is formidably
shielded in her underwater lair.

Early in the morning, Beowulf, accompanied by a band of Danes and Geats, goes to the dreadful pool. Arming himself with Hrunting, a fine sword generously offered him by Unferth (now more friendly), the hero addresses a *bēot* to Hrothgar and plunges into the pool. As he nears the bottom, the troll grabs him and pulls him into her lair, a waterless sea-cave. The sword Hrunting fails Beowulf utterly in the terrible fight, but his armor protects him better against the monster's short sword. Suddenly Beowulf spies, among the armor and weapons in the den, a giant sword, a sword too massive for any other man to lift. (Readers familiar with Wagner's *Ring* cycle will recognize a kinship with the revelation of Nothung, Siegmund's sword, in *Die Walküre*.) Beowulf takes the sword and strikes the female demon a fatal blow. Then he finds the lifeless body of Grendel lying in the den and hews off his head—perhaps an echo of the primitive superstition that decapitation with a magic sword is the only sure way of getting rid of an ogre. The pool has meanwhile grown so bloody that the Danes, assuming Beowulf to be dead, return disconsolate to Heorot. But the Geats remain. When Beowulf returns to the surface carrying the severed head of Grendel, the Geats are elated that he is still alive and, moreover, victorious. At Heorot, amid more feasting and ring-giving, Beowulf recounts the details of his underwater adventure and hears in turn a lengthy homily on pride delivered by Hrothgar. The next morning Beowulf and the Geats take leave of Hrothgar and return to Geatland.

Upon his return to his own country, Beowulf reports in full to Hygelac what has happened in Denmark, and, with uncommon political insight, suggests that the Danes' future will be fraught with internecine war. He shares Hrothgar's gifts with Hygelac and Hygd, the young Queen, both of whom love and honor him as a son.

Thus ends the first half of the poem, an epic presentation of the ideal warrior and loyal retainer, of Beowulf's Young Manhood. A few words should be added, at this point, about some of the problems connected with the etymology, history, and folklore surrounding Beowulf himself.

There are two leading theories as to the meaning of the name Beowulf. One group derives the name from Old English *bēow* (or *bēaw*), meaning "grain" or "barley," and interprets the name accordingly as being associated with an ancient harvest divinity. A refinement of the theory, not generally accepted, personifies in Grendel and his dam the destructive force of the sea from which Beaw, a divine deliverer, rescues mankind. The second major theory, which has attracted many supporters, explains Beowulf as the "beewolf" (the wolf that is the enemy of the bee)—in other words, the bear. What would seem to reinforce this interpretation for many scholars is the close resemblance *Beowulf* shows to the widely circulated folk tale of "The Bear's Son." In this tale an unappreciated boy develops into a man of tremendous strength and saves a kingdom from a demon by tearing him in bearlike fashion (as Beowulf destroys Grendel). Among the many Icelandic analogues of "The Bear's son," two are of unusual interest: in *The Grettissaga* (*c.* 1300), based upon the career of a historical outlaw of the late tenth and early eleventh centuries, the hero, Grettir the Strong, vanquishes a troll-wife who has been spiriting people away and eating them, then kills a giant in a cave under a waterfall; in the fourteenth-century *Hrolfssaga* the hero, Bothvar Bjarki by name, comes from Gautland to rescue the Danish King Hrolf from a winged monster who, like Grendel, seems invulnerable to ordinary swords (this monster, through some slip, *is* killed by a sword but later has to be "re-killed" by a magic sword with a golden hilt). Bjarki is mentioned in a number of histories, among them the work that introduces Amleth (Hamlet) into the literary scene—the early thirteenth-century *Historia Danica* of Saxo Grammaticus. Although some scholars have seen an etymological relation (or confusion) between "Beowulf" and "Bjarki," the intricate problem is far from settled.

Commentary on the Action: Beowulf's Old Age

The second part of *Beowulf* is set in Geatland many years later. Hygelac has led a disastrous expedition against the Franks around 520 (an event also recorded in Gregory of Tours' sixth-century *History of the Franks*) and is dead. After his son Heardred was killed in battle with the Scylfings, a Swedish dynasty, the Geatish throne descended to Beowulf, who has ruled wisely for fifty years. A new scourge now lays waste the land—a firedragon who for three hundred years has been guarding a treasure in a burial mound and is enraged because he has been robbed of a cup by one of Beowulf's subjects. (Dragons, by their nature, the poet says, seek out buried treasure and hoard it—a tradition exemplified in Fafnir and also mentioned in the Old English gnomic verse that says, "The dragon lieth on the grave-mound, old, exultant in treasure.") Unable to find the thief, the *Beowulf* dragon belches forth his flames throughout the countryside; the devastation is overwhelming, and Beowulf's own hall is consumed.

The aged Beowulf must once again defend a people against evil. After ordering an iron shield to be made for himself, Beowulf sets out with eleven others to confront the dragon (the thief, who shows the way, is the thirteenth in the party). Although he foresees that he will die, the hero bravely advances to the entrance of the dragon's barrow and challenges him to combat. The dragon emerges and a violent struggle ensues. When Beowulf, his sword again having failed him, seems on the verge of defeat, the Geatish thanes who came with him flee to the forest—all, that is, except Wiglaf, the son of Weohstan. Beowulf and Wiglaf, lord and thane, together overcome the dragon and slay him, but not before the king has sustained his death-wound.

Before he dies, Beowulf bestows his armor and his rings upon Wiglaf and orders the dragon's treasure to be given to the Geats. Then he requests that his body be placed on a mound near the sea and burned. Beowulf dies, his soul departing "to the joys of the just." After Wiglaf has poured out his wrath upon the deserters, he dispatches a messenger to announce that Beowulf is dead. The messenger predicts that the Swedes, long-time enemies of the Geats, will take advantage of this great loss to renew their attacks and will eventually cause the downfall of the Geatish nation. At Wiglaf's command the dragon is hurled into the sea, the treasure removed from the barrow, and the funeral pyre built as Beowulf had asked. Beowulf's ashes are then buried in a magnificent mound, and the treasure, as useless now as ever, is buried with him. Twelve warriors circle the mound and lament the death of their lord.

Structure of Beowulf

It has been necessary to examine the complicated action of *Beowulf* in some detail. As the preceding commentary indicates, and as the reader has no doubt discovered for himself, *Beowulf* contains many elements not directly connected with the central story of the fights with Grendel and his dam and with the firedragon. There are numerous characters who do not play any part in Beowulf's immediate adventures: Scyld, the founder of Denmark; Breca, the boyhood companion and rival of Beowulf; Ingeld (who has not yet been discussed), the Heathobard prince who becomes Hrothgar's son-in-law; Hrothulf, who seizes the Danish throne after Hrothgar's death.

The poet, it was observed, sometimes halts the advance of the main narrative in order to retell an old story, like the "Lay of Sigemund" and the "Lay of Finnsburg." Important characters occasionally deliver long speeches reviewing the past or predicting the future; Hrothgar, for example, addresses a sermon to Beowulf on pride, illustrated with Danish historical events, and Beowulf himself rehearses the exhausting wars that preceded Hygelac's accession to the Geatish throne. Moreover, the poet in his own person indulges in brief allusions to, or extended comments on, what has already occurred or is yet to come. One of the most distinguished *Beowulf* scholars and editors has written of the poet's "rambling, dilatory method—the forward, backward, and sideward movements" which one encounters even at the poem's most critical moments.* The reader may justifiably question whether all the hints and glances, episodes and digressions, are in fact integrated into an artistic whole.

Modern scholarship has been to some pains to find an artistic unity in *Beowulf*—though there are dissenters, to be sure, who still see the poem as a not wholly artistic fusion of disparate materials (see OEB 94–129, for a summary of recent interpretations). It becomes increasingly clear that Beowulf's personal career must be viewed in the larger context of Danish and Geatish history, a history reflected in the contrasting moods of Parts One and Two of the poem. The young Beowulf is brave, daring, optimistic; the older Beowulf, while relinquishing none of his courage or dignity, has grown tired and melancholy—perhaps disillusioned because of the endless parade of human misfortune which he has observed and in which he has been compelled to intervene. He may deliver the Danes and the Geats from monsters and dragons, but he cannot save them from their own folly and avarice. Beowulf's heroic life is hopelessly enmeshed in the tragic destinies of the two peoples he has served so long and so well. †

By viewing the hero's life, or rather segments of that life, as part of a historical pattern, the *Beowulf* poet displays a kinship with other epic poets of the Western world. In the *Iliad* Homer focuses upon one sequence: the furious withdrawal of Achilles from the Trojan War and his equally furious return to battle. Yet Homer

---

* Fr. Klaeber (ed.), *Beowulf and the Fight at Finnsburg* (3rd ed.; Boston: D. C. Heath and Company, 1936), p. lviii. Reprinted by permission of the publisher.

† See Brodeur, *The Art of Beowulf*, pp. 117 ff. To this very important study of *Beowulf* the present discussion of the poem is profoundly indebted.

recalls the abduction of Helen, which precipitated the war, and looks ahead to the defeat of the Trojans and to the individual fates awaiting some of the Greek and Trojan survivors. Although the theme of *Paradise Lost* is the disobedience and punishment of Adam and Eve, Milton's enveloping action includes the earlier rebellion of Satan, the Creation, and the whole future of fallen mankind. Such a narrative method enables the epic poet to delineate his central figure or episodes with concentrated vigor, yet, at the same time, to enlarge the dimensions of his poem and encompass a tremendous range of human experience.*

The broadened setting for Beowulf's adventures is partly established at the very beginning of the poem in the poet's account of Scyld Sceafing and the Scyldings who followed him to the Danish throne. It is important that the poet expound upon the greatness of the Danes and that he pay tribute to Heorot, the symbol of royal honor and good fellowship. Yet, even as Heorot stands in its fullest opulence and glory, the *Beowulf* poet heralds the terrible end of the Scylding dynasty. Not from Grendel, but from man-made woe:

> The great hall rose
> High and horn-gabled, holding its place
> Till the battle-surge of consuming flame
> Should swallow it up; the hour was near
> That the deadly hate of a daughter's husband
> Should kindle to fury and savage feud.
>
> (ll. 81–86)

The poet alludes to a long-festering feud between the Danes and the Heathobards, a feud which Hrothgar would like to settle by marrying his daughter Freawaru to the Heathobard Prince Ingeld. But later on, Beowulf, back in Geatland after delivering Hrothgar from Grendel, confides to Hygelac his well-grounded fear that Ingeld's smoldering hatred will be fanned into full blaze by some old Heathobard warrior whose memory of earlier violence may still rankle. Both sides will break their oaths, and the bloody slaughter will be renewed. The poet foresees worse disaster to the Danes from the imminent treachery of Hrothulf, a nephew of Hrothgar. The reader will recall Queen Wealhtheow's plea that Beowulf protect her sons, Hrethric and Hrothmund. After Hrothgar's death, however, Hrothulf,

---

* The poet's possible indebtedness to Virgil has been explored by Tom Burns Haber in *A Comparative Study of the Beowulf and the Aeneid* (Princeton: Princeton University Press, 1931).

a presumably loyal kinsman, usurps the throne from Hrethric, the rightful heir, and plunges the Scyldings into intrigue, war, and ultimately destruction. The "Lay of Finnsburg," which recounts a previous breach of faith suffered by the Danes, is partly intended as a parallel to Hrothulf's infamous act.

The Geats, like the Danes, face certain doom. When Queen Wealhtheow, in the midst of the celebration following the defeat of Grendel, rewards Beowulf with jewelry, the poet leaps several years ahead to remind us that the hero's uncle Hygelac wore one of these gems, a ring, on his last military excursion:

> The mighty prince
> Carried the ring　　o'er the cup of the waves,
> The precious jewel,　　and sank under shield.
> Then his body fell　　into Frankish hands,
> His woven corselet　　and jewelled collar,
> And weaker warriors　　plundered the dead
> After the carnage　　and welter of war.
> The field of battle　　was covered with corpses
> Of Geats who had fallen.　　slain by the sword.
> (ll. 1206–14)

The death of the good King Hygelac after a storm-tossed reign marks the first phase of the Geatish collapse. The second stage occurs when Beowulf, donning his armor for the last time, predicts that his own life may be taken by the dragon:

> It shall fare with us both　　in the fight at the wall
> As Fate shall allot,　　the lord of mankind.
> Though bold in spirit,　　I make no boast
> As I go to fight　　with the flying serpent.
> (ll. 2525–28)

The hero's misgivings are borne out. For the first time, says the poet, "It was not his portion to prosper in war." The last chapter of the tragic decline of the Geats, still to be written when the poem ends, is foretold by the messenger who carries the sad tidings of Beowulf's death. As he rehearses the long record of hatred between the Geats and the Swedes, he prophesies that the Swedish people, learning that Beowulf "lies lifeless and still," will resume active warfare. Many a Geat will march into foreign captivity; the sound of the harp will be drowned out by the ugly clamor of "The dusky raven despoiling the dead."

Pagan and Christian Elements

The *Beowulf* poet has made this story of monster-slaying part of
an elaborate panorama of early Scandinavian culture. But the poem,
as stated earlier, derives much of its flavor from the ingenious manner in which the heroic qualities of pre-Christian Germanic civilization are brought into harmony with Christianity. The integration
of the two worlds, save for minor lapses, is quite successful.

Echoes of the earlier heroic age abound in *Beowulf*. There are
frequent glimpses of the feasting and gift-giving that bound the lord
and his thanes in mutual loyalty. Before confronting Grendel, Beowulf utters the characteristic "boast" concerning his victories in the
blood-soaked fields. Hrothgar's *scop* sings of the Volsung champion
Sigemund, whose dragon-killing prowess resembles Beowulf's. As he
prepares to pursue Grendel's mother, Beowulf reacts to Hrothgar's
grief over the death of Æschere by voicing the traditional tribal
commitment to revenge:

>   Better for man
> To avenge a friend   than much to mourn.
> All men must die;   let him who may
> Win glory ere death.   That guerdon is best
> For a nobleman   when his name survives him.
>   (ll. 1385–89)

On that occasion he wears a battle helmet ornamented with a boar,
reminding one of the helmet found in the Sutton Hoo cenotaph
which included gilded boar-heads at the ends of its bronze eyebrows.
When the loyal Wiglaf reproaches the cowardly Geatish retainers
who have fled the field leaving Beowulf to die, he epitomizes the idea
of *comitatus*:

>   And each of your clan
> Shall fail of his birthright   when men from afar
> Hear tell of your flight   and your dastardly deed.
> Death is better   for every earl
> Than life besmirched   with the brand of shame.
>   (ll. 2887–91)

Beowulf receives a heathen burial; he is cremated and placed in a
treasure-laden barrow. The body of Scyld, a kindred spirit, had
been sent out to sea in a treasure-laden ship. The poet and his audience had at least an antiquarian interest in these pagan ideals and
rituals.

Although it was once thought that *Beowulf* was originally a completely pagan poem and that all the Christian passages were interpolated much later by monks, it is now generally accepted that Anglo-Saxon Christianity permeates the poem and transfigures the pagan elements. If the *scop* at Heorot remembers Sigemund and Finnsburg, he also chants of the Creation, of "how the Maker wrought/The shining earth with its circling waters." It is this hymn that infuriates Grendel, whom the poet labels a "fiend from hell" bearing the curse of Cain. The prayers offered by the Danes to their gods are futile, for they do not know how to worship "the Lord of heaven," who is the true "wielder of glory." Wyrd, all-powerful Fate, is frequently mentioned, but the poet usually—though not consistently—subordinates Wyrd to God. Grendel, we are told, was "fated" to slay many more, but God decreed otherwise:

> But all-wise God
> And the hero's courage   had conquered Fate.
> The Lord ruled   over the lives of men
> As He rules them still.

(ll. 1055–58)

God's intervention enables Beowulf to prevail against Grendel's dam. "Often his arm," the hero reports, "has aided the friendless." Pagan history and myth are often made to point a Christian moral. Scyld, a good king, passed "to the peace of God"; but the proud Heremod, cited in Hrothgar's homily to Beowulf, misused God's gifts and accordingly suffered "eternal torment of woe." The poem serves in a sense as a conduct book for the "Christian" prince—something of a "mirror for magistrates" (a type of literature immensely popular in the Middle Ages and the Renaissance) wherein a ruler may find models from the past to imitate or to reject.

Perhaps the most striking evidence of the two worlds operating together and at times conflicting with each other is to be found in the character of Beowulf himself. Here is a wise and reflective sovereign who labors to merit the Christian reward of eternal bliss; yet he is also from first to last a fierce warrior who never thinks of renouncing the prizes of this world. He fights for his personal honor, but he is also wholeheartedly committed to the ideal of service to his own people and to humanity at large. His private glory is indeed founded on the fact that he saves a people from the "foe of God," and he readily offers thanks to his Maker without whose favor he could not even challenge the monsters, let alone conquer them. While it would be too much to claim that Beowulf is a complex personality drawn with great subtlety, it would seem that the poet has at least created a superman who somehow remains recognizable as an individual even though he performs feats that defy the abilities of flesh-and-blood heroes. This the poet accomplishes by keeping the hero poised between the primitive Germanic and the Christian components of his nature. When Beowulf dies, his companions pay him a tribute that seems to strike exactly the right balance:

> So the folk of the Geats,   the friends of his hearth,
> Bemoaned the fall   of their mighty lord;
> Said he was kindest   of worldly kings,
> Mildest, most gentle,   most eager for fame.
>
> (ll. 3179–82)

The Poet's Art

Beowulf is clearly a poem of considerable historical and cultural significance. Yet it primarily lives as a great story which captivates the reader through an almost endless progression of intensely realized moods, feelings, pictures, and personal conflicts: the revelry that rings through Heorot chillingly interrupted by the first onslaught of Grendel; the helplessness of the Danes as the fiend slays and carries away thirty warriors; Grendel's nightly raids through twelve bitter years; Beowulf's journey from Geatland over the "swan's road," a kenning for *ocean* suggesting efficiency and grace, subtly differentiated from "whale's road," used earlier to connote the size and strength of Scyld's empire; the beautifully controlled crescendo of suspense as Grendel stalks ever closer to his fated encounter with Beowulf; the fight between Beowulf and Grendel which causes the beer to spill and the benches to spring loose from their moorings; jubilation, short-lived, after Beowulf tears off Grendel's arm and sends him howling home to die; the sudden, vengeful visit of Grendel's dam, who snatches up the warrior Æschere and flees to her haunt in the fen; pursuit through "wind-swept ridges and wolf-retreats," climaxed by the horror of finding Æschere's head lying on a cliff; Beowulf's emergence in triumph from the blood-drenched pool with Grendel's head, a load too heavy for four men; the touching, though unsentimental, parting of Beowulf and Hrothgar; the voyage back to Geatland amid groaning timbers and blowing gales, with the Danish coast receding into the landscape; the world-weary

lament of the last survivor as he buries in the earth the treasure inherited from his clan; Wiglaf trying in vain to awaken the dead
Beowulf; an aged woman wailing in sorrow as the flames rise up
from Beowulf's funeral pyre. *Beowulf* is, indeed, a triumph of the
storyteller's art, a work that registers a host of unforgettable experiences and emotions.

Many facets of this art are exemplified in the "Breca" episode,
and it may be well to conclude with a closer look at this remarkable "digression." The court orator Unferth, it will be recalled,
"addled with beer," insults Beowulf in the presence of the entire
Danish court with the accusation that he was once defeated in a
swimming match with Breca. Is this weakling, Unferth demands, fit
to be the savior of Denmark? Beowulf, with steadily mounting fury,
offers his own account of the swimming match, one that puts Unferth
to shame and, at the same time, reinforces our faith in the hero's
qualifications. During the match, he tells the assembly, he was assailed by nine grisly *nicors* (sea monsters), whom he had to van-
quish one by one. Not only did Beowulf fight off the monsters, but
he also saved Breca's life and swam, fully armed, all the way to Fin-
land. Back into Unferth's teeth he flings the insult:

>   And little I've heard
> Of any such valiant   adventures from you!
> Neither Breca nor you   in the press of battle
> Ever showed such daring   with dripping swords—
> Though I boast not of it!   But you stained your blade
> With blood of your brothers,   your closest kin;
> And for that you'll endure   damnation in hell. . . .
>   (ll. 581–87)

No need, Beowulf declares with contempt, for Grendel to fear any
hurt from the likes of Unferth or from any of the other Danes. But
Beowulf promises to treat them all to a sample of Geatish courage.
This brave reply silences Unferth.

What marvelous use the poet has made of this "digression"! He
has, first of all, introduced us to Unferth, the most complicated and
mysterious character in the entire poem. Perhaps Unferth, as Hrothgar's official spokesman, is shrewdly goading Beowulf into making his
"boast." On the other hand, Beowulf, in the course of his reply,
charges him with committing the unforgivable crime of slaughtering
his kinsmen. Later on, Unferth, "unmindful/Of words he had spoken
while heated with wine," offers his own sword for the hero to use

against Grendel's dam. Yet the poet also hints that Unferth is a party to Hrothulf's conspiracy against the Scyldings. What are we to make of this ambiguous figure? It is a fascinating problem. Unferth is, at all events, a vital personality. But the "Breca" episode also provides insight into Beowulf the impetuous youth somewhat given to rash escapades; it is thus one of the rare occasions when Beowulf is almost as much man as he is myth. Dramatic and vigorously told, the story of the swimming match foreshadows the hero's far more important battles with monsters of satanic evil. Moreover, the exchange with Unferth underscores Beowulf's self-confidence and intense national pride which can readily erupt in passionate indignation. The "Breca" episode shows the technique of the epic poet at its best; it is a digression that effectively contributes to the forward movement of the narrative.

To the twentieth-century reader much of *Beowulf* will remain obscure, for it is indeed a difficult task to uncover the secrets of an age so remote in time and so different in orientation. The "Age of Beowulf" was marked by the happy interplay of old and new, of Germanic sternness and Christian charity. Out of this meeting of two great cultures emerged the epic *Beowulf*—a unified work of art realizing in full measure the potentialities inherent in the unique historical moment that gave it birth.*

RELIGIOUS HEROIC TALES †

Whereas the materials of *Beowulf* are drawn from pagan culture and converted to Christian use, the two poems *Andreas* and *Judith* show a somewhat different method of composition. Here the subject matter is religious: one is a saint's legend; the other, a story from the Apocrypha. Yet both are to a large degree modeled after the

* In addition to Dorothy Whitelock, Arthur G. Brodeur, and Charles W. Kennedy, whose works on *Beowulf* I have already cited, I should like to record the names of other scholars to whose studies I am especially indebted: Kemp Malone, Adrien Bonjour, William W. Lawrence, Cecil M. Bowra, Hector M. Chadwick, and R. W. Chambers. See Bibliography. Above all, the great edition of Fr. Klaeber has been an almost constant guide.

† The quotations in this chapter from *Andreas* are from *Early English Christian Poetry* by Charles W. Kennedy. Published 1952 by Oxford University Press. Reprinted by permission of Oxford University Press, Inc., and Hollis and Carter, Ltd. Those from *Judith* are from *The Earliest English Poetry* by Charles W. Kennedy. Copyright 1943. Reprinted by permission of Oxford University Press, Inc.

Germanic heroic tale, with the result that they sometimes reflect values not usually associated with poems of Christian origin and intent.

Andreas (c. 800?)

Andreas seems to have been based ultimately upon a Greek text of the *Acts of St. Andrew and St. Matthew*—probably through an intervening lost version in Latin. In the Old English narrative poem, which some scholars have regarded as a deliberate imitation of *Beowulf*, St. Andrew is called upon by God to rescue St. Matthew and other Christians from imminent death at the hands of the cannibal Mermedonians. Andrew at first doubts that he can reach Mermedonia in time, but he secures free passage (he was penniless) on a ship which, unknown to him and his followers, is piloted by God and two angels. After a terrible storm, one of the most vividly written episodes in the poem, Andrew awakens with his companions to find himself safely arrived on the Mermedonian shore. Realizing at last who the Captain was and knowing that his earlier hesitation indicated lack of perfect faith in God's power, Andrew proceeds with his holy work. After rescuing Matthew and undergoing many afflictions, he calls down a flood upon the Mermedonians, wins their loyalty in spite of Satan's efforts to keep them in darkness, and converts them to Christianity. When Andrew's sojourn is over, the Mermedonians are indeed sorry that their beloved teacher must leave.

The *Andreas* poet suffuses this religious tale with a heroic atmosphere reminiscent of pre-Christian Anglo-Saxon life. In addition to the description of the storm at sea, a specialty of Old English poets, there is the traditional assembly of the heathen warriors in full battle regalia. But some of the echoes of Germanic civilization seem incongruous in so Christian a context (as they almost never do in *Beowulf*). Andrew dispenses bounty in the "radiant ring-hall," much in the manner of a Germanic prince. When, during the storm, the Captain (God) offers to leave Andrew's men ashore while the saint continues to Mermedonia, the men answer eloquently, if not altogether appropriately, according to the best traditions of the *comitatus:*

> If we desert you   whither shall we wander
> Lordless and lonely,   lacking all good?
> We shall be loathed   in every land,
> Hated of all men   where valiant heroes

> Sit in assembly   holding debate
> Who best has bolstered   his lord in battle
> When hand and buckler   were bearing the brunt,
> Hacked with swords,   on the field of fate.
>
>   (ll. 407–14)

The poet is grimly ironic as the Mermedonians are drowning; theirs is "a bitter beer feast" with "drink for all from the break of day!" Shortly thereafter, the drowned Mermedonians, in striking contrast, are miraculously restored to receive the waters of baptism.

Despite the occasional inappropriateness of some of its pagan trappings, *Andreas* succeeds by and large in communicating the fervor of the hero's Christian faith. The technique is relatively straightforward for the most part. In the account of the sea voyage, however, particularly in the long dialogue between Andrew and the divine Captain (a dialogue in which Andrew's knowledge and devotion are rigorously tested), it is possible to interpret the voyage as a symbol of man's pilgrimage to God. This image, which recurs frequently in later literature, is specifically developed by the Old English poet Cynewulf, and many scholars believe that some such allegory is intended by the anonymous poets of the Old English elegies, *The Wanderer* and *The Seafarer*.

Judith (9th Century?)

In the *Beowulf* manuscript, there is a fragment of a poem, *Judith*, based upon a story in the Roman Catholic Old Testament (apocryphal in Protestant and Jewish versions) and celebrating the courage of the Hebrew heroine Judith during a war with the Assyrians. Inasmuch as New Testament critics and commentators always found parallels between Old and New Testament narratives, it should come as no surprise that the Old English poet has infused this Hebrew patriot with Christian beliefs—as when she invokes the Trinity for protection in her difficult undertakings. Some scholars have tried to link the Judith of the poem with actual ninth-century or tenth-century Anglo-Saxon queens, but evidence is far from conclusive.

In the surviving 350 lines, which constitute approximately the last quarter of the complete poem, the Assyrian military leader Holofernes is besieging the Jewish city of Bethulia. After an evening of realistically described debauchery, he staggers into his tent thinking to enjoy the embraces of the beautiful widow Judith. But Judith has come with the intention of assassinating an enemy of her people. She cuts off the Assyrian's head, carries it (with the assistance of her maid) to the despondent Hebrews in Bethulia, and thereby inspires her people to win a glorious victory over the enemy hosts. The hungry wolf and the "corpse-greedy" raven feast upon the Assyrian dead.

There is, as the above summary suggests, abundant excitement in *Judith*. The nature of the material renders heroic treatment perhaps more plausible for *Judith* than for *Andreas,* and the reader rarely, if ever, feels that the poet is straining after a discordant style or mood. Even the brutality of the murder seems appropriate in the total context:

> The maid of woven tresses
> Smote the fierce-hearted   with bloodstained blade,
> Half severed his neck;   he lay in a swoon,
> Wounded and drunken.   Not yet was he dead,
> Not wholly lifeless.   Then grimly again
> The bold maid hacked at   the heathen hound,
> Till his head rolled out   over the floor-boards,
> And behind lay lifeless   the loathsome trunk.
>
> (ll. 101–8)

Here is a poet of unusual force.

This chapter, with emphasis on the epic *Beowulf,* has been concerned with defining the so-called heroic tradition and with tracing, through various complete poems and poetic fragments, some of the ways in which the themes and values of early Germanic life found expression in Old English verse. It should not be inferred, however, that only the poems discussed in this chapter reveal the influence of the heroic tradition. Subsequent discussion will show that ironic understatement, love of the sea, the ecstasy of battle, the spirit of *comitatus,* the commitment to revenge—these and other features generally identified with heroic poetry continually recur in other lyric and narrative verse of the period. In fact, they survive well into the later Middle Ages and beyond. The lord-thane relationship will be carried over into the institution of medieval knighthood, and the most renowned figure in English literature—Hamlet, Prince of Denmark—will be tormented by an alleged duty (stressed in many medieval romances but condemned by medieval philosophy) to avenge the foul murder of a kinsman.

IV: ELEGIAC, CAEDMONIAN, AND CYNEWULFIAN POEMS

We should have reason to place a high value upon the Anglo-Saxon contribution to poetry even without *Beowulf*. There are three groups of Old English poems which, next to that epic, have most consistently interested scholars and general readers: first, those personal lyrics known as "elegies"; second, a number of religious poems associated with the poet Caedmon, whose life is so beautifully described by the Venerable Bede; and, finally, a group of poems written by Cynewulf and his "school"—also religious, but different in style from the works of the Caedmonian poets.

ELEGIAC POETRY *

The "traditional" English elegy, like Milton's *Lycidas* or Gray's *Elegy Written in a Country Churchyard,* is usually a lament for the dead. The Old English poems commonly referred to as "elegies," however, are not directly concerned with personal death. Different from each other as the individual poems may be, they are all more or less reflective lyrics rising out of some personal—or perhaps imagined—situation or mood. While they are usually inspired by a state of exile made more poignant by intensely felt recollections of earlier joys, Old English elegies frequently attain to the level of a philosophic generalization, often Christian in spirit, about the frailty of human life and the impermanence of worldly happiness and security. Scholars at one time saw the elegies as expressions of the customs and values of early Germanic life; *The Wanderer,* for instance, was taken to be an outpouring of grief over the dissolution of the *comitatus,* and the Christian emphasis at the conclusion of the poem was believed to have been added later. Now, however, most scholars feel that the Christian element in many of the elegies forms an integral part of the total artistic and philosophic design. Some would

---

* The quotations from elegiac poems are from the translations of Charles W. Kennedy, *Old English Elegies* (Princeton: Princeton University Press, 1936). Reprinted by permission of the publisher.

even read *The Wanderer* and *The Seafarer* as specifically Christian allegories.

Deor (9th or 10th Century *)

Deor is one of two Old English poems (the other is *Wulf and Eadwacer*) with stanzaic organization and a refrain, and there is good artistic reason for its structure. The speaker, Deor, is a *scop* who has been ousted from his lord's favor by a gifted rival, Heorrenda. But the poet skillfully and dramatically delays giving us this information until the very end of the poem. In the first five of the poem's six stanzas the poet alludes to well-known misfortunes recorded in Germanic history and legend: the binding of Weland, the rape of Hild, the oppression suffered by the Goths under the tyrant Eormanric. He concludes each stanza with the statement, "þaes ofereode, þisses swa maeg." ("That passed away, so may this.") In the sixth stanza he makes a generalizaticn: God in His wisdom grants rewards to some, but to others He dispenses "a burden of woe." Only then does Deor feel entitled to speak of his own sorrow, and he does so with a dignity and restraint that leave no room for self-pity. Having seen his private disappointment in the larger context of the pervasive mutability of human affairs in a universe governed by God, the poet once more concludes, "That passed away, so may this." Anglo-Saxon audiences undoubtedly derived pleasure from *Deor,* as they did from *Widsith,* by virtue of the allusions to familiar stories that they loved. The poem may not afford this kind of pleasure to twentieth-century readers, but we may still respond to the timelessness of the theme and to the high quality of the poetic craftsmanship.

The Wanderer

The Wanderer ostensibly describes with superb realism and emotional intensity the spiritual progress of a lonely *eardstapa* ("earth-treader," wanderer), at one time a thane in the service of a generous lord but now a weary exile uprooted from his clan and adrift on the frozen seas. Remembering the days when his lord still lived and distributed gifts in the mead-hall, he dreams that he again places head and hand on his lord's knee to pledge eternal loyalty as in days gone by. But the feverish excitement of his imagined bliss yields to a

* For an interesting discussion of the date of *Deor,* see Malone, in *A Literary History of England,* ed. Albert C. Baugh, pp. 48–49.

heart-rending awakening to present reality—bleak solitude in the midst of an endless gray expanse of ocean. The wanderer turns hopefully to his "old comrades" (their identity is difficult to establish, though "seagulls" is a possible interpretation)* only to see them vanish into air "With no word of greeting to gladden his heart." He then sounds the classical *ubi sunt* theme—a lament over the inevitable decay of all earthly beauty and glory—which will continually recur in religious lyrics of the Middle Ages:

> Where now is the warrior? Where is the war-horse?
> Bestowal of treasure, and sharing of feast?
> Alas! the bright ale-cup, the byrny-clad warrior,
> The prince in his splendor—those days are long sped
> In the night of the past, as if they never had been!

When he has (like Deor) extracted the lesson that suffering is not his private lot, that wretchedness indeed "fills the realm of the earth," the *eardstapa* matures into a *snottor on mode* (wise man). He transcends the temporary sorrows of this world to seek mercy and comfort "From his heavenly Father, our Fortress and Strength."

The poem is almost certainly Christian, but there is considerable disagreement as to details of interpretation (see OEB 132–147). Some scholars believe that the Christian illumination is attained by the wanderer himself; others think that the Christian poet is moralizing upon the experience of a pagan wanderer; a third group of readers argues that the poem was never intended to be taken as a realistic account of an actual or even fictitious experience, but that the poet was creating a poetic homily in a form purely allegorical. In any case, *The Wanderer* remains a moving expression of Christian consolation offered to the lacerated in body and heart.

The Seafarer

The Seafarer (which has been rendered into Modern English by several poets, including Ezra Pound) is a dramatic lyric presumably about a wind-driven mariner to whom the sea is alternately terrifying and alluring. He is numb with hunger and cold; instead of the cheerful laughter of friends in the mead-hall, he hears only the roar of the waters, "The scream of the gannet, the shriek of the gull." Yet something deep within him pushes him relentlessly on over the foam-

---

* Graham Midgely, in *The Review of English Studies,* New Series, X (1959), 53–54.

ing waves and forces him to repudiate the delights and comforts of land:

> The beat of the harp, and bestowal of treasure,
> The love of woman, and worldly hope,
> Nor other interest can hold his heart
> Save only the sweep of the surging billows;
> His heart is haunted by love of the sea.

Convinced that the gifts of the earth are unstable, the seafarer rushes ahead in expectation of joys everlasting:

> Let us muse in our hearts on our heavenly mansions,
> Thitherward planning our pilgrimage,
> Seeking the way to the blessed stronghold
> Of life and joy in the love of the Lord.

Once again there is a difficult problem of interpretation. An earlier theory that the poem is a dialogue between an old and a young sailor has been pretty generally discredited, and scholars now see *The Seafarer* as a dramatic monologue. The central figure is clearly not the young boy, familiar from the novels of Robert Louis Stevenson and others, who is drawn to the sea as a place of romantic adventure; nor is he the victim of the sentimental sea-fever that pervades some of the best-known poems of John Masefield. The seafarer in the Old English elegy is more likely a *peregrinus,* a voluntary exile who has renounced the transitory pleasures of this world in order to win, after prodigious physical and spiritual labors, the eternal felicity of the next.* Yet some scholars, as in the case of *The Wanderer,* hold that the poem is not about seafaring at all; that it, too, is a poetic homily employing Christian allegory (see OEB 135–148). Be that as it may, the universal appeal of *The Seafarer* results mainly from the fact that the real or allegorical central figure experiences a stirring human conflict between his eagerness to struggle and his nostalgia for the old life which he has deliberately rejected. This vividly realized interplay of emotions adds depth and richness to his personality and helps to establish *The Seafarer* as perhaps the greatest of Old English elegies.

---

* Dorothy Whitelock, "The Interpretation of The Seafarer," in *The Early Cultures of North-West Europe,* ed. Cyril Fox and Bruce Dickins (Cambridge: Cambridge University Press, 1950), pp. 261–72. See also Stanley B. Greenfield, in *Studies in Philology,* LI (1954).

The Ruin

The Ruin, an impressive fragment of thirty-three lines, differs from the elegies thus far discussed in that it does not begin with the personal sorrow of the poet or of a fictitious speaker. In *The Ruin* the reflections on the great theme of mutability are occasioned by a real or imaginary visit to the site of a once splendid city (perhaps Bath) now made desolate by the ravages of time:

> The clasp of earth and the clutch of the grave
> Grip the proud builders, long perished and gone,
> While a hundred generations have run.

Although the extant lines of the poem contain no mention of God, we again find the courts and mead-halls, "Where of old once the warrior walked in his pride," shattered by the all-leveling Wyrd (Fate). Thus, *The Ruin,* in spirit at least, resembles those elegies that are explicitly Christian in emphasis.

Elegiac Elements in Beowulf

Several portions of the epic *Beowulf* are tinged with the elegiac mood; there is, for instance, the brief portrait of a grieving father whose son has died on the gallows leaving behind an empty and wind-swept wine-hall. But one extended passage of some forty lines (ll. 2231–70) can be virtually detached from the poem as a whole and considered separately as a self-contained elegy, for it has close affinities with the lyrics just discussed.

The lines in question make up the "Lament of the Last Survivor," which was mentioned in the preceding chapter. The lone survivor of a wealthy tribe carries his riches to a mound near the sea and, realizing that his own end is near, buries this mocking reminder of more fortunate days:

> Keep thou, O Earth,   what men could not keep—
> This costly treasure   it came from thee!
> Baleful slaughter   hath swept away,
> Death in battle,   the last of my blood;
> They have lived their lives;   they have left the mead-hall.

Proud helmet and warrior have turned to dust; the harp is forever silenced. Day and night the last survivor bemoans his misery until he is himself claimed by death. Within the total context of *Beowulf* his plaint gains added significance, for this very treasure, which will be taken over after his death and guarded by a firedragon, will provoke one of Beowulf's subjects to theft and thereby set in motion a new cycle of human woe and destruction.

The Wife's Lament and *The Husband's Message*

There are two dramatic monologues almost unique in Old English literature in that they are love poems. Both deal with a husband and wife who have been separated—*The Wife's Lament,* recalling with pain a love no longer warm; *The Husband's Message,* holding out the bright hope of joyous reunion in the near future. A third poem, the fragment *Wulf and Eadwacer,* may be the impatient exhortation of an unfaithful wife to her lover, but the lines are beset with too many difficulties to be profitably discussed in these pages.*

The speaker in *The Wife's Lament* is an imprisoned woman who has apparently lost the trust of her absent husband as a result of the malicious plotting of his kinsmen. In her dreary cave underneath an oak she remembers a once vibrant love:

> With blithe hearts often of old we boasted
> That nought should part us save death alone;
> All that has failed and our former love
> Is now as if it had never been!

She envies lovers who still enjoy each other. But the life of man, she reflects, is always threatened by misfortune. With fine perceptiveness the poet unobtrusively shifts the wife's thoughts to the man who has forsaken her, and there are at least two plausible interpretations of her attitude. She may be thinking compassionately that his suffering must be greater than hers, for he is probably in some bleak and distant land, "Remembering always a happier home." Or she may be expressing, with understandable vindictiveness, the wish that he, too, should suffer even as he has caused her to suffer. In either case, the woman's point of view, so rarely explored by Old English poets, is set forth with remarkable sensitivity.

The Husband's Message makes delightful use of *prosopopoeia*—a rhetorical device, found in classical literature, in which an inanimate object is personified. In *The Husband's Message* a piece of wood carries to a loyal wife an important message carved into it by her absent husband. But in the opening lines (which some scholars re-

---

* The interested reader may consult John F. Adams, *"Wulf and Eadwacer: An Interpretation," Modern Language Notes,* LXXIII (1958), 1–5. (OEB 155.)

gard not as part of *The Husband's Message* but as a separate poem
entirely [Riddle 60]), the wood gives a charming account of its
earlier history as a tree growing near the sea. Little did the wood
then suspect that it would one day be granted the power of speech;
now, for her ears only, it can "talk." After confirming the mutual
love between husband and wife, the wood commands her to sail
quickly across the ocean into the husband's waiting arms. The message itself seems to have been carved in five runic letters (S, R, EA,
W, and D), which have occasioned a good deal of scholarly discussion. A probable explanation is that the little autobiography spoken
by the wood anticipates and explains the runic message and that the
names of the letters, taken together, comprise a brief five-word cipher
which communicates the husband's rapturous exhortation to join
him. If *The Husband's Message,* like most of the elegies, poses for-
bidding problems of text and interpretation, it furnishes at the same
time abundant compensations in its intimacy and warmth.*

THE CAEDMONIAN POEMS

Bede has frequently been mentioned as one of the major sources
for our knowledge of the early history of England. This great scholar,
who has been justly called the "father of English learning," serves as
a convenient point of departure for a consideration of Caedmon and
his poetic "school"—a group of religious poets who flourished in
Northumbria, presumably during the late seventh and early eighth
centuries.

Caedmon (fl. 657–80)

A celebrated passage in Bede tells of Caedmon, who had had no
schooling and who "did not learn the art of poetry from men, but
from God." At a monastery in Northumbria there lived "a certain
brother" who would self-consciously leave the banquet hall during
evening entertainments for fear that he would have to take his turn
at singing. On one such occasion a miracle occurred. Caedmon left
the hall, went out to the stable to take care of the horses, and, at
the proper time, lay down to rest:

* See Ralph W. V. Elliot, in *The Journal of English and Germanic Philology,*
LIV (1955), 1–8. In the old Germanic runic alphabet the name of each letter was
a word with definite associations. For a brief explanation of the runic alphabet,
see Charles W. Kennedy, *The Earliest English Poetry,* pp. 11–14, 361–64.

A person appeared to him in his sleep, and saluting him by his name, said, "Caedmon, sing some song to me." He answered, "I cannot sing; for that was the reason why I left the entertainment, and retired to this place because I could not sing." The other who talked to him, replied, "However, you shall sing."—"What shall I sing?" rejoined he. "Sing the beginning of created beings," said the other. Hereupon he presently began to sing verses to the praise of God, which he had never heard. . . .*

Caedmon awakened, remembered what he had composed in his dream, and added more to his song. When he repeated the verses before a group of learned authorities, it was concluded that Caedmon had indeed received a divine gift. He joined the monastery of the Abbess Hilda, at Whitby, where, Bede says, he continued to write poems on scriptural subjects.

The nine-line *Hymn,* paraphrased by Bede in Latin and found elsewhere in Northumbrian and West Saxon manuscripts, is largely a series of metaphors praising God as Creator. Other anonymous poems on scriptural subjects were at one time ascribed to Caedmon by literary scholars, but the *Hymn* is the only extant work still generally credited to him. His poems, however, apparently enlisted a sizable group of disciples and imitators. Although the works of the Caedmonian "school" are somewhat uneven in quality, they are almost always executed with a vigor characteristic of poetry in the heroic tradition. Particularly is this true of *Genesis B* and *Exodus.*

Genesis †

The Old English *Genesis* actually consists of two poems in one, both fragments. Lines 1–234 belong to the Caedmonian *Genesis A* (*c.* 700); lines 235–851 are interpolated into the manuscript from the so-called *Genesis B,* which was translated, perhaps as late as the tenth century, from a ninth-century Old Saxon poem; *Genesis A* resumes at line 852 and continues to the end. The scribe compiling the manuscript probably wanted to put together a continuous and complete narrative, and for that reason may have inserted *Genesis B*

* Bede, *The Ecclesiastical History of the English Nation,* Book IV, chap. 24. (Everyman's Library; London: J. M. Dent & Sons, Ltd.; New York: E. P. Dutton & Co., Inc., 1954.) Reprinted by permission of the publishers.

† The quotations from *Genesis* are from *Early English Christian Poetry* by Charles W. Kennedy. Published 1952 by Oxford University Press. Reprinted by permission of Oxford University Press, Inc., and Hollis and Carter, Ltd.

bodily into the middle of the earlier *Genesis A*. At any rate, the total *Genesis,* comprising 2,935 lines, renders the war in heaven, the fall of Satan, the temptation of Adam and Eve, and subsequent Biblical events through Abraham's offering of Isaac. There is some duplication of material between the two poems.

It is, ironically, the non-Caedmonian *Genesis B* that has received the most attention from scholars and general readers. Unlike the author of *Genesis A,* who rather closely paraphrases his Biblical source, the *Genesis B* poet shows real narrative power. His Satan emerges with much of the magnificent insolence of Milton's Satan in the initial books of *Paradise Lost*. Enraged at the prospect of humbling himself before a God whose supremacy he refuses to acknowledge, Satan boasts of his own strength and rouses his followers to rebellion —much in the manner of a Teutonic chief rallying his thanes:

> My hands have might
> To work many wonders. I have strength to rear
> A goodlier throne, a higher in heaven.
> Why must I yield or fawn for his favour
> Or bow in submission? I may be God
> As well as He. Brave comrades stand by me,
> Stout-hearted heroes unfailing in strife.
> (ll. 279–85)

After being hurled with the rest of the fallen angels into the fiery abyss of hell, the restless fiend plots the overthrow of man. First trying, and failing, to undermine Adam, he then turns to Eve. Again like Milton's Satan, he tempts her by playing upon her aspirations to divinity, as well as by promising her dominion over her husband. "Eat of this fruit," he bids her:

> Then your eyes shall have light to look afar
> Over all the world, even unto the throne
> Of your Lord in heaven, and have His favour.
> Over Adam thereafter you shall have sway
> If you have the will and he trusts your words.
> (ll. 567–71)

That Milton may have been acquainted with *Genesis B* is an intriguing possibility; there is at least a chance that he knew Junius, the seventeenth-century scholar who first printed this remarkable Old English poem.

Exodus *

The Caedmonian poem *Exodus* depicts with much originality and strength the career of Moses as lawgiver and military leader. The main action begins with the Israelites preparing to leave Egypt. After tracing their journey through various lands and describing their camping places, the poet reaches the narrative climax of his tale—the crossing of the Red Sea by the Israelites and the drowning of the Egyptian army. Moses speaks wisely to his people about the joys of the future life. Then, after gathering together the spoils of victory, the Israelites raise their voices in thanksgiving to the Almighty God who has delivered them.

The *Exodus* poet has fused Germanic and Christian elements with imagination and boldness. Moses possesses some of the characteristics of a Teutonic warrior, and there are the traditional harbingers of battle—wolves and birds of prey hungrily anticipating a splendid feast. But, interestingly enough, no actual battle takes place. The poet skillfully creates tension by shifting from the Israelites to the advancing Egyptians and back to the Israelites, who grow ever more despondent; and Moses prepares his men for combat with the usual prebattle exhortation to courage. Suddenly, however, God intervenes. The waves are raised up "as a rampart," the Israelites march safely through, and the Egyptians—in one of the most exciting moments in Old English poetry—suffer terrifying destruction:

> The waves mounted up, the storm rose high to the heavens, the mightiest outcry of an army. The foemen screamed aloud with doomed voices; the air grew dark above them; blood stained the flood. The protecting walls were pulled down; the greatest of drownings scourged the sky. . . . The flood foamed; the fated men fell; water rushed on the land; the air was in turmoil.†

"They fought against God," the account tersely concludes. There *is* a battle after all; not between opposing armies, but between a "heroic" God and the forces of darkness.

The phrase "blood stained the flood," quoted in the foregoing passage, translates the Old English *flod blod gewod*—one of many indi-

---

* The quotations from *Exodus* are from the prose translation of R. K. Gordon in his *Anglo-Saxon Poetry* (rev. ed.; Everyman's Library; London: J. M. Dent & Sons, Ltd.; New York: E. P. Dutton & Co., 1954). Reprinted by permission of the publishers.

† Gordon, *op. cit.*, p. 129.

cations of the *Exodus* poet's interest in unusual sounds and images. He says elsewhere in the poem that "the sword roared like a wild beast," and at one point he coins a striking word, *laughter-smith,* meaning "one who makes laughter." Not all the poet's experiments with metrics and diction are successful, but there are many signs in *Exodus* that a fresh creative mind is at work.*

Other Caedmonian Poems

In *Genesis B* and *Exodus* the "school" of Caedmon achieved poetry of substantial and enduring merit. Completing the picture are two Caedmonian works of less sustained interest and importance: *Daniel* and *Christ and Satan.*

Daniel, like *Genesis,* consists of two separate poems—*Daniel A* (c. 700) and *Daniel B,* which possibly dates from the ninth century. (A third, *Azariah,* has close affinities with *Daniel B.*) The poem offers an account of the reign of Nebuchadnezzar and of Daniel's interpretations of the King's ominous dreams. It continues with the rescue of the three young men from the fiery furnace. The final episode in the poem describes Belshazzar's feast, but the manuscript breaks off as Daniel prepares to explain the mysterious handwriting on the wall. Especially well done is the simple presentation of the deliverance of the three believers from the fire by an angel of God. "Under the fiery vault he covered the noble youths with his embraces. The darting of the flickering flame could do no hurt to their beauty, when the Sovereign saved them." †

The 733-line work known as *Christ and Satan* is in three parts: a lament of the fallen angels; Christ's Harrowing of Hell, which incorporates other scriptural material; and Satan's temptation of Christ in the wilderness. Of particular interest is the conception of Satan, portrayed here as an abject, self-pitying creature who is a far cry from the indomitable fiend of the greater *Genesis B.* When this enfeebled Satan tempts Christ in the wilderness (the theme of Milton's *Paradise Regained*), he receives a resounding curse that banishes him to an eternal hell:

> Know how broad and boundless, how bitter is hell.
> Measure it with your hands; take hold on its bottom;
> Explore till you know its limitless expanse.

* I am particularly indebted to the critical discussion by Edward B. Irving, Jr., in his *The Old English Exodus* (New Haven: Yale University Press, 1953).

† Gordon, *op. cit.,* p. 134.

Measure it from above even to the abyss;
Measure how broad the black mist stretches.
When your hands have measured the height and the depth,
The compass of hell, the grave-house grim,
Then shall you find you have fought against God! *

(ll. 699–707)

THE POETRY OF CYNEWULF AND THE CYNEWULFIANS

Except for Caedmon's *Hymn*, all of the verse discussed thus far is of unknown authorship. It is therefore gratifying to encounter one Old English poet, Cynewulf, with whom a number of definite poems may be identified. Cynewulf embedded his signature, in runic letters, in the texts of four important works: *The Fates of the Apostles, The Ascension* (also called *Christ II*), *Juliana*, and *Elene*.† Scholars have at one time or another ascribed additional poems to Cynewulf, but today there is general agreement that these unsigned poems— *Guthlac A* and *B*, *Christ I* and *III*, *Phoenix*, *Dream of the Rood*, and *Andreas* (discussed in Chapter III)—are not his. They do, however, bear sufficient thematic and stylistic resemblance to Cynewulf's four signed poems to have earned the convenient description "Cynewulfian."

The name is about all we know definitely of Cynewulf as a person, but he seems to have been a cultured Anglian cleric of the late eighth or early ninth century. ‡ In an autobiographical section near the end of *Elene*, Cynewulf confesses that in his youth he was soiled and shackled by sin, ignorant of the Cross, until God, in His infinite grace, granted him in old age the glorious gift of knowledge and sacred song; but one cannot tell how literally to take this ostensibly personal revelation.

About his verse we can speak with more assurance. Cynewulf's works reveal a degree of learning and literary sophistication not usually found among the Caedmonian poets, some of whom—the later ones—he may have influenced. Whether Cynewulf himself inaugurated a "school" or merely reflected an already established poetic

* From *Early English Christian Poetry* by Charles W. Kennedy. Published 1952 by Oxford University Press. Reprinted by permission of Oxford University Press, Inc., and Hollis and Carter, Ltd.

† On the Cynewulfian signature, see Charles W. Kennedy, *The Earliest English Poetry*, pp. 361–64.

‡ The old theory that he was the Bishop Cynewulf of Lindisfarne has been questioned by Kenneth Sisam. See OEB 73.

mode cannot be determined. Like other poets in the tradition, he drew his subjects not so much from the Bible as from the liturgy and from saints' lives—the latter incorporating many marvelous incidents, akin to episodes in Oriental lore, in which the hero undergoes fantastic tortures but miraculously escapes unharmed. The most distinctive feature of Cynewulfian verse is its highly intricate use of images. In fact, some of the most memorable lines produced by Cynewulf and his group are elaborately developed symbols and allegories.

The Fates of the Apostles

In what is perhaps the least effective of his four poems, Cynewulf records briefly the life, works, and manner of death of each of the twelve apostles. While his original readers may have responded to the allusions to familiar stories with the same sort of pleasure experienced by the audiences of *Widsith* and *Deor,* for modern readers the chief interest is Cynewulf's runic signature, preceded and followed by a request that whoever reads the poem should pray for the safe passage of the poet's soul on its long journey into the unknown. Thus Cynewulf did not sign his poems out of vanity, but rather from a fervent hope that his audience might help him to attain salvation.

The Ascension (Christ II) *

Of the three-part Cynewulfian poem collectively known as *Christ,* scholars today generally assign only the second part to Cynewulf. *Christ II* is a masterful reworking of a homily on the Ascension composed by Pope Gregory the Great. In attempting to convey the rapture of the Ascension of Christ, Cynewulf achieves some of his most dazzling images. At one point Christ allegorically becomes a radiant bird who alternately flies heavenward to "the realm of angels" and swoops downward to inspire mankind on earth. In another daring figure Christ's redemption is symbolized as a series of six "leaps" (the suggestion comes from a phrase in the *Song of Songs*): Incarnation, Nativity, Baptism, Crucifixion, Burial, and Resurrection. Developing the symbol still further, Cynewulf says that man, too, must leap to God:

* Quotations are from *Early English Christian Poetry* by Charles W. Kennedy. Published 1952 by Oxford University Press. Reprinted by permission of Oxford University Press, Inc., and Hollis and Carter, Ltd.

As here on earth's soil God's Son Eternal
Mounted by leaps above the high hills,
Bold on the mountains, so we mortal men
In our hearts' musings must mount by leaps
From strength to strength, and strive for glory,
That we may ascend by holy works
To the highest heavens, where are joy and hope,
A goodly band of thanes.

(ll. 744–51)

After incorporating his runic signature into a vivid account of the
Last Judgment, Cynewulf concludes the poem with a beautiful metaphor envisioning life as a sea journey. The passage inevitably recalls
The Wanderer and *The Seafarer,* but in *The Ascension* there can be
no doubt that seafaring is intended as a Christian allegory:

Now is it most like as if on ocean
Across cold water we sail in our keels,
Over the wide sea in our ocean-steeds,
Faring on in our flood-wood. Fearful the stream,
The tumult of waters, whereon we toss
In this feeble world. Fierce are the surges
On the ocean lanes. Hard was our life
Before we made harbour o'er the foaming seas.

(ll. 849–56)

The harbor, of course, is salvation; with God's grace our "ocean-
stallions" may find safe anchor there. "Let us fix our hope," Cynewulf urges, "Upon that haven which the Lord of heaven,/In holiness
on high, has opened by His Ascension."

Juliana

In a poem based upon a Latin prose life of St. Juliana (who lived
during the reign of the Roman Emperor Maximian [305–11]),
Cynewulf rehearses the unspeakable torments and eventual martyrdom suffered by a beautiful Christian virgin who will not compromise
her faith. After she refuses to marry the Roman prefect Heliseus
(Eleusius) because he is unwilling to accept Christianity, Juliana
is stripped, scourged, hanged by the hair, thrown into prison, and
immersed in a cauldron of boiling lead. When all these afflictions have
failed to break her spirit, she is beheaded. Meanwhile, her fortitude
has won many converts from the ranks of the pagans who witnessed
her ordeals; and shortly after St. Juliana is buried, the cruel Helis-

eus, with twenty-four of his followers, drowns in a furious storm at sea.

The most interesting scene in this lively poem is that in which Satan, disguised as an angel of God, appears in Juliana's prison cell and tries to persuade her to save herself by submission; but Juliana seizes him and extracts a lengthy confession of the methods he employs to destroy men's faith. In a well-known image, characteristic of Cynewulf, Satan pictures the soul of man as a besieged city. When he encounters a brave Christian whose spiritual armor is impregnable, the Devil must flee, "abased and humbled," to seek out one "less bold under banner" whom he might more readily ensnare. He quickly sizes up his victim, spying out a secret fault that may be obscured by the most virtuous of intentions. Then, Satan tells her, he unleashes his attack:

> Through corruption I weaken the gate in the wall;
> When the tower is pierced and an entrance opened,
> Then into his soul in a storm of darts
> I loose the arrows of evil thought.*

So great is the intrinsic power of the metaphor, even though Cynewulf may not have been the first to use it, that it has appealed almost automatically to poets in nearly every era. Indeed, it became almost a commonplace in the devotional literature of the Middle Ages. Interestingly enough, Petrarch and the sonnet-writers of the Renaissance who followed him, including Spenser, Sidney, and Shakespeare, adapted the image to describe the attempts of a lover to batter down the resistance of a cold-hearted mistress.

Elene

Elene (apparently based upon a Latin text which is not extant) is an ambitious narrative, cast in a heroic mood, in which Cynewulf tells of the Roman Emperor Constantine's vision of the Cross on the eve of battle with the ferocious Huns (A.D. 312); his subsequent victory and commitment to the service of God; and the dispatching of his mother Elene (St. Helena) across the sea to search for the true Cross. Arriving in Jerusalem, Elene at first can elicit no information from the Jews; one of their leaders, however, a man ironically named Judas, is finally forced to direct her to Calvary. With the

* From *The Earliest English Poetry* by Charles W. Kennedy. Pp. 211–12. Copyright 1943. Reprinted by permission of Oxford University Press, Inc.

help of a sign from God, whom Judas now worships as a Christian, Elene recovers three crosses, the true Cross being identified by virtue of its miraculous restoration of a corpse to life. At Constantine's behest Elene builds a temple on the site and adorns the Rood (Cross) with gold and gems. From Judas, now baptized as Cyriacus and serving as a Christian priest, Elene secures the nails used in the Crucifixion, orders these to be fastened on Constantine's bridle, and bids all Christians to celebrate the anniversary of the finding of the Cross. Thus ends the narrative proper. The story of the Cross is followed by the autobiographical passage, which was cited earlier; then comes the runic signature and an exciting description of the Last Judgment, when the unregenerate sinners shall be held fast in a blazing hell and the blessed, as well as the wrongdoers who have repented, shall be cleansed by purgatorial flames.

The poem, which is continually interesting, contains several moments of rare power. It is hard to imagine an Old English poet breathing fresh life into the traditional battle scene; yet Cynewulf does just that, even while using the time-worn ingredients of war spears glittering in the light, and the ever present wolves and ravens clamoring for prey. The poet again pours old wine into new bottles when he evokes a striking picture of Elene's sea-crossing:

> There might he see who beheld that sailing
> Sea-wood scud under swelling sails,
> Sea-steeds plunge and break through the billows,
> Wave-ships skim. The warriors bold
> Were blithe, and the queen had joy of the journey.*
>
> (ll. 244–48)

There are also some breath-taking flashes in *Elene,* as when, in Constantine's dream, the Cross sparkles in the sky to give the Emperor new hope, or when the nails of the Cross suddenly shine from the dark depths of the earth "like heavenly stars."

Guthlac A and B

Andreas (see Chapter III) is a saint's life derived from Greek sources, and *Juliana* and *Elene* celebrate the careers of Roman Christians who attained sainthood. But two Old English poems in the Cynewulfian manner, probably not by Cynewulf, treat the life and

* From *Early English Christian Poetry* by Charles W. Kennedy. Published 1952 by Oxford University Press. Reprinted by permission of Oxford University Press, Inc., and Hollis and Carter, Ltd.

death of a native English saint, Guthlac, who in 699 became a hermit in a desolate part of Lincolnshire. The poems are known as *Guthlac A* and *Guthlac B,* but their chronology and precise interrelationships are not at all certain. Assisted by a guardian angel, Guthlac successfully resists the many physical and spiritual assaults made upon him by demons who would destroy his faith. Although *Guthlac A* and *Guthlac B* are both probably based on Felix of Croyland's mid-eighth-century Latin *Vita,* some of the most interesting passages—notably that in *Guthlac A* which deals with the corruption of the monasteries—seem to be independent additions made by the English poet or poets. (There is also an Old English prose life of Guthlac.)

Guthlac A, after a prologue extolling the hermit's way of life, dwells mainly upon the saint's trials and triumphs. Particularly noteworthy is the section in which the fiends, having failed to undermine Guthlac through physical affliction, attempt to destroy his confidence in the purity and integrity of the clergy. Are there not members of monastic orders, they suggest, who secretly harbor corrupt thoughts? But Guthlac defends his brothers and displays a remarkable understanding of human weakness. God Himself, he says, created youth; and young men cannot be expected to possess the maturity which age alone confers:

> They cannot in their first zest have the ways of old age, but they delight in the pleasures of the world, till length of years comes upon their youth, so that the spirit loves the appearance and presence of an elder age. . . . Men display wisdom to the people, leave pride, when the spirit flees from the lasciviousness of youth.*

Furthermore, Guthlac declares, these devils, in their perversion and cynicism, think only of the sins of the few who are guilty; they never acknowledge the virtue of the many righteous men who serve God faithfully. Apparently monasticism had its critics relatively early in English history, but it also found staunch defenders who could cherish the strength of the monastic ideal in spite of the weakness of individual monks.

Guthlac B touches upon the saint's triumph over the fiends who persecute him, but its chief concern is with his final sickness and death. The death scene is wonderfully serene; Guthlac breathes his

* Translation by R. K. Gordon in *Anglo-Saxon Poetry* (Everyman's Library; London: J. M. Dent & Sons, Ltd.; New York: E. P. Dutton & Co., 1954), p. 293. Reprinted by permission of the publishers.

last as a miraculous light floods the hermitage and shines radiantly upon his face:

> The black northern sky was dark under the clouds; it wrapped the world in mist; covered it with darkness; night came rushing down over the world, over the land's adornments. Then came the greatest of lights in holiness from heaven, shining clearly, radiant over the city-dwellings. He who was destined bravely awaited his end in blessedness, pierced by the arrows of death. An excellent glorious light shone bright about the noble man the livelong night; the shadows drew off, dispersed through the air. The gleaming splendour, the heavenly candle, stayed round that sacred house from the dusk of evening till dawn; the glowing sun came from the east over the deep sea-path.*

After Guthlac's death his devoted servant faithfully carries over the seas to the saint's virgin sister the message that her brother's soul will meet hers in the eternal joy of their heavenly home. As he sails on his mission, the servant laments the passing of his good master and reflects upon the hardships that he himself, now an exile, must undergo. Both his situation and his response recall the elegiac mood of the lonely *eardstapa* ("earth-treader") in *The Wanderer*.

Christ I and III †

The work collectively known as Christ includes two Cynewulfian poems, together with *The Ascension* (*Christ II*). *Christ I* consists of a series of hymns chiefly associated with the Advent season. *Christ III*, one of the strongest descriptive pieces in Old English literature, is a poem on the Last Judgment. *The Ascension*, it will be remembered, is one of the four signed poems of Cynewulf, but the prevailing opinion is that neither *Christ I* nor *Christ III* is his (but see OEB 175).

Christ I, or the *Advent Lyrics*, is an elaboration of eleven liturgical anthems (or antiphons) celebrating the various implications of the coming of Christ. Included are lyrics based upon the image of Christ as the cornerstone rejected by the builders; of God as the keeper of the keys of life which will liberate mankind from a dark dungeon; of Jerusalem as the "City of Christ," where the souls of the righteous

---

* Translation by R. K. Gordon, in *Anglo-Saxon Poetry*, p. 307. Reprinted by permission of E. P. Dutton & Co., Inc., and J. M. Dent & Sons, Ltd.

† The quotations are from *Early English Christian Poetry* by Charles W. Kennedy. Published 1952 by Oxford University Press. Reprinted by permission of Oxford University Press, Inc., and Hollis and Carter, Ltd.

will find rest; of the Rising Sun, "True Son of the Father," illuminating those who have long been "Attired with darkness in eternal
night." One of the most unusual figures is founded upon the prophecy of Isaiah that the Lord will penetrate the firm bars that surround
the earth; it is the Virgin Mary who will be the great door through
which Christ shall enter:

> Now is fulfilled what the prophet foresaw.
> Thou art the wall-door through which the dear Lord
> Once fared unto earth. Just so Christ found thee
> Adorned with power, pure and elect;
> The King of angels, the Lord of life,
> After Him left thee locked with a key,
> An Immaculate Maiden.
>
> (ll. 328–34)

Christ I has yet another claim to distinction: in the midst of the
lyrics there is (ll. 164–214) a passage of dialogue between Joseph and
Mary, an extraordinary departure which some scholars have regarded
as the first dramatic scene in English literature—evidence that the
Advent Lyrics were perhaps intended to be sung, with some dramatic
representation, as part of the liturgy. Medieval drama (see Chapter
XV) seems to have been liturgical in its origins.

Christ III, one of several Old English poems on Doomsday, has
considerable power. The poet manages to paint a convincing picture
of hot flames raging in a world totally deprived of light:

> There is din through the deep Creation. Before the Lord
> The greatest of raging fires flames over earth.
> The hot blaze surges, the heavens shall fall;
> The steadfast light of the stars shall fail.
> The sun shall be blackened to the hue of blood
> Which shone so brightly for the sons of men
> Over the ancient earth. The moon herself
> That by night illumined mankind with her light
> Shall sink from her station; so also the stars
> Swept by the whirlwind through the storm-beat air
> Shall vanish from heaven.
>
> (ll. 930–40)

Then, raised as a sign of God's might, shall stand the Cross, bringing
a shining promise to those who believe. To sin-stained men, however,
it shall bring only terror:

It shall bring them no grace that the brightest of beacons,
The Rood of our Saviour red with His blood,
Over-run with bright gore, upreared before men.

(ll. 1083–85)

In those ancient scars and open wounds the "dark workers of evil"
will behold an agonizing reminder of the supreme good which they
have perverted into an instrument of their damnation.

Physiologus

Physiologus, or *Bestiary,* is an example of allegorical use of natural
history to illuminate Christian teaching. The Old English poem,
which may or may not be a complete unit and which bears a much
debated but indeterminate relationship with the Continental *Physiologus* (in Latin), consists of brief sketches of the Panther, the Whale,
and the Partridge—the last poem surviving in a form too fragmentary for profitable interpretation. The Panther, full of kindness and
friendly to all creatures except the Dragon, slumbers for three days
after tasting of food; on the third day he awakens and exudes a
lovely music and a sweet fragrance. The poet interprets the allegory:
the Panther is Christ. The Whale, on the other hand, is full of de-
ceit. He rests motionless in the sea, causing weary sailors to mistake
his bulk for an island. After they have anchored on him and kindled
what they think will be a comforting fire, the Whale plunges downward and brings death and destruction to the sailors and their ships.
Interestingly enough, this myth and its interpretation provide the
substance of one of Milton's great epic similes—in which Satan,
stretched out in the fiery gulf of hell, is compared to the sea-
beast Leviathan who tempts sailors to their doom. The practice of
allegorizing animals lasted well into the Renaissance.

Phoenix *

Phoenix is the most elaborate attempt on the part of an Old English poet to allegorize natural history. Here the ancient classical and
Oriental myth of the self-perpetuating bird is reshaped into a symbol
of Christian immortality. Although the first portion (or about half)
of *Phoenix* is basically a translation of a Latin poem commonly at-

* The quotations from *Phoenix,* and from the *Dream of the Rood,* are from
Early English Christian Poetry by Charles W. Kennedy. Published 1952 by
Oxford University Press. Reprinted by permission of Oxford University Press,
Inc., and Hollis and Carter, Ltd.

tributed to Lactantius (fl. *c.* 300), the Old English poet has not hesitated to amplify upon his source with images and interpretations of his own.

The poem begins with an exotic description of the eastern paradise where the bird makes its home. In its unchanging beauty and mildness the paradise inevitably resembles Eden:

> Serene that country, sunny groves gleaming;
> Winsome the woodlands; fruits never fail
> Or shining blossoms. As God gave bidding
> The groves stand forever growing and green.
> Winter and summer the woods alike
> Are hung with blossoms; under heaven no leaf
> Withers, no fire shall waste the plain
> To the end of the world.
>
> (ll. 33–40)

The fair bird, who bathes twelve times daily in the cool waters and soars aloft to carol the most wonderful music ever heard, lives for a thousand years. Then he flies westward, builds a nest in some secret woodland tree, and assembles in the boughs of the tree the sweetest of fruits, herbs, and plants. Fired by the heat of the sun, the nest is consumed:

> The pyre is kindled, the fire enfolds
> The home of the heart-sick. The yellow flame
> Fiercely rages; the Phoenix burns,
> Full of years, as the fire consumes
> The fleeting body. The spirit fades,
> The soul of the fated. The bale-fire seizes
> Both bone and flesh.
>
> (ll. 218–24)

From his own ashes the Phoenix renews his life; then, amid the hymns of the birds who surround him (the apostles) and the uplifted glances of men below, the Phoenix returns to his eastern home to dwell in resplendent beauty for another thousand years. The poet proceeds to interpret, in more explicit detail, the Phoenix and his flight. The regenerating flames merge quite naturally with the fires of the Day of Judgment.

As one might surmise, the allegory operates on several levels. The death and rebirth of the Phoenix stand for the resurrection of the soul out of the purgatorial flames of Judgment, as well as for the death and Ascension of Christ. In any event, *Phoenix* as a whole represents a graceful adaptation of pagan myth to the uses of Christian doctrine.

Dream of the Rood

This chapter concludes with a discussion of the most exalted of the Cynewulfian poems—indeed, one of the greatest religious lyrics in our language.

The *Dream of the Rood* (Vision of the Cross) is conceived as a dream-vision, a literary genre so magnificently employed by some of the major poets of the Middle Ages: Chaucer; the *Pearl* poet; William Langland; and, of course, Dante. The dreamer in the Old English poem beholds the towering Cross, encrusted with gold and silver but swiftly turning to reveal on its right side the wet stains of outwelling blood. Suddenly the Cross begins to address him. By means of *prosopopoeia,* the technique used by the poet of *The Husband's Message,* the Rood unfolds its history. The Cross tells how it was cut down, carried to the hilltop, and fastened firmly in the ground. How proudly it stood as Christ, the young warrior, put off his garments and mounted to redeem mankind! Christ is portrayed not as an agonized sufferer, but as a fearless champion who inspires bravery in the very wood that bears him:

> When the Hero clasped me, I trembled in terror,
> But I dared not bow me nor bend to earth;
> I must needs stand fast. Upraised as the Rood
> I held the High King, the Lord of heaven.
> I dared not bow! With black nails driven
> Those sinners pierced me; the prints are clear,
> The open wounds. I dared injure none.
> They mocked us both. I was wet with blood
> From the Hero's side when He sent forth His spirit.

In lines remarkable for their compressed strength, the poet flashes the majesty of Christ against the blackness that at that moment eclipsed the whole of the universe in sorrow—a passage climaxed with an unadorned, "Christ was on the Cross," penetrating in its overtones of both tragedy and triumph:

> Black darkness covered with clouds God's body,
> That radiant splendour. Shadow went forth
> Wan under heaven; all creation wept
> Bewailing the King's death. Christ was on the Cross.

The Cross painfully recalls the dirges sung by the last mourners at evening; it remembers how Christ, still embracing it, was flung into a pit; then it reveals how God's friends recovered it and graced it with treasures. The Cross is now the only way by which mankind can approach God, and it charges the dreamer to transmit his vision to the world and to prophesy the Second Coming. Since that vivid dream, the poet tells us, he has prayed earnestly to the Cross, which sustains him throughout the loneliness of this fleeting life on earth. His fondest hope is that he may revere it well:

> This is my heart's desire, and all my hope
> Waits on the Cross. In this world now
> I have few powerful friends; they have fared hence
> Away from these earthly gauds seeking the King of glory,
> Dwelling now with the High Father in heaven above,
> Abiding in rapture.

Each day he dreams that the Cross will transport him to the heavenly kingdom of everlasting joy where he may dwell forever. The poet has used the rhetorical device of *synecdoche,* whereby the part may be taken for the whole; the Cross stands for Redemption.

The Cross, with its dramatic implications of cosmic suffering and personal redemption, has understandably become one of the most compelling of Christian symbols. The unknown poet of the *Dream of the Rood* responded to that symbol with tremendous faith and intellectual conviction, and because of his extraordinary poetic endowments he could communicate his vision with incandescent beauty.

V: OLD ENGLISH PROSE AND MISCELLANEOUS VERSE

The great period of Old English poetry extended roughly from the last quarter of the seventh century through the first quarter of the ninth, and it is largely identified with the period of Northumbrian and Mercian cultural supremacy. English literary prose, however, was born in Wessex late in the ninth century when King Alfred the Great determined to bring Latin learning within the grasp of all his subjects. As noted in Chapter II, the translations which he made himself, as well as those which he supervised, opened the door for original prose composition in English—notably in the tenth and eleventh centuries by two exceptionally gifted clerics, the Abbott Ælfric and Bishop Wulfstan.

In addition to the works of Alfred and his followers, we consider in this chapter a few poems or groups of poems that do not properly fit into the four major categories (heroic, elegiac, Caedmonian, and Cynewulfian) examined in Chapters III and IV. Two of these miscellaneous poems, the *Battle of Brunanburh* and the *Battle of Maldon,* belong chronologically with the prose, for they were inspired by historical events of the tenth century. In all probability the other verse to be dealt with here—Charms, Riddles, and Gnomes—is generally of much earlier date than the prose, though all three verse collections seem to span almost the whole of the Old English period.

OLD ENGLISH PROSE

In almost any civilization, prose as a form of conscious art flowers much later than verse, and England furnishes no exception. Although English was employed as the language of ordinary daily communication, Latin remained for a long time the vehicle for serious literary composition in such fields as theology, history, philosophy, and biography—a situation exemplified in the varied output of Bede and other clerical writers. Many learned works, however, were inevitably translated or paraphrased into English, and eventually Englishmen, lay as well as clerical, began to produce original prose in vernacular

English. One man was primarily responsible for the emergence of English literary prose: the enormously versatile King Alfred, no less a hero in peace than in war.*

King Alfred (849–899)

Alfred the Great was a rare combination of warrior, administrator, and scholar. Having halted, though temporarily, the ruthless Danish invaders, Alfred embarked upon a program of political and intellec- tual reform designed to make his Wessex the center of ninth-century English culture and to restore some of the glory that was England's during the period of Northumbrian ascendancy. According to the biography written by Bishop Asser, his contemporary, the King him- self had not learned to read until the age of twelve; but recognizing the power and dignity that knowledge confers, he pursued learning diligently and invited scholars and teachers to his court in order to help him implement an educational program for the whole country.

A vital part of Alfred's program was to make important Latin works available to his subjects in the vernacular and thereby estab- lish English as the national language of instruction. His plan is well described in the Preface to his translation of Pope Gregory's *Pastoral Care,* a handbook for clergymen which stresses the teaching function of the Christian ministry. Recalling the former intellectual prestige of his country during the seventh and eighth centuries, Alfred de- plores the decay of learning in his own time. He would therefore "translate some books which are most needful for all men to know into the language which we can all understand. . . ." English, he urges, should become the basic vehicle for teaching; further study in Latin he recommends for those desiring a more advanced education.

Among other books "most needful for all men to know," which Alfred either translated himself or directed others to translate, were Bede's *Ecclesiastical History,* St. Augustine's *Soliloquies,* Orosius' *Universal History,* and Boethius' *Consolation of Philosophy.* The two last-named works are of particular interest. With the *Universal History* of Orosius, a Spanish priest of the fifth century, Alfred in- cluded two fascinating pieces of geographical literature: one by the Norwegian explorer Ohthere, who sailed the Arctic Ocean and the White Sea; the other by the traveler Wulfstan (not to be confused

* On Old English literary prose, see Kemp Malone, in *A Literary History of England,* ed. Albert C. Baugh, pp. 96–105. For fuller treatment see George K. Anderson, *The Literature of the Anglo-Saxons,* chaps. VIII–XIII.

with Bishop Wulfstan), who visited the regions east of the Baltic. The celebrated work by Boethius, a Roman patrician and Christian of the sixth century who is comforted in his prison cell by a great lady personifying Philosophy, was to exercise a tremendous influence on medieval thought; Chaucer, for example, not only translated Boethius but drew heavily upon his conceptions of fortune and tragedy. The literary value of Alfred's translations is actually less than their significance for the intellectual history of England.

The Anglo-Saxon Chronicle *(891)*

Not the least of Alfred's achievements was to arrange for the systematic assembly of the so-called *Anglo-Saxon Chronicle*. This compilation, together with Bede's *Ecclesiastical History*, constitutes an invaluable source of information about early English history. It consists of four distinct chronicles preserved in seven different manuscripts—a consideration which has led some scholars to prefer the name *Old English Annals*. The first entry is Caesar's invasion of Britain in 55 B.C.; the last is the accession of Henry II in 1154. The early materials were derived from Bede and other sources; contemporary entries do not, in all probability, antedate the year 600. The literary style is not distinguished, even when the chroniclers recount, as they frequently do, events steeped in blood and horror; only in periods during the ninth, late tenth, and eleventh centuries does the prose reach any level of narrative excitement. Poems, too, are occasionally included in the *Chronicle*, the *Battle of Brunanburh* being the most effective.

Ælfric *(c. 955–c. 1020)*

Alfred the Great had broken the ground for the development of English prose, but it was the Abbott Ælfric, of Winchester and, later, Oxfordshire, who became the first authentic prose master in our language. Excellence of style, however, was incidental to Ælfric's main purpose, which, not surprisingly, was to provide his countrymen with moral edification founded upon the teachings of Christianity.

Included among Ælfric's voluminous output are a translation of the first seven books of the Bible into English and, perhaps more important, a total of 120 *Homilies*—in three groups of forty each—translated "for those men to read who do not know Latin." The style, though often inclining towards alliterative prose, is wonderfully straightforward and lucid. In the following extract Ælfric discourses upon the meaning of miracles. For him, familiar "daily miracles" are more glorious than the unusual miracles that God performs on special occasions:

> The fact that each day God Almighty feeds the whole world, and guides the good, is a greater miracle than was that of filling five thousand men with five loaves; yet men wondered at that, not because it was a greater miracle, but because it was unusual.*

It is not enough, he continues, to wonder at God's miracles; we must understand their spiritual significance. In the early days of Christianity, he points out in another homily, miracles were necessary in order to impress the heathen and help win them over. "The man who plants trees or herbs continues to water them until they are rooted; when they begin to grow, he stops the watering."

One other work of Ælfric's, of slight literary value, should be noted: the charming *Colloquy on the Occupations,* in Latin but with an interlinear English translation, designed to teach Latin to English boys. In this dialogue, a teacher introduces his pupils to several representatives of English economic life: a farmer, a hunter, a merchant. Each answers questions about his daily work and its problems. These informal glimpses into English society at the beginning of the eleventh century make the *Colloquy* a valuable cultural document.

Wulfstan (d. 1023)

Among the more spectacular developments of recent Old English scholarship has been the emergence of Wulfstan from almost total obscurity into pre-eminence as a religious, diplomatic, and literary light. As Bishop of London (996–1002), Bishop of Worcester (1002–16), and Archbishop of York (1003–23), he helped formulate codes of law for King Ethelred and King Cnut. Although his chief interests were practical rather than literary, Wulfstan's fame rests primarily upon his powers as a homilist. He generally treats doctrinal matters in a spirit of ethical and religious reflection, but he makes skillful use of thunderous rhetorical effects such as rhyme, repetition, and alliteration. His description of hell sounds very effective in Old English. "ðaer is ece bryne grimme gemencged. ðaer is ece gryne. paer is wanung . granung a singal sorh [where is eternal

* *Select Translations from Old English Prose,* eds. Albert S. Cook and C. B. Tinker (Boston: Ginn and Company, 1908). Reprinted by permission of the publisher.

fire cruelly prepared, and where is eternal horror; where is moaning and groaning and ever continuing pain]." *

Oddly enough, Wulfstan is mainly remembered for one celebrated homily which is not typical of his style—the terrifying *Sermo Lupi ad Anglos* ("Sermon of Wulfstan to the English People"). In this passionate outpouring, Wulfstan unleashes a crushing attack upon the many sins he finds rampant among his people and pleads with his listeners to repent lest they be consumed in the flames of hell at the impending end of the world. Here Wulfstan departs from his usual custom and dwells upon sharply observed, concrete details of everyday life. It is the most topical of his great sermons. †

A few other prose works may be cited: the so-called *Blickling Homilies,* a group of nineteen sermons contained in a manuscript dating from about 970; some homilies found in the Vercelli Book; and a fragment of an Old English version of *Apollonius,* a classical romance which reappears in English literature as one of the tales in John Gower's poem *Confessio Amantis* and, more important, furnishes the plot of Shakespeare's *Pericles.*

HISTORIC BATTLE POEMS

The history of England during the tenth century was marked, it was pointed out, by continuing war with the Danish invaders. Out of this long and ultimately tragic struggle came two battle poems which pay a final tribute to the heroic spirit of the Anglo-Saxons: the *Battle of Brunanburh,* a robust celebration of an English victory; and the *Battle of Maldon,* a moving account of a noble defeat.

Battle of Brunanburh (c. 937)

The stirring narrative poem about a battle fought at Brunanburh appears in the *Anglo-Saxon Chronicle* for the year 937. At Brunanburh—the exact location of which is unknown, though Bromborough, in Cheshire, is a possibility—Æthelstan, grandson of Alfred the Great, routed the armies of Constantine, King of the Scots, who was allied with the Norsemen and Danes. Æthelstan later called himself "King of all England," and Brunanburh became a symbol of English unity and strength.

---

* See Dorothy Bethurum, *The Homilies of Wulfstan* (New York: Oxford University Press, 1957).
† *Ibid.*

The *Battle of Brunanburh,* well known through a modernization by Tennyson, utilizes effectively some of the devices of the earlier heroic poetry. In reciting, for example, the carnage inflicted upon Constantine and his men, the poet indulges in familiar ironic understatement, or litotes. "Slender warrant had/*He* to be proud of/The welcome of war-knives." With characteristic greediness the eagle, the raven, and the wolf prepare to feast upon the dead Scots (the translation is Tennyson's):

> Many a carcase they left to be carrion,
> Many a livid one, many a sallow-skin—
> Left for the white-tailed eagle to tear it, and
> Left for the horny-nibbed raven to rend it, and
> Gave to the garbaging war-hawk to gorge it, and
> That gray beast, the wolf of the weald.

As late as the tenth century there was still plenty of vigor in a rousing Old English description of a battle.

Battle of Maldon (c. 991)

The events of the battle fought at Maldon are reported in several of the manuscripts of the *Anglo-Saxon Chronicle.* In 991 a band of vikings, perhaps led by the Norwegian Olaf Tryggvesson, landed on the coast of Essex and were met by the ealdorman Byrhtnoth and his English forces. Although Byrhtnoth led a heroic defense, he was slain in battle and his army defeated. Afterwards, one of the chroniclers states, peace was made with the enemy, and Olaf was received by the King.

The *Battle of Maldon,* the beginning and the end of which are missing, is a fine poetic rendering of Byrhtnoth's valiant fight in a losing cause. The poet rehearses the gathering of the troops, the pre-battle exchange of taunts, and the furious din of the fighting itself. When Byrhtnoth falls in the field, the poet reproaches the cowardice of the thane Godric, who gallops off to safety on the horse of his stricken leader. The young Ælfwine, in contrast, reaffirms the spirit of the *comitatus.* None shall reproach *him,* he proclaims in a bēot ("boast"), with fleeing home while his lord lies dead. One by one the other warriors take up the call to heroic action—even the aged companion Byrhtwold, whose exhortation is indeed inspiring:

> Heart must be hardier, courage the keener,
> Mood must be the bolder, as our band lessens!

> Here on the ground our good lord lies,
> Butchered in battle. Ever will he rue it
> Who now from this war-play thinks to turn away.
> I am old in years. I will never yield;
> But here at the last beside my lord,
> By the leader I loved, I look to lie.*

Here the uncompromising code of loyalty embraced by the early Germanic warrior has been elevated to sublime heights.

CHARMS, RIDDLES, AND GNOMIC VERSE †

This account of Old English literature ends on a relatively informal note. The three groups of poems to be discussed at this time —Charms (or Spells), Riddles (or Enigmas), and Gnomic Verse— all shed an interesting light, in one way or another, upon the daily life and thought of the Anglo-Saxons.

Charms

The Germanic invaders brought with them to England a battery of charms and magic spells designed to ward off a variety of evils— a swarm of bees, bad weather, theft of cattle, and many more. The usual procedure is to declare, in prose, a suitable recipe to furnish relief, then to recite a poetic incantation. The charm against a sudden pain, *Stice,* first prescribes a mixture of feverfew, red nettle, and plantain—all to be boiled in butter. Next the exorcist calls upon the spears which plague the body to depart:

> Out, little spear, if herein it be!
> The smith sat, forged his little knife,
> Sore smitten with iron.
> Out, little spear, if herein thou be!
> Six smiths sat, wrought war-spears.
> Out, spear, not in, spear! ‡

Finally a knife is to be plunged into the magic liquid.

Like so much of early Germanic culture, the charms were in time

---

* From *The Earliest English Poetry* by Charles W. Kennedy. Copyright 1943. Reprinted by permission of Oxford University Press, Inc.

† Quotations are from the translation of R. K. Gordon in *Anglo-Saxon Poetry.* Reprinted by permission of E. P. Dutton & Co., Inc., and J. M. Dent & Sons, Ltd.

‡ P. 95.

Christianized, and the resultant blend of paganism and Christianity is frequently curious. This incongruity is especially well illustrated in the remedy against barren land, *Æcerbot*. Four sods are to be taken from four sides of the land and sprinkled with a strange mixture, including honey, yeast, milk, parts of trees and herbs, and holy water. After the sods are sanctified in the name of the Trinity, they are carried to church where the priest sings four masses over them. The poetic incantation is addressed partly to God and the Virgin Mary, partly to "Erce, Erce, Erce, mother of earth." Unfortunately, however, the presence or absence of Christian elements does not help us to date individual charms with accuracy.

Riddles

The riddle, a literary performance of classical derivation, flourished in Latin late in the seventh century before imitations began to appear in English. The nearly one hundred English riddles contained in the *Exeter Book* seem to be based in part upon Anglo-Latin riddles composed by Aldhelm and other English scholars. Modern scholars have not determined, however, the extent of the indebtedness to Latin models; and, as usual, little can be said about authorship and dates for particular riddles.

The *Exeter* Riddles encompass a vast range of subjects drawn from everyday life: birds, animals, weapons, household utensils, foodstuffs. The speakers—note the *prosopopoeia*—do not explicitly reveal their identities; through a series of ingenious clues, often in the form of striking paradoxes, they tease and mystify (though scholars have solved most of the puzzles). The Anchor, for example, declares that if he is at rest, he is mighty in conflict. The Plough confides that his nose is down. "I go deep and dig into the ground." Mead (the alcoholic drink of the Anglo-Saxons) boasts that he can cast a young man to the earth, even in daylight. The delightful "Riddle of the Bookworm" may be quoted in full:

> A Moth ate words. That seemed to me a strange event, when I heard of that wonder, that the worm, a thief in the darkness, should devour the song of a man, a famed utterance and a thing founded by a strong man. The thievish visitant was no whit the wiser for swallowing the words.*

The "Riddle of the Shield" contains sharp images of war and violence. The "Storm" Riddles are extended dramatic poems:

* P. 335.

The wave struggles foaming against the cliff; the dark mountain rises above the deep; behind, moves a second dark sea, mixed with the ocean. . . . There is the ship full of clamour, the shouting of mariners; quietly the high stone-cliffs abide the strife of the waters, the dashing of the waves, when the towering surge presses on to the rocks. . . .*

"Declare what my name is," the Storm demands, "or who shall raise me when I may not rest, or who shall hold me in when I am still." Once again the sea has inspired an Old English poet to the boldest reaches of his descriptive powers.

Gnomic Verse

Gnomic poetry is made up of *sayings:* "short, pithy, homespun generalizations about the common concerns of life, whether proverbial, descriptive, or moralizing." † Old English gnomic verse is frequently incorporated into the texts of other poems; a notable example is Beowulf's, "Better for man/To avenge a friend than much to mourn." We are concerned here, however, with two collections of gnomic poems, the so-called *Exeter Gnomics* and the *Cotton Gnomics* —both named for the manuscripts in which they are found.

Old English gnomic verse covers many areas. Some "gnomes" simply describe physical phenomena. "Frost shall freeze, fire consume wood; earth shall grow, ice form a bridge; water shall wear a covering, wonderfully lock up the sprouts of earth." Others draw upon nature to point up a moral for men. "As the sea is serene when the wind wakes it not, so peoples are peaceful when they have settled a dispute." Often the gnome is merely a piece of wholesome advice. "It is meet that a woman be at her table; a roving woman causes words to be uttered. . . . A shamed man shall walk in the shade; a pure man's place is in the light." A number of the gnomes are, of course, explicitly Christian. "Foolish is he who knows not his Lord, since death often comes unlooked for." Finally, there are precious vignettes that achieve remarkable freshness, like the famous scene of the Frisian wife greeting her husband who has just returned from sea:

Dear is the welcome one to the Frisian wife when the ship comes to rest. His vessel has come, and her husband is at home, her own provider; and she bids him come in, washes his sea-stained garment and

* P. 326.
† Kemp Malone, in *A Literary History of England,* ed. Albert C. Baugh, p. 43.

gives him fresh clothes. Pleasant it is for him on land whom his love constrains. . . . Long is the sailor on the voyage; yet ever shall one await a beloved, await what he cannot hasten for.*

The gnomic formula has here been expanded into a scene of intimacy and charm.

*   *   *   *   *   *

Old English literature reflects several centuries of early English life, but what are its literary values for the modern reader? By now it should be quite clear that the literature of the Anglo-Saxons— even the relatively few samples that have survived in manuscript— can claim ample variety and strength. One still responds to the humor of the riddles, the narrative power of the Caedmonian poems (especially *Genesis B*), the haunting lyricism of elegies like *The Wanderer* and *The Seafarer,* the intricate but expertly wrought symbolism in the poems of Cynewulf, the ecstasy of the *Dream of the Rood,* the lucid and dignified prose of Bede (in Latin) and Ælfric— these would constitute a respectable achievement in any age. And above all, of course, there is the magnificent artistry of *Beowulf,* an epic which sums up the diverse qualities of its own period and at the same time attains the universal significance of all great works of the human spirit.

* P. 343.

PART TWO
THE MIDDLE ENGLISH PERIOD
(1066–1485)

VI: GENERAL VIEW OF THE MIDDLE ENGLISH PERIOD

The Middle English period, an age which in time produced Chaucer and witnessed the birth of modern drama, may be said to have begun in 1066 with the Battle of Hastings. On that historic occasion the Normans, originally a band of Scandinavian pirates who had obtained land in what is now northwest France, conquered England and brought it into the orbit of French culture. Under the leadership of William, Duke of Normandy, described in the *Anglo-Saxon Chronicle*, perhaps with some exaggeration, as a "very stern and fierce man," the Norman invaders proceeded to reshape the destiny of England. Anglo-Saxon political institutions were overhauled by Norman administrators; the English language was remolded through contact with French; and society at large underwent great changes, often reflected in the literature of the period.

THE NORMAN CONQUEST

The political and military situation in pre-Conquest England is a subject too complicated and too widely debated for detailed examination in these pages, but the broad outline is relatively clear. During the tenth and eleventh centuries, England had been plagued by the Danish wars as well as by domestic unrest. The nation had been governed by a succession of English and Danish kings; and while some of them, notably Cnut (1017–35), were strong and intelligent leaders in the tradition of Alfred the Great, the over-all prestige of the monarchy had diminished. The kingship was finally vested in Edward the Confessor (1041–66), the last of the Anglo-Saxon line. Edward himself had been educated by monks in Normandy, and he appointed Normans to important secular and religious offices in England. Moreover, he left no direct heir—a circumstance that weakened the position of his successor, Harold II, and helped William, Edward's illegitimate cousin, to establish a vaguely plausible claim to the English throne. The active role played by the Normans in the government of England, the boldness of William the Conqueror, the fatigue of Harold's troops (who had just traveled four days after defeating the vikings at Stamford Bridge, in the North), the efficiency of the Norman cavalry—all these factors, together with sheer good luck, contributed to the Norman victory at Hastings. On Christmas Day, 1066, William II, Duke of Normandy, was crowned King William I of England.

The new monarch systematically embarked upon an economic and social reorganization of the conquered country. He rewarded his Norman followers with the lands of the defeated English nobility— at least those lands belonging to the diehards who held out against him—and thereby introduced feudalism into England. William also ordered the compilation of the first comprehensive survey of English property, a record known as the *Domesday Book* (1085). On the relationship between the ecclesiastical and secular arms of the government, the King had definite views. Although he co-operated with the pope in seeking monastic reform and drew England generally closer to Rome, he insisted upon a separation of the secular from the ecclesiastical courts and firmly upheld the independent authority of the former. The king, William maintained, should hold the highest position and make the major appointments. William managed to exercise personal control over the affairs of state, and even when he delegated powers to his justiciars (political and judicial officers appointed by the king), he kept himself fully informed as to what was going on throughout England. Estimates of his character vary, but he governed the country effectively.

The Norman empire, which was built by William I (1066–87) and by his immediate successors—William II (1087–1100), Henry I (1100–35), and Stephen (1135–54)—began to decline near the end of the twelfth century. In 1204 the ineffectual King John lost Normandy to France (an event of special significance, it will be shown, for the history of the English language); and in 1215 his domestic powers in England proper were seriously challenged by the rebellious barons who forced from him the Magna Carta. The fourteenth and fifteenth centuries were marked by the exhausting "Hundred Years' War" (1337–1453) between England and France. England not only lost the war, but from the deposition of the weak Richard II (1399) through the blood-soaked reign of Richard III (1483–85) —a period later immortalized by Shakespeare in two cycles of histories—"this scepter'd isle" was torn by civil strife, particularly the War of the Roses (1455–85) between the rival houses of Lancaster

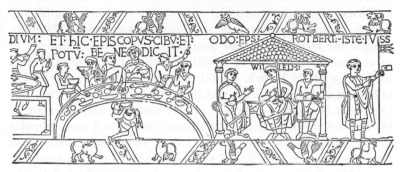

WILLIAM SAILING TO ENGLAND.

BISHOP ODO OF BAYEUX SAYING GRACE AT
BANQUET AFTER LANDING.

WILLIAM HOLDING COUNCIL WITH HIS
BROTHERS, ODO AND ROBERT.

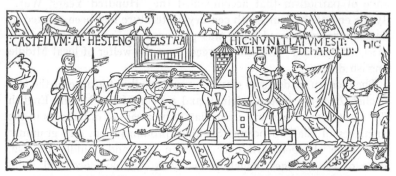

FORTIFICATION OF WILLIAM'S CAMP AT HASTINGS

MESSENGER BRINGS TIDINGS TO WILLIAM
OF HAROLD'S MOVEMENTS.
Courtesy of The Bettmann Archive

Scenes from the celebrated Bayeux Tapestry.

and York. At last, however, on the field of Bosworth (1485), the War of the Roses came to a military end. The Duke of Richmond gained the English throne and, reigning as Henry VII, ushered in the era of the Tudors. With this event the Middle English period may be said to have ended.

Although the political implications of the Norman Conquest were of exceptional importance, the most significant effect of the Conquest—at least for students of English literature—consisted in the impact it had upon the structure and future growth of the English language. The Conquest led in time to an expansion of the literary potentialities of English beyond anything the language had previously known.

The re-establishment of literary English was not accomplished easily. After the cultural leadership of Alfred's Wessex receded in the face of almost constant social and military pressures, English and French began a long struggle for linguistic supremacy. Naturally enough, the masses, who had been born in England, continued to speak English, while the new nobility, which had its roots in France, read and wrote in French. English was the language of day-by-day utilitarian discourse; French was the language of belles-lettres. But the loss of Normandy to France (1204) weakened the allegiance of the Anglo-Norman lords to the Continent and gave a fresh stimulus to English nationalism. By about 1250, it would seem, English had begun to supplant French, and to a large extent Latin, in nearly all areas. The displacement of French was further accelerated by the wave of patriotism that accompanied the "Hundred Years' War." By the end of the fourteenth century a literature had been created in English that surpassed what was produced in French. After about 1450, a "standard" English emerged from the welter of local Middle English dialects.*

The modern reader who glances even casually at a page of the Old English *Beowulf*, in the original, and a page of the Middle English *The Canterbury Tales* will immediately be aware of differences in the languages of the two poems. Spelling, pronunciation, and grammar —all have changed strikingly between Old and Middle English. Some of the changes, which probably would have occurred independently of the Conquest, have been in the direction of simplicity— for example, the substantial loss of inflections. Others have complicated the language, as in the frequently revolutionary spelling conventions introduced by the Anglo-Norman scribes. But the most

---

* On the subjection and re-establishment of English, see Albert C. Baugh, *A History of the English Language* (2nd ed.; New York: Appleton-Century-Crofts, Inc., 1957), secs. 81–110.

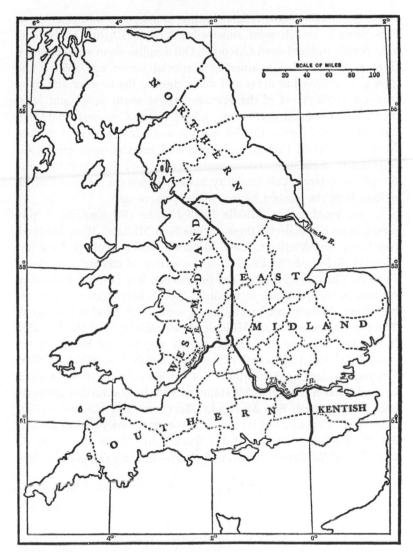

The dialects of Middle English. (Reprinted by permission from *A History of the English Language,* Second Edition, by Albert C. Baugh. Copyright © 1957, Appleton-Century-Crofts, Inc.)

prominent feature of Middle English was its new and enlarged vocabulary. Besides additional prefixes and suffixes, more than ten thousand French words found their way into the English language —particularly into areas dominated by the Anglo-Norman ruling class: government, law, religion, army, music, art, medicine, dress. Sometimes a French word superseded its Old English equivalent; e.g., *people* replaced *leod*. Often the Old English form was dislodged from general use but retained in a special sense; e.g., *dēman* and *dōm* have survived as *deem* and *doom* despite the broader and more frequent employment of the French-derived words *judge* and *judgment*. Post-Conquest borrowings, added to pre-Conquest retentions, have enriched Modern English with synonyms—sometimes derived from Old English, French, and Latin and invested with subtly differentiated meanings: *rise-mount-ascend; fast-firm-secure; holy-sacred-consecrated*. This flexibility has broadened the range of English writers from the age of Chaucer to the present day.

As suggested earlier, Middle English (like Old English) is preserved in several dialects; these include East Midland, West Midland, Northern, and Southern. East Midland, which evolved from the Mercian dialect of Old English, is the source of modern "standard" English. The other Middle English dialects, less familiar to modern readers, partially survive in localized speech habits; even today one may have difficulty understanding a man from Scotland or Kent. The pre-eminence of East Midland stems mainly from the fact that it was the language of London, which was rapidly becoming the commercial and intellectual center of English life. When William Caxton, the first English printer, set up his printing press in 1476, he used London English as his standard and thereby further strengthened the position of East Midland.* Moreover, East Midland was the language of Chaucer. But it was by no means the only dialect used by Middle English writers. Notable works—like *Piers Plowman, Sir Gawain and the Green Knight,* and *Pearl*—were also created in other dialects.

The foregoing sketch of the historical and linguistic background of the Middle English period has indicated some of the ways in which English life was modified after the Norman Conquest. The remainder of this chapter will be devoted to several matters of more direct relevance to Middle English literature—first, to some of the philosophic and literary ideals that found expression in Middle English poetry, prose, and drama; then, to the genres (types) and metrical forms which English writers appropriated from European (mostly French) models.

---

* On Caxton, see George H. McKnight, *Modern English in the Making* (New York: Appleton-Century-Crofts, Inc., 1928), pp. 56–59.

The Sirth Booke. Fo.rrliii.

Fortune's Wheel from the 1544 edition of Lydgate's *The Fall of Princes*. (Reprinted from *Shakespeare's Tragic Heroes* by Lily B. Campbell. Copyright, 1960, by Barnes & Noble, Inc.)

MEDIEVAL THOUGHT

If one expects to find in medieval life the comfortable simplicity and uniformity that have frequently been ascribed to it, he will be disappointed. The Middle Ages, like many other periods in history, is full of contradictions. Brutality and sentimentalism, luxury and self-denial, coarseness and refinement—all flourished simultaneously.* Some poets liked to picture Fortune at her turning wheel, capriciously juggling human happiness in the manner of her Anglo-Saxon counterpart, Wyrd. Yet it was possible for the medieval man, if he was strong enough, to believe that the universe was ultimately governed by just and immutable laws. Beneath the very real chaos of his worldly existence he could perceive order and beauty, and he epitomized these deeply cherished qualities in three ideals to which, in varying degrees, he could pay homage—God, King, and Fair Lady.

Religious Thought

It is impossible in these pages to do justice to the fullness and complexity of medieval religious thought. But inasmuch as the Christian view of the universe permeates the most enduring literature of the Middle Ages, it is necessary to indicate some of the main tenets of medieval Christianity.

God, Himself absolute perfection, placed Adam and Eve in a world where they enjoyed, and could continue to enjoy, abundant satisfactions, including closeness to God. But Adam and Eve disobeyed their Creator and, as a consequence of their sin, were expelled from Eden. Their descendants, sharing the guilt and the punishment, were denied Paradise; man was required to work until he died. In this world man may not always suffer physical or even mental anguish, but he is wearied by what a distinguished interpreter of medieval thought has called "the incessant pursuit of an ever fugitive satisfaction." † His earthly attainments—wealth, power, pleasure— pale into insignificance when compared to the higher and more lasting delight that comes from closeness to God. Moreover, what man thinks of as pain in this life has no abiding significance when he considers the endless bliss of heaven. But even if man in his mortal life gains the wisdom to renounce the empty and sometimes per-

---

* On medieval anomalies, see J. Huizinga, *The Waning of the Middle Ages* (London: Edward Arnold, 1924), pp. 1–21. See MEB 17.

† Etienne Gilson, *The Spirit of Medieval Philosophy,* trans. A. H. C. Downes (London: Sheed & Ward; New York: Charles Scribner's Sons, 1936), p. 271.

verted values of the world, his vision of God is inevitably partial. Here he acquires a *knowledge* of God through His works and His glorious gifts, but he does not see God face to face and cannot understand the operations of His providence.

The sin of disobedience whereby Adam and all humanity fell from the state of grace was so great an offense to God's majesty that the Son of God, in His infinite love, offered Himself as a sacrifice. If an individual reciprocates Christ's love through obedience to God's commandments and if he accepts the teachings of the Church, he will attain salvation. It will be his privilege in the next world to achieve the full felicity missing on earth. In the brilliant and unfailing light of eternity, St. Augustine (354–430) paraphrases St. Paul, we shall see God not reflected, as in a mirror, but with our own eyes. This life becomes a school which prepares man for the life everlasting.

God's greatness was manifest throughout His created universe. Consequently, some authors, for figurative purposes, chose to speak of the world as a symbol. By the visible forms and motions of everyday life could be expressed intangible spiritual mysteries. The red rose, for example, was a convenient figure for the blood of the martyrs; the twelve months could be used to represent the apostles; and the pelican, which was popularly believed to feed its young with its own blood, could serve as a poetic analogy with Christ's love for man. This kind of symbolizing, it will be recalled, provided the artistic framework of the Old English *Phoenix* and *Physiologus*, in which animals were imaginatively used to help clarify certain theological concepts. Sometimes, of course, the writer became so absorbed in the ingenuity of the symbol that he lost sight of the idea which the symbol was supposed to illustrate. At its best, however, as in the Middle English *Pearl, Piers Plowman, Everyman,* and, to a certain extent, *The Canterbury Tales,* symbolism and its partner, allegory, could be vastly enriching. In Dante's *The Divine Comedy* (*c.* 1307–21), the most sublime poem of the Middle Ages, the poet's journey from the Forest of Error through Inferno (Hell), Purgatorio (Purgatory), and Paradiso (Paradise) stands symbolically for the gradual ascent of mankind to the divine presence and the seat of grace.

The bulk of the extant literature from the Middle English period is concerned, explicitly or implicitly, with the problem of sin and redemption. One insistent theme recurs: the vanity and treachery of this transitory world as opposed to the perfect bliss of the world to come (the motif, it will be recalled, of the Old English elegies *The Wanderer* and *The Seafarer*). Death is seen not as an affliction, but rather as the culmination of a long journey—the release from all the shortcomings attendant upon man in his mortal state and the deliverance into eternal joys.

Political Thought

Just as God expressed the unity of the cosmic order, so the king was widely regarded as the natural expression of the unity of the social order. Although some medieval writers exploited the analogy to justify the political *status quo,* even to the extent of denying the right of the people to seek redress from tyrannical oppression, the king was expected by and large to fulfill his obligations to God and to his subjects.

The commanding position of the medieval king is illustrated in the system of *feudalism* that William the Conqueror introduced into England. He rewarded his followers with the lands of displaced English nobles, but these lands remained in his jurisdiction. The lords and their descendants held the estates in perpetuity so long as they furnished the king with knights, young men who were trained to fight on horseback, for his military campaigns. The lords could meet their military commitments by similarly subinfeudating, or subleasing, part of their estates to lesser nobles in return for military service. This vassalage continued down the social scale. The serfs and villeins were obligated to provide physical labor on the manor of their immediate lord in exchange for food, protection from external enemies, and, under the law, justice within the estate on which they lived. Each member of the hierarchy, from king to villein, thus had definite responsibilities which as a Christian he could not renounce; medieval literature is frequently concerned with clarifying these duties. When feudal obligations conflict with private feelings, as when Launcelot loves Guinevere, the wife of his king, the resultant moral dilemma can produce absorbing drama.

The profound respect for kingship which characterized the Middle English period had its roots, at least in part, in the Anglo-Saxon tradition of the *comitatus.* Just as the Germanic lord commanded the unwavering love and loyalty of his thanes, the feudal king expected complete allegiance and devotion from his subjects. The sanctity of the crown remained the ideal of political theorists well into the Renaissance and served as an indispensable element in the philosophy underlying the plays of Shakespeare.

Chivalry and Courtly Love

A third focus of medieval loyalty, at least at court, was the Lady. She it was who inspired a profusion of medieval poetry and prose, and the attitude toward her received expression in two complicated institutions, chivalry and courtly love.

Knighthood, initially a practical means of supplying cavalrymen for the king's wars, was eventually glamorized into an elegant ideal called, after the French *chevalier* (horseman, knight), "chivalry." It was soon not enough for the true knight to be merely a capable horseman. He was expected, like the Knight in *The Canterbury Tales*, to exemplify courage, piety, generosity, and, above all, "courtesy." In theory, at least, chivalry was identified with virtue; and later, with increasing emphasis placed upon the protection of the weak, the chivalric ideal became as compelling in peace as in war.

Although it is difficult to gauge the extent to which the chivalric code was actually incorporated into the behavior of flesh-and-blood knights and ladies, certainly the institution of chivalry contributed much color and excitement to ceremonies like the tournament and the induction into knighthood. By 1300 chivalry had receded into a golden memory. Nevertheless, some of its values influenced writers throughout the Middle Ages and, in modified form, contributed to the Renaissance concepts of the courtier and the gentleman. The religious implications of chivalry are constantly stressed in Middle English literature. Sir Gawain, hero of one of the greatest of the medieval romances, is a Christian knight—courageous, courteous, and deeply pious.

One development conventionally associated with chivalry is the highly controversial doctrine known as "courtly love." This institution apparently was given its major impetus late in the eleventh century through the love lyrics of the troubadours in Provence (southern France), though it seems also to have had close links with Arabian love literature, especially an eleventh-century treatise, *A Book Containing the Risala Known as the Dove's Neck Ring about Love and Lovers*. Courtly love reached its zenith at Poitiers, in western France (*c.* 1174), in the court of Eleanor of Aquitaine and her daughter, the Countess Marie. Its rules were codified for Marie by Andreas Capellanus (Andrew the Chaplain) in his Latin *The Art of Courtly Love.* Scholars do not agree as to whether courtly love was a real way of life, a parlor game, or just a pleasant literary convention—though in the present volume we are more concerned with it as a literary convention. In part of his book Andreas records "judgments" allegedly rendered by Eleanor and Marie, who may have conducted mock court sessions at which lovers were "tried" according to the intricate laws of love. A typical case: A lover must obey his mistress in everything and he must love her eternally; these are "laws." But what is the poor soul to do if she should command him to stop loving her? Or, to cite another problem, what gifts is a lady allowed to receive from a lover without being considered mercenary? Chaucer loved to parody such absurd discussions.

The rules of courtly love have a bearing upon medieval literature, particularly the romance. True love, according to Andreas, is impossible between husband and wife, but under no circumstances is marriage to be considered an excuse for not loving. The courtly lover, like Sir Launcelot and Tristram, is required to worship at the shrine of a beautiful lady, generally (like Guinevere or Iseult) the wife of somebody else. After being singled out for the favors of his mistress, he must swoon, send her the appropriate gifts, and obey her every whim. Moreover, he risks anything—even his life—to defend her reputation. The passion is, by definition, adulterous, but whether or not it is in every case supposed to be consummated is a moot question. Secrecy, of course, becomes imperative in the relationship; and medieval romance abounds in references to "derne [secret] love," a phrase Chaucer frequently makes fun of. At one point courtly love seems to be partially reconciled with the chivalric ideal. This kinship appears in Andreas' insistence that the courtly lover is never promiscuous. He remains faithful to his one lady; she, in turn, inspires him to perform acts of courtesy in behalf of all womanhood.

Despite the efforts of some poets in the Middle Ages, and later, to make courtly love appear respectable, the code could not possibly be accommodated into medieval Christianity, which sanctified marriage. Indeed, some writers, notably Malory, emphasize the destructive force of courtly love.

MIDDLE ENGLISH LITERARY CONVENTIONS

The foregoing discussion has dealt with some specific religious, political, and social-aesthetic ideals whereby life in the Middle Ages assumed a degree of unity. It would be a mistake, however, to lay too much emphasis upon the unifying elements in medieval life and thought. The reader approaching Middle English literature for the first (or the five-hundredth) time will be most impressed by its enormous diversity.

Old English literature, varied as it may have been, could be grouped according to a relatively small number of pervasive types; but the *Wells Manual* (see MEB 10), the most authoritative guide to Middle English writings (from 1050 to 1400), lists no fewer than sixteen major classifications for the literature of the later period. There is also considerable metrical variety in Middle English. Old English verse was almost without exception unrhymed, nonstanzaic, and alliterative; Middle English poets, on the other hand, frequently utilized complicated rhyme schemes and stanza forms. Although writers, especially in the North, did not altogether abandon Old English literary conventions, they nevertheless imported French genres and prosody; and they often tried to imitate, with varying success, the elegance of polite French literature. Chaucer, for one, absorbed many lessons from his study and imitation of French—and Italian—poetic masters. The Middle English period was one of experiment and discovery in literature.

The range of Middle English literature can be partially suggested by means of the following lists, not intended to be exhaustive, of the dominant types and verse forms employed by Middle English writers:

Literary Types

Allegory: the more or less extended use of metaphor, symbol, or personification for the purpose of communicating indirectly a hidden meaning—often a veiled personal identity, political opinion, or religious or moral doctrine.

Dream Allegory: an allegory set in the framework of a dream or vision.

Exemplum: a moralized tale that usually, though not necessarily, embellishes a sermon or homily.

Fabliau: a short, humorous, and sometimes bawdy story, usually in verse, which deals with middle- or lower-class life.

Lay (*Lai*): a short poem, usually a romantic narrative, intended to be sung or recited by a minstrel.

Miracle Play: a dramatization of some extraordinary power exhibited by a saint. The term, in English usage, is also applied to a play based upon Bible scenes.

Morality Play: an allegorical drama in which some or all of the characters are abstractions, frequently of particular virtues and vices
who struggle for possession of the soul of man.

Mystery Play: a term, in French usage, designating a play based upon
Scripture or sacred history. In English usage, however, this kind
of play is more often called "miracle."

Romance: a tale of chivalric adventure, in verse or prose. Romances
in verse are sometimes called "metrical romances."

Satire: a work in verse or prose (in classical literature it had always
been in verse), aiming to expose, and sometimes to correct, personal, social, or spiritual follies or vices.

Prosody

Couplet: a pair of successive lines that rhyme (*aa, bb, cc, dd*).

Heroic Couplet: a pair of successive lines, in iambic pentameter
(regularly five feet, or ten syllables), that rhyme—as in the
General Prologue to *The Canterbury Tales*.

Octosyllabic Couplet: a pair of successive lines, in iambic tetrameter
(regularly four feet, or eight syllables), that rhyme—as in Chaucer's *The Book of the Duchesse*.

Rhyme Royal: a stanza of seven iambic pentameter lines that rhyme
ababbcc—as in Chaucer's *Troilus and Criseyde*.

Terza Rima: three-line stanzas with interlocking rhyme (*aba, bcb,
cdc, ded*). The form is rare in English prosody, but it is used in
Part II of one of Chaucer's minor poems, *Complaint to His
Lady*.

Ballade (sometimes spelled "balade" and not to be confused with the
folk ballad): a poem consisting of one or more three-stanza
groups, each group within a given ballade usually ending with
the same refrain. The form is used by Chaucer in several minor
poems—e.g., *Balade de Bon Conseyl*.

Envoy: usually a half-stanza that frequently appears at the end of
a ballade.

VII: THE MIDDLE ENGLISH ROMANCE

The "escape" literature of medieval aristocrats—indeed, the most widely read and enjoyed of all literary genres employed during the Middle Ages—was the *romance*. Within the highly palatable framework of daring deeds performed by knights in shining armor, the authors of the romances (almost all of whom were anonymous) gave expression, often in prose but still more often in verse, to some of the most cherished religious, political, and courtly ideals of the Middle English period.

Surviving from the Old English period is the fragment of a prose romance, *Apollonius*. But the medieval romance may be said to have really begun in France near the end of the eleventh century. At first even writers living in England generally wrote their romances in French. Then, around 1250, the English language began to re-emerge as the principal vehicle for literary expression, and romances in English made their appearance. The French influence, however, did not stop, for most of the early English romances, and some of the later ones, too, were either translations or adaptations (generally inferior) from French originals. Unlike their French counterparts, English romances rarely dealt with delicate sentiments precisely analyzed, but inclined instead to unusual situations or striking plots— exiled princes, hunts, rash promises, battles with pagans or dragons, trials by combat, fairies, enchanted swords, magic girdles. Not that these elements were absent from French romance, but the pervading atmosphere was different. "As a general rule," it has been said, "the English took the adventurous, sensational part of the French romances, and let the language of the heart alone." * Yet English writers, while creating a unique climate in which a native romance literature could flourish, never completely outgrew their dependence upon French plots, characters, and themes.

It has long been customary for scholars, following the lead of the thirteenth-century French poet Jean Bodel, to classify the vast number of medieval romances according to national themes, or "matters."

* William P. Ker, *English Literature: Medieval* (New York: Henry Holt and Co., 1912), p. 72.

The "matter of Greece and Rome," for example, deals mainly with the exploits of Alexander the Great and with the Trojan War and its aftermath, as treated by Homer and Virgil; the "matter of France" includes romances about Charlemagne and his Frankish knights; the "matter of England" treats the careers of English and Germanic heroes of history and legend; the "matter of Britain" centers upon King Arthur and the Knights of the Round Table. There are, in addition, countless other romances which do not fit into any of the major cycles—for example, the group commonly known as "Breton lays." By far the most important focus of the romances, both in English literature and elsewhere, has been the mysterious, partly historical, partly mythical figure of King Arthur. It is, therefore, with the "matter of Britain" that this discussion of medieval romance will begin.

ARTHURIAN ROMANCE THROUGH MALORY

The tales surrounding King Arthur illustrate the curious web of history and fable which entangles nearly all folk heroes. A real Arthur apparently lived during the sixth century, and he seems to have acquired substantial renown for his valiant leadership of the Welsh in their hopeless defense of the island against the invading Anglo-Saxons. He eventually became a legend. Little by little the legend grew until it spread far beyond the confines of Ireland and Wales, where it had probably originated. Arthur was in time raised to the rank of king and credited with fabulous achievements in peace and war. He was made the central figure in a twelfth-century Latin history of Britain by Geoffrey of Monmouth. After his literary fame crossed the Channel into France, Arthur returned to his own land as a literary hero at the beginning of the thirteenth century—for the first time in an English version, Layamon's *Brut*. Later in the thirteenth century he recrossed into Germany and soon established himself as the common literary property of much of the Western world. In the second half of the fourteenth century one of his knights, Sir Gawain, played the leading role in the most enjoyable of Middle English Arthurian romances, *Sir Gawain and the Green Knight*. King Arthur received his fullest treatment in Middle English in an important prose work by Sir Thomas Malory, published in 1485 under the title *Morte d'Arthur*. Arthur's fame, however, has continued well beyond the Middle Ages. Even a partial list of English and American writers who have, since Malory, made use of Arthurian subjects furnishes impressive evidence of his enduring literary appeal: Spenser, Dryden, Tennyson, William Morris, Edwin Arlington Robinson, John Masefield, and—in the comic novel *A Connecticut Yankee in King Arthur's Court*—Mark Twain. Moreover, Arthur's popularity has not been confined to literary artists. The German composer Richard Wagner derived three massive music-dramas from Arthurian legend: *Lohengrin, Tristan and Isolde,* and *Parsifal.* More recently this sixth-century Briton and his brave knights have adorned motion-picture and television screens throughout the United States.

Piecing together the details of the germination and early development of the Arthurian tradition has provided scholars with a difficult and fascinating challenge. Surprisingly enough, there is no mention of Arthur in any contemporary record. The historian Gildas writes of the battle of Mount Badon, the site of an actual victory won by the Britons around 500. But despite the fact that this battle was to be hailed by later writers as the occasion of Arthur's most astounding triumph, Gildas pays tribute to a Roman, Ambrosius Aurelianus, as leader of the Celtic forces, and says nothing at all of an Arthur. The earliest known reference to Arthur occurs in a Welsh poem composed about the year 600, the *Gododdin* (edited in Welsh as *Canu Aneurin*). Describing the excellence of a particular Briton, the poet remarks that he was a ferocious warrior, "though he was not Arthur." The Welsh historian Nennius, writing around 800, explicitly names Arthur and calls him simply a *"dux bellorum"* [leader in battles], who participated in twelve victories over the Anglo-Saxons. In addition to crediting Arthur with killing 960 of the enemy singlehanded, Nennius records two Arthurian marvels. The first has to do with a heap of stones, one of which contains a footprint of Arthur's dog. Wherever men may take the stone, the next day it is always miraculously back on top of the heap. The second marvel concerns the burial mound of Arthur's son. Men frequently measure it, finding it "sometimes six feet in length, sometimes nine, sometimes twelve, sometimes fifteen. However you measure it on one occasion, you will never find it of the same measure again." The historical work *Annales Cambriae* (*c.* 955) contains two Arthurian entries: one, under the date 516, is a mention of the battle of Mount Badon, where Arthur wore a cross on his shield; the other entry is a notation of the battle of Camlan (537), where Arthur and Medraut (Mordred) fell. Arthur appears briefly in a tenth-century Welsh poem, *The Spoils of Annwn,* and looms more significantly in the collection of Welsh tales translated in the nineteenth century by Lady Charlotte Guest as the *Mabinogion*—most conspicuously in the prose love story *Kulhwch and Olwen* (*c.* 1100), which is perhaps the earliest extant full-scale Arthurian romance. The first indication that Arthur's fame had spread to England is provided by the historian William of Malmesbury. In his *Gesta Regum Anglorum* (1125), he writes that it is high time the truth were told concerning this great leader, a man "worthy not to be dreamed of in fallacious fables, but to be proclaimed in veracious histories, as one who long sustained his tottering country, and gave the shattered minds of his fellow-citizens an edge for war." Then William relates that the tomb of Walwen (Gawain) was discovered in southwest Wales, "but the tomb of Arthur is nowhere beheld, whence ancient ditties fable that he is yet to come." *

Clearly, then, a tremendous myth about Arthur had accumulated, partly through written accounts but chiefly through oral transmission. It remained for some writer with a bold imagination and a convincing literary style to organize the scattered materials of the myth somewhat more systematically into a single book. Such a writer was Geoffrey of Monmouth, the man who really gave impetus and direction to the "matter of Britain."

Geoffrey of Monmouth (*c. 1100–c. 1155*)

One of the most valuable works in the early history of Arthurian legend is an imaginative chronicle, in Latin prose, by Geoffrey of Monmouth, a canon at Oxford. His *History of the Kings of Britain* (1137) purports to be a true record of British events from the time of the alleged founding of the nation by a mythical "Brutus," great-grandson of Aeneas. But Geoffrey's engaging chronicle is really a superb and deliberate compound of fact and fantasy. The author claims that his work is based upon "a secret book in the British tongue" given to him by his good friend Walter, Archdeacon of Oxford. Walter's book, however, has never been discovered; and it is generally believed that Geoffrey invented his source simply to add one more touch to a first-class literary joke. The linking of Britain with Troy, a legend picked up by later British writers, represents an effort on the part of Geoffrey to enhance the prestige of his country.

* See Edmund K. Chambers, *Arthur of Britain* (London: Sidgwick & Jackson, Ltd., 1927), which should be supplemented by Roger S. Loomis, *Arthurian Tradition and Chrétien de Troyes* (New York: Columbia University Press, 1949), pp. 12–24.

In Geoffrey's *History* we meet shadowy kings from the remote past who reappear later in literature—figures like Gorboduc, Cymbeline, and Lear. About halfway through, Geoffrey introduces Merlin the Magician, destined to become (like Launcelot, Perceval, Gawain, and others) the central character in many Arthurian romances. One of Merlin's feats is to bring King Uther Pendragon to the bed of the beautiful Igraine after transforming him into the likeness of her husband. From this adulterous union King Arthur is born, and his adventures make up the remainder of Geoffrey's book. Many essentials of the full-blown Arthurian legend are already present in Geoffrey: Arthur's conquest of Britain and invasion of Gaul, his war with ancient Rome, the treachery of Mordred, the infidelity of Queen Guinevere—here with Mordred, not Launcelot, who is not yet a character in the Arthurian romances. Geoffrey even mentions Arthur's departure, after his death, for Avalon. Moreover, the action has begun to acquire chivalric trappings. Geoffrey succeeded in tying together the scattered threads of Arthurian legend, but at the same time he did not hesitate to add a yarn or two of his own.

Wace (c. 1100–c. 1175)

Though immensely popular, Geoffrey's *History* was limited in circulation to the learned who could read Latin. Several translations or adaptations soon appeared in French, the most notable being a verse chronicle by Wace, a Norman poet of elegance and taste.

Wace's *Roman de Brut* (1155)—the name is derived from Brutus, that supposed founder of Britain—is more than just a bare translation of Geoffrey, for Wace had an eye for picturesque detail and was endowed with a poet's imagination. Where Geoffrey, for example, merely records the fact that Arthur embarked for Rome from Southampton, where the wind was fair, Wace vividly captures the bustle and clamor of a busy port. He shows us the loading of the ships, allows us to listen to the private farewells, and generally intensifies the excitement of the scene. More important, Wace adds to the narrative by introducing the Round Table and by enlarging upon the suggestion that after his final battle Arthur departed for Avalon, where—some say—he is being healed of his wounds in preparation for a return as "the hope of Britain." Wace is apparently aware of the problem of separating truth from fiction, for he cautiously tries to cite authorities for his statements. Many Arthurian wonders, he writes, have been told so many times that their validity cannot be ascertained. "Not all lies, nor all true, [not] all foolishness, nor all sense; so much have the makers of fables fabled to embellish their stories that they have made all seem fable." Wace is, on the whole, somewhat skeptical.

Chrétien de Troyes (*fl. 1160–1190*)

Both Geoffrey and Wace had treated King Arthur in a comprehensive biographical fashion that allowed little room to develop the unique literary possibilities of single episodes or to highlight individual knights in Arthur's retinue. It was left for Chrétien de Troyes, a gifted French poet at the court of the Countess Marie, to refine the loosely knit Arthurian chronicles into unified, cleanly constructed, and continuous tales.

Chrétien has left five Arthurian romances of unusual merit: *Erec, Cliges, Perceval, Yvain,* and *Launcelot.* In addition to focusing upon specific heroes, Chrétien's poems inject the French courtly ideal into the rugged world of the Arthurian knights. The characters often epitomize the virtues which Andreas Capellanus recommends as the standard equipment of the courtly lover. For example, when Chrétien's hero Yvain falls in love with the widow of a knight whom he has slain, he is smitten suddenly as if by a disease. "For I am doomed to be her slave, since such is the will of Love." Launcelot falls passionately in love with Guinevere, who is Arthur's queen, and places himself completely at her service. Her illicit love inspires Launcelot to become the model of knightly perfection, and this role he is destined to play throughout the course of later Arthurian romance. Not all of Chrétien's innovations could be comfortably absorbed into the rather different moral tradition upheld by English writers, but his contribution to the subsequent development of the "matter of Britain," both in England and on the Continent, cannot be overemphasized.

Layamon (*fl. 1189–1207*) *

There was still no version of Arthurian material for the common people until an English priest, Layamon, enchanted by Wace ("How he could write!" Layamon says), produced a *Brut* in English. Layamon's *Brut* is much more than a translation; the poet more than doubles the fifteen thousand lines he found in Wace.

Written in a combination of alliteration and rhyme that links Old
English verse with the alliterative revival of the fourteenth century,
Layamon's *Brut* is conceived and executed in a rough English spirit
fundamentally alien to the gracefulness of Wace and Chrétien. Where
Wace has a bare line or two on the introduction of the Round Table,
Layamon provides a vigorous narrative of the circumstances that
made it necessary, and he fully describes the details of its construction. Arthur's knights begin to squabble over who is more entitled to
a place of honor at the original tables:

Each one had in his heart   over-proud feelings,
And felt that he was better   than his fellow.
That folk was from many lands;   there was great envy:
When one held him[self] high,   the other held him[self] much
    higher.

(ll. 777–80)

A brawl erupts: the men hurl trenchers and bowls at each other, then
leap with knives at the throats of their fellows. Finally Arthur, with
a fierceness more appropriate to a Germanic warrior than to a courtly
king, quells the rioters with his sword. He decrees a terrible punishment for the instigator of the bloodshed:

Take me that same man   who this fight first began,
And put a withy on his neck   and drag him to a moor,
And throw him in a low-lying fen,   where he shall lie.
And take all his next of kin,   whom ye can find,
And smite off their heads   with your broad swords;
And the women that ye can find   nearest him of kin,
Carve off their noses   and ruin their beauty;
And thus will I wholly destroy   that kin that he came from.

(ll. 817–24)

After the knights are made to swear, on pain of death, never again
to stir up a quarrel, Arthur goes to Cornwall and commissions a skilled
craftsman there to build a round table as a preserver of harmony and
as a symbol of equality among his knights.

Layamon, who is intensely patriotic, loves the folk traditions of his
native England. Picking up Wace's observation that Arthur, upon his
death, left for Avalon, the English poet draws upon Celtic lore for
an elaborate account of the fairies who bear the dead king away to
dwell with Queen Argante (Morgan). This "fay most fair" will make
Arthur's wounds whole so that he may one day come again to his

kingdom. Layamon seems more convinced than Wace of the truth of
the prophecy concerning Arthur's return:

> Then was it come to pass　　what Merlin once said,
> There would be very great sorrow　　at Arthur's departure;
> The Britons believe yet　　that he is alive,
> And dwelleth in Avalon　　with the fairest of fays;
> And the Britons still look ever　　for Arthur to come.
> There was never man born,　　of any maiden chosen,
> Who knoweth of the truth　　more to say of Arthur.
> But there was once a prophet,　　Merlin by name;
> He foretold in words,　　—his sayings were true,—
> That an Arthur must still come　　to help the Britons.
>
> (ll. 1075–84)

Although Layamon's *Brut* interests us primarily for its Arthurian
material, it should be noted that the poet, like his predecessors, covers
a long span of British history and legend. Particularly valuable is
the long narrative of the probably fictitious Leir (Lear) and his
daughters, which Layamon expands from the briefer version found in
Geoffrey.

The Alliterative Morte Arthur (*c. 1360*) *

After enjoying an artistically fruitful period in Germany during the
thirteenth century, notably in the poems of Wolfram von Eschenbach
and Gottfried von Strassburg (whom Wagner used as sources, respectively, for *Parsifal* and *Tristan and Isolde*), Arthurian romance
flourished abundantly in England in the fourteenth century. But only
two of the countless Middle English Arthurian poems written during
the three hundred years after Layamon's *Brut* are of substantial
literary merit. One of these is the great *Sir Gawain and the Green
Knight* (see Chapter X); the other is the alliterative *Morte Arthur,*
so called to distinguish it from a less important stanzaic *Morte
Arthur*. The alliterative *Morte Arthur* served as one of the sources
for Malory's big prose work.

The anonymous poet of the alliterative *Morte Arthur* generally dispenses with romance and magic, those inevitable ingredients of earlier
Arthurian chronicles and romances. He creates instead an epic world
of flesh-and-blood heroes who act on a grand scale and feel passions

---

* Quotations are from *Medieval English Verse and Prose,* in modernized
versions by Roger S. Loomis and Rudolph Willard. Copyright, 1948, Appleton-
Century-Crofts, Inc. Reprinted by permission of the publisher.

broadly. Observe, for example, the gusto with which Sir Gawain prepares to charge the forces of the treacherous Mordred. One seems to be in the world of *Beowulf* and Brunanburh:

> Then grimly Sir Gawain   grips his weapon,
> Against that great battalion   he addresses him forthwith;
> Hastily rightens the chains   of his rich sword;
> He brandishes his shield;   he holds back no longer,
> But quite unwisely and madly   the quickest way charges.
> The wounds of those adversaries,   for the vengeful dints,
> All well full of blood   where he passes by;
> And though he were in great woe,   he wanders but little,
> But wreaks, to his worship,   the wrath of his lord.
>
> (ll. 3813–21)

When this noblest of Arthur's warriors is slain, the evil Sir Mordred knows an instant of remorse. Praising Sir Gawain as "the graciousest man that under God lived," Mordred weeps bitterly that it was *his* fate to have killed him:

> Yet that traitor as quickly   tears does let fall,
> Turns him forth quickly,   and talks no more,
> Went weeping away,   and curses the hour
> That his wierd [Wyrd]   was wrought to work such destruction;
> When he thought on this thing,   it pierced his heart.
> For the sake of his kinsman's blood,   sighing he rides off,
> When that renegade wretch   remembered within him
> The reverence and revelry   of the Round Table,
> He cried out and repented him   of all his cruel works. . . .
>
> (ll. 3886–94)

And Arthur, too, feels the epic grief of a Hector or an Achilles as he clasps the dead Gawain in his arms and senses that his own doom is forthcoming:

> "Alas!" said Sir Arthur,   "now my sorrow increases!
> I am utterly undone   within mine own lands;
> O, doubtful dread death,   thou dwellest too long!
> Why drawest thou on so slowly?   thou drownest my heart!"
> Then faints the sweet king,   and aswoon falls down,
> Staggers up swiftly,   and lovingly kisses him,
> Until his burly beard   was berun with blood,
> As though beasts he had quartered   and brought out of life.
> Had not Sir Ewain come,   and other great lords,
> His bold heart had burst   for sorrow at that moment.
>
> (ll. 3965–74)

Arthur himself is not a supernatural being, but a mortal hero of exceptional magnitude. The "Avalon" in which he is buried is no haunt of fairies; it is fixed in solid English Glastonbury, and the king is buried according to Christian law. The alliterative *Morte Arthur* concludes with a fitting tribute to Arthur as a kinsman of Hector of Troy.

Sir Thomas Malory (c. 1410–1471) *

Malory's superb prose rendering of the "matter of Britain" was completed (*c.* 1469) in prison, where Malory was frequently consigned for various reasons, and printed (1485) by William Caxton, the first English printer, as *Morte d'Arthur*. In a well-known preface, Caxton deplores the fact that Arthur, one of the Nine Worthies, is better appreciated among other peoples—the Dutch, Italian, Spanish, Greek, French—than among the English; but "no man is accept[ed] for a prophete in his owne contreye." In spite of skeptics who doubt Arthur's historicity, Caxton believes that the hero really lived, though not everything written of him may be true. Caxton prints Malory's book not because it is true, he asserts, but because it is moral. It teaches readers "the noble actes of chyvalrye, the jentyl and vertuous dedes that somme knyghtes used in tho[se] dayes, by whyche they came to honour, and how they that were vycious were punysshed and ofte put to shame and rebuke." †

Caxton may have had a moral purpose in bringing out the book, and his insight into Malory's art remains essentially valid. It would seem doubtful, however, that Malory himself was greatly concerned with the didactic possibilities of the "matter of Britain." The episodes involving the Grail, while effective, impress a reader as having little of the spirit of holiness and religious wonder characteristic of their counterparts in French literature. There are ample opportunities for Malory to point up the parallels between Arthur's Britain and his own contemporary political scene, but these potentialities are virtually unexplored. When he observes that the English were overly hasty in forsaking Arthur and joining the rebellious Mordred, Malory makes only the vaguest of political generalizations:

> Lo, ye all Englysshemen, se ye nat what a myschyff here was? For he that was the moste kynge and nobelyst knyght of the worlde, and

* Quotations from Malory are from *The Works of Sir Thomas Malory*, ed. Eugène Vinaver (Oxford: Clarendon Press, 1947). Reprinted by permission of the publisher.
† P. cxiii.

moste loved the felyship of noble knyghtes, and by hym they all were upholdyn, and yet myght nat thes Englyshemen holde them contente with hym. Lo thus was the olde custom and usayges of thys londe, and men say that we of thys londe have nat yet loste that custom. Alas! thys ys a greate defaughte [default] of us Englysshemen, for there may no thynge us please no terme.*

Personal comments of a moralistic nature are indeed rare. Even in the famous discussion of the month of May, when every lusty heart begins to blossom, Malory simply looks back sentimentally to the days of old when there was "stability" in love. Of the chivalric ideal as a spiritualizing force there is scant, if any, suggestion. If Malory has a "cause" of any sort to espouse, he is certainly not very persistent or convincing.

One must further qualify Caxton's remarks in the light of recent Malory scholarship. The evidence of the Winchester MS (discovered in 1934), of earlier date than Caxton's printed text, strongly indicates that Malory must have written not one continuous Arthurian prose epic with a unified structure and theme, but eight individual romances which Caxton conveniently assembled into a single volume. As a matter of fact, the definitive modern edition of Malory is called "The Works of Sir Thomas Malory" rather than the conventional, but perhaps misleading, "Morte d'Arthur." Although the question is not entirely settled to the satisfaction of all medievalists, Malory's literary art is in any case more impressive if we consider his Arthurian tales as eight separate romances instead of as a single large narrative. Malory has justly been hailed as a pioneer in the field of the *nouvelle*, or short novel, "the real, if unacknowledged, starting-point of modern fiction." †

If Malory was primarily interested in telling a good story, he chose materials that admirably suited his needs. His plots, which are derived from numerous English and French sources (Malory apparently had access to a good library while in prison), feature a variety of heroes involved in a wide range of adventures composed for the most part out of the daring and the unusual in Arthurian legend. Malory traces the early career of Arthur, including an account of his miraculous birth, his coronation, and his acquisition of the sword Excalibur from the mysterious outstretched hand in the lake. We travel with Arthur as he wages his triumphant military campaign

* P. 1229.
† P. lviii.

¶Here foloweth the fyrth boke of the noble and worthy prynce kyng Arthur.

¶How syr Launcelot and syr Lyonell departed fro the courte for to seke auentures/ & how syr Lyonell lefte syr Launcelot slepynge & was taken. Capitulm.j.

 Anone after that the noble & worthy kyng Arthur was comen fro Rome into Englande/all the knyghtes of the rounde table resorted vnto ye kyng and made many iustes and turneymentes/ & some there were that were good knyghtes / whiche encreased so in armes and worshyp that they passed all theyr felowes in prowesse & noble dedes & that was well proued on many. But in especyall it was proued on syr Launcelot du lake. For in all turneymentes and iustes and dedes of armes / bothe for lyfe and deth he passed all knyghtes & at no tyme he was neuer ouercomen but yf it were by treason or enchauntement. Syr Launcelot encreased so meruayllously in worshyp & honour / wherfore he is the first knyght ye the frensshe booke maketh mencyon of / after that kynge Arthur came from Rome / wherfore quene Gueneuer had hym in grete fauour aboue all other knyghtes / and certaynly he loued the quene agayne aboue all other ladyes and damoyselles all the dayes of his lyfe / and for her he

i ii

A page from Malory's *Morte d'Arthur*, 1529 edition printed by Wynkyn de Worde.

against the ancient Romans and the Saracens. The chivalrous Sir Launcelot wins tournaments, delivers prisoners from unjust captivity, and rescues distressed ladies from wicked knights and evil enchanters. Sir Tristram achieves a deathless fame in literature through his celebrated love affair with Iseult, wife of King Mark of Cornwall (who, unlike the noble king in Wagner's *Tristan and Isolde,* is thoroughly unsympathetic). Sir Galahad, "a clean virgin above all knights," is among the few—his sinful father, Launcelot, is not—who are granted sight of the Holy Grail, the vessel which Christ used at the Last Supper. When he arrives at the Grail Castle, Galahad is empowered to heal the long-festering wounds of the maimed king. (The figure of the maimed king often recurs in folklore and has sometimes been incorporated into Christian allegory as a symbol of Christ, as in the Middle English lyric *He Bare Him Up, He Bare Him Down.*) Malory's concluding pages recount the most poetic phase of the Arthurian legend: the fateful love of Launcelot and Guinevere, the revolt of Mordred, the death of Arthur, and the final disintegration of the once indomitable Order of the Round Table.

As is to be expected of a chivalric romance, especially one so heavily indebted to what Caxton calls "certain books of French," courtly love is prominently exhibited in Malory's stories. There are many instances of adultery and its inevitable partner, secrecy: Uther Pendragon and Igraine, Arthur and the wife of King Lot, Tristram and Iseult, and, of course, Launcelot and Guinevere. Launcelot, who knows all the courtly rules, behaves in the prescribed courtly fashion. He commits perjury in order to protect Guinevere's reputation, and at one point swears, in a masterful evasion, that the Queen has not given herself to any *knights,* plural. He is also moved, quite properly, to transmute the inspiration afforded by his lady's love into unflinching service in behalf of all ladies. One of these, Elaine, the fair maid of Astolat, desperately wants Launcelot to become either her husband or her lover, but the perfect knight naturally refuses both of these unknightly alternatives. After Elaine has died of a broken heart, Launcelot must appear before Guinevere and "stand trial"—much in the manner, presumably, of knights at the court of Eleanor of Aquitaine and the Countess Marie. And he justifies himself completely: " 'For, madame,' seyde Sir Launcelot, 'I love nat to be constrayned to love, for love muste only aryse of the harte selff and nat by none constraynte.' " * A perfect speech! On the basis of so

* P. 1097.

admirable a declaration, the courts of love at Poitiers would surely, like Guinevere, have exonerated him.

The Englishman Malory, however, is not really at home in the misty French world of courtly love. An earlier age had glorified the *comitatus;* and Renaissance writers—Shakespeare, for example, in *Two Gentlemen of Verona*—would again and again extol the fraternal bond between man and man (evidenced in the deep friendship between Hamlet and Horatio) as being far superior to the love between man and woman. Accordingly, Malory's Arthur recognizes that romantic love must yield to the higher ideal of knightly fellowship. To this belief the suffering king gives recognition in beautiful prose that is at once archaic and colloquial:

> "And therefore," seyde the kynge, "wyte you well, my harte was never so hevy as hit ys now. And more I am soryar for my good knyghtes losse than for the losse of my fayre quene; for quenys I myght have inow, but such a felyship of good knyghtes shall never be togydirs in no company. And now I dare say," seyde kynge Arthur, "there was never Crystyn kynge that ever hylde such a felyship togydyrs. And alas, that ever sir Launcelot and I shulde be at debate!" *

But comradeship, though finer than love, is itself, as Arthur's speech implies, a perishable value. Knighthood and courtly love turn out, in fact, to be incompatible; and the chivalric order is destroyed, ironically, through the unworthiness of the very lady who should have inspired it and held it together. Guinevere herself acknowledges the destruction which her faithlessness has wrought. This she does, most dramatically, as Launcelot visits her for the last time in her cloister:

> Thorow thys same man and me hath all thys warre be wrought, and deth of the moste nobelest knyghtes of the worlde; for thorow oure love that we have loved togydir [i]s my moste noble lorde slayne. †

In a very moving scene, Guinevere dismisses Launcelot from her sight without even so much as one parting kiss, for she has renounced the world and committed her contrite soul to God. And Launcelot, at last aware of the vanity of human life, spends his remaining days on earth in fasting, penance, and prayer.

It has been suggested that the dissolution of the brotherhood of the Round Table, which Malory depicts so memorably, constitutes an early approach in English literature to tragedy in the post-medieval

* Pp. 1183–84.   † P. 1252.

sense of the term. The medieval concept of tragedy, as excmplified in Chaucer's *Troilus and Criseyde* and *The Monk's Tale* (see Chapters XII and XIII), was largely derived from Boethius and was often involved with the image of Fortune and her wheel: one may prosper for a time, but with a single spin Fortune can hurl the mighty into the depths of misery. Now, however, we generally demand of tragedy as an art form that the hero be something more than a passive victim of a capricious Fortune and that he to some degree make his fate out of the stuff of his own soul.

According to present-day aesthetic standards, Malory's characters are for the most part free agents entangled in a web of conflicting loyalties and passions. Launcelot loves and owes allegiance to Arthur, his friend and king, but he strongly desires Guinevere; Gawain prizes Launcelot, but he values Arthur deeply, just as he values his own two brothers whom Launcelot has slain; Arthur strives to preserve the knightly order, but he also cherishes his waning domestic happiness; Guinevere enjoys a sinful relationship with Launcelot, but she cannot escape the agonizing conviction that she is wronging her husband, undermining knighthood, and separating her soul from God. All of these characters are in a sense caught in the toils of an inescapable destiny; yet we feel, in each case, that they are responsible for their own acts. In Malory, as in later tragedy, destiny and individual freedom serve to reinforce each other. Malory does not provide easy solutions that can avert final catastrophe, but he brings sympathetic understanding to the delineation of the moral struggles carried on by his characters. By probing into the inner conflicts of essentially believable human beings, Malory lifts his narrative far above the usual standard of medieval romance.

NON-ARTHURIAN ROMANCE

Although the medieval romances dealing with the "matter of Britain" have received the major share of scholarly and critical attention, the non-Arthurian "matters," in varying degrees, also found their way into Middle English literature and have continued to attract readers. These romances, to repeat, comprise the "matter of England," the "matter of Greece and Rome," and the "matter of France." To the three non-Arthurian cycles, a fourth group is frequently added, the "Breton lays." Although the Breton lays are sometimes discussed together with the "matter of England," it would seem that they more properly constitute a special category and therefore deserve separate treatment. Finally, there are some romances that belong to none of the national "matters," romances that can be classified only under the vague heading of "miscellaneous." It is with a few specimens chosen from the vast body of non-Arthurian romance that the following pages will be concerned.

The "Matter of England"

A number of entertaining, though often crudely executed, Middle English romances are built upon the careers of English and Germanic heroes of history or legend. Some of these romances are appealing for the light they shed upon English life, others for individual moments that are diverting or quaint. A few are remembered simply because they introduce into English literature motifs or characters later explored by more gifted writers. Two of the earliest and most interesting romances that make up the "matter of England" are *King Horn* and *Havelock*—both of which treat the ever popular folk and romance theme of the exiled prince who returns to his land, regains his rightful place, and marries a beauteous princess who for a long time had been unaware of his royal lineage.

King Horn (*c.* 1250?), derived from an earlier work (*c.* 1180) by an Anglo-Norman poet known only as Thomas, tells the story of a young prince who, after the death of his father, is uprooted from his native Suddene (Isle of Man), in the Irish Sea, by an invading army from Scandinavia. These invaders, oddly enough, are called "Saracens"—evidence, perhaps, that overtones of the Crusades often crept into romances predominantly secular in character. At any rate, Horn and twelve companions are cast adrift in a rudderless boat (a recurrent device in medieval literature employed, for example, in accounts of the life of St. Constance, notably in Chaucer's *The Man of Law's Tale*) and carried by wind and tide to the land of Westernesse. There Horn meets the princess Rimenhild, who tries to win his love. With Horn, however, duty comes first; he longs for knightly adventure before permitting himself the comforts of a wife. Meanwhile, one of his companions, Fikenhild, reveals the love affair to Rimenhild's father, the King, who banishes Horn forthwith. The banishment, unwelcome though it may be, at least gives the hero his long-awaited opportunity for military action, and he fights valiantly in behalf of the King of Ireland. He must return, however, from this second exile (disguised as a pilgrim) in order to rescue Rimenhild from a hateful suitor. After Rimenhild's father pardons him, Horn takes off for Suddene and reconquers his native land from the "Saracens." But all is not yet well! During this absence, his enemy Fikenhild has struck again, this time abducting Rimenhild; and Horn therefore has one more rescue on his agenda. At long last comes the happy ending: Horn and Rimenhild are married, and, when bride and groom return to Suddene, the reader can only hold his breath and pray that Horn is not infected with the knightly wanderlust for a while. The narrative is sprightly throughout, and recent criticism (see MEB 90–91) has been attentive to it as literature, seeing the poem, for example, as a study in the coming of age of a medieval knight, and analyzing the significance of some of its imagery patterns. Horn was a very popular figure in medieval literature. Not only does he reappear in a later English version (*Horn Childe and Maiden Rimnild*) whence he journeys into a French adaptation (which was in turn readapted into English in the fifteenth century), but he figures prominently in Middle English folklore ballads.

Havelock (*c.* 1250?), an ingratiating romance based upon a mid-twelfth-century Anglo-Norman history by Geoffrey Gaimar, deals with the adventures of a dispossessed prince of Denmark. The child king, Havelock, is deposed by Earl Godard, a scheming regent who first slits the throats of the boy's sisters and then arranges (so he thinks) to have the boy himself drowned by a fisherman named Grim. The poet meanwhile has contrived a parallel plot involving Havelock's eventual bride, the English princess Goldborough. She has been imprisoned in Dover Castle by a wicked English regent, Godrich, who holds on to her wealth by delaying her marriage until he can find the strongest man in England to be her husband. The paths of hero and heroine are to converge. Grim, who has taken pity on Havelock and reared him in a humble fisherman's cottage, perceives a mysterious light about the young man's head, becomes aware of his royal birth, and sails with the prince to England. There Havelock displays incredible physical prowess and, later, secures employment as helper to the Earl of Lincoln's cook. Godrich is naturally delighted at the opportunity to marry Goldborough off to Havelock, the strongest man in England; for the hero, presumably a churl, will not be able to get control of her fortune. Goldborough herself resents the low match until, like Grim, she observes one night that luminous glow emanating from the face and body of the sleeping Havelock, once again the sure sign that he is a prince and that she has therefore not been disgraced by marrying him. In time Havelock conquers both Denmark and England, and he and Goldborough can live happily ever after. Unlike most other romances, *Havelock* is almost exclusively concerned with refreshing scenes of ordinary life involving characters (like Grim and the cook) of homely grace. In addition to its warmth, *Havelock* also contains scenes of earthy humor. When Havelock, his identity still undisclosed, outwrestles the local English champions and defeats them in a stone-throwing contest, the rival athletes, who are good losers, nudge each other, laugh, and decline further competition: " 'We dwellen her [here] to longe!' "

Other romances on English and Germanic heroes encompass a variety of subjects and moods. The robust hero of *Richard Coeur de Lion* (*c.* 1300), the English crusader-king Richard I, gets his name by thrusting his arm down the throat of a lion, tearing out the beast's heart, dipping it in salt, and swallowing the morsel whole. Later Richard embarks upon the Crusades, where he displays prodigious bravery, but few of the feats ascribed to him by the poet have any historical warrant. The long and ambitious romance, while not distinguished from the literary point of view, is notable for exhibiting a fierce patriotism: England is glorified beyond measure while the French are buried with contempt. *Guy of Warwick* and *Bevis of Hampton* both date from around 1300 and were extremely popular at one time. These romances (in which some have seen parallels to *Hamlet*) deal with heroes who, in addition to experiencing a variety of typical knightly adventures, help defend the faith against infidels. In a comical scene in *Bevis of Hampton,* the Bishop of Cologne tries to baptize the hero's page, Ascapard, a thirty-foot giant; but the latter leaps angrily from the specially built font:

> For Ascapard was made a tun;
> And when he should therein be done,
> He lept out upon the brench [brink],
> And said, "Churl! wilt thou me drench [drown]?
> The devil of hell mot fetche thee!
> I am too much [big] christened to be!"

In the alliterative *William of Palerne* (*c.* 1350) the prince of Spain, who has been turned into a werewolf by a wicked stepmother, carries off William, son of the King of Apulia. Eventually, however, the prince is restored to his proper form, and William, after many exciting adventures, concludes a happy marriage with the prince's sister. *The*

Tale of Gamelyn (*c.* 1350), which tells the story of an ill-used younger brother, is the ultimate source of the Oliver-Orlando plot in *As You Like It.* The tale appears in some manuscripts of *The Canterbury Tales* and has occasionally been linked with the Cook, whose own tale is never finished. But *The Tale of Gamelyn* is almost certainly not by Chaucer.

Breton Lays

Among the most delightful poems of the Middle Ages are the short romances commonly called, without any precise reason, *Breton lays.* Scholars do not know who originated the form, nor can they agree as to whether it has any distinguishing characteristics. It seems, however, that the genre was perfected in the twelfth century by a French poet living in England, identified only as Marie de France (fl. 1167–84). The vogue died out in France, but it enjoyed a revival in England during the fourteenth century.

The name "Breton lay" is derived from Bretagne (Brittany), an old province in northwest France that presumably furnished the setting for most of the lays. Chaucer's Franklin introduces his tale, itself a Breton lay, with a vague statement as to the ancestry of the form:

> Thise olde gentil Britouns in hir [their] dayes
> Of diverse aventures maden layes,
> Rymeyed [rhymed] in hir firste Briton tonge;
> Whiche layes with hir instrumentz they songe,
> Or elles redden [read] hem for hir plesaunce,
> And oon of hem have I in remembraunce. . . .*

This does not tell us much, but it suggests that the lays were often sung, with an accompaniment, or, at least, recited rather than read. As for the "diverse aventures" that comprised the subject matter —we get some help from the opening lines of *Sir Orfeo,* a charming English Breton lay:

> Sum ben of wele and sum of wo,
> And sum of joy and merthe also,
> Sum of trechery and sum of gyle,
> And sum of happes that fallen by whyle;

---

* From F. N. Robinson, ed., *The Works of Chaucer* (2nd ed.; Boston: Houghton Mifflin Company, 1957), Group F, ll. 709–14. Reprinted by permission of the publisher.

> Sum of bourdys [jests], and sum of rybaudry,
> And sum ther ben of the feyré [faery].
> Of alle thing that men may se,
> Moost o love forsothe they be.

There is, of course, nothing in these lines that could not be applied to just about the entire body of medieval romance literature; and it is possible, as at least one literary historian believes, that a romance becomes a Breton lay for no better reason than that it contains a reference to Brittany or that the poet *says* it is a Breton lay.* And yet there may be a certain atmosphere that consistently pervades the Breton lay and confers something of a unique quality upon the genre. Breton lays are usually short, simply constructed, and cheerful. Being of Celtic folk origin, they sometimes make use of the supernatural in the form of fairy lore and enchantment. Moreover, as the lines from *Sir Orfeo* have suggested, Breton lays may often be pure love stories.

In *Sir Orfeo* (*c.* 1320) the classical fable of Orpheus and Eurydice is stripped of its heartbreak and terror and transmuted into a lovely Celtic fairy tale with a happy ending. One day, in the merry month of May, "when clustered blossoms deck the bowers," the beautiful Queen Heurodis (Eurydice) is enchanted by the King of the Fairies and whisked away to his castle in a bright country far away. No gloomy Hades this, but a wonderful place sparkling with unearthly light:

> Al that lond was ever light:
> For when it schuld be therk [dark] and night,
> The rich stones light gonne [shed forth],
> As bright as doth at none the sonne.
> No man may telle no thenche in thought
> The riche werk that ther was wrought.
> Bi al thing, him think that it is
> The proude [splendid] court of paradis.

The grief-stricken King Orfeo entrusts his land to a steward and, armed only with his incomparable harp, wanders barefoot for ten long years in search of his beloved. He finally stumbles upon a host of dancing knights and maidens and is astonished to find Heurodis in their company. He follows them to the castle of the King of

---

* Albert C. Baugh, in *A Literary History of England,* ed. A. C. Baugh (New York: Appleton-Century-Crofts, Inc., 1948), pp. 195–97.

Fairies, gains admittance as a poor minstrel, and, of course, charms the King with the ravishing strains of his harp. The King of Fairies offers the minstrel a boon, but when the latter asks for Heurodis, the King hesitates to bestow so lovely a rose upon the foul creature he takes Orfeo to be. But it is indeed foul, says Orfeo, to break a promise. The King of the Fairies is properly touched at an indisputable point of honor, and he answers like a true knight and a good sport:

> The king seyd: "Sethen it is so,
> Take hir bi the hond, and go;
> Of hir Ichil thatow [that thou] be blithe."

Orfeo and Heurodis return to their land with none of the anguish that darkens the Greek myth in which Orpheus looks back and loses Eurydice forever. Still disguised as a poor minstrel, Orfeo tests the integrity of his steward by claiming to have found Orfeo's corpse torn by lions and wolves and to have picked up the harp that was lying in the snow. The steward swoons, providing thereby ample proof of his love. Orfeo can then reveal his true identity and, with his queen, resume the reign. After their death, the faithful steward succeeds to the throne.

Many elements are engagingly combined in *Sir Orfeo:* the power of minstrelsy, a motif that in English literature goes back as far as the Old English *Widsith;* the abducted queen, a favorite theme of fairy tales; the journey to the other world, a modified version of the classical underworld of dark shapes; the disguised prince returning to his realm, a narrative device that is at least as old as the *Odyssey* (in which Odysseus, to test his wife Penelope, conceals his return to Ithaca)—all this, as was said before, handled lightly and good-humoredly. *Sir Orfeo* is a success.

Sir Launfal (*c.* 1350?) is one of several English adaptations from a similarly titled lay of Marie de France. The hero, a knight of the Round Table, enjoys the love of a beautiful fairy who pledges him to secrecy. But the lascivious Queen Guinevere, frustrated after unsuccessful attempts to seduce Sir Launfal, at last goads the knight into revealing his love for the more radiant mistress. As a result, the fairy deserts Sir Launfal. Later the jealous Guinevere, in revenge, alleges to King Arthur that Sir Launfal has molested her with amorous advances. On the verge of being executed, the knight is rescued in a sensational manner by the fairy mistress, who bears him away to live with her in endless pleasure.

Other Breton lays may simply be mentioned here: *Emare, Sir Degare, The Earl of Toulouse, Lay le Freine*—all tales that end happily after a variety of threatening circumstances have nearly produced disaster. The masterpiece among Breton lays, *The Franklin's Tale*, will be more fully discussed later as part of *The Canterbury Tales*.

The "Matter of Greece and Rome"

During the Middle Ages, England, like France and Italy, produced several romances based upon heroes and events of classical antiquity. The principal stories involved Alexander the Great, the Trojan War, the siege of Thebes, and Aeneas—though in England, only tales of Alexander and Troy were popular.

Alexander's popularity as a hero of romance was mainly grounded upon his magical birth and his thrilling adventures as conqueror of exotic India. Both of these themes are derived ultimately from a Greek prose biography of Alexander written in the second century by an author whom scholars have designated as "Pseudo-Callisthenes." This Greek book traveled the inevitable road of translation—first into Latin, then into French and other Continental languages. When it finally appeared in English, particularly in *King Alisaunder* (*c.* 1300), a long poem in octosyllabic couplets, some of its earlier excitement had been diluted—evidence, it has been suggested, that the Alexander legend, unlike the "matter of Britain," was circulated primarily by means of a written scholarly tradition rather than an oral popular tradition.* Two fragments, *Alexander A* and *Alexander B,* survive in West Midland alliterative verse from around the middle of the fourteenth century, but whether they are both the work of the same author is uncertain.

The Troy legend received its impetus from two Latin prose documents, from the fourth and sixth centuries respectively, which had been translated from two earlier Greek works purporting to be eyewitness accounts of the Trojan War. The two Greek writers (Dares Phrygius and Dictys Cretensis) obviously lived several centuries too late to have participated in the war, but their pretense made for a lively story. As might be expected, the first treatment of the Troy legend in a modern language is in French—a long Norman-French poem, the *Roman de Troie* (*c.* 1155–60), by Benoît de Sainte-More. In this interesting work Benoît tells, perhaps for the first time, the

* Baugh, *A Literary History of England,* p. 182.

story of Troilus and Briseida (Criseyde). Although Benoît handles the love affair as merely a diverting episode in the midst of his more usual scenes of violent combat, the lovers are later to occupy the center of the stage in two great English works—one by Chaucer, the other by Shakespeare. Benoît's *Roman de Troie* was adapted into Latin prose (1287) by a Sicilian, Guido delle Colonne, and the Troy legend prospered from then on. The first English romance inspired by Benoît and Guido was the *Seege of Troy,* dating from the beginning of the fourteenth century. Several other accounts have been preserved in English, including the enormous *Troy Book* (1412–20), composed by Chaucer's most prolific fifteenth-century imitator, John Lydgate.

Little need be said of the remaining two classical themes that were explored by writers of medieval romance. As mentioned before, the legend of Thebes, immortalized in three overwhelming plays of the Greek tragedian Sophocles (*Oedipus the King, Oedipus at Colonus,* and *Antigone*), received scant attention in England. The only English romance that draws directly upon the story is Lydgate's *Siege of Thebes* (1420–22). The material is reflected obliquely, however, in Chaucer's *The Knight's Tale.* Finally, the legend of Aeneas is almost completely absent from Middle English romance except for Chaucer's inclusion of Dido in the *Legend of Good Women.*

The "Matter of France"

The "matter of France," at least as it flourished on the Continent, falls into three main divisions: the *geste du roi* ("exploits of the king"), romances in which Charlemagne appears in either a major or minor capacity; the *geste de Doon de Mayence,* romances dealing with some of Charlemagne's rebellious vassals and named after the alleged forefather of the rebels; and the *geste de Garin de Monglane,* named for the legendary progenitor of William of Orange and featuring the adventures of William and his family.

The most important group by far—indeed, the only segment of the "matter of France" to be represented in the extant body of Middle English poetry—is the *geste du roi,* and its chief glory is the French epic *Chanson de Roland* ("Song of Roland"). This stirring narrative, which may date from around 1100, concerns itself primarily with the stubborn heroism of Charlemagne's nephew, Roland, as commander of the French rearguard at Roncevaux, where he and the army are ambushed by the Saracens. The legend of Charlemagne also lent itself to light treatment—for example, in the French comic epic *The Pilgrimage of Charlemagne to Jerusalem* (*c.* 1115).

That the "matter of France," extremely popular on the Continent, was largely ignored in England may perhaps be attributed to the growing hostility between the two countries. Near the beginning of the fourteenth century an English version of the *Song of Roland* appeared in four-stress rhymed couplets. One of the most rewarding English romances on Charlemagne is *Sir Ferumbras,* dating from the end of the fourteenth century. This work, like most of the Charlemagne romances, emphasizes the conversion of the Saracens to Christianity, Ferumbras himself accepting the faith after being defeated by Oliver, one of Charlemagne's most valiant knights. *Sir Ferumbras* is of additional interest because it is preserved in the anonymous author's own handwriting—a rare phenomenon among medieval manuscripts. The so-called Otuel Group is made up of five English romances which deal directly or indirectly with material related to Charlemagne's expeditions to Jerusalem and Spain. The group takes its name from a particularly well-told story about a Saracen, Otuel, who accepts Christianity while engaged in single combat with Roland. During the struggle, the Holy Spirit in the shape of a dove alights upon Otuel's helmet; from that moment on, Otuel fights bravely in Charlemagne's Christian army.

Miscellaneous Romances

Remaining to be considered are a few romances which belong to no "matter," or national grouping, and which are of slight literary value. Nevertheless, these noncyclic romances increase our understanding of the attitudes and tastes of the medieval reading public. *Floris and Blancheflor* (*c.* 1250) narrates the separation of two childhood lovers and their reunion, years later, in the harem-prison of the Sultan of Babylon. The latter is so moved by their willingness to die for each other that he releases them, and the romance ends with a happy marriage. *Amis and Amiloun* (late thirteenth century?), an English metrical version of a well-known medieval story, celebrates a perfect friendship between two men (like Damon and Pythias). John Barbour's *Bruce* (1376), a patriotic romance that honors the exploits of the Scot Robert Bruce against the English early in the fourteenth century, heralds a long tradition of Scottish nationalistic verse extending at least to Robert Burns. *The Squire of Low Degree* (*c.* 1450), probably based upon an earlier work, is undistinguished as literature;

but it is enlivened by interesting incidental descriptions of food, drink, clothes, and general manners in mid-fifteenth-century England.

* * * * * *

With rare exceptions—it is, of course, the exceptions that have concerned us most—medieval romances offer little in the way of sustained plot or characterization. They are usually made up of a series of loosely connected episodes, some of which recur again and again in romance literature. Supernatural elements regularly play an important, and frequently a decisive, role in shaping the outcome of the overelaborate action. The knights, more often than not, are little more than puppets; they mechanically slay their dragons, rescue their damsels, or fight in their tournaments—generally in strict obedience to the rules of chivalry and courtly love. The women, for their part, are even less real—unmotivated, vaguely beautiful creatures for whom their chosen lovers would willingly lay down their lives. A *Havelock* or a *Sir Orfeo,* neither of which, incidentally, deals with courtly love, is pretty nearly the best one can expect; writers who can breathe genuine artistic life into the genre—Malory with his awareness of human tragedy; the Gawain poet with his dazzling control of plot, setting, and character—these are indeed rarities. Chaucer's *Troilus and Criseyde* and *The Knight's Tale,* while ostensibly romances, seem to burst through the boundaries of their professed form and rise to the level of philosophic poems of the highest order.

If we find it hard to understand how so generally unoriginal and repetitious a literary vehicle as the romance could have engrossed the attention of sophisticated medieval readers, we might find a parallel in the widespread twentieth-century taste for the detective story or, better still, the western. These contemporary favorites abound in typical situations and characters, yet manage to be individually interesting—at least for one quick reading. If the hero of medieval romance transported readers back to the glorious age of chivalry, the twentieth-century cowboy, an equally unrealistic figure, glamorizes that period in real or imaginary history when a different sort of knight, also on horseback, rode far and wide to bring law and order to the wild West. The fictional cowboy, too, finds inspiration in a lovely girl, whom he serves faithfully and well. But by no means do the rules of cowboy errantry permit him to marry.

VIII: MIDDLE ENGLISH PROSE

The prose writers of the Middle Ages comprise a relatively small portion of English literary history. For one thing, English authors were perhaps too deeply absorbed in the newly discovered example of French rhyming verse to pay sufficient attention to the needs of a native literary prose. Then, too, the disruption of the English linguistic and cultural scene—the decline of Wessex, the growing importance of London, the use of French among the upper classes and Latin among the clergy—militated against the development of English prose even more effectively than it delayed the rebirth of English poetry. To be sure, the tradition of English prose as established in the ninth, tenth, and early eleventh centuries by Alfred and Ælfric was kept alive in sermons and other devotional works of the early Middle Ages; and English, as has been noted, never relinquished its place as the language of ordinary daily life. But, generally speaking, the extensive use of prose for belles-lettres, especially in works of a more secular nature, had to await the fifteenth century and the growth of an educated and leisured gentry that was relatively free from the ties that had bound the Anglo-Normans to France.

Oddly enough, these conditions were, in a sense, healthy for English prose. Without much in the way of a learned prose tradition behind them, the newly prominent English gentlemen first had to master their rapidly changing language in order to articulate regularly their everyday purposes and thoughts; then they had to shape the English language into a more versatile tool. Civic ordinances, wills, letters, hunting treatises, recipes—all these, and many more, while they may not have constituted "literature" in any significant measure, nonetheless provided the raw materials out of which men of letters could fashion a strong and supple instrument for communication at the level of art. "Prose had almost everything to learn," writes a literary historian about the fifteenth century, "and there were no great writers whose influence was all-pervasive, so that prose in this century developed by much trial and error and owed much to 'unprofessional' as well as to professional writers." *

* Henry S. Bennett, *Chaucer and the Fifteenth Century* (New York: Oxford University Press, 1947), p. 180.

It should not be inferred, however, that Middle English prose fails to rise above practical or pedestrian interests. Certainly the example of Malory should prove that greatness was not beyond its reach. Nor should Malory's well-deserved fame obscure the fact that there were other prose writers of enduring excellence—the anonymous author of that wonderful early work, the *Ancrene Riwle;* John Wyclif and his followers, who achieved the first complete English translation of the Bible; Richard Rolle of Hampole, who captured in writing the almost unbearable intensity of his private visions; Sir John Mandeville, author of an engaging book of travels, realistic and fantastic; the Paston family, which bequeathed us, unintentionally, an enormous volume of letters that illuminate English life in the fifteenth century. Even these (except for the *Paston Letters*) more self-conscious "literary" productions, it will be seen, are rooted in the simple, vigorous idiom of English colloquial speech. The ornate Latinistic style associated with Cicero, while not missing from Middle English prose, was to invade the language in full force only at the time of the Renaissance.

RELIGIOUS PROSE

The religious prose of the Middle English period is voluminous, and it covers a vast area. It includes sermons, proverbs, conduct books, saints' lives, *exempla* (moralized tales), translations, mystical treatises, and tracts advising parish priests as to the performance of their duties. Not all of this material has proved to be of permanent interest; the chances are, in fact, that the authors, in most cases, cared little about what posterity might think of their literary art. Yet, in spite of the pervasive medieval attitude which extolled the needs of the soul above the delights of the senses and of the mind, a number of these English prose works manage to convey their moral instruction in a fairly attractive manner. Moreover, at least three prose creations of the Middle English period have substantially enriched our literary heritage. These valuable works—a conduct book, a translation, and some "mystical" pieces—satisfy a profound religious impulse on the part of their authors and, at the same time, exhibit a very high standard of literary accomplishment. The major part of this discussion will therefore be devoted to the *Ancrene Riwle,* the "Wyclif" Bible, and the meditations of Richard Rolle.

The Ancrene Riwle (*c. 1200*) *

The widely circulated *Ancrene Riwle* ("Rule for Anchoresses") exists in some seventeen different manuscripts in English, French, or Latin; but the original manuscript, probably in a West Midland dialect, has not survived. The book was written, anonymously, to provide moral instruction for three young sisters, presumably from a comfortable family, who were preparing to live a cloistered life. If the circumstances surrounding its origin do not sound inviting to the modern reader, let it be said at once that the *Ancrene Riwle* is one of the wittiest and most charming books ever written. Nearly every page reflects a warmth and a practical wisdom uncommon among medieval religious works and rare enough in any age.

The moderate and large-minded author of the *Ancrene Riwle* speaks of the strict inner discipline of religion and never allows the outer forms to become burdensome. His advice is a unique blend of moral earnestness, compassion, and urbanity. The anchoress, he insists, must not break a vow. "If, however, she does not vow it, she may, nevertheless, do it, and leave it off when she will." Let her parlors be closed on all sides, lest the heart fly out and the soul turn sick; the young girls he is addressing surely do not want to get the name "of roving-eyed anchoresses, or of having catching looks or expressions, which some, at times, alas, put on contrary to their nature." If she must have a pet, let the anchoress choose something small, a cat; by no means should she cumber herself and her thoughts with a cow:

> For then must she think of the cow's fodder, and of the herdman's hire, blandish the bailiff, defend her when men impound the cow, and yield therefore any damages. Christ knoweth this is a loathly thing, when a complaint is made in town of an anchoress's cattle. However, if any must needs have a cow, look that she trouble no man, or harm any man, or that the anchoress have her thought fixed on the cow. An anchoress ought not to have anything that draweth her heart outward.†

The same refreshing mixture of spirituality and practicality is apparent in the entertaining metaphors with which the author makes

---

* Quotations from the *Ancrene Riwle* are, with one exception (noted below), from *Medieval English Verse and Prose,* in modernized versions by Roger S. Loomis and Rudolph Willard. Copyright, 1948, Appleton-Century-Crofts, Inc. Reprinted by permission of the publisher.

† P. 51.

an old piece of moral advice ring with a fresh sound. The anchoress, he warns, should not talk too much. "The hen, when she hath laid, can do nothing but cackle. And what doth she get from it? The stealthy man cometh right away, and taketh from her her eggs." Thus the devil "beareth away from the cackling anchoress, and swalloweth up, all the good that she hath gained. . . . The wretched peddler maketh more noise to cry up his soap than doth a rich mercer about all his precious merchandise." Sometimes the author echoes the bestiary, which (like the Old English *Physiologus,* discussed earlier) allegorized natural history. Anchoresses must be thin like the pelican so that they may fly heavenward, with a high and holy life; they must not weight themselves down to the earth like the bulky stork (ostrich):

> And though she maketh semblance, and much noise with her wings, that is, she letteth on as though she flew, and were a holy anchoress, yet, whoever beholdeth her laugheth her to scorn, for her feet, as doth the stork's, which are her lusts, draw her to earth.*

Even more rewarding are the author's countless homely details garnered from actual life, like that marvelous vignette of mother and child at play:

> Our Lord, when He suffereth us to be tempted, playeth with us, as the mother with her young darling: she flies from him, and hides herself, and lets him sit alone, and look anxiously around, and call Dame! dame! and weep a while, and then leapeth forth laughing, with outspread arms, and embraceth and kisseth him, and wipeth his eyes.†

Into this passage the author has distilled a lifetime of knowledge and experience, all of it mellowed by a quiet humor and a rich love.

Still another facet of the *Ancrene Riwle,* and further evidence of the author's wealth of understanding, is the clarity and insight with which various aspects of human nature are depicted. At several points the author seems to anticipate the "character" writers of the seventeenth century who, in imitation of the Greek author Theophrastus, turned out miniature verbal portraits of typical personalities. Observe, for example, the epigrammatic bite of this description of the glutton. The passage occurs as the author reminds the anchoresses of the Seven Deadly Sins:

* P. 52.
† From *A Literary History of England,* ed. Albert C. Baugh, p. 131. Copyright, 1948, Appleton-Century-Crofts, Inc. Reprinted by permission of the publisher.

The greedy glutton is the devil's manciple, for he sticketh ever in the cellar or in the kitchen. His heart is in the dishes, his thought is all in the table-cloth; his life is in the tun, his soul in the pitcher. He cometh into the presence of his lord besmutted and besmeared, with a dish in one hand, and a bowl in the other. He talketh much with words, and staggereth like a drunken man who seemeth about to fall; he beholdeth his great belly, and the fiend laugheth so that he bursteth.*

There is a similar, though less formal, piece on the oily-tongued seducer, who makes poisonous inroads into a young girl's thoughts with his speeches of love and who lingers in her mind "when she ought to attend diligently to something else." Especially skillful is the portrait of the backbiter, who spews out his venom under the cloak of friendship:

He casteth down his head, and beginneth to sigh ere he may say anything, and maketh a drooping cheer, and moralizeth long in general that he may be the better believed. But when it cometh forth wholly, then is it but yellow poison. "Alas and alack!" she saith, "woe is me, that he, or she, hath caught such a reputation!" †

Too bad, the backbiter continues, that everybody—not through *my* doing, of course—knows the worst. "They say that it is evil, and it is even worse. So grieved and sorry am I that I must admit it, but, in truth it is so; and that is great sorrow." And one could go on citing one delicious morsel after another. The charms of the *Ancrene Riwle* are well-nigh inexhaustible.

But the *Ancrene Riwle* has more to recommend it than simply charm, humor, or even wisdom. The author rises at times to a kind of rapture, perhaps nowhere better illustrated than in the haunting parable of the kingly wooer who offers himself to an unwilling beauty besieged by enemies within an earthen castle. Having sent messengers bearing jewels and all means of sustenance for this poor persecuted creature, the King at last appears himself and tenderly pleads his case:

"My Lady, thou art warred upon, and thy foes are so strong that thou mayst no wise, without succour of men, escape their hands, that they put thee not to shameful death. I will, for love of thee, take this fight upon me, and save thee from them that seek thy death. I know, however, in truth, that I shall receive in their midst a death-wound, and I will accept it heartily, to win thy heart. Now then I beseech thee, for the love that I have made known to thee, that thou love me, at

* P. 55.   † Pp. 58–59.

least after that same death, whom thou wouldst not when I was alive." *

One recalls Cynewulf's *Juliana,* in which Satan explains how he besieges the fortress of man's soul. But the author of the *Ancrene Riwle* carries the figure further and shows how the traditional materials of chivalry and courtly love may be transfigured by the power of medieval Christianity:

> This king is Jesu Christ, God's Son, who all in this wise wooed our soul, which the devils had beset. And He, as a noble wooer, after many messengers and many good deeds, came to prove His love, and showed through knightly prowess that He was worthy of love, even as sometimes knights were wont to do. †

"He entered a tournament," the parable concludes, "and for His lady's love, He, like a bold knight, had His shield pierced in every part in the fight."

John Wyclif (c. 1328–1384) and His Followers ‡

Except for a few partial translations, like Ælfric's *Heptateuch,* dating from the Old English period, the Bible was accessible in fourteenth-century England only in Latin versions. It remained for the scholar and theologian John Wyclif, an outspoken critic of Church policy and doctrine, to provide the impetus behind the first complete translation of the Bible into English, a version that somewhat misleadingly goes under his name.

Wyclif's interest in translating the Bible into English was part of a persistent campaign against many aspects of ecclesiastical organization and thought. It is impossible in these pages to discuss in detail his differences with the Church, the most serious of which was his attack upon the doctrine of transubstantiation (a position for which Wyclif himself was censured and for which many of his followers were physically persecuted). Of more immediate concern to us is the effect of Wyclif's attitude upon the English literary scene. Wyclif argued that the Church held a monopoly on learning; that it sustained its monopoly by permitting the Bible to circulate only in Latin, which

---

* P. 60.
† *Ibid.*
‡ Quotations from Wyclif's disciple Purvey and from the "Wyclif" Bible are from *Medieval English Verse and Prose,* in modernized versions by Roger S. Loomis and Rudolph Willard. Copyright, 1948, Appleton-Century-Crofts, Inc. Reprinted by permission of the publisher.

ordinary men could not read; and that it further obscured "the points that be most needful to salvation" by means of a pulpit style that was too formal, too eloquent, and too erudite. The Wyclifites both advocated and tried to practice, in sermons as well as in written prose, a plain style that would be sincere, logical, and robust. It should be noted that the Wyclifites, in exalting the Scriptures and urging the adoption of an unadorned literary style, anticipated some of the attitudes emphasized in the Protestant Reformation—particularly as it came to be embodied in English Puritanism of the sixteenth and seventeenth centuries. Many Wyclifites stumped the country as Lollards, or "poor priests," sounding a call to evangelical Christianity.

Although the extent of Wyclif's participation in translating the so-called Wyclif Bible has been strenuously debated, he undoubtedly was the main inspirational force behind it. The "Wyclif" Bible (1385) was brought out a year after Wyclif's death by one of his disciples, Nicholas of Hereford; and although it was not printed in its entirety until 1850, it gained increasing popularity and has often been referred to as the only complete English Bible before the sixteenth century. The 1385 version was an overly literal rendering of the Latin, but about ten years later John Purvey, another Wyclifite, issued a much improved translation. In his interesting General Prologue to the revision, Purvey justifies certain liberties taken in order that the translation should be "according to the meaning and not only according to the words." He once again defends the right of "one simple creature of God [to] translate into English for the profit of English men." Is it not true, Purvey asks, that Frenchmen, Bohemians, Bretons [?]—all have the Bible and other devotional literature translated into their native tongues?

> Why Englishmen should not have the same in their mother language, I cannot understand, unless for falseness and negligence of clerics, or because our people is not worthy to have so great grace and gift of God in punishment of their old sins.*

As for the translation itself, let the following single example, well known in so many other versions, serve to indicate the high literary quality achieved by those, including Purvey, who were responsible for the "Wyclif" Bible:

> If I speak with tongues of men and of angels, and I have not charity, I am made as brass sounding or a cymbal tinkling. And if I have

* P. 284.

prophecy and know all mysteries and all cunning, and if I have all faith so that I move hills from their place, and I have not charity, I am naught. And if I depart all my goods into the meats of poor men, and if I bitake my body so that I burn, and if I have not charity, it profiteth me nothing. Charity is patient, it is benign; charity envieth not, it doth not wickedly, it is not blown, it is not covetous, it seeketh not those things that be his own, it is not stirred to wrath, it thinketh not evil, it joyeth not on wickedness, but it joyeth together to truth; it suffereth all things, it believeth all things, it hopeth all things, it sustaineth all things. Charity falleth never down, whether prophecies shall be voided, either language shall cease, either science shall be destroyed. For a party [part] we know, and a party we prophesy; but when that shall come that is perfect, that thing that is of party shall be avoided. When I was a little child, I spake as a little child, I understood as a little child; but when I was made a man, I avoided those things that were of a little child. And we see now by a mirror in darkness, but then face to face; now I know of party, but then I shall know as I am known. And now dwell faith, hope, and charity, but the most of these is charity.*

(I Corinthians, 13:1–13)

In addition to enjoying the revised "Wyclif" Bible as literature, readers may have the satisfaction of discovering how much of its vocabulary and rhythm were to be incorporated more than two hundred years later into the greatest and most familiar of all English translations, the King James Bible (1611).

Richard Rolle (c. 1300–1349) and Other "Mystics" †

A number of Middle English writers have often been referred to by literary historians as "mystics." Mysticism is extremely difficult to define, and no attempt will be made in these pages to discuss the subject in any detail. Let it merely be noted that the mystical experience, although it may never be identical for any two individuals, seems essentially to be grounded in some sort of intense personalized communion between the mystic and God. As might be expected, the medieval mystics did not generally find favor either with Church officials or with Wyclifite reformers, for there was always the danger

---

* P. 286.

† Quotations from Rolle are from *Medieval English Verse and Prose*, in modernized versions by Roger S. Loomis and Rudolph Willard. Copyright, 1948, Appleton-Century-Crofts, Inc. Reprinted by permission of the publisher. The quotation from Dame Julian is from Dame Julian of Norwich, *Revelations of Divine Love*, ed. Grace Warrack (London: Methuen and Co., 1901).

that an alleged communion was spurious, hence potentially disruptive to Christian discipline.

Richard Rolle, the hermit of Hampole, seems to have been more widely read in his time than any other Middle English writer; his prolific mystical works in poetry and prose, both Latin and English, have survived in some four hundred different manuscripts. His principal English prose works, including *The Bee and the Stork, Meditations on the Passion,* and *The Form of Living,* were all composed in a Yorkshire dialect and probably belong to the last years of his life. *The Bee and the Stork* echoes the bestiary in its allegorical use of natural history. The bee, never idle and always fighting against the one who would steal her honey, is the righteous man holding firm "against devils that strive to steal from us the honey of a life of poverty and of grace"; the "stork," on the other hand, cannot fly on account of its heavy weight, which roots it in earthly thoughts. The reader will recall this image from the *Ancrene Riwle*—with the same confusion of stork and ostrich. In *The Form of Living* Rolle makes extended use of the fire-of-love metaphor which recurs throughout mystical literature:

> [God] makes them gather up their heart, and fasten it only on Him. He opens to the eye of their souls the gates of heaven, so that the same eye looks into heaven. And then the fire of love verily lies in their heart and burns therein, and makes it clean of all earthly filth. And from then on they are contemplative men, and ravished in love.*

Rolle said that he actually felt and smelled the fire burning in his heart and chest.

One of the subjects that attracted Rolle and other mystics was, understandably, Christ on the Cross. In his *Meditations on the Passion,* where Rolle achieves his most intense writing, he speaks directly to Christ in prose remarkable for its descriptive power:

> The press of the people was terribly strong; they hurled Thee and harried Thee so shamefully, they spurned Thee with their feet, as if Thou hadst been a dog. I see in my soul how pitifully Thou goest: Thy body is so bloody, made so raw and blistered; Thy crown is so sharp that sitteth on Thy head; Thy hair moveth with the wind, clotted with blood; Thy lovely face so wan and so swollen with buffeting and with beating, with spitting and spouting. †

Just as vividly, Rolle portrays the sorrowing Mother following among the crowd: "Like a woman beside herself, her hands she wrung; weeping and sighing she cast out her arms; the water from her eyes dropped at her feet." Her sufferings ought to be Rolle's own sufferings, for he, like the rest of fallen mankind, has caused them. Let the Mother, he begs, pity him now in his spiritual poverty and allow him to share in her grief:

> Give to me of thy sighings, who sighest so sorely, so that I may sigh with thee who began that woe. I ask not, dear Lady, castles, or towers, or other worldly weal, the sun, the moon, the bright stars. But all my desire is for the wounds of pity, pain and compassion for my Lord Jesu Christ. Worst and unworthiest of all men's holding, I have appetite for pain, to beseech my Lord for a drop of His red blood to make bloody my soul, a drop of that water to wash it with.*

Rolle is historically the most important of the mystical writers of the fourteenth century, and he may have been the most gifted artistically. Other mystics, however, deserve brief notice. The anonymous author of the *Cloud of Unknowing* (*c.* 1350?) turned away from the concrete and the finite, addressing himself to readers already to some degree initiated into the contemplative life; he speaks of the "cloud" that separates the soul from God, a cloud through which God's rays may occasionally penetrate. Walter Hilton (d. 1396) wrote the *Scale* (or *Ladder*) *of Perfection,* a quiet work somewhat in the homely style of the practical author of the *Ancrene Riwle;* like that earlier work, the *Scale of Perfection* was primarily intended as a conduct book for one desirous of living as a recluse.

Two autobiographical treatises, both by women, are of unusual interest. Dame Julian of Norwich (*c.* 1342–?) records in her *Revelations of Divine Love* (a work which exists in a shorter and a longer version) how, in the year 1373, she lay upon her sickbed, close to death. Her sight failing, she fixed her gaze steadfastly on the face of the crucifix. Suddenly, she beheld a light emanating from the cross:

> After this the upper part of my body began to die, so far forth that scarcely I had any feeling;—with shortness of breath. And then I weened in sooth to have passed.
>
> And in this moment suddenly all my pain was taken from me, and I was as whole (and specially in the upper part of my body) as ever I was afore. . . .

* P. 117.

Then came suddenly to my mind that I should desire the second wound of our Lord's gracious gift: that my body might be fulfilled with mind and feeling of His blessed Passion. For I would that his pains were my pains, with compassion and afterward longing to God.*

At that moment, she continues, "I saw the red blood trickle down from under the Garland hot and freshly and right plenteously, as it were in the time of His Passion when the Garland of thorns was pressed on His blessed head who was both God and Man, the same that suffered thus for me." This was the first of the sixteen "showings" she describes in her Revelations.

Finally, there is *The Book of Margery Kempe*—a fascinating, highly controversial self-revelation, originally dictated at an unknown date and revised between 1436 and 1438. Margery Kempe, an illiterate though well-to-do "creature," as she calls herself, was born in Lynn about 1373. After the birth of the first of her fourteen children, she began to have visions of Christ on the Cross. For a long time, however, she continued her abandonment to vanity and to the "lusts of the flesh" that had hitherto marked her life. The visions grew in number and intensity, provoking her to a series of great outbursts, or "cryings," which were a source of pride to her but were sometimes offensive to those around her. During the course of her busy career, Margery visited Jerusalem, stood up boldly to an examination for heresy conducted by the Archbishop of York, and repeatedly endured, she says, public ridicule and slander. Even while recounting some of her most serious experiences, Margery is never indifferent to the impression she is creating—particularly among the young men, many of them clerics, who cast admiring glances at her face and figure. Whatever one makes of this strange woman, there is no denying that *The Book of Margery Kempe* is written in a robust, colloquial style that is well suited to the boisterous temperament it reflects.

Saints' Legends and Exempla

Rounding out this survey of Middle English religious prose are two literary genres from which medieval readers in England and on the Continent derived a good deal of pleasant moral instruction— saints' lives and *exempla* (moralized tales).

Of the many saints' lives produced during the period, two collections, one early and the other late, are of special interest: the so-called Katherine Group (*c.* 1200) and the *Legenda Aurea* (*Golden*

* P. 123.

Legend), translated around 1438 and again (much expanded) by
Caxton in 1483. The Katherine Group consists of five pieces, three of
which—*St. Katherine, St. Margaret,* and *St. Juliana* (the Old English
poet Cynewulf had told her story)—celebrate the martyrdoms for
virginity suffered by uncompromising Christian heroines. As is customary with many saints' lives, these works relate a series of tortures
from which the heroines are delivered; Katherine, for example, is
stripped, beaten, imprisoned, starved, and torn by spike-covered
wheels that are turned simultaneously in opposite directions. None
of these afflictions, however, harms her body or weakens her commitment to resist the blandishments of that "heathen hound," the
Emperor of Alexandria. Although she is finally beheaded, her example
has converted many heathens to Christianity; and her death accomplishes still further miracles. *St. Margaret* and *St. Juliana* follow a
similar pattern. All three lives are written in alliterative prose of a
West Midland dialect, but the question of single or separate authorship has not been decided. A fourth member of the Katherine Group,
Hali Meidenhad, is a frequently amusing homily contrasting the
serenity of the virgin state with the harrowing trials of marriage—a
quarreling husband, a screaming child, a burned dinner, and so on.
The vitality of the piece has led some scholars to ascribe it to the
author of the *Ancrene Riwle,* but this hypothesis is doubtful. Completing the Katherine Group is a full-scale allegory, *Sawles Warde*
(The Safeguarding of the Soul), in which the house (body) is depicted as the dwelling place of a most precious treasure (the soul),
which must be preserved through the good management of Wit and
the diligence of the Four Cardinal Virtues. *Sawles Warde* is an adaptation of the *De Anima* of Hugh of St. Victor. A similar theme is treated
in the morality play, *The Castle of Perseverance* (see Chapter XV).

    The Golden Legend is a translation into English (*c.* 1438) of a
famous Latin collection of *legenda* (readings) originally by Jacobus
de Voragine, a Spaniard. Enormously popular in its time, it contains
several well-told stories of heroic martyrdom. Included among these
is a moving account of the murder of St. Thomas à Becket, Archbishop of Canterbury, that "hooly blisful martir" whose shrine is the
object of the pilgrimage in *The Canterbury Tales*. The Archbishop is
killed, as he kneels before the altar, by four knights, who are acting,
perhaps, with the tacit approval of King Henry II. The dramatic possibilities of this event were realized by the twentieth-century poet
T. S. Eliot in his play *Murder in the Cathedral.*

The best-known anthology of prose *exempla* is the *Gesta Roman-orum,* a work with a long history. Originally collected in Latin, prob-ably in England, during the late thirteenth or early fourteenth century, it received wide circulation on the Continent; and around 1440 two English versions appeared independently of each other. The *Gesta Romanorum* retained its popularity through the Renaissance, a third translation being published late in the fifteenth century and a fourth brought out by the English printer Wynkyn de Worde in 1524(?). In this generally diverting book a short tale is customarily narrated and its "morality," or allegorical meaning, is then explained. Sometimes the tales seem to have originated in spirited little jokes (not always decent), and their religious applications may strike a reader as farfetched. Nevertheless, the tales are sufficiently entertain-ing, with their combination of the homely and the exotic, to have served later English writers, notably the dramatists, with a veritable mine of plot material. In the *Gesta Romanorum* occurs a parable— it has Buddhist analogues—in which a maiden is accepted in marriage by an emperor's son because, when asked to choose from among vessels of gold, silver, and lead, she selects the lead. The situation, with the roles of the hero and heroine reversed and with the allegori-cal overtones considerably diminished (if not, perhaps, even dis-carded), comprises the Portia-Bassanio plot in *The Merchant of Venice.* One *exemplum* that has been elevated into supreme art will be discussed later: Chaucer's terrifyingly dramatic *The Pardoner's Tale.*

SECULAR PROSE

Although English prose continued to be written in an unbroken tra-dition after the Norman Conquest, there is relatively little secular prose extant from the Middle English period—and for good reason. Before the advent of Caxton and his printing press (1476), when manuscripts had to be laboriously transcribed by hand, it was all but inevitable that works which were not deemed of sufficient reli-gious significance should run risks of neglect. One must also take into account the heavy destruction visited upon manuscripts of all sorts, between 1535 and 1660, by political and religious wars and raids, by fires, and by floods. Consequently, we do not have an extensive body of English secular prose dating from before the fifteenth century.

During the fifteenth century, at about the same time that printing was being introduced into England, there was emerging a new reading public of comfortable landholders clamoring for all kinds of books of a semipractical nature: chronicles, books of parental advice (like the *Book of the Knight of La Tour Landry,* translated from the French about 1450), books of general etiquette, and even a few works on natural science and political theory. Prose romances, like Malory's *Morte d'Arthur,* were, of course, always in demand. There was also, to repeat, a sizable body of "nonprofessional" writing, best exemplified in the family letters left by the Pastons, the Celys, the Stonors, and others. If the prose is not usually of compelling interest as literature, it holds many attractions for linguists and for historians of manners.

Of this many-faceted secular prose of the Middle English period, the two specimens which (next to Malory's masterpiece) have most captivated modern readers are Mandeville's *Travels* and the *Paston Letters.*

The Travels of Sir John Mandeville (c. 1356) *

Who has not surrendered to the magic of faraway places? Perennially fascinating has been *The Travels of Sir John Mandeville,* written originally in Norman French and soon translated into both English and Latin.

It was at one time widely believed that Mandeville, like Gulliver or Baron Munchausen, was a fictitious character—part of a colossal literary hoax invented by the real author, thought to be either a Liège physician named Jean de Bourgogne or else a Liège chronicler named Jean d'Outremeuse. On the basis of recent scholarly investigations, however, it now seems likely that the real author *was* John Mandeville, a man born, as he himself tells us, at St. Albans, England. There were several John Mandevilles from that region who could have written the book, but one is safer not trying to choose from among the various candidates.

Cultivating a literary genre as old as Homer's *Odyssey,* Mandeville records his alleged visits to the Holy Land and to more remote regions of Asia and Africa. He refines and organizes his materials— some gathered from firsthand observation, most from wide reading in medieval geographies—with the imaginative power of a first-rate

* The present discussion incorporates the conclusions of Josephine Waters Bennett concerning the date and authorship of the *Travels.* Earlier scholarship assigned the *Travels* to between 1366 and 1371. See her important book, *The Rediscovery of Sir John Mandeville* (New York: Modern Language Association of America, 1954). (MEB 110.)

literary artist. Some of his exploits are pure fable. He meets the men whose heads grow beneath their shoulders (one of the wonderful tales with which Othello woos Desdemona) and speaks of the Ethiopians who have but one foot, so large "that the shadow thereof covereth the body from sun or rain when they lie upon their backs"; he dazzlingly describes the palace of the Great Khan, where delicious aromas are exuded from walls of panther skin; he tastes of the miraculous waters of the Fountain of Youth:

> And there by the land of Lombe is the city of Polomes [Quilon, on the Malabar Coast], and under that city is a hill that men call Polombe and thereof taketh the city its name. And so at the foot of the same hill is a right fair and clear well, that hath a full good and sweet savor, and it smelleth of all manner of sorts of spices, and also at each hour of the day it changeth its savor diversely, and who drinketh thrice on the day of that well, he is made whole of all manner of sickness that he hath. I have sometime drunk of that well, and methinks yet that I fare the better; some call it the well of youth, for they that drink thereof seem to be young always, and live without great sickness.

Some men, he goes on to say, believe that the well must come from the earthly paradise itself.

Lest the reader think, however, that Mandeville is capable only of wild flights into fantasy, it should be pointed out that he is also a serious thinker. He can imbue with significance even the strangest of customs. He speaks of the island of Raso, where men are hanged as soon as they become "sick [dead?]": "It is better that birds, that are angels of God, eat them, than worms of the earth." Mandeville discourses at length on the roundness of the earth; and he records with fine perceptiveness and unusual tolerance the religious practices of distant peoples. The inhabitants of the island of Synople wear no clothes at all out of the conviction—so they once explained to Alexander the Great—that man should bear in mind that he is born naked and will return naked into the earth. Alexander may amass riches and conquer the world, but not even he can take his wealth with him into the grave. Only God, who made all things, is immortal. Mandeville's reflection on the experience discloses a supple mind:

> And Alexander was greatly astonished of this answer, and if it be so that they have not the articles of our faith, nevertheless I believe that

God loveth their service to gree [please] Him, as he did of Job that was a Paynim [pagan], the which he held for his true servant and many other. I believe well that God loveth all those that love him and serve him meekly and truly, and that despise the vain glory of the world as these men do, and as Job did.

Never, Mandeville points out, can we presume to know who is loved or hated of God.

Mandeville's wide scope is again illustrated by the scene in which the Sultan of Egypt lectures him on how far Christians have departed from the example of Christ. "For we wot well," the Sultan observes, "that when that ye serve well your God, that he will help so that no man shall win of you." When Christians serve God better, they shall reclaim the land of Egypt. "But while they live so sinfully, as they do, we have no dread on them, for their God shall not help them." Is it not a disgrace, Mandeville asks his readers, that infidels can reproach us with our sins? The Saracens, for their part, faithfully observe the commandments of the Alkoran, "that God sent them by his messenger Mohammed, to whom, they say, Gabriel, the angel, spake often and told to him the will of God." Christians would do well to emulate their steadfastness.

Readers will find Mandeville not only an enchanting entertainer but a wise and sensitive guide immensely interested in the diversified spectacle of life as he saw or imagined it.

The Paston Letters

Unpublished until 1787, the 1,088 private letters of the Pastons of Norfolk furnish an intimate glimpse into the daily life of a typical well-to-do English family of the fifteenth century. At the beginning of the correspondence, in 1422, the Pastons were ordinary farmers; by 1509, when the extant letters end, they had steadily risen to wealth and pre-eminence through a series of skillful economic and legal maneuvers—a threat here, a bribe to a judge there, a hard marriage bargain somewhere else. We learn much, and at first hand, about social conditions of the time: arduous travel, inadequate police protection, unreliable servants, incorrigible children. Here is part of a typical list of errands Agnes Paston wants attended to in London (January 28, 1457):

> To pray Greenfield to send me faithfully word by writing how Clement Paston hath done his endeavor in learning. And if he hath not done well nor will not amend, pray him that he will truly belash

him till he will amend; and so did the last master and the best that
ever he had at Cambridge. And say to Greenfield that if he will take
upon him to bring him into good rule and learning so that I may
verily know he doth his endeavor, I will give him ten marks, for his
labor, for I had liefer he were fairly buried than lost for default. . . .

Item, to do make [have made] me six spoons of eight ounces of
troy weight, well fashioned and double gilt.

And say to Elizabeth Paston that she must use herself to work
readily, as other gentlewomen do, and somewhat to help herself
therewith. . . .

And if Greenfield have done well his devoir to Clement, or will do
his devoir, give him the noble.*

Nothing is too small to include, and the style, here as elsewhere in
the letters, is straightforward and readable.

Not having been intended for publication, the letters also speak
with unusual candor about the more personal affairs of the Pastons.
Something of the "business" of marriage appears in the prolonged
efforts (at last successful) to marry off Elizabeth Paston on terms
that should offer the greatest economic advantage. An exception to
numerous instances, recorded in the letters, of young girls literally
sold to the highest matrimonial bidder, is the fervent love between
Margery Paston and a mere bailiff, Richard Calle; the lovers triumphantly ignore the objections of Margery's mercenary parents
and, as if in a romantic play or novel, eventually marry. To social
historians the letters are, of course, invaluable; but students of literature, particularly if they are mildly addicted to eavesdropping, can
enjoy them, too.

Other Secular Prose

This chapter is to be concluded with a bare mention of a few
works which in one way or another reflect some of the political
and intellectual interests of the Middle English period. Thomas Usk
(d. 1388) wrote, presumably while in prison (he was later executed)
for supporting John of Gaunt, *The Testament of Love*—a political allegory justifying his conduct and calling upon "Margaret of virtu" to
have pity on him. Usk obviously was indebted to Boethius as well as
to Chaucer's *Troilus and Criseyde,* and his *Testament* was at one
time erroneously ascribed to Chaucer. Sir John Fortescue (*c.* 1394–

* From *Medieval English Verse and Prose,* in modernized versions by
Roger S. Loomis and Rudolph Willard, p. 431. Copyright, 1948, Appleton-
Century-Crofts, Inc. Reprinted by permission of the publisher.

c. 1476), Chief Justice of the King's Bench, wrote much in both Latin and English, his principal contribution being *On the Governance of England,* the first book in English on the theory and practice of constitutional government. The most important translator— after the Wyclifites and Caxton—was John Trevisa (1326–1402), who, in addition to making numerous translations of religious works, turned into English two monuments of earlier Anglo-Latin scholarship originally written near the end of the twelfth and the middle of the thirteenth centuries, respectively. In 1387 Trevisa translated Ranulf Higden's *Polychronicon,* a history of the world; and in 1398 he translated the *De Proprietatibus Rerum* of the friar Bartholomaeus Anglicus, a compendium of medieval scientific and natural knowledge. Finally, there is a work of a somewhat more insular character, *The Chronicle of England* by John Capgrave (1393–1464) —a history, extending from the Creation to the year 1417, which includes the interesting piece of information that Henry V "after his coronacion was evene turned into anothir man and all his mociones inclined to vertu." This tradition, which was to be popular among English writers, receives its most brilliant expression in Shakespeare's *Richard II–Henry V* cycle: Prince Hal, after a youth given over to wantonness, rejects "the tutor and the feeder of my riots," Sir John Falstaff, and emerges as a mature and responsible sovereign.

IX: LYRICS AND FOLK BALLADS

If Middle English prose, however interesting and historically important, has proved to be only intermittently satisfying when judged as literary art, the case with Middle English poetry is altogether different. Chaucer alone would be sufficient to insure its fame. But even if he were excluded from consideration, the record would still be impressive.

Without forgetting that there was a relatively unbroken poetic tradition which dates back to the Old English period and which somehow survived both the Danish and the Norman invasions, one may nevertheless point to many literary events in the Middle English period which attest to a renewal of poetic vigor. First of all, the period gave birth to the rhymed English lyric and to the English and Scottish folk ballad. Next, it produced, during the fourteenth century, two poets of undisputed greatness—the *Gawain* (or *Pearl*) poet and the author of *Piers Plowman,* in all probability William Langland. Both of these writers, significantly enough, drew much of their strength from the alliterative tradition of Old English verse, a legacy which they adapted to their own artistic purposes. Finally, the Middle English period saw many debates, satires, and didactic poems, some of which, like *The Owl and the Nightingale* and at least portions of the works of John Gower, achieve real literary distinction.

This and the two following chapters will accordingly be devoted to an examination of the non-Chaucerian poetry of the Middle English period. To be considered first are two groups of shorter poems that have attained wide familiarity among modern readers: lyrics and folk ballads.

LYRICS *

Of the many controversies currently engaging the interest of literary historians and critics, perhaps none is more violent than that

---

* Quotations from medieval lyrics, except when otherwise noted, are from the three volumes edited by Carleton Brown for the Oxford University Press: *English Lyrics of the XIIIth Century; Religious Lyrics of the XIVth Century;* and *Religious Lyrics of the XVth Century.* Copyrights are 1932, 1924, and 1939, respectively. Reprinted by permission of the publisher.

which centers upon the interpretation of medieval and Renaissance literature as a whole as "secular" or "religious-allegorical." Although the ramifications of the quarrel extend into Old English literature (as was seen) as well as into a romance like *Sir Gawain and the Green Knight,* the medieval lyric has stimulated more than its share of scholarly debate. The problem has arisen in a somewhat different form as a result of fresh speculations as to the "beginnings" of the English lyric of the Middle Ages.

According to the traditional view, the secular English lyric originated in the *carole*—a sprightly ring dance, of French derivation, which the participants punctuated at intervals with hand clapping or a vocal refrain. In time the "leader," or perhaps one of the other dancers, seems to have assumed more responsibility and independence by introducing new verses, sometimes even composing new dance-songs for the group. Becoming somewhat of a self-conscious artist, this poet, presumably, would then transplant the folk qualities of the *carole* into more formal songs of his own composition. The next step in the evolution of the lyric was the emergence of the "professional" poet responsive to the forms and conventions of the more sophisticated Continental verse of his day.

Recently, however, the old, well-established theory of the ring-dance origin of the Middle English lyric has been challenged. It has been argued, on the basis of various textual and musical evidence provided by the manuscripts in which the songs are found, that the earliest Middle English carols were composed by ecclesiastical authors for specific use in church processions. Viewed in this light, the medieval lyrical tradition would become "not vernacular, secular, and foreign; but Latin, religious, and native." * Whatever facts future scholarship may uncover concerning the origins of the lyric, it remains extremely difficult to classify lyrics consistently as "secular" or "religious," even though this convenient distinction will be observed in the following discussion. Oddly enough, one cannot always be sure, at first, whether a given love poem is addressed to the poet's mistress or to the Virgin Mary. "As Y Me Rod This Ender Day" ("As I Rode the Other Day") introduces a maid's complaint about a fickle boy, but it is also the first line of a later poem on the five joys of the Virgin. Moreover, the poems about Mary often contain sensuous images scarcely distin-

---

* See Rossell Hope Robbins, "Middle English Carols as Processional Hymns," *Studies in Philology,* LVI (1959), 559–82. See MEB 125.

guishable from those occurring in poems which deal frankly with sexual passion.

It is clear in any case that the earliest extant rhymed English lyrics were not based upon the *carole*. They are found in twelfth-century manuscripts and are ecclesiastical, rather than popular, in inspiration. *Cnut's Song,* consisting of just four lines, was reportedly written in the eleventh century by the great Danish and English King Cnut as he rowed past the Isle of Ely and enjoyed the singing of the monks at the abbey service. St. Godric (1065–1170), whose unusually long life embraced the varied careers of peddler, merchant, and shipowner before his retirement as a hermit near Durham, is the author of an important *Hymn to the Virgin.* The *Hymn,* one of three credited to Godric, contains two quatrains (four-line stanzas) with musical notation. It anticipates the cult of the Virgin which found expression in much of the later religious verse of the Middle English period.

When English lyrics really began to blossom in the thirteenth and fourteenth centuries, they had already assimilated many of the themes and attitudes of French troubadour verse (though the French influence has been accounted slight after the thirteenth century). The dividing line between popular and courtly verse, like that between the secular and the religious lyric, is therefore blurred.

Secular Lyrics

From the testimony of the historian Gerald of Wales (*c.* 1146–*c.* 1220) we learn that folk singing, in fairly elaborate counterpoint, was a highly developed art in twelfth-century Wales and northern England. Some clergymen frowned upon such singing as a frivolity, deeming it a perversion of a sacred gift that should be employed exclusively in the service of God. Gerald, who enjoys a good joke, tells the story of a priest in Worcestershire who was kept awake all night by noisy carolers in the churchyard. At services the next morning the priest scandalized his parishioners by absent-mindedly intoning the refrain of a love song, "Sweetheart, thy favor," instead of *Dominus vobiscum.* Thereafter, Gerald would have us believe, the singing of that particular song was forbidden throughout the diocese. In view of the clerical opposition to caroling, a point delightfully underscored in Robert Mannyng's *Handlyng Synne* (see Chapter XI), it is perhaps surprising that the only samples of Welsh song that have survived are scribbled in book margins or incorporated into sermons.

Courtesy of The Bettmann Archive

Facsimile of the *Cuckoo Song* manuscript in the British Museum.

This phenomenon, of course, would be easily explained should the liturgical origins of the carols be established. Be that as it may, clerics must have used snatches of popular songs to help members of the congregation memorize and retain spiritual teachings.

Many early secular lyrics are *reverdies*—songs heralding the "re-greenment" of nature in the spring (in the manner of the opening lines of *The Canterbury Tales*). The development of the genre follows an interesting course. One of the oldest *reverdies* is the celebrated *Cuckoo Song*, usually dated *c.* 1230–40 (though a later date, *c.* 1300, has been proposed). The song, an intricately scored six-voice canon, is of enormous significance, musical as well as literary:

> Sumer is icumen in,
>   Lhude [loudly] sing cuccu!
> Groweþ sed [seed] and bloweþ med [meadow]
> and springþ þe w[o]de [forest] nu.
> Sing cuccu!

In the *Cuckoo Song* spring arouses the mating instincts of animals, but this theme is more explicitly developed in *Lenten Is Come with Love to Town*. A third *reverdie*, entitled *Alysoun*, is a love song with an engaging refrain:

> An hendy hap [fair fate] ichabbe yhent [won],
> ichot [I know] from hevene it is me sent—
> from alle wymmen mi love is lent [turned],
> & lyht on Alysoun.

The *reverdie* which begins, "When þe nyhtegale singes þe wodes waxen grene," approaches the realm of the courtly lyric. Love, the poet sings, has pierced his heart with a sharp spear and now drinks his blood night and day. Just one speech, one "swete cos" from her mouth, will heal his sickness. The poem beginning, "Wiþ longyng y am lad [led]," is not a *reverdie* at all, but a full-fledged courtly lament by a lover held in the excruciating bondage of unrequited passion— a theme to be exploited in a later age by sophisticated pastoral poets and by Petrarch and his imitators on the Continent and in England. The *reverdie* had traveled a long road from its simple beginnings. Nor was its development completed. It will be shown presently how the *reverdie* could merge into the religious lyric.

In the fourteenth and fifteenth centuries, when the extant secular lyrics bulk larger than before in the total picture, the subjects range from begging songs, drinking songs, and seduction songs to formalized pleas for "merci" and to fanciful catalogues, minutely detailed, of the charms of the female body. To this period belong the gay and ribald student songs, in Latin and vernacular languages, some of them known to music-lovers in Carl Orff's twentieth-century setting of the *Carmina Burana*. Two amorous poems stand out. *The Lover's Mass* is a parody in which secular love songs are assigned titles which correspond to certain sections of the liturgy. In the moving dialogue *The Nut-Brown Maid,* the son of an earl pretends that he is a squire of low degree in order to test the devotion of the baron's daughter who loves him. He alleges that he is an outlaw forced into exile, and in the alternate stanzas assigned to him he paints a dismal picture of the hardships he will have to endure, concluding each time with the refrain,

> For I must to the greenwood go,
> Alone, a banished man.*

Her unvarying protestations of love—she will go with him or, if he rejects her in favor of another, die of a broken heart—always end with her own touching refrain:

> For in my mind, of all mankind
> I love but you alone.

After she has proved her steadfastness in the face of all trials, the knight reveals that he has been testing her and, highly pleased, offers to marry her. The two join in pointing out the moral:

> Here may ye see that women be
> In love meek, kind, and stable.
> Let never man reprove them then
> Or call them variable. . . .

This entertaining lyric is linked structurally with the ballad and the debate. Thematically, it may suggest Walter's testing of Grisilde in Chaucer's *The Clerk's Tale* and seems to have been inspired, at least in part, by the long-standing medieval and Renaissance controversy as to whether women are as worthy as men—in *The Nut-Brown Maid* they are.

Religious Lyrics

The religious lyrics of the Middle English period outnumber the surviving secular lyrics by at least three to one. Again the word "surviving" must be emphasized; for, as has been said on other occasions, the major scribal effort in the pre-Caxton days when there was no printing press in England was directed to the preservation of

* Quotations from *The Nut-Brown Maid* are from *Medieval English Verse and Prose,* in modernized versions by Roger S. Loomis and Rudolph Willard. Copyright, 1948, Appleton-Century-Crofts, Inc. Reprinted by permission of the publisher.

works of a specifically religious character. Generally speaking, one may classify medieval religious lyrics according to whether they are primarily *moral* or *devotional*. As a rule, the moral lyrics tend to be somewhat more didactic in theme and method. The devotional lyrics, on the other hand, are more likely to spring from impulses no less artistic than religious. In the best of the devotional lyrics there is a happy fusion of theology and poetry.

The obsessing preoccupation of the moral lyrics, as of the Old English elegies, is with the impermanence of earthly joy and glory. But whereas the Old English poets took their illustrative material from the once proud warrior and the desolate mead-hall of the Germanic past, the Middle English lyrists drew upon a wealth of material from classical literature and from romance. Sometimes, in fact, they incorporated Latin into their English poems. (Poetry written in two languages is called *macaronic* verse.) *Ubi sunt qui ante nos fuerunt?* asks one poet. Where are those who came before us? Where are the beautiful ladies? The brave knights?

> Eten and drounken and maden hem glad;
> Hoere [their] lif was al wiþ gamen [games] I-lad . . . .

This particular poet seems almost to exult in the misfortunes visited upon these rich lords and ladies whose souls were lost "in a twincling of on eye":

> Al þat joye is went away,
> Þat wele [happiness] is comen te weylaway [woe],
> To manie harde stoundes [hours, times].

But Friar Thomas of Hales, in his *Love Rune* (probably written early in the thirteenth century), invests the *ubi sunt* theme with sympathy and understanding. As he answers a young girl who has requested of him a love poem, Friar Thomas cannot conceal his admiration and compassion for the magnificent lovers—Paris and Helen, Amadas and Edayne, Tristram and Iseult—whose tragedies he remembers:

> Hwer is paris & heleyne
>   þat weren so bryht & feyre on bleo [in hue],
> Amadas & dideyne,
>   tristram, yseude and alle þeo [those]. . . .

Where are powerful Hector and Caesar, who were at one time so gloriously endowed with the prizes of the world? Friar Thomas offers the inevitable advice: let the maiden, whose mind is set on love, hold fast to Christ—that fairest, richest, and most steadfast of wooers. The poem *Earth upon Earth,* a variation on the *ubi sunt* theme, grimly reminds vain man that he is born of dust and will return to dust. The best-known medieval *ubi sunt* poem is not English but French. It ought to be mentioned here, however, if for no other reason than that an English poet of the nineteenth century, Dante Gabriel Rossetti, translated it so effectively. The poem, of course, is François Villon's fifteenth-century ballade on dead beauties, with its poignant refrain, *Mais où sont les neiges d'antan?* ("But where are the snows of yesteryear?")

Vastly superior to the moralizing lyrics are the devotional poems —in most cases imaginative meditations on two closely related subjects of intense emotional appeal, the Crucifixion and the grief of the Virgin Mother. The two themes converge in the early *Sunset on Calvary,* a lyric of four lines in which the dark setting and the tragic event reinforce each other perfectly:

> Nou goth sonne under wod,—
> me reweth, marie, þi faire Rode [face, complexion].
> Nou goþ sonne under tre,—
> me reweþ, marie, þi sone and þe [thee].

The pun on "sun" and "Son" is a common one, but it functions here with fresh power and dignity. There may also be a play on words involving "Rode," which means "complexion" but could also mean "cross" (rood). Some medieval lyrics, like *The Divine Paradox,* abound in intellectual subtleties akin to the wit of John Donne and the other metaphysical poets of the seventeenth century. The mystical *He Bare Him Up, He Bare Him Down* contains a simple refrain of haunting beauty:

> Lully lullay, lully lullay,
> The falcon hath borne my mate away.

In this poem the crucified Christ, portrayed as a bleeding knight whose body lies in a bed draped with bright red gold, is associated with the maimed king of the Grail legend and of folklore.

The bleeding Christ is the subject of one of two fine macaronic poems with a Latin refrain, *Quia amore langueo* ("Because I languish in love"). In this poem, which begins, "In a Valey of This Restles Minde," the dreaming poet beholds Christ sitting under a tree, his wounds dripping with the blood of the Crucifixion; Christ begs with transcendent ardor for man's soul in marriage:

> "Fair love, lete us go pleye!
> Applis ben ripe in my gardayne,
> I schal þee cloþe in a newe aray,
> Þi mete schal be mylk, hony, & wiyn." *

"Tarie þou not, my faire spouse mine, *Quia amore langueo.*" The ripe apples in Christ's garden may well be the divine counterpart of the fruit with which Satan tempted Eve. Christ, too, is offering a "temptation"—this time a temptation to partake in the joys everlasting. One is reminded of the parable of the kingly wooer in the *Ancrene Riwle*. The situation in the second *Quia amore langueo* poem, beginning "In a Tabernacle of a Toure," is somewhat similar. Here, however, it is the Virgin Mary who languishes in unrequited love. She appears as a crowned queen and pleads with sinful mankind that her enduring love be returned:

> "My love abydeth, thyne ys away;
> My love the [thee] calleth, thow stelest me fro [stealest from me];
> Sewe [sue] to me, synner, I the pray,
>   *Quia amore langueo.*"

The love imagery, which runs throughout the poem, culminates in the impassioned cry, "'Take me for þy wyfe and lerne to synge, *Quia amore langueo.*'" In *An Appeal to All Mothers*, a very human Mary describes her grief in the universal language of motherhood:

> Your childur the[y] dawnse upon your kne
> With laghyng, kyssyng and mery chere;
> Be-holde my childe, be-holde now me,
> ffor now liggus [lies] ded my dere son, dere.

The greatest of the devotional lyrics is the superbly concentrated *I Syng of a Myden Þat Is Makeles* [matchless; or perhaps "without a mate"]—a lyric inspired not by Calvary, but by Bethlehem. The first of the five simple quatrains that make up the poem announces the theme: Mary's unassuming acceptance of Christ as her son:

> I Syng of a myden
> þat is makeles,
> kyng of alle kynges
> to here sone che [she] ches [chose].†

* In F. J. Furnivall, *Political, Religious, and Love Poems*, Early English Text Society, 1866.

† Carleton Brown, in his *Religious Lyrics of the XVth Century* (from which these quotations are taken), prints the poem in five two-line stanzas rather than quatrains.

After the quiet majesty of this first quatrain, the poet describes in three successive variations on the simile, "As dew in aprylle . . . ," the serenity of the Incarnation:

> He cam also stylle
> þer [where] his moder was
> as dew in aprylle,
> þat fallyt [falleth] on þe gras.

The dew falls first on the grass, then on the flower, and, climactically, on the spray (the blossoming bough). The progression symbolizes spring reaching the height of its regenerative powers, together with the growing force of Christ's own renewal of mankind. In the final quatrain the poet restates with marvelous restraint the worthiness of Mary to receive the supreme honor:

> Moder & mayden
> was never non but che—
> wel may swych a lady
> godes moder be.

The *reverdie* has here become much more than a tribute to the rebirth of spring, for the poet has joyously identified it with an exalted moment in Christian history.*

FOLK BALLADS

Ballads are described by Joseph Addison, in *The Spectator* for 1711, as "the darling Songs of the common People." They are narrative poems that tell their stories in a unique way—concisely, dramatically, and impersonally. The narrative is generally developed by means of dialogue and is usually focused upon one striking episode; earlier and later events, if mentioned at all, are not treated in detail, but are briefly alluded to and, in many cases, deliberately left unexplained.

Serious ballad-collecting dates from the eighteenth century, when Bishop Thomas Percy discovered accidentally and saved from destruction a mid-seventeenth-century manuscript of 191 narrative and lyric poems. These he published as *Reliques of Ancient English Poetry* (1765). In 1802–3 Sir Walter Scott, who was steeped in the folklore of Scotland and northern England, brought out his *Min-*

---

* For a detailed analysis of the poem, one which stresses the complexity of its puns and the aesthetic and theological connotations of its images, see Stephen Manning, "I Syng of a Myden," *PMLA,* LXXV (1960), 8–12.

strelsy of the Scottish Border. The great modern collector was Professor F. J. Child of Harvard; his *English and Scottish Popular Ballads* (1882–98) contains variant texts of 305 ballads. To all three of these pioneers we owe a heavy debt.

Percy, Scott, and Child regarded ballads primarily as written poems. Only in the twentieth century—thanks largely to the pioneer work of Cecil Sharp, a trained musician—did students begin to realize the importance of the music and, consequently, start an intense and systematic search for ballad tunes. These tunes are still being recorded from the lips of untrained singers living in the backwoods of the British Isles and America. That ballad-hunting is fraught with unexpected problems can be gleaned from some of the experiences related by eminent collectors. Imagine an impatient scholar in the mountains of Kentucky, desperately trying to preserve his dignity and his temper as he holds out a stick of chewing gum to entice a suspicious ten-year-old down from a tree. Why? Because an old man in the community seems to remember the boy's grandmother singing a version of some song that sounded different from any version anyone else in those parts had ever sung, and he *thinks* the boy in the tree may know the song, too.*

Today not only are ballads the object of widespread scholarly research, but they are enjoying a tremendous vogue among the general public. They have found their way into the performing and recording repertoires of professional concert, radio and television, and night-club singers. Poets continue to write *literary* ballads (like Coleridge's *The Rime of the Ancient Mariner* or Keats's *La Belle Dame Sans Merci*)—artful poems that in one way or another try to imitate the form, the manner, or the subjects of folk ballads. Moreover, serious twentieth-century composers, among them Ralph Vaughan Williams, Aaron Copland, and Virgil Thomson, have carried on the tradition of earlier composers who employed folk materials in large-scale orchestral and choral works. And less serious composers, recognizing the commercial possibilities of the ballad style, regularly flood the popular-music market with adapted or made-up ballads.

Ballad Texts and Subject Matter

Although a few ballads (like *Judas*) are as old as the thirteenth century, the majority belong to the fifteenth, sixteenth, and seven-

---

* See, for example, Dorothy Scarborough, *A Song Catcher in Southern Mountains* (New York: Columbia University Press, 1937).

teenth centuries. After the introduction of printing, ballads were frequently hawked in the streets by enterprising peddlers, like Shakespeare's Autolycus in *The Winter's Tale* (IV, iv). The sheets on which the ballads were printed were called "broadsides," and it became customary in the late sixteenth and early seventeenth centuries to rush to press with a new broadside ballad celebrating some lively piece of current history—a military victory, a hanging, a public scandal. (Broadsides were also used to disseminate, sometimes in ballad form, hotly contested points of view on political or theological issues.) The number of broadside ballads constantly being unearthed by scholars seems almost inexhaustible.

How did the ballads originate? It was at one time widely accepted, and the theory still has its adherents, that ballads were composed *communally;* that they grew more or less spontaneously out of some group experience and expressed emotions and attitudes shared by the group. Most scholars now believe, however, that ballads—at least in their initial forms—were conceived and sung by individual poets, who remain anonymous. As the ballads circulated orally, other singers would vary both words and music because of the unreliability of their memories, the special interests and demands of their local communities, or, simply, their own creative impulses and abilities. As a result, a given ballad may appear in several forms at different times and places; and one version, whatever its relative literary merit, is as "authentic" as another. Professor Child, for example, included in his collection twenty-seven versions of *The Twa Sisters,* and at least forty more have been subsequently recorded. In the most familiar versions of *Edward,* a young man tells his mother that he has killed his father, but in one of Child's variants (*Son Davie*) the victim is the hero's brother. Some versions lack the final chilling suggestion that it was the mother herself who instigated the murder. Moreover, *Edward* has a Swedish counterpart, the *Velisurmaaja* ("Brother-Killer")—a circumstance which demonstrates the important point that many ballad plots are international.

Edward centers upon a violent domestic crisis, and in this feature it resembles many other notable ballads. The hero in *Lord Randal* has, for some mysterious reason, been poisoned by his sweetheart. A bride in *The Cruel Brother* is stabbed by her brother on her wedding day simply because the bridegroom "got consent frae her kin each one, / but forgot to spiek to her brother John." *Bablyon* has overtones of incest: an outlaw kills two girls in quick succession for refusing to marry him, but he takes his own life in horror when he learns indirectly from a third girl that all three are his sisters. Terrifying effects are often achieved or enhanced through use of the supernatural. The young wife in *The Daemon Lover* abandons her husband and two babies in order to sail away with her former lover —only to discover that the latter has a cloven foot and is speeding her to death and damnation. In *The Wife of Usher's Well* a grief-stricken mother prays for the return, "in earthly flesh and blood," of her three sons, recently drowned; the sons do come home, but they must leave at the crowing of the cock the next morning, never to visit this world again. To be sure, domestic situations are occasionally depicted with a light touch. The quick-witted wife in *Get Up and Bar the Door* wins a silly wager from her husband, and the shrew in *The Farmer's Curst Wife* is snatched away by Satan from her all-too-grateful husband, to be promptly returned when she proves too disagreeable even for Hell. Yet the best of the ballads on domestic themes remain miniature tragedies.

Besides the stark domestic dramas, ballad literature includes riddles, as when a knight tests the wit of his prospective bride or the Devil tries to befuddle a chaste girl; historical ballads growing out of the border wars between England and Scotland, like *Chevy Chase;* ballads about Robin Hood, who fights lustily for the poor, feuds with the Sheriff of Nottingham, and matches brawn and skill with tradesmen and artisans; religious ballads like *Judas, St. Stephen and Herod,* and the numerous miracles of the Virgin; ballads about last-minute rescues, like *The Maid Freed from the Gallows;* ballads on King Arthur, Sir Orfeo, Horn, and other heroes of romance; ballads extolling love that survives death—in the exquisite *Barbara Allan,* a love that begins with death; and sea ballads, like *The Golden Vanity* and *Sir Patrick Spens.*

Literary Qualities

The typical ballad stanza has four iambic lines—one and three (unrhymed) with four feet, and two and four (rhymed) with three feet. About a third of Child's ballads have refrains within or following each stanza. The refrain can be a recurring bit of description or dialogue, an irrelevant phrase, or a string of nonsense syllables. Ballad refrains help shape the musical accompaniment and control the pace of the action.

Normally the ballad-maker plunges directly into the midst of a

dramatic situation. He does not develop his story in a smooth sequence, but by a series of flashes—a process aptly characterized as
"leaping and lingering." He pauses briefly over a scene, then jumps
without warning to something else, "like those clocks whose hands
point only to the five-minute intervals on the dial." * Rather than
relaxing over descriptive or psychological details, he scores a broad,
suggestive stroke and sweeps on to the next narrative peak.

Sir Patrick Spens opens with the king drinking blood-red wine in
Dumferling and looking for a sailor to man his ship—we are not
told *why*. An old knight recommends Sir Patrick, whereupon the
king writes a letter. In the middle of the third stanza we are transported from Dumferling to a new scene in which the hero, walking
on the sand, has received the letter. With a bitter laugh and a blind-
ing tear he reads it; we infer that somebody (the old knight perhaps?) has hatched an evil plot against him. Quickly Sir Patrick
assembles his men, one of whom anxiously predicts a deadly storm
and pleads with his lord not to embark. The poet does not even
pause to present Sir Patrick's answer; we must surmise that the
warning went unheeded. In fact, from this point on there is no dialogue at all—just the poet's objective reporting of the tragedy. The
actual shipwreck is revealed indirectly through a grim understatement: the proud Scots were loath to get their elegant cork-heeled
shoes wet, but look at their hats floating. Then we move to the shore,
where the richly bedecked ladies await the return of their men—and
a long wait they have!

> O lang, lang may the ladies stand,
> > Wi thair gold kems [combs] in their hair
> Waiting for thar ain deir lords,
> > For they'll se thame na mair.

Finally, there is a sudden and bold shift back to the drowned nobles
and their leader. One glimpse is all the poet provides:

> Haf owre [over], haf owre to Aberdour,
> > It's fiftie fadom deip,
> And thair lies guid Sir Patrick Spens,
> > Wi the Scots lords at his feit.

Tension, of course, counts a good deal in a dramatic poem like
the folk ballad, and one way of augmenting the tension is through the

* F. B. Gummere, *The Popular Ballad* (Boston and New York: Houghton
Mifflin and Company, 1907), pp. 90–92.

device of "incremental repetition." In *Babylon*, for example, the outlaw on three different occasions proposes marriage in almost identical language:

> He's taen the first sister by the hand,
> And he's turned her round and made her stand.

> "It's whether will ye be a rank robber's wife,
> Or will ye die by my wee pen-knife?"

And the three sisters one by one refuse:

> "It's I'll not be a rank robber's wife,
> But I'll rather die by your wee pen-knife."

Twice he makes good his threat:

> He's killed this may [maid], and he's laid her by,
> For to bear the red rose company.

But the pattern is broken because the third sister, after refusing according to the established formula, adds a piece of information: she has a brother in the woods who will avenge her death. What is his name? asks the outlaw. "Baby Lon" is her reply. The ghastly recognition follows:

> "O sister, sister, what have I done!
> O have I done this ill to thee!
> O since I've done this evil deed,
> Good sall never be seen o' me."

Thereupon he uses the penknife on himself. The repetitions have set up a rhythm which both the reader and the outlaw absorb almost without thinking. It is the unexpected variation that jolts the reader into attentiveness and completely shatters the formulaic responses of the outlaw. Readers will realize, of course, that incremental repetition is not a structural phenomenon peculiar to ballads but a rhetorical technique employed in many types of poetry; a case in point is the great lyric *I Syng of a Myden That Is Makeless,* in which the poet scores his most triumphant effect through delicate mutations of the "dew in aprylle" figure. Nevertheless, folk ballads seem to depend upon incremental repetition to an unusual degree, and the variations carry the plot forward with unflagging momentum.

A common type of incremental repetition, one which is partially developed in *Babylon*, is the so-called climax of relatives. Since this pattern is more easily illustrated than explained, it would be well to conclude with a look at the famous ballad *Lord Randal*. Here incremental repetition is used to the extent that each stanza is identical with its predecessor—except for a slight but crucial variation amounting to little more than a word or two. The entire poem consists of a series of questions asked by a mother and of answers supplied by her son, the questions and answers being the only new elements in the otherwise unchanging four-line stanza:

> "O where ha you been, Lord Randal, my son?
> And where ha you been, my handsome young man?"
> "I ha been at the greenwood; mother, mak my bed soon:
> For I'm wearied wi hunting, and fain wad lie down."

When she has gradually learned that her son was poisoned by his truelove, the mother (and here the poet comes to the "climax of relatives") asks in three successive stanzas, "What d' ye leave to your mother, Lord Randal, my son? . . . to your sister? . . . to your brother? . . ." He bequeaths, respectively, his cows, his gold and silver, his house and lands. The pattern of the repetition having been well fixed in our minds, we are now primed for the last inevitable question:

> "What d' ye leave to your true-love, Lord Randal, my son?
> What d' ye leave to your true-love, my handsome young man?"
> "I leave her hell and fire; mother, mak my bed soon:
> For I'm sick at the heart, and I fain wad lie down."

"Hell and fire." The unexpectedness of the phrase, coming as it does in the context of the familiar and lilting cadence that has operated throughout the poem, lends to the curse a particularly shattering impact. And the subtle replacement, found in many versions of the final stanza, of "wearied wi' hunting" with "sick at the heart" further enhances the power of Lord Randal's tragedy.

X: THE ALLITERATIVE REVIVAL: SIR GAWAIN, PEARL, AND PIERS PLOWMAN

It was observed earlier that alliteration, which had been an indispensable tool of Old English poets, was largely supplanted by rhyme after the Danish and the Norman invasions, but that it never entirely disappeared from English prosody. Around the beginning of the thirteenth century, Layamon combined alliteration and rhyme in his *Brut,* and the five pieces which comprise the early Katherine Group were written in an alliterative prose that has at times been mistaken for verse and actually printed as such. Alliteration seems always to have been a device particularly congenial to English writers and, of course, is still used selectively by modern poets and prose writers striving after certain artistic effects.

And yet, after the survival of the Old English alliterative tradition has been properly acknowledged, one is still not quite prepared for the phenomenal outburst of alliterative poetry that occurred in west and northwest England during the second half of the fourteenth century. This "revival" was no less extraordinary in quality than in quantity, for it included three poems that must be numbered among the greatest achievements of the Middle English period. Two of them, *Sir Gawain and the Green Knight* and *Pearl,* are found in the same manuscript and are most probably by the same anonymous poet, an artist to whom we refer simply as the *Gawain,* or *Pearl,* poet. The third poem, *The Vision of William Concerning Piers the Plowman,* which exists in three distinct and unique texts, is usually considered to be the work of a William Langland.

THE GAWAIN (PEARL) POET *

(*fl. 1360–1400*)

To a West Midland writer who was active sometime in the second half of the fourteenth century are ascribed four alliterative poems of

---

* Quotations from *Sir Gawain* are from *Sir Gawain and the Green Knight,* translated by Theodore Howard Banks, Jr. Copyright, 1929, F. S. Crofts & Co., Inc. Reprinted by permission of Appleton-Century-Crofts, Inc.

Quotations from *Pearl* are from Sophie Jewett, *The Pearl* (New York:

high quality, all found (untitled) in a single manuscript in the Cotton collection of the British Museum. They have been named, in the order in which they appear, *Pearl, Purity* (or *Cleanness*), *Patience,* and *Sir Gawain and the Green Knight.* In addition to these four poems, this exceptional poet has been generally credited with a fifth poem, *St. Erkenwald,* which is found elsewhere. Although scholars have made numerous attempts to identify the artist, or at least to reconstruct the kind of personality and background he must have had, the results remain inconclusive.

The greatest works in the manuscript, *Sir Gawain* and *Pearl,* are remarkable even as metrical achievements. Each stanza of *Sir Gawain* consists of two parts: the first part has an irregular number of four-stress, unrhymed, alliterative long lines (as distinguished from the shorter lines usually found in Old English poems); the second part has five short lines, cross-rhyming *ababa*—the first line with only one stress and the remaining four lines with three stresses ("bob and wheel"). Still more intricate, metrically, is *Pearl.* Its 101 stanzas are arranged in twenty groups; nineteen groups contain five stanzas and one group contains six. The five stanzas in a particular group all end with the same word, and this word also appears in the first half-line of each stanza in the group, thereby linking the five stanzas together. Furthermore, since the twelve-line stanzas rhyme *abababababbcbc,* the device of the linking word (which is also the rhyme word) necessitates that the c-rhyme remain constant throughout a given group of five stanzas. Yet within these rigorous and, to an extent, artificial confines the *Pearl* poet manages to attain surprising variety without sacrificing the impression of order and of inner harmony that he wishes to convey.

Sir Gawain and *Pearl* will be examined more closely, but first a word about the three other valuable works normally assigned to the author. *Purity,* a verse homily, draws upon a wealth of Biblical illustration to make its point that one cannot approach the Divine Presence with an unclean body or soul; it includes episodes dealing with the Flood, the destruction of Sodom and Gomorrah, and Belshazzar's Feast—the last constituting an especially rich piece of descriptive and narrative writing. *Patience,* by retelling in lively fashion the story of *im*patient Jonah, shows how *not* to react to changes in human fortune. *St. Erkenwald* recounts the legend of the Bishop of the East

Thomas Y. Crowell, 1908). Reprinted by permission of Miss B. Fraser, on behalf of the late Edith Jewett.

Saxons who miraculously secured salvation for a righteous heathen judge (long since dead) by weeping over his corpse; St. Erkenwald's tears serve as the waters of baptism, which release the soul of the heathen from Limbo.

Sir Gawain and the Green Knight

The outstanding Arthurian romance in English is built upon the physical and moral ordeal undergone by Sir Gawain, a knight of rare courage and purity. The hero emerges from his "chivalrous Pilgrim's Progress" * with one minor blemish upon an otherwise spotless character.

Gawain's two principal adventures, the so-called Beheading Game and the Temptation to Adultery, may have ultimately been derived from Celtic and French sources, but the English poet has successfully welded them into an original and effective whole (whether he was the first to do so is still a matter of scholarly dispute). The Beheading Game is introduced when the fantastic Green Knight bursts into King Arthur's New Year's celebration at Camelot and dares anyone to strike him a blow with an axe, provided that one year later he be allowed to return the blow. Although Arthur himself is willing to match strength with the Green Knight, Sir Gawain graciously accepts the challenge. He beheads the Green Knight (naturally this supernatural creature does not die), and, twelve months later, he sets out to keep his tryst with the phantom adversary at the distant Green Chapel.

Now the Temptation motif enters the story. The hero is entertained en route in grand style at a castle belonging to a Lord Bercilak. The host proposes an exchange-of-gifts game, a kind of parallel to the exchange-of-blows offer extended by the Green Knight. On three successive days Bercilak will go hunting while Gawain remains behind at the castle, and at the end of each day the two men are to exchange whatever they have won on that particular day. While Bercilak is away at the hunt, his beautiful wife exercises all of her abundant charms in an effort to seduce Sir Gawain. For two days Gawain behaves with exemplary courtesy, each night bestowing upon Bercilak the kisses he has received from the lady and receiving in turn the spoils of the hunt. On the third day, however, as the hour of his de-

---

* William P. Ker, *English Literature: Medieval* (London: Williams & Nordgate; New York: Henry Holt and Co., 1912), p. 141. (A new edition with a supplementary note was published in 1945.)

parture for the Green Chapel draws nearer, Sir Gawain suffers a lapse—a lapse not of manners, but of courage. He accepts from the lady a silk girdle (sash), which he believes will protect him in his encounter with the dreaded Green Knight and, in violation of his bargain, conceals the gift from Bercilak. When Gawain reaches the chapel, the Green Knight strikes three blows at the hero's neck. Two are feints because Gawain resisted the first two temptations, but the third blow nicks him slightly as a visible mark of that one ever-so-tiny break in his moral armor. The whole affair, it turns out, had been planned by the old crone who was chaperoning Lady Bercilak and who is actually the magician Morgan le Fay; she apparently had held a grudge against Guinevere and, in addition, wanted to test the true mettle of the knights of the Round Table—her motivation is somewhat obscure. Bercilak, of course, is the Green Knight. At the end of the romance, Arthur's knights have a pleasant laugh at Gawain's adventure and, in tribute to his valor, agree to wear a green band around their waists thereafter.

The interdependence of the two episodes has long been recognized as evidence of the *Gawain* poet's narrative skill. It has been further suggested, however, that the hunting exploits of Bercilak are structurally related to the temptations Sir Gawain simultaneously experiences in his bedroom. On the first day Bercilak hunts the deer, an animal described in medieval hunting treatises and in books of heraldry as noble game—wise, politic, tactful, quick to foreknow his hazards and adroit in avoiding embarrassing situations. These are precisely the qualities Sir Gawain displays in the face of his temptation on the first day. Anticipating trouble, he pretends to be asleep; and when he finally is engaged by his hostess in conversation, the tone is gay, delicate, and bantering. The boar, Bercilak's quarry on the second day, is also noble game, but he is renowned for boldness and ferocity in conflict. Gawain, like the boar, faces his pursuer directly on the second day. He abandons his pretense of sleep and discards his light tone, preferring to speak more resolutely and to resist more directly. The fox, of course, enjoys a long-standing reputation for duplicity; this animal, who is hunted on the third day, makes a false turn, and, fearing for his life, he "shunts," that is, makes an instinctive movement of avoidance. All of these details are brought out in the poet's description of the hunting down of Reynard, and they bear close affinities with Gawain's sly, fear-inspired behavior of the third day. When Bercilak returns from the hunt, he hands the pelt of the fox to Sir Gawain with an angry comment about the baseness of his quarry:

> "By Mary,		mine's of less worth.
> The whole of the day	I have hunted, and gotten
> The skin of this fox—	the fiend take its foulness! . . ."
>
> 					(ll. 1942–44)

Later, in the Green Chapel, Gawain also "shunts"—just once and no more. If this interesting theory about the connections between the hunting scenes and the temptation scenes is correct, and it would seem plausible enough, then the subtlety of the poet's art becomes still more impressive.*

If the *Gawain* poet is an accomplished storyteller, he is also a virtuoso scene painter. He describes brilliantly the dazzling décor and sumptuous cuisine at Arthur's feast, as well as the resplendent beauty of Bercilak's castle. Observe the opulence of the room to which Gawain is conducted:

> To a bright room they brought him,	the bed nobly decked
> With hangings of pure silk		with clear golden hems.
> And curious coverings		with comely panels,
> Embroidered with bright fur		above at the edges;
> On cords curtains running		with rings of red gold;
> From Tars and Toulouse		were the tapestries covering
> The walls; under foot		on the floor more to match.
>
> 					(ll. 853–59)

The poet conveys the full excitement of Bercilak's hunt, down to the most minute details of the slitting open of the deer. More than once he uses scenery to suggest Gawain's mental state. While Gawain waits for his year to elapse before embarking upon his journey to the Green Chapel, the four seasons come and go with amazing rapidity—an apt reflection of the speed with which time would pass for one anticipating almost certain death. The dreariness of Gawain's situation (he does not know that the Virgin protects him) is further reinforced by the freezing weather that afflicts him on the long road:

> With sleet nearly slain,	he slept in his armor
> More nights than enough	on the naked rocks,
> Where splashing the cold stream	sprang from the summit,

---

* See Henry L. Savage, *The Gawain-Poet: Studies in His Personality and Background* (Chapel Hill, N. C.: University of North Carolina Press, 1956), pp. 31–48.

And hung in hard icicles high o'er his head.
Thus in peril and pain and desperate plights,
Till Christmas Eve wanders this wight through the country

Alone.
Truly the knight that tide
To Mary made his moan,
That she direct his ride
To where some hearth-fire shone.

(ll. 729–39)

One even catches a glimpse of the birds huddling on the bare twigs, poor creatures "that piteously piped for pain of the cold." The reader enjoys a sense of direct participation in the action, so completely is each scene realized.

But the crowning distinction of *Sir Gawain* is the vitality of its two leading characters. The poet succeeds in making the Green Knight a figure both terrifying and comic. At his sensational entrance into Camelot, Arthur's knights "sat stone-still . . . in swooning silence." And no wonder!

From his throat to his thighs so thick were his sinews,
His loins and his limbs so large and so long,
That I hold him half-giant, the hugest of men,
And the handsomest, too, in his height, upon horseback.
Though stalwart in breast and in back was his body,
His waist and his belly were worthily small;
Fashioned fairly he was in his form, and in features

Cut clean.
Men wondered at the hue
That in his face was seen.
A splendid man to view
He came, entirely green.

(ll. 138–49)

"Men wondered at the hue. . . ." Could anything be more artfully matter-of-fact? After the detailed physical description, the poet *then* adds, almost as an afterthought, that the formidable stranger happened to be green: his skin, hair, beard, clothes, armor, horse, and axe. The one startling exception was his bright red eyes. The attitude of the poet coincides beautifully with the air of utter nonchalance assumed by the Green Knight; it is as if neither were aware that the visitor is causing a stir—a pose that makes the event seem all the more spectacular. Asked whether he has come to do battle, the Green

Knight answers contemptuously that he cannot condescend to fight such beardless babes as are in Arthur's retinue—whereupon he lays down his sinister challenge. Upon receiving Gawain's mighty blow he calmly retrieves his bloody head from the floor (where it has been kicked around for a while), holds it aloft by the hair, restates the terms of the contract, and rides off undaunted into the night. This expert at psychological warfare later makes certain that the first sound Gawain hears while approaching the Green Chapel should be the awful grating of an axe on a grindstone. To add to Gawain's apprehensiveness, the Green Knight casually uses the axe to vault a stream that separates the two antagonists. His superb bravado contrasts charmingly with Gawain's uneasiness.

Sir Gawain himself is almost unique in medieval romance: he is an ideal knight who is not fearless and a champion of purity who is never dehumanized into an abstraction. With touching simplicity the poet indicates the deep spirituality of the young man during the lonely progress to his mysterious rendezvous (the passage is quoted in the original and then in the Banks translation):

> Hade he no fere bot his fole   bi frythes and dounes,
> Ne no gome bot God   bi gate wyth to karp. . . .
> [Save his foal, he'd no fellow   by forests and hills;
> On the way, no soul   but the Savior to speak to.]
>   (ll. 695–96)

Painted upon his shield is a five-pointed star, a symbol of his wholehearted commitment to Christian piety. The star stands for his five faultless wits, his five strong fingers, his constant attentiveness to the five wounds of Christ, his absorption in the five joys of Mary, his five supreme virtues—five different collections of worthy fives. When he prays for protection, it is not a prayer for victory, but a request for some lodging where he might worship and hear mass. In the temptation scenes, which are handled with restraint and wit, Gawain chooses to hold firm to the moral values of Christianity rather than find release in the adulterous union sanctioned by courtly love. He manages to preserve his chastity, however, without ever being discourteous to his alluring hostess; he is thus a perfect knight who realizes that it is more important, if he is faced with a choice, to be a good Christian.

Yet Gawain is not perfect. In accepting the superfluous magic girdle, he fails to display sufficient faith in his own physical and

spiritual resources and in the bounty of his God; his second error is
to conceal the gift from Bercilak. Human weaknesses, yes, but weaknesses nevertheless. Gawain's courage again fails him, this time less
crucially, when he "shunts" (like the fox) beneath the raised axe of
his opponent. Recovering quickly, however, he answers the Green
Knight's taunts with a wistful joke which may refer obliquely to his
earlier evasiveness with his host. The passage is quoted in the original:

> Quoth Gawayn, "I schunt [flinched] ones [once]
> & so wyl I no more;
> Bot thaʒ [though] my hede falle on the stones,
> I con not hit restore."

(ll. 2280-83)

Fortunately, the hero's head need *not* be (like the Green Knight's)
replaceable, for he amply vindicates his good name and is spared. Yet
though acclaimed by all knighthood for his brave performance, Gawain insists on retaining the girdle as a constant reminder of his
frailty:

> "And thus when I'm proud   of my prowess in arms,
> The sight of this sash   shall humble my spirit."

(ll. 2437-38)

Even the most upright men, the poet seems to be saying, need to
guard against pride.

It is perhaps inevitable that a perfect work of art like *Sir Gawain
and the Green Knight,* a romance in which plot, setting, characterization, and theme are so unerringly controlled and integrated, should
have given rise to numerous critical interpretations of a rather involved nature. Some link the Green Knight with the sun god who,
like Bercilak, goes out daily on his appointed rounds and returns at
night to his abode. A second group of critics associates the Green
Knight with the god of vegetation and traces the Beheading Game
back to a seasonal fertility ritual commonly practiced among pre-
Christian peoples and not far removed from the English folk plays
about St. George (see Chapter XV). A third group, taking a different tack, interprets the romance as a Christian allegory, with the
Green Knight representing Death or the Devil (the Devil, interestingly enough, wears green in Chaucer's *The Friar's Tale*). The poem
has also been seen as a tribute to the Order of the Garter, whose
color is green. A recent and generally moderate position explains

Gawain as making a pilgrimage from innocence to knowledge (see MEB 142–148).

A rich poem may indeed mean many things, and some or all of the elements just described, Christian as well as pagan, may be present in varying degrees. This much, however, can certainly be said: *Sir Gawain* meets the requirement of the medieval romance for idealization while it remains firmly rooted in the realities of human feeling and conduct. It fulfills a serious moral purpose—the glorification of uncompromising chastity, courage, and truth—without ceasing to be first-rate entertainment. Both morally and artistically *Sir Gawain and the Green Knight* is a continuing source of stimulation and pleasure.*

Pearl

Pearl is an exquisite dream-vision, and on that basis alone it is an unforgettable literary experience. It is also an elusive poem which has unceasingly held the attention of scholars and critics desirous of solving its many arresting problems of interpretation.

For a long time the poem was considered a mere personal elegy, with the Pearl representing the bereaved poet's two-year-old daughter. But readers in increasing numbers, especially in recent years, have come to interpret the poem as some sort of religious allegory. For one reader the Pearl symbolizes purity; for another, the Eucharist; a third finds in the experience of the dreamer a parallel to the mystic's emergence from depression, or "spiritual dryness," into a renewed sense of oneness with God. According to a theory which is currently attracting considerable attention and sympathy, the dreamer in the garden is fallen man; the Pearl is equated with his lost innocence that will eventually be restored; the statement that the Pearl, when it was lost, was not two years old is taken to mean that the fall from grace occurred early in the history of mankind. Meanwhile, there have been sporadic returns to the more traditional interpretation which sees the Pearl as a child. The various symbolic readings, however, need not exclude the possibility that *Pearl* (like *Deor* and Milton's *Lycidas*) may have a core of human emotion to provide its driving force; that this emotion may or may not be involved with the death of a real or imagined child; that the poem nonetheless can be made the vehicle for earnest reflection about the state of man. *Pearl*

---

* For a balanced and lucid evaluation of the poem and its literary setting, as well as informative commentary on the action, see James R. Kreuzer's Introduction to his edition: *Sir Gawain and the Green Knight*, trans. James L. Rosenberg (New York: Rinehart & Co., 1959).

certainly succeeds artistically on both the personal and allegorical levels.*

As the poem begins, the poet returns to a lovely garden where he once lost a very dear Pearl, "precious, without spot":

> Once, to that spot of which I rime,
> I entered, in the arbour green,
> In August, the high summer-time
> When corn is cut with sickles keen;
> Upon the mound where my pearl fell,
> Tall, shadowing herbs grew bright and sheen,
> Gilliflower, ginger and gromwell,
> With peonies powdered all between.
> As it was lovely to be seen,
> So sweet the fragrance there, I wot,
> Worthy her dwelling who hath been
> My own pearl, precious, without spot.
>
> (ll. 37–48)

His Pearl appears in a dream, radiantly adorned with faultless white gems:

> A crown with pearls bedight, the girl
> Was wearing, and no other stone;
> High pinnacled of clear white pearl,
> Wrought as if pearls to flowers were grown.
>
> (ll. 205–8)

Deeply moved, the dreamer cries out in grief. "Art thou my pearl for which I mourn,/Lamenting all alone at night?" Since her departure he has been "a joyless jeweler."

At this point the Pearl rebukes him and introduces a theological discussion. He has no right, she says, to mourn when he has really gained and not lost:

> Thou hast lost nothing save a rose
> That flowered and failed by life's decree:
> Because the coffer did round it close,
> A precious pearl it came to be.
> A thief thou hast dubbed thy destiny
> That something for nothing gives thee, sir;
> Thou blamest thy sorrow's remedy,
> Thou art no grateful jeweler.
>
> (ll. 269–76)

* For a survey of scholarship on *Pearl*, see MEB 150–157.

Moreover, he is guilty of three ill-considered assumptions. First of all, he thinks she is with him merely because he sees her with his eyes. Next, he believes that he can dwell with her in her country. Finally, he imagines that he is free to cross over at will into her domain. These errors reveal the defects in his vision and understanding. There is no cause, he is told, for grief; the Pearl has, after all, been enthroned as one of heaven's peerless queens. But how, the dreamer asks, could a creature so young and inexperienced have won salvation?

> Our life not two years didst thou lead
> Nor learned to please God, nor to pray,
> No Paternoster knew nor creed;
> And made a queen on the first day!
>
> (ll. 483–86)

Again she chides him, this time with the expertly told parable of the laborers in the vineyard whose master pays them the same wages no matter how long they may have worked. Both the child and the adult can be saved, the former by virtue of innocence and the latter through suffering and repentance. If anything, newborn innocence, "a pearl unblemishéd," offers a more secure claim:

> The sinful soul of mercy fain
> Finds pardon if he will repent,
> But he who sinless doth remain
> Is surely saved, being innocent.
>
> (ll. 669–72)

At last the dreamer seems to realize the immensity of the gulf separating him from his Pearl. He has but one request: let her show him the celestial city.

The "one short hour" during which the dreamer is permitted to look with his flawed eyes upon the new Jerusalem enables the poet to create one of the most magnificently sustained passages in our literature—a beatific vision modeled upon the Revelation of St. John. Having described the brightly burning city, all gold "like gleaming glass that glistens clear," he moves gradually to the Heavenly throne itself:

> Of sun or moon they had no need;
> For God Himself was their lamp light,
> The Lamb their lantern was indeed;
> From Him the city shone all bright.

> Through wall and dwelling my looks might speed,
> Such clearness could not hinder sight.
> Of the high throne ye might take heed,
> With draperies of radiant white,
> As John the Apostle doth endite;
> High God Himself did sit thereon.
> From the throne a river welled outright
> Was brighter than both sun and moon.
>
> (ll. 1045–56)

At the climactic moment, after beholding the Lamb smiling gloriously as the blood gushes down His white side, the dreamer would plunge into the untainted stream that cuts him off from his Pearl; but such an action is unpleasing to God. The poetry is rapturous in its intensity, then sudden in its falling off as God checks the dreamer's presumption:

> Delight that flooded eye and ear
> My mortal mind beatified;
> When I saw her, I must reach my dear,
> Though she beyond the brook abide.
> Nothing, I thought, could keep me here,
> No crippling blow hold my strength tied;
> I would plunge, whatever interfere,
> And swim the stream, though there I died.
> But ere the water I had tried,
> Even as I would my vow fulfill,
> From my purpose I was turned aside;
> It was not to my Prince's will.
>
> (ll. 1153–64)

Finding himself once again awake and alone in his garden, the poet accepts his exile "from that life, glad and undefiled" and takes comfort in his new-gained submission to the will of his Prince.

Whatever its detailed theological import, *Pearl* gives immediacy and freshness to the Christian view of the vanity of this world and the transcendent beauty of the next. The Pearl may well be, as some critics have stressed, a shifting symbol which serves in various contexts and with various other images to point up the fundamental contrast between the values of the earthly and the heavenly kingdoms. The poet must learn that temporal standards of merit and reward do not coincide with God's eternal justice. Above all, the poet must transfer his love from the material to the spiritual reality, from the pearls of courtly princes to the Pearl of the celestial Prince. To be sure, he does not gain his illumination without first suffering through the agony of bereavement and then undergoing an almost complete re-education. It is not easy, after all, for a human being caught up in a great sorrow, whether personal or universal, to become reconciled to the stern necessities imposed by the Almighty Judge. Yet out of this very interplay of personal weakness and divine strength the *Pearl* poet has fashioned a truly sublime lyric.

WILLIAM LANGLAND (*c. 1332–c. 1400*)

The Vision of William Concerning Piers the Plowman is among the world's most puzzling works. It is a satire, a social history, a religious allegory, and much more. Often imitated in its own day (especially by satirists) and still exerting a tremendous appeal, this big, sprawling poem contains so perplexing a mixture of the dull and the inspired as to defy sustained critical analysis. "Almost every opinion expressed about it," writes one scholar, "has been contradicted; the only ones that pass unchallenged are very general, that it is important, and great, and significant." *

Even the authorship of *Piers Plowman* is unsettled. A once popular view, now on the decline, though immortalized in the *Cambridge History of English Literature* by its most distinguished champion, would ascribe the three different versions of the poem to as many as five different poets. Without entering here into the many intricacies of the famous "Piers Plowman Controversy" (let the interested reader consult the MEB for relevant studies), we shall assume—with most contemporary scholars—that all three texts are the work of one man, a West Midlander (probably from Ledbury, in Shropshire) who has been named, on the basis of certain external and internal evidence, "William Langland." Although it is difficult to date the *Piers Plowman* texts with precision, scholars generally incline to *c.* 1362 for the A-text; to *c.* 1377 for the B-text; and to 1393, 1398, or—a recent and plausible suggestion—1387 for the C-text.

Each of the texts is divided into *passus*, or cantos: the A-text has eleven, the B-text twenty, and the C-text twenty-three. These texts should be regarded not as variants of the same poem but as succes-

---

* George Kane, *Middle English Literature: A Critical Study of the Romances, the Religious Lyrics and 'Piers Plowman'* (London: Methuen & Co., Ltd., 1951), p. 182.

sive attempts on Langland's part to develop and clarify his vast theme. The A-text, the shortest of the three, comes to about 2,500 lines. The B-text reworks and expands the materials of the A-text and continues with fresh material; it comprises some 7,200 lines in all. The C-text, just slightly longer than its predecessor, is a further revision, in some parts a complete rewriting, of the B-text. Although the B-text is undoubtedly Langland's supreme achievement and is the source for most of the quotations in the present discussion, *each* text has its distinctive qualities. Consequently, a rounded appreciation of the poet's aims and accomplishments demands that the entire cumulative poem be taken into account. The A-text is more or less straightforward; the B-text abounds in literary embellishments—anecdotes, excursions into bypaths of description and characterization, and vivid images designed to give a sense of immediacy to abstruse doctrinal points; the C-text finds the poet more concerned with theological and moral matters in themselves, often pruning his verse by reshaping concrete verbal pictures into a language more abstract and prosaic.

Courtesy of The Bettmann Archive

Plowing in the Middle Ages. Text reads: "God speed the plow and send us corn enow."

However one chooses to evaluate the individual texts, *Piers Plowman* in its totality is a series of extraordinary visions concerning the way in which man can attain salvation. In the opening vision the poet Will (whose name may also signify the human will, or the source of moral action) clothes himself as a hermit and falls asleep by the bank

of a brook on Malvern hillside. There he dreams of a "faire felde ful
of folke," which symbolizes the world as it is—a place teeming with
vitality but at the same time rife with hypocrisy and corruption.
Meanwhile, far away in the distant east stands a tower on a high
hill—the tower of Truth, we soon learn, and the dwelling place of
God. In the valley below is a dungeon, the home of the Devil, the
Father of Falseness. Into the busy scene swarm countless figures,
some realistic and some allegorical. Among them is a beautiful lady,
Holy Church, who scolds Will for sleeping when there is such urgent
work to be done. She further points out the gorgeously bedecked
Lady Meed (Reward, but more often Bribery), who is to marry
False. The scene shifts. Lady Meed is brought to trial in London,
but she is stoutly defended by everyone except Conscience and
Reason. Here the first vision ends.

Before long, however, the poet is asleep again, and this time he
dreams of a sermon preached by Conscience back in the original
field. So moving is this exhortation to repentance that even the Seven
Deadly Sins begin to confess—all but Gluttony, who is lured into an
alehouse en route to Church. The confessions completed, a huge mob
starts on a pilgrimage to the shrine of Holy Truth. No one, however,
knows where Truth lives; and when the pilgrims ask directions of a
palmer, who has been on many pilgrimages in his time, the answer
is both disappointing and ironic: Who has ever heard of a palmer
interested in visiting Holy Truth?

At this stage of the poem Piers (Peter) the Plowman makes his
first appearance. *He* knows where Truth is and will gladly serve the
pilgrims as a guide as soon as he finishes plowing his half-acre—the
implication being that man, whatever his destiny, ought not abdicate
his responsibility to live a good life wherever he happens to be placed.
A number of the pilgrims help him plow, but others malinger or get
sidetracked. Truth hands Piers a pardon containing just two Latin
lines saying that those who do good will go to eternal life while those
who do evil will go to eternal fire. Such a pardon, ironically, is too
simple to appeal to a priest who happens to see it, but the dreamer
is convinced that to do well is the key to salvation. The vision concludes with a passage in Latin to the effect that the vision of William
concerning Piers the Plowman is finished and that the life of Do-well,
Do-bet (Do-better), and Do-best is beginning: *"Explicit hic Visio
Wilhelmi. . . ."*

The rest of the poem, which is almost impossible to summarize,

consists of an extensive search for Do-well, Do-better, and Do-best—
the precise meaning of which constitutes one of the most widely
explored subjects in literary scholarship. According to one well-
established interpretation (see MEB 171), Do-well, Do-better, and
Do-best symbolize three stages of man's spiritual journey, namely, the
active life, the contemplative life, and the mixed life. Do-well labors
actively in the world, plowing his half-acre and fulfilling his duties.
Do-better stands for monastic renunciation and study. Do-best, the
personification of the mixed life that is both active and contemplative,
returns to the world with a deepened responsibility to lead and inspire. Piers himself, according to this theory, embodies in turn each
of the three ideals according to what the world at a given juncture
most acutely needs. Recent criticism, however, has questioned the
validity of the separation of the active and contemplative lives. One
scholar argues that to do well, whatever one's sphere of activity, is
Langland's primary concern and that Do-better and Do-best are
simply higher manifestations of the same kind of exemplary conduct
that is prescribed for Do-well. Another critic, drawing upon a vast
body of medieval Christian doctrine, suggests that the "active" and
the "contemplative" lives are not mutually exclusive; that the active
life, far from being equated with external activity, really means a
life of asceticism—the beginning of the spiritual life proper, which is
then heightened through contemplation. It is possible, of course, that
these symbols change their significance from time to time during the
course of the poem. Piers himself seems to change, but he never
loses any part of what he has been. With each new role that he assumes Piers grows, always accumulating fresh doctrinal and emotional values. He can therefore be, among other things, the honest
worker, the spiritual guide, the perfect priest, the instrument of grace,
Christ's authoritative spokesman (the Church), and even Christ himself. The allegory in *Piers Plowman* is indeed complex.

What makes the poem even more difficult to follow is that the pilgrimage toward the good life does not proceed smoothly. It is repeatedly interrupted by false starts, by intentional (and perhaps un-
intentional) digressions, by disillusionments and frustrations. For
Langland, after all, is more poet than systematic theologian, and he
accordingly takes more delight in people and things directly seen and
experienced—Glutton's alehouse, for example, comes marvelously to
life—than in abstract doctrinal argument. Though thoroughly orthodox, he examines Christianity with the full force of his complicated

and, in a sense, undisciplined personality. It is turbulent and dramatic, this restless probing of his; and however unsatisfying he may be from the point of view of closely reasoned theology, no reader can deny his enormous poetic power.

Turning, then, from the vexing question of the poem's theology, we may observe some of the ways in which Langland transforms the alliterative long line, generally associated with formality and ornateness, into a vehicle for wide-ranging emotional effects. The poet can speak with vigor and sternness, particularly when denouncing ecclesiastical or social abuses. Unlike Chaucer, he rarely displays, even on the surface, an affection for his satirical targets. Langland's monk is a "rider, a roamer by streets," who will one day be punished for his corrupt living:

> There shal come a kyng   and confesse yow religiouses [religious orders]
> And bete yow as the bible telleth   for brekynge of yowre reule.
> (B, Passus X, 317–18)

Hermits "with hoked staves" take their wenches to Walsingham; pilgrims and palmers return from visits to Rome "with many wise tales" and have leave to lie for the rest of their days. From fee-hungry lawyers, we are told in an image rooted in everyday experience, it is impossible to extract the barest syllable without paying:

> Thow myghtest better mete [measure] the myste   on Malverne hulles [hills]
> Than get a momme of here [their] mouthe   but money were shewed.
> (B, Prologue, 214–15)

Langland is indeed a master at finding the specific figure of speech that lends immediacy and strength to philosophic abstractions. In one place he compresses the grandeur of God into three simple lines; the first suggests great height, the second provides a breath-taking instance of what God can do, while the third reduces Death himself to abject obedience:

> The tour ther [where] Treuthe is inne   i-set is above the sonne,
> He may do with the day-sterre [morning star]   what him deore lyketh [whatever he likes];
> Deth dar [dare] not do   thing that he defendeth [forbids].
> (A, VI, 82–84)

Sometimes the poet moves boldly from one mood to another. The sublime vision of the dance of the Four Daughters of God merges into the personal as the dreamer awakens and addresses his wife and daughter, then quickly soars back into a fervent affirmation of Christian faith:

Tyl the daye dawed   this damaiseles daunced
That men rongen [rang] to the resurexioun   & right with that I
    waked
And called Kitte my wyf   and Kalote my doughter—
"Ariseth and reverenceth   goddes resurexioun
And crepeth to the crosse on knees   and kisseth it for a juwel!
For goddes blissed body   it bar for owre bote [help]."

(B, XVIII, 424–29)

Among the poem's greatest episodes is the Harrowing of Hell, in which Christ, from the midst of a magnificent light, commands the infernal creatures to unbar the gates:

"Dukes of this dym place   anon undo this yates,
That Cryst may come in   the kynges sone of hevene!"
And with that breth helle brake   with Beliales barres.

(B, XVIII, 317–19)

Claiming from Satan all the souls in hell, Christ announces triumphantly that the "doctour of deth" must now drink his own bitter brew. But Christ has not come to exult in his superior strength; he strikes a note of profound tenderness for mankind:

For I, that am lorde of lyf   love is my drynke,
And for that drynke today   I deyde upon erthe.
I faughte so, me threstes [I thirst] yet   for mannes soule sake;
May no drynke me moiste   ne my thruste [thirst] slake,
Tyl the vendage [vintage] falle   in the vale of Josephath,
That I drynke righte ripe must [new wine]   *"resureccio mortuorum*
    [resurrection of the dead],"
And thanne shal I come as a kynge   crouned with angeles,
And han [take] out of helle   alle mennes soules.

(B, XVIII, 363–70)

It is this consuming sympathy for human beings that prevents the poem, in spite of the wrath poured into its fierce invectives against evildoers, from taking on an unrelieved harshness. The poet, in fact, loves the whole of the created universe—witness this warm vision of life in all its variety:

> [Ich] seih the sonne and the see   and the sand after
> Wher that briddes [birds] and bestes   by here [their] makes
>   [mates] yeden [went about],
> Wilde wormes [snakes] in wodes   and wonderful foules
> With fleckede fetheres   and of fele [many] colors;
> Man and hus make [his mate]   ich myghte see bothe,
> Poverte and plente   both pees and werre,
> Blisse and biter bale   both ich seih at ones.
>
> (C, XIV, 135–41)

Langland has an intimate understanding, perhaps based on his own experience, of the genuinely poor who suffer in all seasons, "Thorough derth, thorough drouth alle her dayes here," and he begs Christ to take pity on them. Yet his simple description of charity encompasses the whole ladder of society, rich as well as poor:

> I have seyn hym in sylke   and somme tyme in russet
> Both in grey and in grys [costly fur]   and in gulte herneys [gilt
>   armor or outfit].
>
> (B, XV, 214–15)

Too often Langland's imitators directed their attention exclusively to the elements of satire and social protest in *Piers Plowman*. Langland's scope is far more vast than that.

We may never untangle the mysteries of the authorship of *Piers Plowman,* just as we may never solve all of the staggeringly difficult problems involved with the interpretation of the poem. But no matter. *Piers Plowman* at its best throbs with the excitement and exaltation which only the very greatest poetry is capable of producing. And if Langland is impatient or inconsistent or vague concerning some of the details of his theology, he certainly has no doubts as to the essence of the Christian way of life. Seldom has that essence been so wonderfully distilled as when the poet, aging and weary, asks Kynde (Nature) to recommend the best trade for him to practice and receives from her the answer that is electrifying in its simplicity:

> "Conseille me, Kynde," quod I,   "what crafte is best to lerne?"
> "Lerne to love," quod Kynde,   "and leve of alle othre."
>
> (B, XX, 206–7)

XI: DEBATES, DIDACTIC VERSE, AND SATIRE

The *Gawain* poet and the author of *Piers Plowman* produced moral poems that have endured as great works of art. For some poets, however, the instructional purpose became so explicit as to obscure any artistic impulse they may have felt. In this last of the three chapters on non-Chaucerian poetry, we direct our attention to "miscellaneous" verse aimed at providing spiritual edification—debates, didactic poems, and satires. What was said earlier of medieval religious prose applies almost equally well to this poetry: seldom is the didactic or satiric intention realized without loss, at least from the modern point of view, of literary quality.

Having characterized the poems in this tentative fashion, one must immediately make an important qualification. Readers are naturally more interested in the exceptions to the above rule, and most of the works to be considered here are at least partially successful as literature. One of the most serious of the poets, John Gower, is remembered chiefly as an entertainer, a purveyor of tales which may not in all cases adequately reinforce the high moral principles they are designed to illustrate. Moreover, the most extraordinary poem of the lot, that early debate *The Owl and the Nightingale,* seems to have no didactic intention whatsoever.

DEBATES *

A widely used teaching device during the Middle Ages was the *debate*. This literary genre, which seems to have been derived from the eclogues of Theocritus and Virgil, received fresh impetus in the twelfth century through the popularity of Peter Abelard's *Sic et Non*. The debate was a disputation on subjects serious or trivial: Body vs. Soul, Youth vs. Age, Rose vs. Lily, Water vs. Wine, Heart vs. Eye—and so on. Very often its method was merely to present

---

* Quotations from *The Owl and the Nightingale* and from *The Debate of the Body and the Soul* are from *Medieval English Verse and Prose,* in modernized versions by Roger S. Loomis and Rudolph Willard. Copyright, 1948, Appleton-Century-Crofts, Inc. Reprinted by permission of the publisher.

conflicting sides of an argument and let the reader or the student arrive at the proper decision on his own. Frequently, of course—as in the question, which is more beautiful, the rose or the lily?—there is no "final" decision; the main interest is in debate for its own sake as a test of the poet's dialectical powers. In the alliterative poem *Wynnere and Wastoure* (*c.* 1352), Wynnere (Thrift) disputes with Wastoure (Extravagance) as to the relative merits of their ways of life, but the work breaks off after King Edward III, acting as arbiter, has advised the parties, in effect, to live and let live. The brisk dialogue that characterizes some of the more effective debates invites the tempting speculation that the form may have also served as a kind of drama substitute during a period when there was little, if any, acted drama.

The Owl and the Nightingale (c. 1200)

The earliest, and surely the greatest, specimen of Middle English literary debate is *The Owl and the Nightingale*. The poet wanders into a secluded valley and overhears a violent quarrel between two birds. Each claims to be the better singer and, by extension, the more useful servant of man. The solemn owl objects to the daylight twitterings of the nightingale:

> Better than thou I sing at least;
> Thou chatterest like an Irish priest.
> (ll. 321–22)

The pleasure-loving nightingale, for her part, cannot stand the melancholy hooting of the owl and counters with an equally pungent simile:

> Thou singest like a hen in snow
> Where all she sings is song of woe.
> (ll. 413–14)

The owl accuses the nightingale of encouraging love and fostering lust through her sensual music:

> Once thou sangest, I know the spot,
> Nigh to a bower, and lewdly sought
> To lead a lady's heart astray,
> And sangest high and low thy lay
> And taughtest her the way of shame,
> Adultery, and evil fame.
> (ll. 1049–54)

Both hurt and angered by this charge, the nightingale answers that
she is proud to sing roulades celebrating love, a delightful experience
that is beyond the comprehension of the owl; but it is chaste love
between husband and wife that she would extol. If others pervert
her beautiful song to evil purposes, is that *her* fault? Moreover, she
says, the owl is always bragging about her reputation for wisdom.
Well, the nightingale is skeptical:

> An ape can hold an open book
> And turn the pages o'er and look,
> But for all that he has no more
> Of learning than he had before.
> Even so at the stars thou starest,
> But never a wiser head thou wearest.
>
> (ll. 1325–30)

If at one point relatively early in the poem the owl gets so puffed
up with rage that she looks as if she had just swallowed a frog, is it
any wonder after so prolonged an exchange of insults that armed
combat should seem imminent? Fortunately, the wren, who in a
showdown would have supported the nightingale, proposes arbitration. The birds agree to seek a judgment from the wise Master
Nicholas of Guildford (or Guilford), perhaps the author of the poem,
but neither the eavesdropping poet nor the reader ever learns how
the debate is resolved.

Commentators on this fine poem have disagreed almost as vehe-
mently as the birds themselves. Is Nicholas of Guildford the author?
Is the poem a plea for preferment written by a John of Guildford in
behalf of Nicholas? Are the owl and the nightingale merely ill-
tempered birds? Or are they embodiments, respectively, of asceticism
and pleasure, philosophy and art, religious poetry and love poetry,
the contemplative life and the active life? The poet has usually been
thought either neutral or "pro-nightingale," but it has recently been
argued (see MEB 189) that the "Nightingalians" are misty-eyed
romantics and that the poet clearly supports the owl, a staunch de-
fender of Christian values against the specious arguments of a sen-
sualist.

In any case, the poet (Nicholas of Guildford, John of Guildford,
or someone else) displays a lively mind, an expert command of
metrics, and a superb sense of comedy—qualities particularly impressive at so early a stage in the development of English poetry.

That the poet uses the four-stress couplet attests to his receptiveness to French influence, but the poem as a whole is thoroughly English. Like the prose *Ancrene Riwle*, also of early date, *The Owl and the Nightingale* demonstrates that there was a significant native English literary tradition that may have been enriched by contact with the Normans but was by no means blotted out after the Conquest.

The Debate of the Body and the Soul (1250–1300)

One of the recurring themes of medieval literary debate, both in England and on the Continent, is the mutual confrontation of body and soul. This disputation sometimes takes place over a corpse awaiting burial, an occasion admirably suited to a discussion of the past existence and future destiny of the two disputants. Extant from the Old English period is a poem, *Soul and Body,* in which first a wicked and then a righteous soul address their dead bodies. The bodies, however, are silent, a consideration that excludes the Old English poem from qualifying as a debate.

In the Middle English *Debate of the Body and the Soul,* a dream-vision, the soul of a dead knight pauses over the body lying upon the bier and heaps recriminations upon it. The soul upbraids the body for its life of vanity and pomp, echoing once again the familiar *ubi sunt* theme:

> "Thou, that wert ever wont on prancing steed
>   To ride abroad, by country or by town;
> Thou, that wert known for many a shining deed
>   Of high emprise, a knight of fair renown:
>   How are thy swelling honors stricken down,
> Thy heart of lion-daring lowly bowed!
>   Where now is thy imperious voice, thy frown
> Of withering hate? Thou, that wert once so proud,
> What dost thou lying here, wrapt in a vulgar shroud?"
>
> (ll. 19–27)

But the body, acknowledging its mortality, blames the soul for the sorry life it has led. The soul was given man in order to be a keeper and guide; if the sins of the body bring damnation upon the soul, let the soul reproach no one but itself. To its dismay the soul soon learns that it *is* held accountable for the body's transgressions and must consequently be torn asunder by fiends:

Some thrust its jaws apart, and cried, "Drink, drink!"
  While molten lead was poured adown its throat.
Then came there one, the master-fiend, I think,
  And with a burning spear its heart he smote.
  Then through sides, back, and breast, they plunged red-hot
Falchions of steel, till all their points did meet
  In the heart's core; and they did cry, and gloat
Upon its pangs—"This heart, that once did beat
So hot with pride, ho! feels it now another heat?"

(ll. 271–79)

"O Jesu Lord!" cries the soul from the depths of its agony, but too late. The fiends hurl their victim into a murky pit to dwell in everlasting damnation. Awakening from his dream with cold drops of sweat on each hair, the poet urges sinners to repent while there is still time. The moral has been driven home with unusual vividness.

The Cuckoo and the Nightingale (1392?)

The Cuckoo and the Nightingale (also called *The Book of Cupid, God of Love*) crosses the paths of three great English poets. It was probably written by Sir Thomas Clanvowe, an imitator and perhaps a friend of Chaucer; its theme was used by Milton in his sonnet *To the Nightingale;* and it has been superbly modernized by Wordsworth (from whose version the quotations in the present discussion are taken).

After an invocation to the God of Love, the poet tells how he lay sleepless and recalled the legend that he who hears the nightingale before the cuckoo will be lucky in love. Betaking himself to a lovely green lawn that is powdered with daisies, he falls asleep and overhears a dispute between a cuckoo and a nightingale about the value of love. The cuckoo, who refuses to accept the so-called law that one must either love or die, considers love the source of all human misery:

"For thereof come all contraries to gladness,
  Thence sickness comes, and overwhelming sadness,
  Mistrust and jealousy, despite, debate,
  Dishonor, shame, envy importunate,
  Pride, anger, mischief, poverty, and madness. . . ."

To the nightingale, on the other hand, love is the inspiration of all that is admirable in life:

> "For thereof comes all goodness and all worth;
> All gentiless and honor thence comes forth;
> Thence worship comes, content and true heart's pleasure,
> And full-assurèd trust, joy without measure,
> And jollity, fresh cheerfulness, and mirth. . . ."

The poet's experiences in love would seem to bear out the cuckoo's point of view, but his sympathies are naturally with the nightingale. Deeply agitated, the poet picks up a stone and hurls it at the hateful cuckoo—whereupon the latter, still mocking, flies away in terror. The nightingale, whose heart had been on the verge of breaking, gratefully promises the poet, her faithful friend, that she will make amends and grant him success in love—next year:

> "And one thing will I counsel thee also,
> The Cuckoo trust not thou, nor his Love's saw;
> All that she said is an outrageous lie."
> "Nay, nothing shall me bring thereto," quoth I,
> "For Love, and it hath done me mighty woe."

Taking leave of the poet and bidding him ease his pains by looking every day upon the daisy, the nightingale excitedly assembles the rest of the bird kingdom and extracts a pledge that the cuckoo will be made to stand trial before a parliament. As the nightingale loudly celebrates her devotion to Love, the poet awakens.

If the situation recalls *The Owl and the Nightingale*, it bears even closer affinities with Chaucer's *Parlement of Foules*, a poem (to be discussed later) in which the ambiguous nature of love is explored by numerous birds sitting in debate. *The Cuckoo and the Nightingale* is indeed suffused with something like the gentle irony that has become identified with the Chaucerian manner, and it was at one time even ascribed to Chaucer by some readers. There is still the possibility that John, and not Thomas, Clanvowe wrote this pleasant debate and that a date early in the fifteenth century (*c.* 1403?) is plausible.

DIDACTIC VERSE

In addition to the literary debate, a versatile genre that could be readily adapted to serve a moral purpose, the Middle English period is deluged with other types of verse more explicitly designed to instruct men in virtuous living. The range of the verse includes proverbs, homilies, scriptural paraphrases, allegories, *exempla* (moralized tales), and metrical lives of saints, notably Chaucer's *Second Nun's Tale*.* This discussion will be primarily concerned with four works: the *Proverbs of Alfred*, the medieval *Bestiary*, Robert Mannyng's *Handlyng Synne*, and John Gower's *Confessio Amantis*.

Proverbs of Alfred (*12th Century?*)

Although Alfred the Great was a man of many and varied accomplishments, there is no evidence that he had anything to do with the popular collection of early Middle English sayings that enjoys the prestige of his name. The *Proverbs of Alfred*, which survives in three thirteenth-century manuscripts that pretty clearly represent reworkings of an older version, contains advice on a variety of matters practical and philosophical, including how to choose and manage a wife, bring up children, and live a good Christian life. The work echoes the pithy wisdom of Old English gnomic verse; it also calls to mind the worldly instruction given by Polonius (in *Hamlet*) and by Benjamin Franklin's "Poor Richard." Occasionally a precept is phrased in a fresh way, as in the counsel against telling everybody your troubles: "If thou dost harbour sorrow, let not thine arrow know it; whisper it but to thy saddle-bow, and ride abroad with song." Metrically the *Proverbs of Alfred* is of some interest because it uses both alliteration and rhyme and thus represents a transitional stage between Old English and Middle English verse. As evidence of the wide circulation of proverbs attributed to that glorious king of the West Saxons, the reader may observe that both parties to the dispute in *The Owl and the Nightingale* see fit to bolster their arguments—some eleven times all told—with quotations from "Alfred."

Bestiary (*c. 1240*)

The *Bestiary*, like the Old English *Physiologus*, is a series of short poems allegorizing various animals. But whereas the *Physiologus*, at least in the form in which it has been preserved, includes sketches of only the Panther, the Whale, and the Partridge, the Middle English poem contains accounts of the Panther, the Whale, and eleven other beasts—all but one (the Dove) freely adapted from an eleventh-century Latin *Physiologus* by Theobaldus. In the *Bestiary* the

---

* A work in the same tradition is the *South English Legendary*. This compilation, probably begun in the last quarter of the thirteenth century, includes saints' legends and other narratives appropriate for particular seasons of the ecclesiastical calendar.

Whale, as in the Old English *Physiologus,* stands for Satan, who deceives sailors into thinking he is an island haven—then plunges with them into the depths of the sea. The Lion, whose actions and "signification" are almost identical with those of the Panther in the Old English poem, habitually lies still for three days after birth until his father rouses him with a mighty roar. The signification comes as no surprise:

> When our Lord was dead,   and buried as His will was,
> In a stone He lay still,   till it came the third day;
> His Father strengthened Him   that He rose from the dead then,
> To bring us to life.*

The Elephant represents Adam's fall and, at a later stage, his redemption through Christ. In the Middle Ages, as has been repeatedly shown, the whole world could be viewed symbolically, and all objects in it—stones, flowers, animals—could be assigned specific roles in a larger spiritual drama.

Handlyng Synne (*1303*)†

One didactic poem makes teaching vastly entertaining. Robert Mannyng of Brunne wrote his *Handlyng Synne,* he tells us in his Prologue, because too many men listen to tittle-tattle at the alehouse and are drawn into evil ways. His poem will show what deeds are sinful, though men may think them harmless. Especially quaint is Mannyng's explanation of the title of his work:

> In that tyme [1303] turnede y thys
> On [into] englyssh tunge out of frankys [French],
> Of a boke as y fonde ynne;
> Men clepyn [call] the boke "handlyng synne."
> In frenche ther a clerk hyt sees,
> He clepyth [calleth] hyt "manuel de pecches."
> 'Manuel' ys handlyng with honde;
> 'Pecches' ys 'synne,' y undyrstonde.
> These twey wurdys [words] that beyn otwynne
> Do hem to gedyr, ys "handlyng synne."
>
>   (ll. 77–86)

---

* From *Medieval English Verse and Prose,* in modernized versions by Roger S. Loomis and Rudolph Willard. Copyright, 1948, Appleton-Century-Crofts, Inc. Reprinted by permission of the publisher.

† Quotations are from *Robert of Brunne's 'Handlyng Synne,'* ed. Frederick J. Furnivall (Early English Text Society, 119, 122; 1901–1902).

The French *Manuel* that Mannyng freely translated was by the Anglo-Norman William of Wadington.

The poem proper—some 12,600 lines in octosyllabic couplets— is enlivened by numerous *exempla*, little stories told to illustrate particular sins or points of doctrine. When he has a good story to tell, Mannyng warms up—as in the account of the adulterous wife whose skeleton split in two, or the tale, intended to illustrate that words without belief are powerless, of the witch, the bag, and the bishop. The witch pronounces a charm that causes her bag to suck men's cattle, but the bishop, who does not believe as she does, is unable to work the charm even though he recites the identical words. To emphasize the importance of using the correct liturgical formula in christening a child, Mannyng tells of an ignorant midwife who lost an infant through not saying the right words. Thereafter she was forbidden to come where children were born. "The poyntes of bapteme," Mannyng warns midwives, "y rede [advise] yow lere."

Deservedly famous is Mannyng's *exemplum* of the dancers at Colbek (Cologne). Dancing and caroling in the churchyard, he solemnly begins, is a sacrilege. Then follows the story of the carolers who offended the priest during mass with their dancing and who were cursed by him to dance for a full year without stopping:

> As sone as the preste hadde so spoke,
> Every hande yn outher so fast was loke,
> That no man myght with no wundyr [miracle]
> That twelvemonthe parte hem asundyr.
>
> (ll. 9087–90)

On and on they whirl, singing their carol with the ironical title, "Why stonde we? why go we noght?" The priest's own daughter, Ave, is among them; and when her brother attempts to remove her from the dance, her arm is severed from her body. Three times the arm refuses to stay buried. Meanwhile, the carolers are oblivious of their surroundings:

> Ne mete ete [they ate no meat], ne drank drynke,
> Ne slepte onely a-lepy wynke [they slept not a single wink];
> Nyght, ne day, they wyst [knew] of none,
> Whan hyt was come, whan hyt was gone;
> Frost ne snogh, hayle ne reyne,
> Of colde ne hete, felte they no peyne;
> Heere [hair] ne nayles never grewe,

Ne solowed [soiled] clothes, ne turned hewe;
Thundyr ne lyghtnyng dyd hem no dere [hurt],
Goddes mercy dyd hyt fro hem were [protected them];
But sungge that songge that the wo wroght:
"Why stonde we, why go we noght?"   (ll. 9145–56)

When the year is up, the dancers go their separate ways, hopping continually with the same step they had used. The story recurs in Robert Burton's *The Anatomy of Melancholy* (1621) and in other works. But Mannyng's tale has never been more expertly told, particularly with his ingenious moral, restated at the end with much softness and humor:

Thys tale y tolde yow, to make yow aferde,
In cherche to karolle, or yn cherche yerde,
Namely agens the prestys wylle;
Leveth [stop], whan he byddeth yow be stylle.
                              (ll. 9249–52)

It is sacrilege to dance in the churchyard; so you had better stop—when the priest tells you to!

John Gower (c. 1330?–1408) *

Once considered Chaucer's equal as a poet, Gower now gets somewhat less than his due. We know relatively little of his life, except that he had some financial importance and was a personal friend of Richard II and Henry IV. His diminished reputation, which some recent critics have been attempting to restore (see MEB 193–196), rests upon three massive moralizing poems written, respectively, in French, Latin, and English. The French *Mirour de l'Omme* ("Mirror of Man"; known also by the Latin titles *Speculum Meditantis* and *Speculum Hominis*), written before 1381, offers a detailed account of the Seven Deadly Sins and the corresponding Virtues. According to Gower's own note (in Latin) appended to most manuscripts of his English poem *Confessio Amantis,* the *Mirour de l'Omme* endeavors to teach the proper way by which a sinner might return to the knowledge of God. The Latin *Vox Clamantis* ("The Voice of One Crying"), starting out as an unfavorable commentary on the Peasants' Revolt of 1381, develops into a full-scale exposure of contemporary social and moral corruption. It treats, to refer again to the note to *Confessio Amantis,* the many misfortunes which befell Eng-

* Quotations are from *The Works of John Gower,* ed. G. C. Macaulay. 4 vols. (Oxford: Clarendon Press, 1899–1902).

land during the reign of Richard II, a time in which the whole realm suffered—including the evil king himself, who fell from his lofty eminence into the pit which he himself had dug.

The "moral Gower," as Chaucer called him, is chiefly remembered for his English *Confessio Amantis* (1390), or "The Confession of a Lover." The work is actually a huge collection of *exempla*, moralized tales, but the framework is quite charming. The poet, realizing that he has not remedied the ills of the world through the unrelieved seriousness of his earlier poetry, tells us in his Prologue that he will change his style and his subject matter:

> Bot for men sein, and soth [truth] it is,
> That who that al of wisdom writ
> It dulleth ofte a mannes wit
> To him that schal it aldai rede,
> For thilke cause, if that ye rede,
> I wolde go the middel weie
> And wryte a bok betwen the tweie;
> Somewhat of lust [pleasure], somewhat of lore. . . .
> Prologue (ll. 12–19)

After a lengthy survey of the contemporary social and religious scene, Gower ends the Prologue and begins the poem itself. He relates that he was wandering one day in May, "Whan every brid hath chose his make," and reflecting upon his own disappointment in love:

> For I was further fro my love
> Than Erthe is fro the hevene above. . . .
> (Book I, ll. 105–6)

He complains bitterly of his life-in-death:

> And evere I wisshide after deth,
> Whanne I out of my peine awok,
> And caste up many a pitous lok
> Unto the hevene, and seide thus:
> "O thou Cupide, O thou Venus,
> Thou god of love and thou goddesse,
> Wher is pite? wher is meknesse?"
> (Book I, ll. 120–26)

Venus appears, but will do nothing for him until she is certain that he is her genuine servant and no impostor. She calls upon Genius,

the Priest of Love, to hear the poet's confession. In order to help
Gower get started, Genius announces that he will expound the many
sins of which the poet may be guilty, with an *exemplum* to illustrate
each of his sermons.

There follows an almost unending flow of homilies and tales. Perjury, for example, is illustrated by the false oath of eternal love
sworn by Jason to Medea, whom he later forsakes. The vice of "Sur-
quiderie," or Presumption, is exemplified in the story of Narcissus, a
woman-hater, who falls in love with his own reflection in the stream
and kills himself with a stone because his love cannot be returned.
It is clear that Gower has little interest in the tales except for the
morality they impart; consequently, he offers a number of com-
petently written stories that are almost always lucid, but he never
immerses himself in the narrative—as Mannyng does, for example—
in order to achieve genuine excitement. Still and all, the *Confessio
Amantis* is eminently readable. It is, moreover, a storehouse of material for greater writers to adapt. The Tale of Florent and the
Loathly Hag, told to illustrate disobedience in love, is an analogue of
Chaucer's *The Wife of Bath's Tale;* the Tale of Constance, in the
Confessio Amantis, a story emphasizing detraction, becomes *The
Man of Law's Tale* in Chaucer. Gower's long account of Apollonius
of Tyre, illustrating incest, is the source of Shakespeare's *Pericles,*
in which Gower himself appears as narrator.

The *Confessio Amantis* is of additional interest to students of
Chaucer, for near the end of Gower's poem Venus praises Chaucer as
her favorite poet:

> And gret [greet] wel Chaucer, whan ye mete,
> As mi disciple and mi poete:
> For in the floures of his youthe
> In sondri wise [sundry ways], as he wel couthe [knew how],
> Of ditees and of songes glade,
> The whiche he for mi sake made,
> The lond fulfild is overal:
> Whereof to him in special
> Above alle othre I am most holde. . . .
>
> (Book VIII, ll. 2941–49)

Because this tribute was omitted in some later manuscripts, it has
been inferred that Gower and Chaucer must have quarreled, but the
evidence is far from conclusive.

Other Didactic Poems

A few works, while not claiming much distinction as literature, deserve brief mention because they represent important facets of medieval literary taste. The *Poema Morale,* also called *Moral Ode* (*c.* 1170), is a vigorous exhortation to repentance and is marked by a particularly moving description of the terrors of Hell and the joys of Heaven. This versified homily is of importance to literary history because it employs for the first time in English the "fourteener," a fourteen-syllable (seven-foot) iambic line that was frequently used during the Renaissance. (In practice, the line almost inevitably breaks into two lines, the first with four feet and the second with three, as in the typical ballad stanza or in "Mary Had a Little Lamb.") The *Ormulum* (*c.* 1200), so named for its author Orm, contains some 20,000 lines of scriptural paraphrase interspersed with pedestrian sermonizing and overelaborate explication. But the work, which is of modest interest as a cultural document, commands the attention of historians of the English language because Orm wrote in a Northeast Midland dialect and painstakingly practiced a system of phonetic spelling which provides valuable information about late twelfth-century pronunciation in the poet's area. Like many another work of the period, the poem usually called *Sinners, Beware,* which dates from before 1250, attempts to warn readers of the consequences of evil-doing; as literature, it is chiefly notable for its six-line stanzas rhyming *aabaab*—additional corroboration for the rapid assimilation of French metrical forms into English after the Norman Conquest.

SATIRE

Each age produces its own abuses and its own corrective satire. Generally speaking, the most angry satire is that which is directed against individuals or groups whose conduct shows a marked falling off from lofty aims. In the Middle Ages some of the ripest targets for satiric attack were the monks and, especially, the friars who failed to uphold the ideals of poverty, obedience, and humanitarian service exemplified by St. Francis of Assisi (1182?–1226). The ecclesiastics we meet in Middle English satires and in the pages of Langland and Chaucer generally have worldly ideas.

There were, of course, other stock subjects for satire—some, perhaps all, of ancient literary lineage: the greed of lawyers, the follies of women, the corruption of city life, the fopperies of the court. Moreover, Middle English satirists, like satirists in any age, had their personal antagonisms against particular individuals.

The Land of Cockayne *

As early as the second half of the thirteenth century, *The Land of Cockayne* pictured the Cistercian monks living in a never-never land of luxury and greed. In Cockayne, a fair island west of Spain, rivers flow oil, honey, milk, and wine. On that island is an abbey— wondrously gay:

> There are chambers good and halls;
> All of pasties are the walls,
> Of flesh and fish and tender meat,
> The most delicious man may eat.

And wonder of wonders, there are flying geese, ready roasted and dressed—garlic and all! The younger monks are particularly given to pleasures, and the poet assures us with an almost Chaucerian irony that virtue is amply rewarded:

> And the monk who slumbers best
> And gives his body ample rest,
> There is a goodly certainty
> That he'll be abbot speedily.

Anyone wanting to enter the country of Cockayne must wade for seven years in the dung of swine, up to his very chin. One recalls how in the Old English *Guthlac* the fiends attempted to destroy the saintly hermit's faith by reciting the abuses of monks, but Guthlac, unlike the angry poet of *The Land of Cockayne*, had sprung eloquently to the defense of his brothers. There is a possibility that the Middle English satire was the work of a Franciscan friar, in which case the condemnation of the Cistercians may be partially explained as the outburst of one friar against members of a rival order.

Piers the Plowman's Creed (c. 1394)

Langland's great poem inspired several satires, among them the Wyclifite *Piers the Plowman's Creed*. In this work the author por-

* Quotations from *The Land of Cockayne, Piers the Plowman's Creed,* and *London Lickpenny* are from *Medieval English Verse and Prose,* in modernized versions by Roger S. Loomis and Rudolph Willard. Copyright, 1948, Appleton-Century-Crofts, Inc. Reprinted by permission of the publisher.

trays himself as a suppliant, eager to be instructed in the true faith.
He approaches, in succession, representatives of each of the four
major orders of friars—a Minorite (Franciscan), a Dominican, an
Augustinian, and a Carmelite. What he receives from each, however,
is merely a scathing denunciation of the other three. Coming away
in profound sorrow, he happens upon a simple plowman wearing a
coat of coarse cloth (in contrast to the rich garments worn by the
representatives of the mendicant orders) and with his toes peeping
out of his shoes. The plowman, despite his poverty, addresses the
poet with sympathy and generosity:

> This man looked upon me   and let the plow stand,
> And said, "Simple man,   why sighest thou so hard?
> If thou lack what is needful   to life, I will lend thee
> Such goods as God hath sent.   Go we, dear brother."

Learning of the poet's disillusionment, Piers the Plowman warns him
against being taken in by these false prophets and then teaches him
the fundamentals of the Christian faith. The poet concludes, perhaps
ironically, with a disclaimer of absolute certainty. Since he is no
churchman, he insists, he may have gone astray—in which case he
asks his readers to forgive him. Chaucer's Plowman, in *The Canterbury Tales*, is further testimony to the idealization of the plowman
as a good guide to Christian living.

London Lickpenny

A simple plowman is victimized in *London Lickpenny*, a popular
fifteenth-century satirical ballad that has been erroneously ascribed
to John Lydgate. In an effort to secure justice, the plowman travels
to the law courts in Westminster, but most stanzas end with some
variation of the bitter refrain, "But for lack of money I could not
speed." Not only is he frustrated in his bouts with the judges and
clerks in Chancery, but he is assailed by the cries of cooks, peddlers,
taverners—all of whom lose interest in him when they learn that he
has no money. When his hood is stolen, he cannot wait to return to
the plow. The bargeman who ferries him back is as mercenary as
the rest:

> Then I hied me on to Billingsgate,
> And one called out: "Ho, go we hence!"
> I prayed a bargeman, for God's sake,
> That he would spare me my expense.

"Thou scap'st not," quoth he, "under two pence.
'Tis not yet my will to do an almsdeed!"
Thus, lacking money, I could not speed.

The poet captures very effectively the clamor and excitement of the
city throngs, and he has an especially good ear for the cries of the
street hawkers. "Strawberries ripe!" "Cherries on the rise!" "Hot
sheep's feet!" All of these details are appropriately integrated with
his satiric intention.

Other Satirical Poems *

A good deal of minor satirical verse, which has been edited under
the convenient heading "historical poems," belongs mainly to the
fifteenth century and reflects by and large some of the themes already mentioned. *Money, Money!* resembles *London Lickpenny* in
its assertion that money rules the world—the court, the market place,
the chamber, and every other area of life:

Of whate degre so ever he be,
    Of werteouse [worthwhile] conyng [scholarship] he have,
And wante mone[y], yet men wyll sey,
    That he ys but a knave.

A poem with the refrain, "Huff! A Galaunt," heaps mockery upon
the court gentleman with his elegant hose, shoes, coiffure. The gal-
lant devotes himself to a life of utter recklessness:

Galaunt, by thy gyrdyl ther hangyth a purss;
Ther-in ys neyther peny ner crosse,
But iii dysse [dice], and crystys curse—
    Huff, a galawnt!

A poem written in 1419 recalls specifically the fifty-two follies (i.e.,
crimes) of the Duke of Burgundy, who had assassinated the Duke
of Orleans in 1407. There are several poems on the evil state of England, including the following, dated 1381 and quoted in its entirety:

Man be ware and be no fool:
Thenke apon the ax, and of the stool [block]!
The stool was hard, the ax was scharp,
The iiii yere of kyng Richard.

* Quotations from the poems in this section are from *Historical Poems of the
XIVth and XVth Centuries,* ed. Rossell Hope Robbins (New York: Columbia
University Press, 1959). Reprinted by permission of the publisher.

It is an age, according to another verse satire, in which virtue and truth are perverted, mercy is scorned, and riches are called worthiness:

> And thus for defaute of trewe techinge,
> men wenden [go] to helle by many weies.
> The joye of hevene men setten not bi,
> but al bi wordli [worldly] likinge.

The abuses of the age are admirably summarized in a poem identified by the title *Truth Is Unpopular*. If a man, the poet says, wishes to tell the truth, he had better stay out of ladies' chambers, the dwellings of lords, the courts of law—even out of church. Truth may be found in only one place:

> A man that shulde of trewthe aspyre,
> he must sekyn [seek] esylye [calmly]
> In the bosum of marye,
>   for there he is for-sothe.

XII: CHAUCER (c. 1340–1400): MINOR WORKS AND TROILUS

The greatest English poet of the Middle Ages was born into circumstances extremely well suited to the development of his extraordinary artistic sensibility. Geoffrey Chaucer's London hummed with commercial and intellectual activity, and its language, the East Midland dialect, was rich in potentialities. The poet's family was able to place him in the midst of the most fashionable society—a position numbering among its advantages regular access to books and vogues of the Continent. Moreover, Chaucer himself was blessed with a versatility matched in English literature only by Shakespeare's. While retaining all the high seriousness of medieval Christianity, he never sacrificed his lusty enthusiasm for the abundance of this life. Above all, Chaucer could appreciate people and write about them with compassion and with virtually unequaled humor. Before such prodigious creative energy one finds himself echoing the Restoration poet John Dryden: "Here is God's plenty."

CHAUCER'S LIFE AND LITERARY HERITAGE

While we know relatively little of Chaucer's life, his biography emerges with greater clarity than that of most other writers of his period. He was born around 1340, the son of John Chaucer, a wealthy London wine merchant with good court connections. The boy became a page in the household of the Earl of Ulster and gradually advanced to more responsible positions. We know for certain that Chaucer served in the French Wars and was taken prisoner in 1359 or 1360, part of his ransom being paid by the king himself, Edward III. In 1366, or earlier, Chaucer married Philippa Roet, then a lady in waiting to the queen and later a sister-in-law to the powerful John of Gaunt. With a comfortable annuity provided him, Chaucer rose in royal favor, and in 1367 he was sent abroad on a diplomatic mission. Subsequently, Chaucer visited Europe several times on official business: he was in Italy in 1372 and 1378, and in France in 1376 and 1377. From 1374 until 1386 the poet enjoyed a prosperous career as Comptroller of the Customs and Subsidies on Wool

Howe he þat deuoute was mayden marie
And lat his loue floure and fructifie

¶ Al-þogh his lyfe be queynt þe resemblaunce
Of him hath in me so fressh lyflynesse
Þat to putte othir men in remembraunce
Of his persone I haue heere his lyknesse
Do make to þis ende in sothfastnesse
Þat þei þt haue of him left þought & mynde
By þis peynture may ageyn him fynde

¶ The ymages þt in þe chirche been
Maken folk þenke on god & on his seyntes
Whan þe ymages þei be holden & seen
Were oft vnsyte of hem causith restreyntes
Of þoughtes gode whan a þing depeynt is
Or entrayled if men take of it heede
Thoght of þe lyknesse it wil in hym breede

¶ Þyt somme holden oppynyon and sey
Þat none ymages schuld y maked be
Þei erren foule & goon out of þe wey
Of trouth haue þei scant sensibilite
Passe ov'r þt now blessid trinite
Vppon my maistres soule mercy haue
ffor him lady eke þi mercy I craue

¶ More othir þing wolde y fayne speke & touche
Heere in þis booke but oþuch is my dulnesse
ffor þt al voyde and empty is my pouche
Þat al my lust is queynt wt heuynesse
And heuy spirit comaundeth stilnesse

for the port of London, and in 1385 he was named a justice of the peace for the county of Kent.

After representing Kent as a knight of the shire in the Parliament of 1386, Chaucer went into temporary retirement, probably in Greenwich. It is not clear whether this retirement was voluntary or whether it was necessitated by political developments—the eclipse of his patron Gaunt and the rise of Gaunt's brother, the Duke of Gloucester, to the position of court favorite. At any rate, Chaucer did not return to public life until 1389. By that time Gloucester had been murdered, Richard II had restored Gaunt's authority, and the poet's own financial situation had perhaps deteriorated to the point that he found it necessary to resume his political career. Chaucer was appointed Clerk of the King's Works in and around London, and two years later, in 1391, he became deputy forester in the royal park in Somerset.

Chaucer lived his last years pretty much in obscurity. During this time he continued as deputy forester and, presumably, devoted the bulk of his energies to *The Canterbury Tales,* which he never finished. After Henry IV, Gaunt's son, usurped the throne (1399), Chaucer petitioned him for money in a delightful poem, *The Complaint of Chaucer to His Purse;* and the new king quite naturally responded by granting an annuity and a generous pension to the esteemed poet who had been his father's loyal servant and friend. Chaucer died on October 25, 1400.

In Chaucer's very busy career as a man of affairs, poetry was inevitably a part-time activity. Nevertheless, his occupations at court provided him with a sophisticated audience, composed for the most part of lords and ladies who, as was previously suggested, maintained lively social and literary intercourse with the Continent, especially with France and Italy. And judging from the number of extant manuscripts of his poems—particularly *The Canterbury Tales,* which is found in some ninety complete or partial manuscripts—we have to assume that Chaucer's audience was by no means confined to the nobility.

One of the most conspicuous features of Chaucer's poetry is its indebtedness to Continental models. His output has, in fact, been conveniently—though not altogether accurately—assigned to three periods: the French (1359–72), Italian (1372–86), and English (1386–1400). Chaucer came early under the spell of French dream allegory, especially the extremely popular *Roman de la Rose,* a long poem which was to exert a lasting influence upon his verse. Italy offered him the examples of Dante and Petrarch, whom he acknowledged; he also drew heavily, but without acknowledgment, upon Boccaccio—most notably for the plots of *Troilus and Criseyde* and *The Knight's Tale*. It should be kept in mind, however, that in the Middle Ages, as well as in the Renaissance, a writer could borrow freely from either his predecessors or his contemporaries without incurring charges of plagiarism. Greek and Latin writers had regularly adapted or retold the same traditional myths of Troy and Thebes; and Shakespeare rarely invented an "original" plot (if there is such a thing). One's poetic reputation depended upon how he treated the subject and not upon where he found it. During the English period, to which much of *The Canterbury Tales* belongs, Chaucer concentrated to a large extent upon contemporary English life and manners. But as a distinguished student of the poet has observed, he kept accumulating his various experiences and "took with him into the English period all the lessons he had ever learned." *

CHAUCER'S "MINOR" WORKS

Troilus and Criseyde and *The Canterbury Tales* rank with the masterpieces of world literature. But even Chaucer's lesser works are rewarding—both in themselves and for the light they shed upon his mature accomplishment. Several of these works belong to a genre close to Chaucer's heart, the dream-vision.

The Romaunt of the Rose (Early)

Chaucer never divorced himself entirely from his first love, *Le Roman de la Rose*. That Chaucer translated the work into English he himself tells us in the Prologue to *The Legend of Good Women*, and part of the extant English version, a fragment in octosyllabic couplets, may be his.

In this celebrated poem, a lover tries to pluck the rose of love from an exquisite garden and receives advice along the way from various abstractions, such as Idleness, Mirth, and Danger (Disdain). The French poem was begun, about 1225, by Guillaume de Lorris and finished, about 1275, by Jean de Meun. The contrasting temperaments of these two men furnish an interesting clue to the enigma of

* George L. Kittredge, *Chaucer and His Poetry* (Cambridge, Mass.: Harvard University Press, 1915), p. 27.

Chaucer, who was sympathetic to both. Guillaume de Lorris wished to create a virtual encyclopedia of courtly love—serious, lush, extravagantly romantic. But Jean de Meun, perhaps with tongue in cheek, took a cynical tone towards love and women. The two strains run throughout Chaucer's works, and frequently Chaucer achieves comedy by presenting the romantic and the cynical attitudes side by side. Sometimes, as in the portrait of the Prioress in *The Canterbury Tales* or in *The Miller's Tale*, romantic material is lifted out of its usual context and used with satiric effect.

The Book of the Duchesse (1369–70)

The Book of the Duchesse, a dream-vision in octosyllabic couplets, is a lovely elegy upon the death of Blanche, Duchess of Lancaster and wife of John of Gaunt, Chaucer's friend and patron. Unable to sleep for thinking about love, the poet seeks diversion in Ovid's sad tale of Ceyx and Alcyone. He at last falls asleep and dreams of a splendid hunt that takes place on a bright May morning. Suddenly the dreamer comes across a mysterious Knight in Black (John of Gaunt). The Knight first recites a sorrowful lay (eleven lines rhyming *aabbaccdccd*) which alludes to a great bereavement; then he leads into a lengthy account of the progress of his love for Blanche, "so blysful a tresor" as was never before found in the world. In expertly controlled dialogue, and with remarkable economy, the Knight discloses that he has lost more than the dreamer can possibly know. The latter is puzzled:

> "Allas, sir, how? what may that be?"
> "She ys ded!" "Nay!" "Yis, be my trouthe!"
> "Is that youre los? Be God, hyt ys routhe [a pity]!" *
> (ll. 1308–10)

The dreamer awakens, looks again at the copy of Ovid in his hand, and decides to write a poem about his "queynt" dream.

Though filled with the ingredients of medieval French love poetry —the dream convention, the May setting, the personification of abstractions like Love and Nature—*The Book of the Duchesse* bears the stamp of Chaucer's genius. The poem has real structural unity with its three parallel griefs: the poet's unrequited love, the unhappy love of Ceyx and Alcyone, the tragic sorrow of the Knight in Black.

---

* All quotations from Chaucer are from *The Works of Geoffrey Chaucer,* 2nd edition, ed. F. N. Robinson (Boston: Houghton Mifflin Company, 1957). Reprinted by permission of the publisher.

There is humor, as when Juno's messenger runs to awaken Morpheus, the god of sleep, and has to blow a horn in his ear in order to rouse him. The Knight's grief is poignantly accentuated against the festive backdrop of the spring day and the hunt. The Duchess herself is portrayed as the embodiment of gracious womanhood, and her death is thereby made to seem especially tragic.

Much of the interest of *The Book of the Duchesse* derives from the artistry with which Chaucer develops the character of the dreamer. This traditional figure reveals a personality far more complex than that which the dream-vision normally encompasses. The dreamer's monosyllabic queries used to be regarded as a sign of obtuseness, a quality Chaucer frequently imputes to himself when he appears as a character in one of his own poems. More recently, however, scholars have begun to take a different view of the dreamer's intelligence. It has been cogently argued that the dreamer is actually a man of sympathy and tact, a good listener who feigns naïveté so that the Knight will have an opportunity to "talk out" his grief. One critic (see MEB 247) has advanced the interesting theory that the dreamer at first, understandably, takes the Knight in Black's sad lyric to be the fashionable complaint of a courtly lover, with all the customary exaggerations associated with this literary genre; it comes as a genuine surprise to the dreamer that the lady is in truth dead and that the Knight has not been indulging in fantasy. Chaucer's poem is thus seen as a skillful adaptation of the artificial love-vision to the purposes of authentic elegy, and one may hazard a further conjecture that Chaucer is concerned here with the aesthetic problem of expressing real sorrow through the traditional poetic vocabulary —in other words, of bridging the tremendous gap between feeling and form.

According to one newer interpretation (see MEB 249), *The Book of the Duchesse* is not merely a personal elegy but a kind of allegory in which Blanche symbolizes the virtues and ideals of courtly love which have departed the world. In any event, the poem has considerable charm—principally because it shows the youthful Chaucer, in characteristic fashion, putting conventional materials to unconventional uses.

The Hous of Fame (c. 1379)

In what may be (in point of time) Chaucer's second long poem, the dreamer is snatched away from earth by, of all things, a learned and garrulous eagle.* They soar heavenward towards the House of Fame, the place which all sounds ultimately reach, where the eagle promises his pupil "tydynges of Loves folk yf they be glade." The dreamer is also taken to the House of Rumor, a whirling structure infested with gossip and false report. As he is about to receive enlightenment concerning love from some unidentified "man of great authority," the manuscript abruptly ends. Whether Chaucer left it that way or whether the rest of the poem has been lost, we shall probably never know.

The poem (in octosyllabic couplets) is in three parts. The first, an echo of several French poets, includes a lush description of the Temple of Venus; it is made of glass and the walls are adorned with representations of the story of Dido and Aeneas, which Chaucer retells with due regard for its significance as a tale of tragic love. The second consists entirely of the flight through space with the golden eagle. In the third part we are in attendance at the House of Fame and the House of Rumor; huge mobs petition Fame for either renown or oblivion, and Fame grants or denies the various requests in a most arbitrary manner. Because the poem is incomplete, it is difficult to decide upon any over-all purpose behind its composition. Some scholars believe that the man of authority is about to announce the arrival in England of Richard II's bride, Anne of Bohemia. Others argue that *The Hous of Fame* was originally intended as a prologue to a group of love stories. Another school of critics stresses the autobiographical elements in the poem. It has been recently suggested (see MEB 251) that the poem deals with the relationship of fame to the mutability of the world and that the man of great authority is, appropriately, Boethius.

Whatever *The Hous of Fame* may mean in its totality, the dialogue with the eagle remains for many readers the most fascinating part of the work. The eagle calls the rotund Chaucer a "noyous [troublesome]" burden and reprimands his passenger for having experienced love only through reading and writing. Chaucer, the eagle charges, is such a bookworm that he has been deaf to the world, hearing "neyther that ne this." But the bird dryly adds that Chaucer merely pretends to live as a hermit; his "abstynence ys lyte [little]." The eagle proceeds to demonstrate his intellectual powers

---

* The eagle seems to have been a traditional medieval symbol of contemplation. See John M. Steadman, "Chaucer's Eagle: A Contemplative Symbol," *PMLA*, LXXV (1960), 153–59.

to Chaucer, who has no choice but to listen. The bird expounds an elaborate theory of sound and proudly asks Chaucer what he thinks of it. "A good persuasion," Chaucer answers; later he meditates, with a kind of unwitting pun, on the wisdom of Boethius,

> That writ, "A thought may flee so hye,
> Wyth fetheres of Philosophye,
> To passen everych element. . . ."
> (ll. 973–75)

This airborne interchange between the loquacious eagle and the terrified and bewildered poet is surely one of the great comic scenes in English literature.

The Parlement of Foules (1379–82?)

In *The Parlement of Foules*, a puzzling but richly amusing poem that is yet another dream-vision, Chaucer brings to life a memorable society of birds embroiled in a furious argument about courtly love. The poet, unsuccessful in love, turns for consolation to Cicero's *Somnium Scipionis*—a surprising choice because the *Somnium* is a severe work notoriously unsympathetic to love—and he falls asleep. Scipio Africanus, a character in the *Somnium,* appears to the dreaming poet and offers to conduct him to a garden where he will learn all about love. The serious Scipio is, of course, a superbly inappropriate guide for such an excursion. The gate to the garden (unlike the entrance to Dante's Inferno, after which it is modeled) bears *two* contrasting inscriptions, a shrewd indication of the ambiguity of love's rewards. One promises an eternity of "grene and lusty May" as it opens up "the way to al good aventure [chance]." The other leads "unto the mortal strokes of the spere/Of which Disdayn, and Daunger is the gyde."

In the garden itself it is St. Valentine's Day, when all birds gather in an assembly, presided over by the goddess Nature, to choose their mates. First to be mated is a female eagle of great nobility, and three noble male eagles make elaborate pleas for her hand. Their speeches are in the best courtly manner, full of glowing offers of eternal devotion and sweet entreaties for "merci" and "grace." The lower fowls, naturally, have no patience with this high-sounding language:

> "Com of! they criede, "allas ye wol us shende [ruin]!
> Whan shal youre cursede pletynge [pleading] have an ende?"
> (ll. 494–95)

A heated parliamentary debate follows until Nature, "the vicaire of the almighty Lord," restores order by urging the lady-eagle to choose the most gently born suitor. The bride-to-be is granted a year to make up her mind. Meanwhile, Nature bestows upon each bird in the assembly a mate suitable to its rank in the social hierarchy.

The poem has been interpreted as a personal or social allegory, perhaps referring to the betrothal of Richard II and Queen Anne. An exhaustive recent study (see MEB 253), drawing upon a vast background of medieval literary and philosophic tradition, sees the poem as a many-branched inquiry into the ambiguous, paradoxical nature of human love and its relation to human weal. At all events, Chaucer seems to present the ideal of courtly love and, at the same time, to expose that ideal to the relentless scrutiny of the realists. Chaucer does not necessarily take sides; he is content, at least for the time being, merely to offer us several essentially irreconcilable attitudes toward love and to exploit the comic possibilities of the situation.

The Parlement of Foules is of additional interest because it is Chaucer's first extended venture away from the somewhat monotonous rhythmical pattern of the octosyllabic couplet into the rich stanzaic form of *rhyme royal* (seven-line iambic pentameter stanzas, with the rhyme scheme *ababbcc*). Rhyme royal is the metrical form used in *Troilus and Criseyde* and in some of the tales of the Canterbury pilgrims.

The Legend of Good Women (*c. 1386*)

Chaucer himself reports that Queen Anne took personal offense at his portrait of the faithless Criseyde (to be discussed presently) and ordered the poet to write about exemplary women for a change. He accordingly started out to write a series of narratives about faithful women deceived by men, but for some reason, perhaps his lack of interest in the not very promising subject, Chaucer broke off near the end of the ninth story. *The Legend of Good Women* is a collection of short tales which, while inferior to Chaucer's best efforts, are nonetheless solidly constructed and often gracefully executed. His wronged heroines include Dido, Lucretia, Cleopatra, and Medea. There is excitement in the alliterative verse describing Antony's battles, tenderness in the rendering of Cleopatra's plight, and exuberance in the poet's resounding warning to Jason that he will broadcast to the world that foul hypocrite's shabby treatment of Medea: "Have at thee, Jason! now thyn horn is blowe!" The poem is also of great historical importance because it employs the heroic couplet for the first time in English poetry.

But the chief attraction of *The Legend of Good Women* is its high-spirited Prologue, in which Queen Alceste (Anne?) exacts from the dreaming Chaucer her peculiar kind of penance for *The Romaunt of the Rose* and *Troilus*.* When Chaucer sheepishly protests that he merely transcribed of Criseyde what he had found in his sources and that his purpose had really been to foster truth in love, the outraged Alceste is not appeased:

> And she answerde, "Lat be thyn arguynge,
> For Love ne wol nat countrepleted [disputed] be
> In ryght ne wrong; and lerne that at me!"
>   (F, ll. 475–77)

The Prologue abounds in Chaucerian irony. With staggering incongruity the god of love, expressing disapproval of Chaucer's heresies, cites as an authority for feminine virtue St. Jerome, a violent critic of women and of sexual love, whose writings played a major role in the development of the antifeminist literary tradition. Alceste begs for a lenient sentence for Chaucer on the grounds that, while he may not be much of a poet, he *has* done love some small service—at least among the "lewed folk," that is to say, the vulgar herd. The Prologue also contains passages of refined lyricism; in its fresh description of spring, the time when Zephirus and Flora

> Yaf [gave] to the floures, softe and tenderly,
> Hir swoote breth, and made hem for to sprede,
> As god and goddesse of the floury mede . . .
>   (F, ll. 172–75)

it anticipates the greater Prologue to *The Canterbury Tales*. And Chaucer's account of his joy in beholding the daisy—"day's eye"— at dawn and at evening is sheer magic. In the morning, when it opens its eye to the sun, he is up and walking in the meadow to feed upon the gorgeous whites and reds: "That blisful sighte softneth al my

---

* The Prologue was first written about 1385 and revised some time after 1394. Both versions exist, but scholars are not agreed on which came first. For a comparison of the two, with stimulating comments on Chaucer's method of working and revising, see Kemp Malone, *Chapters on Chaucer* (Baltimore: Johns Hopkins Press, 1951), pp. 80–99. The two versions are called "F" and "G" in the Robinson edition.

sorwe." At the end of the day he rushes to savor its beauty once again:

> And whan that hit ys eve, I renne blyve [quickly],
> As sone as evere the sonne gynneth weste,
> To seen this flour, how it wol go to reste,
> For fere of nyght, so hateth she derknesse.
> Hire chere is pleynly sprad in the brightnesse
> Of the sonne, for ther yt wol unclose.
> Allas, that I ne had Englyssh, ryme or prose,
> Suffisant this flour to preyse aryght!
>
> (F, ll. 60–67)

Short Poems

Sprinkled throughout Chaucer's career are some twenty short poems encompassing a variety of themes and metrical forms. The early *An A B C* is a free translation, in eight-line stanzas, of a French hymn to the Virgin; each of the 23 stanzas begins with a different letter of the English alphabet. The longer *Anelida and Arcite* (c. 1380), a 357-line fragment, includes a charming complaint of a wronged lady to her false lover; the poem is said to be Chaucer's most complicated metrical experiment. *Chaucer's Words unto Adam* (1386?), which consists of just one rhyme royal stanza, playfully threatens the scribe who has garbled the poet's manuscripts of *Troilus and Criseyde* and the translation of Boethius; the poem furnishes an interesting sidelight on the conditions of pre-Caxton book production, when works had to be copied by hand and errors were consequently frequent. *Merciles Beaute* (1390–93?) is made up of three roundels; in the first two Chaucer basks in the typical sentiments and rhetorical figures of the courtly lover, but in the third roundel he informs his lady, with superb impudence, that he and Love have stricken each other off their lists and that he has thrived since the separation:

> Sin I fro Love escaped am so fat,
> I never thenk to ben in his prison lene;
> Sin I am free, I counte him not a bene.

The Complaint of Venus (1391–94) is freely adapted from three ballades by the French poet Otes de Granson; after rehashing the conventional notions concerning love and jealousy, the aging Chaucer wearily deplores the scarcity of rhymes in English. In the celebrated

Complaint of Chaucer to His Purse (1399), a three-stanza ballade in rhyme royal addressed to Henry IV, the poet speaks engagingly to his empty purse, his "hertes stere [heart's steersman]," as a courtly lover might plead with his lady fair:

> For which unto your mercy thus I crye:
> Beth hevy ageyn, or elles mot I dye!

Chaucer's most moving short poem is the serious ballade *Truth: Balade de Bon Conseyl* (1386–90?). Drawing upon the philosophy of Boethius, the poet urges withdrawal from the turmoil of the world and emphasizes that men can liberate themselves only through strengthening their inner resources. The poem also calls to mind the ending of *The Canterbury Tales*. Life in this ballade is seen as a proving ground, a pilgrimage wherein men must put aside the world and journey to eternal blessedness—armed not with external goods but with the freedom that comes only from within:

> That thee is sent, reccyve in buxumnesse [submissively],
> The wrastling for this world axeth a fal.
> Her is non hoom, her nis but wildernesse:
> Forth, pilgrim, forth! Forth, beste, out of thy stal!
> Know thy contree, look up, thank God of al;
> Hold the heye wey, and lat thy gost [spirit] thee lede;
> And trouthe thee shal delivere, it is no drede [without doubt].

Prose

Chaucer also wrote prose, but it has more intellectual than literary interest. His translation of Boethius' *De Consolatione Philosophiae* (*c.* 1380–85) represents a milestone in the development of his mature philosophy. Boethius' great work, composed in prose and in verse while he was in a prison in Rome (he was executed in 524), was one of the books that Alfred the Great translated as part of his educational program for ninth-century Wessex; in a later age it was to be translated, or so the story goes, by Queen Elizabeth I. At any rate, Boethius was one of the most influential figures in medieval thought, for from his book were derived the customary doctrines concerning fortune, free will, and *gentilesse*. Chaucer's poems *Troilus and Criseyde, The Knight's Tale,* and *The Monk's Tale*—to cite only the most prominent examples—reflect the Boethian concepts of fortune and tragedy, about which more will be said later. Chaucer put even Boethius' verse passages into prose.

Two works attest to Chaucer's lively interest in science. In *The Treatise on the Astrolabe* (1391), a fragment translated from a Latin work by an eighth-century Arabian astronomer, Chaucer simplifies for a child (perhaps his son Lewis) the workings of an intricate scientific instrument that was used to measure the altitude of the heavenly bodies. The recently discovered *Equatorie of the Planetis* (1392), which has been ascribed to Chaucer (though his authorship has not been conclusively proved), also deals with the construction and operation of an astronomical instrument.

Finally, two of the tales of the Canterbury pilgrims are in prose: *The Tale of Melibee,* which is told by Chaucer himself, and *The Parson's Tale.* These will be discussed later.

TROILUS AND CRISEYDE (*c. 1385*)

Troilus and Criseyde, written in rhyme royal, is Chaucer's only complete long poem and his greatest sustained narrative. It has an intellectual and psychological range unprecedented in the English language and rarely equaled anywhere. That readers after almost six centuries still differ in their interpretations of Criseyde, as bewitching a heroine as Shakespeare's Cleopatra, is a tribute to the unfailing artistry of Chaucer's conception.

The source for *Troilus and Criseyde* is Boccaccio's *Il Filostrato,* a love poem dealing with familiar material from the Troy legend as popularized in the Middle Ages in the works of Benoît de Sainte-More and Guido delle Colonne. It has recently been tentatively suggested, however, that Chaucer may have been working directly from an intermediate book that had been derived from Boccaccio—*Le Roman de Troyle et de Criseida* (in French prose) by Beauvau, Seneschal of Anjou (see MEB 270). Whatever illumination future scholarship may shed upon this problem, it is at least clear that Chaucer preserves most of the essentials of Boccaccio's fully developed plot; it is equally clear that Chaucer's poem is superior to all previous treatments of the story.

Troilus and Criseyde is a love story set against the background of the Trojan War. Troilus, Hector's valiant brother, openly scoffs at love—until he catches his first glimpse of Criseyde, a lovely widow who has lived in Troy under Hector's protection ever since her father, Calchas, deserted the Trojans and joined the Greek camp. While Troilus suffers all the prescribed agonies of the courtly lover, his friend Pandarus, who is Criseyde's uncle, acts as a go-between. A series of cleverly executed moves by Pandarus finally unites the lovers. All goes well for several years until, in an exchange of prisoners, Criseyde is returned to the Greek camp. Although she has pledged herself eternally to Troilus and promised to come back at the first opportunity, Criseyde soon becomes the mistress of her Greek military escort, the "sudden" Diomede, who takes his pleasure where he finds it. Troilus, at last aware of the betrayal, dies in battle and ascends to the eighth sphere.* From this celestial vantage point he looks down upon the world and laughs.

Chaucer allows his story to unfold slowly and majestically through five long, unhurried books. This relaxed pace adds a spaciousness to the poem and enables the reader to savor each detailed turn in the narrative. There is time for sheer lyricism, as when the hero sings of the torments of love in an exquisite "Canticus Troili" (in Book I) translated from a sonnet of Petrarch. For perhaps the first time in English literature we are confronted with full-bodied scenes and fully realized characters. We witness charming interplays of personalities, as when the quick-witted Pandarus coaxes from the moping Troilus a letter for Criseyde, or when the spirited young widow, alternating between indifference and interest, nimbly parries her uncle's verbal thrusts. At one point Chaucer takes us to the dinner party Pandarus has arranged at the home of Deiphebus, Troilus' brother, and treats us to an evening that positively sparkles with the sophisticated conversation of Trojan high society. Other episodes linger in the memory: Criseyde's first glimpse from her window of Troilus riding back from the field of battle atop his bleeding horse, the ecstasy of the lovers' embrace, the pain of their parting, the sad but half-comic impatience with which Troilus waits at the walls of Troy for Criseyde's return. As the crowning glory, Chaucer has penetrated with rare psychological subtlety into Criseyde's mind and made her minute-by-minute fluctuations come dazzlingly alive.

By medieval standards Chaucer's *Troilus* is a tragedy, though it does not sustain a tone of deep sorrow. At the height of the hero's happiness Pandarus instructs him in the fundamental premise of

---

* In ancient and medieval astronomy the sun, stars, and planets were set in a series of concentric spheres or "heavens" which revolved around the earth and made a sublime music that man in his mortal state cannot hear. Troilus, in other words, has attained a new perspective denied him on earth. See Walter Clyde Curry, *Chaucer and the Mediaeval Sciences* (2nd ed.; New York: Barnes & Noble, Inc., 1960), pp. 245–49. (MEB 231.)

medieval tragedy as derived from Boethius. Tragedy, Pandarus warns, results when Fortune plays a trick and suddenly reduces the prosperous man to wretchedness:

> "For of fortunes sharpe adversitee
> The worst kynde of infortune is this,
> A man to han been in prosperitee,
> And it remembren whan it passed is. . . ."
>
> (III, ll. 1625–28)

Fortune for a while favors the young lovers, but in her typically capricious manner she spins her wheel, casts out Troilus from his lady's grace, and sets up Diomede. Because Fortune works without motive, no one can ever rest secure.

In harmony with the notion of Fortune's wheel is the great Christian theme of the poem, a theme that clearly emerges even though the setting and general orientation are pre-Christian. Pandarus advises Troilus that "worldly joie halt [holds] nought but by a wir [wire]." Troilus is finally made to understand that his affection for Criseyde has been misplaced. He looks down on "this litel spot of erthe" and cries out against the disruptive griefs and lusts of the world:

> And in hymself he lough right at the wo
> Of hem that wepten for his deth so faste;
> And dampned [damned] al oure werk that foloweth so
> The blynde lust, the which that may not laste,
> And sholden al oure herte on heven caste.
> And forth he wente, shortly for to telle,
> Ther as where Mercurye sorted hym to dwelle.
>
> (V, 1821–27)

If a man loves Christ, the only stable lover, he has no need for the imperfect shadows of love that the world offers:

> And loveth hym, the which that right for love
> Upon a crois oure soules for to beye,
> First starf [died] and roos, and sit in hevene above;
> For he nyl falsen no wight [man], dar I seye,
> That wol his herte al holly on him leye.
> And syn he best to love is, and most meke,
> What nedeth feynede loves for to seke?
>
> (V, 1842–48)

Troilus laughs, somewhat disdainfully, at the spectacle of human beings wasting their energies in what was later to be called "Vanity Fair."

But the intensely serious poet is at the same time the prince of comedy. Troilus also smiles in amusement—at himself, at Criseyde, at women in general, at the whole religion of courtly love at whose shrine he worshipped during the foolish days of his life on earth. One suspects that in portraying Troilus, Chaucer may have deliberately exaggerated the swoonings, the fevers, and the frenzies that are the standard equipment of the courtly lover. Pandarus, that elderly busybody (in Boccaccio's version, he is a gay young man, a cousin of the heroine), at times plays a role similar to that of the vulgar birds in *The Parlement of Foules*. As a spokesman for common sense he ridicules the lovesick Troilus unmercifully and assures him that "The town is ful of ladys al aboute." But Troilus, until his final attainment to Christian wisdom, idolizes Criseyde and is morally blinded by the infatuation. That Chaucer laughs at his hero seems to be borne out by the supersubtle distinction whereby Troilus demonstrates that Pandarus is a true friend, not a bawd. The bawd "gooth for gold or for richesse," but the true friend brings lovers to bed out of "gentilesse, compassioun, and felawship, and trist." One can only gasp when the innocent young lover offers in gratitude to bring Pandarus to bed with any of his fair sisters—Polyxena, Cassandra, even Helen. Pandarus may take his choice! Of course Chaucer writes within the framework of the courtly convention, but like all great poets he reserves the right to transform convention. Chaucer has the inimitable power of building a character or an ideology out of materials which, if we look closely, destroy the very structure they appear to reinforce. On one level, the level of Guillaume de Lorris, Chaucer simply reproduces to perfection the courtly code; on another level, the level of Jean de Meun and—more important—of Christian ethics, he damns the system and its devotees. As a thoroughly Christian poet Chaucer must see the courtly code as immoral.

Chaucer's ability to sustain simultaneously both a sympathetic and a critical attitude toward a single situation may account for the differences of opinion as to Criseyde's motivation. Is she merely "tendreherted, slyding of corage," a poor victim of unfortunate circumstances with whom many scholars have sympathized? Is she one of the casualties of war, tossed about by a fate too cruel for her frail nature to resist? Or is she a designing schemer, a strong and independent woman "who wants to yield to destiny—and then to put the blame on destiny"? * By the time Shakespeare wrote his great *Troilus and Cressida,* the heroine had pretty clearly degenerated into a camp follower, and Troilus' infatuation for her had become one more piece of evidence to support the thesis that nothing holds fashion but war and lechery. About Chaucer's Criseyde, however, there is more room for speculation. Does she really love Troilus? Does anybody know? Does Chaucer himself know?

In view of Chaucer's habit in the dream-visions of inventing a literary personality for himself, the narrator in *Troilus and Criseyde* can perhaps be kept separate from the poet Geoffrey Chaucer. The narrator, like the dreamer in a number of the early poems and the pilgrim "Chaucer" who goes to Canterbury, is a fictitious character— good-natured and enthusiastic, but extremely naïve. In *Troilus* this narrator blandly relates the facts of the story as they appear to his unquestioning mind or as they are relayed through the books that he says he is adapting. But the "authentic" Chaucer, poet and student of human nature *par excellence,* sits behind the scenes and looks beneath the surface of the narrative. What the "chronicler" sees with his partial vision need not, and does not, coincide with the mature inter-pretation placed upon the events by the "poet." This discrepancy is largely responsible for the unique irony which characterizes Chaucer at his best." †

"Chaucer the Chronicler" sees Criseyde much as he sees Troilus— an innocent victim of tragedy who wins his sympathetic tears. He *has* to forgive the poor thing "for routhe [pity]." After all, she wept *so* hard when she jilted Troilus:

> Ne me ne list this sely [innocent] womman chyde
> Forther than the storye wol devyse.
> Hire name, alas! is punysshed so wide
> That for hire gilt it oughte ynough suffise.

* Howard Patch, *On Rereading Chaucer* (Cambridge, Mass.: Harvard University Press, 1939), p. 79.

† See Sanford B. Meech, in *English Institute Essays* (New York: Columbia University Press, 1950); E. Talbot Donaldson, "Chaucer the Pilgrim," *PMLA,* LXIX (1954); Robert M. Jordan, "The Narrator in Chaucer's *Troilus,*" *English Literary History,* XXV (1958). The most complete examination of the uses of Chaucer's narrator may be found in Sanford B. Meech, *Design in Chaucer's 'Troilus'* (Syracuse: Syracuse University Press, 1959), pp. 370–85.

> And if I myghte excuse hire any wise,
> For she so sory was for hire untrouthe,
> Iwis, I wolde excuse hire yet for routhe.
> (V, 1093–99)

One critic has recently ventured the suggestion that the narrator, after starting out as a dispassionate scholar transcribing material found in some old books, eventually gets so taken with Criseyde that he falls in love with her and completely forgets to be objective about her behavior.* "Chaucer the Poet," on the other hand, has made Criseyde a not-unwilling accomplice in her own seduction. Criseyde early takes us into her confidence with a spirited defense of the freedom allowed her by widowhood. Is it not pleasant? No jealous or domineering husband to say "check mate." She can certainly have a little fun. "What, par dieux! I am naught religious." If only she is discreet! When her misty thoughts begin to clear, she commits herself to a calculated risk—nothing ventured, nothing gained:

> And seide, "He which that nothing undertaketh,
> Nothyng n'acheveth, be hym looth [hateful] or deere."
> (II, 807–8)

Diomede, it is worth pointing out, speaks the same language: "For he that naught n'asaieth, naught n'acheveth." The two are, indeed, well mated. On that fateful rainy night Pandarus invites her to his house, and Criseyde artfully asks whether Troilus will be there. Of *course* not, Pandarus reassures her. "Chaucer the Chronicler" professes that he does not know—his sources do not *say*—whether she believes Pandarus; "Chaucer the Poet" definitely implies that she does not believe him. So she goes, and by some strange coincidence Troilus is there, too. As she lies in Troilus' arms, the young hero asks Criseyde to yield to him. Her answer should dispel any notion of her innocence. She already has yielded, she tells Troilus; otherwise, she would never have come! "Fox that ye ben!" she chastises Pandarus on the morning after; but when her uncle with characteristic mock heroism offers his sword that she might smite off his wicked head, Criseyde is only too glad to forgive him. "And with here uncle gan to pleye. . . ." Pandarus is comic enough as it is with his colossal energy, his own tragicomic frustration in love, his inexhaustible fund

---

* E. Talbot Donaldson (ed.), *Chaucer's Poetry: An Anthology for Modern Readers* (New York: Ronald Press, 1958), pp. 966–67.

of well-worn proverbs, and his confident vitality. But the crowning touch is beautifully ironic: he has been forced to labor long and hard to mastermind a union which both parties ardently desired and would have made no serious move to impede. What a waste of effort! Pandarus is the real victim, not Criseyde.

When the mature Troilus, from his observation point in eternity, sees how ridiculously he has behaved, Chaucer drops the mask of irony and explicitly states his attitude:

> Swich fyn [end] hath, lo, this Troilus for love!
> Swich fyn hath all his grete worthynesse!
> Swich fyn hath his estat real above [more than royal estate],
> Swich fyn his lust, swich fyn hath his noblesse!
> Swich fyn hath false worldes brotelnesse!
> And thus bigan his lovyng of Criseyde,
> As I have told, and in this wise he deyde.   (V, 1828–34)

This renunciation of the little spot of earth is no tacked-on moral, but the determined Christian answer to the pagan and courtly values which Chaucer both utilizes and supplants; it is the destination toward which the poem, from its beginning, has constantly and inevitably moved. That Chaucer understands his frail characters and their brittle hopes, that he makes them believable, that in all the seriousness of his Christian faith he retains an unrivaled appreciation of the human comedy—all this is precisely what makes him so great. If Criseyde is the pathetic victim that many critics conceive her to be, it is not because she is deceived by Pandarus, Troilus, Diomede, or by a cruel world. It is because Chaucer sees her, like all her fellow human beings in the earthly Kingdom of Satan, as deceiving herself. This self-deception may be tragic, but in the hands of a Chaucer it can also be magnificently comic.

XIII: THE CANTERBURY TALES

We come again and again to the opening lines of the *General Prologue* to *The Canterbury Tales,* and each time the picture of returning spring, with its gentle breezes and life-giving rains, emerges with the freshness of a new discovery:

> Whan that Aprill with his [its] shoures soote [sweet]
> The droghte of March hath perced to the roote,
> And bathed every veyne [of the plants] in swich licour
> Of which vertu [by the power of which] engendred is the flour.

We feel, as one critic has pointed out, that Chaucer "is the first poet ever to have put this picture into words," * even though we know full well that the coming of spring is a perennial subject of poetry— classical, medieval, and modern. It is the time of year that tender shoots begin to grow and that "smale foweles maken melodye,/That slepen al the nyght with open ye [eye]." What a wonderful season for a journey, especially a pilgrimage to the shrine of a Christian martyr like St. Thomas à Becket in Canterbury. The setting is lovely, the purpose of the trip is entirely honorable (though some Wyclifites frowned upon pilgrimages as inciting to thievery and immorality), and the fellowship en route promises to be stimulating.

However it may have taken shape in Chaucer's mind, the idea of bringing together in a pilgrimage "by aventure [chance]" twenty-nine "sondry folk" representing a wide range of fourteenth-century English society was no less than inspired. For one thing, Chaucer could find an opportunity to use several stories he had perhaps written at various stages in his literary career. He could also make a comprehensive study of human beings, his favorite subject, both in isolation and in interaction with other human beings. Moreover, he could find the perfect vehicle for his special brand of irony. Chaucer himself could join the crowd in his customary literary pose of the genial but not very intelligent observer, and if the reactions of "Chaucer the

* Muriel Bowden, *A Commentary on the General Prologue to the Canterbury Tales* (New York: The Macmillan Company, 1948), p. 19.

Pilgrim" should not coincide with those of "Chaucer the Poet"—why, so much the better! *

Each pilgrim, according to the plan proposed by Harry Bailey, the hearty and vigorous host of the Tabard Inn (where the pilgrims meet), is supposed to tell two stories on the way to Canterbury and two stories on the way back. The teller of the best tale—Harry Bailey will be the judge—is to be rewarded at the end of the pilgrimage with a dinner at the Tabard provided by his fellow pilgrims. The *General Prologue* sets the scene and introduces the characters, but between many of the tales Chaucer provides links that enlarge upon the previously defined personalities of the pilgrims and thereby heighten the dramatic interest. There are a number of arguments—between the Reeve and the Miller, for example, and between the Summoner and the Friar—that prepare for subsequent tales. Sometimes a pilgrim introduces a tale with a commentary on his own personal life; frequently the impact of a tale is intensified by the reactions of the listeners after it has been completed. There are occasions when a pilgrim is cut off in the middle of a tale, a fate most amusingly visited upon "Chaucer the Pilgrim" himself. And Chaucer is full of surprises. At the end of the Second Nun's somber narrative of St. Cecilia, two newcomers, the Canon and his Yeoman, burst breathlessly upon the company. Their unexpected arrival, together with the Canon's equally unexpected departure, varies the narrative pace and sets the stage for the Canon's Yeoman's brisk report on one phase of English roguery.

Chaucer's (or Harry Bailey's) ambitious project was never completed, only twenty-four tales—less than a fourth—having come down to us. The tales, which display a number of verse forms (mainly the heroic couplet and rhyme royal), were probably composed at various times during the poet's busy life; and it is pleasant to imagine Chaucer himself reading some of them to his sophisticated friends at court, smiling as his listeners responded or failed to respond to his wonderful subtleties. But whether or not the tales were ever recited by Chaucer, the manuscript apparently did not circulate widely until after his death. The materials of *The Canterbury Tales* seem to have trickled out to scribes in sections, or "Groups," and the precise se-

---

* According to another interpretation, Chaucer the Pilgrim is not a credulous fool but (like Chaucer the Poet) an astute and playful observer who is thoroughly conscious of the irony in what he sees. See John M. Major, "The Personality of Chaucer the Pilgrim," *PMLA,* LXXV (1960), 160–62.

quence Chaucer may have had in mind for the groups cannot be clearly determined. Of the ninety or so complete or partial manuscripts of *The Canterbury Tales,* the famous Ellesmere MS has enjoyed the most authority. Scholars now generally feel that the Ellesmere MS, with the slight modifications proposed by Bradshaw, represents the nearest we can come to Chaucer's final intention.*

Although the problems have not been entirely solved, abundant riches await the reader of this unfinished masterpiece—a collection of tales so varied as to embrace almost every literary type known to the medieval world, and a gallery of characters, the pilgrims themselves and the figures who appear in the actual tales, so brilliantly realized that scholars have often been tempted to look for flesh-and-blood models in Chaucer's own England.

It is true that scholars have unearthed various fourteenth-century figures who may have inspired some of Chaucer's portraits in *The Canterbury Tales.* † The existence of a real Harry Bailey of Southwerk, an innkeeper at that, has been established; and a Madame Argentyne has been found in the records of a fourteenth-century convent—a nun whose name is sometimes considered to be the model for "Madame Eglentyne," the name of Chaucer's Prioress. Flesh-and-blood originals have also been suggested for other Canterbury pilgrims, with varying degrees of plausibility. Chaucer, to be sure, was an acute observer of people—a poet who, like all great creators of character, distilled his observations of human nature into art. There is doubtless some justification for looking for his sources among real people he may have known or heard of.

Yet some of the most telling details in Chaucer's characterizations are derived not so much from real people actually seen as from the rich mine of medieval literary, scientific, and religious thought and tradition. Chaucer could no doubt count upon his original audiences to bring to their reading of his poem a thorough knowledge of medi-

* See Robert A. Pratt, in *PMLA,* LXVI (1951), cited in the Bibliography (MEB 288). The "Bradshaw shift" would place Fragment VII (Group B^2 in the Robinson edition), consisting of *The Shipman's Tale* through *The Nun's Priest's Tale,* immediately after Fragment II (Group B^1), that is *The Man of Law's Tale.* For a lucid summary of the problems connected with the sequence of the tales, see William W. Lawrence, *Chaucer and the Canterbury Tales* (New York: Columbia University Press, 1950), pp. 90–118. (MEB 281.) Robinson's edition, which is followed here, adheres to the Ellesmere MS, without the "Bradshaw shift."

† See especially John M. Manly, *Some New Light on Chaucer* (New York: Henry Holt and Co., 1926).

eval romance, and much of the artistic effect depended upon their recognizing—in the portraits of the Prioress and of Alisoun (the young wife in *The Miller's Tale*), for example—the novel use he was making of the conventional description of the heroine of a romance. And although the Miller or the Pardoner may seem "real" enough, their natures become even more clearly understood when one studies their faces in the light of medieval ideas about physiognomy or when one evaluates their other physical attributes and accouterments against the background of medieval scriptural commentary and exegesis. In a word, Chaucer has put together a diversified and complex world, a world made up of elements chosen from the private experience of the poet as well as from the common intellectual legacy of his age. The portraits are at the same time conventional and individualized, "realistic" and idealized. Nearly every character is the *best* in something or other, even if it is only roguery. When the many ingredients are sifted through the intelligence, wisdom, and artistic sensibilities of a supreme genius, the result is one of the most rewarding literary adventures imaginable—*The Canterbury Tales*.

THE GENERAL PROLOGUE

After the opening *reverdie,* Chaucer assembles the pilgrims at the Tabard and promises to describe each one. Beginning the poem with a long, rhetorical sentence in the "high style" of the conventional (though fresh) description of spring, the poet gradually descends into the more "realistic" style of expository narrative. First we are in the world of classical myth, with Zephyrus, the west wind, recalling the earth to life. Before long, however, Chaucer abandons florid rhetoric in favor of simplicity, as he reminds us, with superb plainness, of St. Thomas à Becket's martyrdom:

> The hooly blisful martir for to seke,
> That hem hath holpen whan that they were seeke [sick].
> (Group A, ll. 17–18)

It is further characteristic of Chaucer's genius that the secular and the spiritual implications of the season become almost inextricable; * the birds are sleepless for love, and men decide that it would be good to go on a pilgrimage:

* See *Chaucer's Poetry: An Anthology for the Modern Reader,* ed. E. Talbot Donaldson (New York: Ronald Press, 1958), p. 876.

(So priketh hem [i.e., the birds] nature in hir corages [hearts];
Thanne longen folk to goon on pilgrimages.

(A, ll. 11–12)

With appropriate respect, Chaucer turns his attention first to the Knight and his entourage. The Knight is the quintessence of chivalry:

A Knyght ther was, and that a worthy man,
That fro the tyme that he first bigan
To riden out, he loved chivalrie,
Trouthe and honour, fredom [liberality] and curteisie.

(A, ll. 43–46)

This idealized hero has fought for Christianity in many major battles across Europe, from the Mediterranean to the Baltic; in fact, he comes to the pilgrimage straight from a military expedition. Yet he is modest in his bearing: "And of his port as meeke as is a mayde." Never has he said a villainous thing to anybody, of whatever social degree. Chaucer summarizes his fine qualities with memorable economy: "He was a verray [true], parfit gentil knyght." The Knight is also eminently sensible and, as we shall discover from his unusual tale, philosophical. His handsome son, the Squire, has curly hair and wears an elaborate costume that is embroidered like a meadow "Al ful of fresshe floures, whyte and reede." In the spring this ardent young man, who spends most of his time singing and playing the flute, sleeps no more than the "smale foweles" mentioned earlier; he is, after all, a lover:

So hoote he lovede that by nyghtertale
He sleep namoore than dooth a nyghtyngale.

(A, ll. 97–98)

Nevertheless, the Squire, for all his romantic excesses, is a dutiful son. The Knight's retinue is completed unostentatiously by a single servant, the Yeoman, attired in the conventional green of his class.

The ensuing ecclesiastical portraits of the Prioress, the Monk, and the Friar are, even for Chaucer, masterpieces of irony. Although Chaucer as unreflecting pilgrim admires them extravagantly, "Chaucer the Poet" knows that they distort in varying degrees the lofty spiritual ideals they are pledged to uphold.

The Prioress, Madame Eglentyne—the name itself smacks of the romances—is all woman. Her smile is "ful [very] symple and coy," her eyes are "greye [blue] as glas," and her mouth is small, soft, and red. "Chaucer the Pilgrim" may be smitten, but "Chaucer the Poet" expects his readers to smile; for these are the customary attributes of the beautiful heroines of medieval romance and are hardly what one should notice in a nun. Madame Eglentyne's greatest delight is to cultivate "curteisie":

> And peyned hir [took pains] to countrefete cheere [behavior]
> Of court, and to been estatlich [dignified] of manere.
>   (A, ll. 139–40)

The Prioress boasts elegant table manners: never does she let a morsel of food drop from her lips, and she handles gravy with particular aplomb. Now there is nothing wrong with good table manners, to be sure, but Chaucer has deliberately selected the details of the Prioress's decorous etiquette from a passage in *Le Roman de la Rose* in which an old woman, La Vieille, is tendering shrewd advice on how a girl can snare a man. The Prioress is very fond of her little dogs—she even feeds them roast meat and bread of the highest quality—but prioresses were expressly forbidden to keep pets. Although she cuts a handsome figure on the pilgrimage, it would appear that she should not really be going on a pilgrimage in the first place. All the things, in short, that the Prioress does so gracefully and for which "Chaucer the Pilgrim" can express only unqualified admiration, she has no business doing at all. In view of the striking femininity Chaucer endows her with, the reader may take ambiguously the *Amor vincit omnia* (Love conquers all things) inscribed on her brooch. The Prioress herself may be confused as to whether the motto refers to spiritual or secular love. True, the Prioress has found eloquent defenders, one of them an eminent twentieth-century scholar who brings to bear her own rich experience as a nun.* Nevertheless, one will always wonder just how gentle the satire really is in this unforgettable portrait.

The Monk, who rides out of his monastery (perhaps, or perhaps not, on official business), violates the rules of his order by hunting and by dressing and eating lavishly. For the texts which urge a monk to remain in his cloister, he does not give a plucked hen or an oyster. "Chaucer the Pilgrim" thinks this "manly man" is even worthy of being an abbott. "And I seyde his opinion was good." Why, after all, should this monk "studie and make hymselven wood [mad]" over books, or toil with his hands merely because Augustine prescribed

---

* See Sister Mary Madeleva, "Chaucer's Nuns," in *A Lost Language and Other Essays on Chaucer* (New York: Sheed & Ward, 1951). (MEB 221.)

physical labor for those in monastic orders? "How shal the world be served?" On one level the question sounds innocent enough: How does a cloistered monk do the world any service? But on another level it is precisely the wrong question to ask regarding a monk's responsibilities. The monk should serve God and not the world; he cannot, of course, win worldly success if he retires from the world, feeds only his soul, and neglects his material comforts. Chaucer's Monk is a fashion plate, with costly gray fur to trim his sleeves and an expensive gold pin to fasten his hood. He certainly is no ascetic pining away in penitent fasting:

> He was nat pale as a forpyned [tormented] goost.
> A fat swan loved he best of any roost.
>
> (A, ll. 205–6)

Hens, oysters, hares, fat swans, roasts—it is scarcely an accident that so much of the imagery in this portrait echoes the animal world or the gourmet's table. Chaucer, in fact, describes his Monk as one would a substantial piece of livestock: "He was a lord ful fat and in good poynt."

If the Prioress cannot fully comprehend her duties and if the Monk chooses to ignore his, the Friar, "a wantowne and a merye," completely overturns the exemplary moral standards of his ecclesiastical profession. St. Francis deliberately chose to go out among the poor and the sick, but Chaucer's Friar avoids "sicke lazars [lepers]" and "poraille [poor people]" and cultivates instead the friendship and hospitality of franklins, tavern-owners, and, of course, "faire wyves" and "yonge wommen." He is positively charming as a confessor, and why not? He does not require contrition and prayer, for he is less interested in true penitence than in collecting a nice fee for himself:

> Ful swetely herde he confessioun
> And plesaunt was his absolucioun:
> He was an esy man to yeve [give] penaunce,
> Ther as [whenever] he wiste to have a good pitaunce.
>
> (A, ll. 221–24)

The Friar's conduct appears still more reprehensible because in hearing confession and selling absolution he is actually interfering with the work of the parish priest and is degrading the penitential system of the Church. But "Chaucer the Pilgrim," so delightfully naïve, is all admiration for this "worthy lymytour [friar licensed to beg within a certain limit, or district]":

> And over al, ther as [whenever] profit sholde arise,
> Curteis he was and lowely of servyse.
> Ther nas no man nowher so vertuous.
> He was the beste beggere in his hous.
>
> (A, ll. 249–52)

"The beste beggere in his hous"! As was said before, nearly everyone "Chaucer the Pilgrim" meets on the way to Canterbury, whether saint or sinner, has arrived at the top in his chosen field.

The next few portraits, while not so detailed as those of the ecclesiastics, reveal much the same sort of Chaucerian irony. The Merchant is involved in "bargaynes" and in "chevyssaunce," ambiguous terms which apply to legitimate borrowing and lending and at the same time imply usury. He also traffics illegally in foreign exchange. He speaks solemnly, and upon only one subject: "th' encrees of his wynnyng," that is, his profits—but he says not a word about his debts. That he conceals them so well argues both for his business acumen and for his faulty management. Chaucer professes not to know his name, a fact which has been taken by some scholars to mean that the poet is exercising prudence. There is good artistic reason, however, for the Merchant's anonymity. Later on, after hearing the Clerk's story of Grisilde, the perfect wife, the Merchant bursts out in a totally unexpected and uncontrollable flood of cynical rage directed against his own wife and against marriage in general; then, just as suddenly, he withdraws again behind his customary mask.

The Clerk of Oxford—poor and, like his horse, underfed ("As leene was his hors as is a rake")—is an unworldly scholar whom Chaucer can simultaneously laugh at and admire. Rather than "robes riche," this earnest young man would have, at the head of his bed, "Twenty bookes, clad in blak or reed." He is a philosopher, but "Chaucer the Pilgrim" teasingly observes, in one of the stalest bromides of his day, that the philosopher's stone (an allusion to alchemy) does not seem to have brought him much gold. The Clerk, however, wins the poet's respect because he is destined for a virtuous career: "And gladly wolde he lerne and gladly teche."

The Sergeant of Law, though very busy, "semed bisier than he was." He knows all the legal precedents from the time of King William I, and this knowledge is directed almost exclusively to successful speculation in real estate. "So greet a purchasour [of land] was nowher noon." When he establishes a claim to a piece of property, nobody can find any loophole in his document—even though his title may rest on questionable grounds. He is, indeed, "war [prudent] and wys."

The Franklin, "Epicurus owene sone," feels that "pleyn delit" is the key to felicity, and his delight is measured according to the delicacies he brings to his table:

> His breed, his ale, was alwey after oon [uniformly good];
> A bettre envyned [stocked with wine] man was nowher noon.
> Withoute bake mete was nevere his hous
> Of fissh and flessh, and that so plentevous [plentiful],
> It snewed in his hous of mete and drynke,
> Of alle deyntees that men koude thynke.   (A, ll. 341–46)

The epitome of hospitality and of middle-class respectability, the Franklin presides over the sessions of the justices of the peace and frequently represents his county in Parliament as a knight of the shire (an office Chaucer himself once held).

The five guildsmen—a Haberdasher, a Carpenter, a Weaver, a Dyer, and a Tapestry-maker—all seem shapely enough to be aldermen and to sit on a dais in the guildhall. Their wives, who are not with them on the pilgrimage, would certainly have no objections to attaining such prestige; it is, after all, pleasant to be called "madame" and to ride first in guild festivals. The guildsmen have brought with them a Cook, who takes on a bit of ugly individuality—especially distressing in one of his vocation—by having a "mormal [running sore]" on his shin. Still and all, he is outstanding in the kitchen: "For blankmanger [creamed stew], that made he with the beste." Chaucer tells us that the Cook is an expert on London ale, an ambiguous tribute that may refer simultaneously to his discriminating taste and to his perpetual drunkenness.

The Shipman—here is another old joke characteristic of "Chaucer the Pilgrim"—rides a horse "as he kouthe," that is to say, as well as he can for a sailor. This "good felawe" (the phrase connotes rascality), it is implied, steals "many a draught of wyn" from aboard the ship from Bordeaux while the owner sleeps. He is long on bravery, but not at all gentle: "Of nyce conscience [tender feeling] took he no keep [heed]." When he fights and wins, he sends his foes home by water; in other words, he drowns his prisoners.

The "Doctour of Phisik," like most medieval physicians, is "grounded in astronomye [astrology]." Medical authorities he has read in abundance: Aesculapius, Dioscorides, Hippocrates, Galen,

Averroës—what an impressive roll call! And yet, the poet comments, "His studie was but litel on the Bible"—apparently a complaint frequently made against doctors in the Middle Ages. He gets rich on plagues and maintains a mutually profitable friendship with apothecaries, a subject for satire in Chaucer's day as now. Because gold (that is, the liquid *aurum potabile*) is a good medicine, the Physician is especially fond of it. As evidence of his wealth he wears handsome clothes lined with taffeta and fine silk. "And yet he was but esy of dispence [slow to spend money]." Chaucer skillfully parodies the dignified phrase which he had earlier applied to the Knight: "He was a verray [true], parfit praktisour."

Bypassing for the time being the incomparable Wife of Bath, we turn to the saintly Parson and Plowman. The Parson, whose tale brings the pilgrimage into a new perspective at the very end of the poem, may be poor in material possessions, but he is rich in holy thoughts and charitable works. He takes his ministry very seriously, for he feels that the good parson must teach primarily by the example of his own good life:

> This noble ensample to his sheep he yaf [gave],
> That first he wroghte, and afterward he taughte.
> Out of the gospel he tho [those] wordes caughte,
> And this figure he added eek [also] therto,
> That if gold ruste, what shal iren do?
>
> (A, ll. 496–500)

The Parson treats sinners with compassion, but he does not hesitate to rebuke the obstinate, be they rich or poor. The Plowman, "Lyvynge in pees and parfit charitee," is a devout laborer in the image of Piers Plowman.

In decisive contrast to the Parson and the Plowman, Chaucer next introduces some thoroughgoing scoundrels. The Miller is a "stout carl [fellow]" who can break down a door with his head. On his nose is a disfiguring wart capped by a tuft of hairs, "Reed as the brustles of a sowes erys [ears]"; his beard, too, is red. To a medieval audience this physiognomy would have suggested a man who is violent, lustful, and dishonest.* He knows all about "synne and harlotries [obscenities]" and boasts a vast repertoire of smutty stories, one of which he will later tell to his fellow pilgrims. The Miller is adept at stealing corn—he has a golden thumb—and he manages to collect his toll

---

* See Curry, *op. cit.*, pp. 71–90.

three times over from those tenants on his lord's manor who bring him grain to grind. The dishonest Manciple purchases supplies for a school of law. Is it not touching, "Chaucer the Pilgrim" asks, that God should grace so ignorant a lout with the ability to cheat the learned scholars? The Reeve, who acts as manager for an absentee landlord, is so clever a manipulator that no auditor on earth can catch him. The repulsive Summoner, his hideous face ravaged with the marks of leprosy and probably venereal disease, is a kind of under-sheriff empowered by the archdeacon to arrest those who were slated to be tried by ecclesiastical courts. He is "lecherous as a sparwe [sparrow]," quick to take bribes (sometimes in the form of sexual favors), and perfectly willing to engage in blackmail or bawdry. No need, he insists, for a Christian to fear the archdeacon's curse, for the soul of a man really resides in the purse: "Purse is the arch-deacon's hell." At this cynical remark even "Chaucer the Pilgrim" recoils in righteous indignation and lapses into a mature moral judgment: "Of cursyng oghte ech gilty man him drede." But in a masterful anticlimax accentuated by a ludicrous rhyme of which Gilbert and Sullivan might be proud, he quickly returns to his usual fatuous self:

> For curs wol slee [slay] right as assoillyng [absolution] savith,
> And also war hym of a *Significavit*.
>
> (A, ll. 661–62)

That is to say, the sinner should fear the terrors of eternal damnation—and watch out for the *Significavit*, the writ which turned an offender over to the civil courts.*

Most loathsome of all the Canterbury pilgrims is the Pardoner—an agent, in most cases a layman, empowered by the Church to grant temporal indulgences in exchange for a donation to some worthy charity. Chaucer's Pardoner allegedly represents the hospital of Rouncivale [Roncesvalles], in Spain, and his wallet is filled with pardons which he claims are "comen from Rome al hoot." A good part of his income is derived from a highly profitable business in "relics." He palms off a pillowcase as the veil of Our Lady, offers for sale as a guarantee of salvation a piece of cloth which—he says—is a fragment of St. Peter's sail, and dazzles even country parsons with his weird assortment of rocks and pigs' bones. Not only is he a eunuch,

---

* See E. Talbot Donaldson, "Chaucer the Pilgrim," *PMLA*, LXIX (1954), 933. (MEB 277.)

but Chaucer hints at a homosexual relationship between him and the Summoner. These two depraved creatures sing in duet a love song, "Com hider, love, to me!" The Pardoner's physical deformity may be taken as an outward sign of deeply ingrained spiritual deformity, for he perverts human love in the same manner that he perverts divine love. And yet, to give the devil his due, "He was in chirche a noble ecclesiaste" who can preach movingly (and profitably) against sin. We shall later be treated to a brilliant demonstration of his salesmanship: he will shock us with a full-bodied confession of his own wickedness, then follow it up with a powerful sermon and tale denouncing avarice.

This discussion of the Canterbury pilgrims will conclude, appropriately, with Chaucer's portrait of the Wife of Bath, who is the most original and complicated personality on the pilgrimage. With her robust sexuality she combines a desperate longing for security and power. Humorous yet pathetic, the Wife of Bath has taken five "housbondes at chirche dore"—not to mention "oother compaignye in youthe"—and is actively in the market for Number Six. She is "somdel [somewhat] deaf" as a result of a domestic tiff with Number Five, her favorite, the details of which are revealed in the Prologue to her own tale. Going on pilgrimages is one of her favorite pastimes, for reasons no less social than religious. Her religion is genuine, but note the impatience with which she always rushes to make her offering first at church; if anyone gets to the altar ahead of her, she is angered "out of alle charitee." Of course we laugh at her, for the Wife of Bath shares with Shakespeare's Falstaff high place among the comic figures in literature. But for all the flamboyance of her dress and behavior, there are (as with Falstaff) overtones of tragedy in this great character. These will be revealed as she unfolds her autobiography.

So much for the *General Prologue*. With unbelievable economy of expression Chaucer has evoked spring, collected his characters, familiarized us with their appearances and manners, and set the stage for their separate but frequently interdependent narratives. Some of the tales seem to have been perfectly tailored to fit the personalities and the backgrounds of the individual pilgrims who tell them; others may have been allotted with little or no attention paid to unifying the tales with their tellers. At all events, Harry Bailey draws lots, and, as a consequence, the privilege of telling the first tale falls to the Knight.

THE KNIGHT'S TALE

The Knight's Tale is a long chivalric romance adapted from a portion of Boccaccio's *Teseide,* an epic celebrating the career of Theseus, Duke of Athens. Two Theban knights, Palamon and Arcite, fall in love simultaneously with the fair Emelye, whom they see only from their prison window in Athens. Their lifelong friendship is immediately disrupted by their rivalry for Emelye. In time Arcite is released from prison on the condition that he never again, on pain of death, set foot in Athens, and years later Palamon manages to escape. The young men, now bitter antagonists, meet by chance in a grove near Athens and are about to fight when Theseus and his company interrupt them. After forgiving the knights for their past enmity to Athens, Theseus schedules a tournament, to be held in fifty weeks, for the hand of Emelye. Arcite wins the tournament, but scarcely has he had time to claim his fair prize when the malign planet Saturn causes him to fall from his horse and die shortly thereafter. Palamon then forgets his ill feelings toward Arcite and retires to Thebes, where he mourns his former friend. Several years later Theseus summons the disconsolate Palamon, who is still wearing black, and gives Emelye to him in marriage, thus making of two sorrows one "parfit joye, lastynge everemo."

If a reader turns to *The Knight's Tale* expecting to find a conventional romance, he will be disappointed. There is little action or conflict in this leisurely and very formal narrative and, except for Theseus, virtually no real characterization. Chaucer deliberately keeps his two rivals as undifferentiated from each other as possible, and he constantly shifts the narrative center from one to the other as if to guarantee that neither should receive a larger share of attention. The activities of the two knights are neatly balanced with an almost mathematical exactness. Both make speeches declaring their love, both curse their destiny, both pray to their respective gods — all this in rhetorical patterns that are astonishingly symmetrical. In terms of the story one could say that Palamon perhaps deserves Emelye more than Arcite does, for on the eve of the tournament Palamon prays to Venus, goddess of love, while Arcite prays to Mars, god of war. But the beautiful Emelye, as depersonalized a heroine as one could imagine, apparently has no interest in either Palamon or Arcite; *her* prayers are offered to Diana, goddess of chastity. The temples of all three of the major deities—Venus, Mars, and Diana—are deco-

rated, interestingly enough, not with scenes of pleasure or content-
ment, but with reproductions of unrest and violence. *The Knight's
Tale* does not celebrate love, war, or chastity.

Does it not seem odd that Palamon and Arcite should cancel a
lifelong friendship in a fiery debate over which one saw Emelye first
and loved her most? The debate is as absurd as the subtle arguments
in the courts of love which it may be parodying. Palamon actually
saw her first, but in a fantastic quibble Arcite claims that he himself
first loved Emelye as a *woman;* to Palamon she was a *goddess.* Before
Arcite's release from prison, an equally ludicrous courtly debate develops: Is it a worse agony to be free, like Arcite, yet banished from
the sight of the beloved? Or is it more painful to enjoy the sight of
the beloved, as Palamon does, from a place of hopeless confinement?
When Theseus finds the knights at each other's throat, he observes
with sober melancholy that men in love make utter fools of themselves:

> Now looketh, is nat that an heigh folye?
> Who may been a fool, but if he love?
> Bihoold, for Goddes sake that sit above,
> Se how they blede! be they noght wel arrayed?
>   (A, ll. 1798–1801)

This is how the god of love rewards her servants! And for Theseus,
as for us, the best joke of all is that the lady "for whom they han
[have] this jolitee" knows nothing about it:

> She woot namoore of al this hoote fare,
> By God, than woot a cokkow or an hare!
>   (A, ll. 1809–10)

Not even in the generally poignant account of Arcite's death does
Chaucer permit us to become emotionally involved. The cold of death
gradually spreads; Arcite prepares to enter the grave "Allone, withouten any compaignye," and with his last breath he whispers a plea
for courtly favors. "Mercy, Emelye!" But the Knight, with his characteristic detachment, has meanwhile injected a jarring note of levity
into his narrative: "Fare wel phisik! go ber the man to chirche!" And
where is Arcite going? Never having been there himself, the Knight
wryly declines to say. Palamon, Arcite, and Emelye have been counters in a game; the time-hallowed emotions of love and heroism are
viewed from a distant perspective that reduces them to triviality.

How, then, should one interpret this unorthodox but very great romance? The key is provided by Theseus in a speech out of Boethius. Before awarding Emelye to Palamon, Theseus justifies the turn of events by appealing to an immutable principle of order that underlies the universe and that always operates, even though we cannot immediately perceive it. The First Mover, he explains, created a chain of love whereby the four elements—fire, air, water, and earth—are kept within prescribed bounds. The Creator, whom the pre-Christian Theseus does not call God but Jupiter, is stable and eternal; but as one proceeds down the scale of creation through the planets toward the earth, he encounters an ever increasing degree of corruption and decay. All things of this earth being transitory, it is inevitable that men should be plagued with misfortunes. To complain is the height of futility, for in ways that transcend human understanding these reversals are ordained to happen by a just providence. Whatever comes his way man must accept ungrudgingly:

> Thanne is it wysdom, as it thynketh me,
> To maken vertu of necessitee,
> And take it weel that [what] we may nat eschue,
> And namely [particularly] that [what] to us alle is due.
>
> (A, ll. 3041–44)

It is foolish, then, to persist in fruitless mourning for Arcite, who, after all, met his end as well as any mortal man has a right to expect. Arcite departed with honor "Out of this foule prisoun of this lyf." Palamon's course becomes clear: let him forego his senseless mourning, thank Jupiter for granting him good fortune, and take Emelye for his wife. By accepting, on faith and without bitterness, the omnipotence and ultimate justice of the Unmoved Mover, men can triumph over the vicissitudes of fortune and learn, as Theseus and Chaucer's Knight have learned, that our earthly loves and hates are insignificant—in fact, they can be rather amusing. We are reminded of the enlightened Troilus smiling at the world from his celestial perch.

THE MILLER'S TALE

After the Knight has completed his philosophic romance, the Host invites the Monk to tell the next tale. But the Miller, so drunk that he totters upon his horse, rudely interrupts and insists on being heard right away. Both *The Miller's Tale* and *The Reeve's Tale*, which follows immediately as an answer to the Miller, are excursions into

the realistic middle-class world of the fabliaux. If these short tales of
sexual intrigue were not handled with such consummate art, we should
be quite right to follow Chaucer's own advice, "Turne over the leef
and chese another tale." In the two tales, however, Chaucer ties together the complicated threads of action and counteraction with
breath-taking clarity and economy.

The main action of *The Miller's Tale* involves the exorbitantly
elaborate strategy employed by "hende [handy, attractive] Nicholas," a poor scholar, in order to enjoy the "deerne [secret]" love of a
young wife, Alisoun. He convinces John the Carpenter, Alisoun's
jealous and blockheaded husband, that a deluge is on the way and
persuades him to prepare for it by climbing to the roof with three
tubs. John, Alisoun, and Nicholas, together with the tubs, await the
flood on the roof until the old man goes to sleep; then Nicholas and
Alisoun climb down and enjoy the "solas" of love. Meanwhile, the
parish clerk, an effeminate youth named Absolon, arrives at Alisoun's
window for a kiss; is victimized by a hilariously dirty practical joke
perpetrated by Alisoun; and, a bit later, takes his revenge by apply-
ing a hot colter (plowshare, borrowed from a smith) to Nicholas, who
has come to the window to have more fun at Absolon's expense.
When Nicholas cries out for water ("Help! water! water! help, for
Goddes herte!"), the carpenter awakens and believes that the deluge
has in truth arrived. He cuts the ropes that hold his tubs, falls to the
ground, and breaks his arm. Little does it avail poor John to explain that he had simply been waiting for Noah's flood, for the man
is obviously "wood [crazy]."

Only a virtuoso could carry off so intricate a narrative with such
speed and efficiency. Just as remarkable, however, is the vitality of
Chaucer's earthy characters. The young Alisoun, "gent and smal" as
any weasel (in ironic suggestion of the heroine of a romance), has a
"likerous [lecherous] ye" and moves with a healthy animalism:

> Wynsynge [skittish] she was, as is a joly colt,
> Long as a mast, and upright as a bolt.
>
> (A, ll. 3263–64)

Nicholas, the lusty scholar, repeats all the clichés of medieval romance. If she does not grant him "mercy," the "solas" of "deerne
love," he will "spille [die]." He is said to occupy a room in the carpenter's hostelry, "Allone, withouten any compaignye"—a phrase that
Chaucer had used in the more serious context of Arcite's lonely death

in *The Knight's Tale.* The practical John has no patience with scholars; proud of his ignorance, he remembers with glee the story of a scholar who was so busy gazing upon the stars that he fell into a marl-pit. Of particular interest is Absolon. He has curly golden hair, sings in a voice "gentil and smal," and sweetens his breath with licorice, cardamom, and clover. One of Chaucer's minor surprises is that this dainty clerk should be capable of executing so indelicate a revenge—a revenge, in fact, that he had planned for a lady. ·

There is some reliance in *The Miller's Tale* on the materials of the medieval mystery, or miracle, plays (to be discussed in Chapter XV). Absolon tries to impress Alisoun by playing Herod upon a high scaffold, Herod being one of the stormiest and most masculine roles in medieval drama; and Noah's flood, which figures so prominently in the plot, was traditionally a scene performed by the guild of carpenters. There is additional comedy in the fact that Chaucer, through the use of puns and *double-entendre*, makes each character in the tale behave in a manner contrary to his avowed religious beliefs. This irony, of which the Miller himself is of course totally unaware, provides the fabliau with a Christian background that subtly reinforces the triviality of the characters and their actions.*

THE REEVE'S TALE AND THE COOK'S TALE

On the heels of *The Miller's Tale* come two fabliaux of a similar nature—first *The Reeve's Tale*, a comic masterpiece; then the fragment known as *The Cook's Tale.*

The Reeve, who is himself a carpenter, takes offense at the Miller's story of a carpenter who is made a fool of and whose wife plays him false. He gets back at the Miller at once by making a miller the dupe in his own bawdy tale. The Reeve's miller, like the pilgrim miller, is thickset and brawny; he, too, is experienced at stealing grain. The miller of *The Reeve's Tale* takes pride in his wife's high lineage and fine breeding: she is the daughter, necessarily illegitimate, of a parson, and has been brought up in a nunnery. The wife, for her part, is intolerably haughty: "And she was proud, and peert as is a pye [magpie]." Alluding to her somewhat "smoterlich [besmirched]" reputation, Chaucer records in an unforgettable comic proverb that "She was as digne [proud, worthy] as water in a dich. . . ." As we might

* See Paul N. Siegel, "Comic Irony in *The Miller's Tale,*" *Boston University Studies in English,* IV (1960), 114–20.

expect, both are riding for a fall. The jealous miller is made a cuckold, the wife receives her comeuppance, and their daughter—whose honor they have been zealously guarding with a shrewd eye for its negotiability at the marriage market—is soiled. All this damage is adroitly engineered by two students, Aleyn and John, whom the miller has not only cheated but regarded with contempt (partly because they speak a northern dialect which the miller, a southerner, finds amusing). The denouement, in which Chaucer may be parodying the romantic convention of the *aubade,* or dawn-song (see MEB 299), involves a rollicking succession of mistaken beds.

The Cook, who is chaffed by Harry Bailey, begins a tale about a hosteler which promises to outdo its predecessors in bawdiness and intrigue. But Chaucer apparently saw fit to finish only some fifty-eight lines, perhaps feeling that three fabliaux in succession might prove monotonous. At any rate, we have no more than a sample of *The Cook's Tale.*

THE MAN OF LAW'S TALE

The fragment containing *The Man of Law's Tale,* with its Prologue and Epilogue, begins with the Host's admonishing the pilgrims that they are losing valuable time in their journey. He quotes Seneca and other philosophers to the effect that time is more precious than coffers of gold:

> "For 'los of catel may recovered be,
> But los of tyme shendeth [ruineth] us,' quod he.
> It wol nat come agayn, withouten drede [without doubt],
> Namoore than wole Malkynes maydenhede,
> Whan she hath lost it in hir wantownesse.
> Lat us nat mowlen [become moldy] thus in ydelnesse. . . ."
>
> (B¹, ll. 27–32)

Having added this ribald touch to the wisdom of the philosophers, Harry Bailey asks the Man of Law for a tale. The latter's introductory remarks deserve notice because in them Chaucer alludes to himself. The Man of Law says that he would be very happy to oblige, but every story he can think of has already been told, in an amateurish way, by Chaucer:

> "And if he have noght seyd hem, leve [dear] brother,
> In o [one] book, he hath seyd hem in another."
>
> (B¹, ll. 51–52)

There follows a brief summary of the stories that Chaucer had versified up to that time (1390?), including some of which we have no record in the Chaucer canon. Chaucer may have been indulging here in a private joke, perhaps allowing the Man of Law to credit him with some of the works of John Gower. At least, the Man of Law declares, Chaucer did not write tales of incest, such as those of Canace and Apollonius of Tyre (both of which appear in Gower's *Confessio Amantis*). This sly reference has been taken as a sign of friendly (or not so friendly) rivalry between the two poets. The upshot is that the Man of Law decides to leave rhyming to Chaucer and tell his own story in prose. That *The Man of Law's Tale* turns out to be in rhyme royal and not prose has been interpreted as an indication that Chaucer changed his original plans.

The Man of Law's Tale is based primarily upon the story of Constance as told in the *Anglo-Norman Chronicle* of Nicholas Trivet (*c.* 1335), though the legend is treated in the *Confessio Amantis* and seems to have been a favorite among many writers, both popular and literary. The heroine Custance (Constance), beautiful daughter of a Roman emperor, is betrothed to the Sultan of Syria and converts him to Christianity. She subsequently is made to suffer at the hands of numerous infidels. The Sultan's evil mother secretly arranges with a band of Saracens to have the wedding guests slaughtered and, in the Sultan's absence, casts her adrift on the high seas in a rudderless boat (a familiar motif of folklore and romance, e.g., *King Horn*). After Custance has landed in Northumbria, a Saxon knight, failing in his efforts to seduce her, commits a murder and plants the bloody knife behind her pillow in order to throw suspicion upon her. And although Alla, the virtuous King of Northumbria, marries Custance and accepts baptism, his mother, Donegild, forges letters declaring Custance to be an elf and her newborn son a horrible "feendly creature"; she later forges additional letters that order Custance's banishment from Britain. Through these afflictions, and many more, Custance remains patient, for she knows that her destiny rests with a benign God who will not forsake her. The whole tale, a strange blend of romance and saint's legend, is constructed upon a philosophic principle similar to that enunciated by Theseus in *The Knight's Tale* —namely, that whatever happens in this world, however reasonless it may seem in our eyes, happens according to the will of a divinity who governs the universe justly and according to plan. In *The Man of Law's Tale* the Boethian doctrine of necessity, with its repudiation of chance, is placed in an explicitly Christian context. *The Man of Law's Epilogue,* often printed as "The Shipman's Prologue," raises a score of problems. It is not certain that the passage was ever designed to follow *The Man of Law's Tale,* and the omission of the Epilogue entirely from the Ellesmere MS suggests that Chaucer, in the process of revising *The Canterbury Tales,* may have intended to cancel it altogether. At any rate, the Epilogue is distinguished by a somewhat angry exchange between Harry Bailey and the Parson, with a healthy assist from the Shipman (in some manuscripts the Summoner or, oddly enough, the Squire). When the Host calls upon "Sir Parisshe Prest" for a tale, "for Goddes bones," the latter objects to his swearing. At this, Harry Bailey accuses the Parson of being a follower of John Wyclif: " 'I smelle a Lollere [Lollard; see p. 126] in the wynd,' quod he." No doubt, the Host continues, the pilgrims are in for a hard time, in the form of a "predicacioun [sermon]":

> "This Lollere heer wil prechen us somwhat."
> "Nay, by my fader soule, that schal he nat!"
> Seyde the Shipman; "heer schal he nat preche;
> He schal no gospel glosen [explain] here ne teche."
> (B¹, ll. 1177–80)

Lest the serious Parson dampen everybody's spirits and sow "cokkel [tares, weeds] in our clene corn," the Shipman promises a rousing tale—and not of philosophy, he reassures the pilgrims. " 'Ther is but litel Latyn in my mawe [stomach]!' " Just what tale, if any, he is supposed to tell at this point, we cannot say; the present *Shipman's Tale* seems originally to have been written for a woman, in all likelihood the Wife of Bath.*

THE WIFE OF BATH'S PROLOGUE AND TALE

The Wife of Bath is in many ways the culmination of the medieval tradition (actually dating from classical times) of literature satirizing women, but the Prologue to her tale, as well as the tale itself, proceeds with an energy that pulverizes her would-be detractors. First the

---

* Donaldson (*Chaucer's Poetry: An Anthology for the Modern Reader,* p. 150) daringly substitutes "Wif of Bath" for "Shipman" in B¹, l. 1179 (quoted above) and leads right in to *The Wife of Bath's Prologue and Tale.* On the various theories bearing upon *The Man of Law's Epilogue,* see Robinson, 2nd ed., pp. 696–97.

Pardoner and later the Friar learn that it is dangerous to interrupt her. With the same ease that she employs to squelch these pilgrims who interfere with the unfolding of her autobiography (which, incidentally, is more than twice as long as the tale proper), she turns the age-old arguments against women inside out and triumphs over them even as she offers living proof of their validity. A remarkable woman indeed—one who, despite the coarseness revealed in almost every word she speaks, somehow manages to win our sympathies.

Everybody has of God some special gift; Solomon, for instance, was blessed with a large number of wives. The Wife of Bath's special gift happens to be lustiness. She simply must have a husband, and in a delicious parody of scholastic argument she justifies herself by appealing to two sources dear to the hearts of medieval logicians—authority and experience. The former she distorts with uncanny skill; the latter is a realm in which she has few, if any, equals. In citing authorities she asserts that "God bad us for to wexe and multiplye," and she is quite sure He never set limits on the permissible number of husbands. Solomon, everybody knows, was no monogamist. The Wife discusses virginity at length, attempting to undermine the theological arguments in favor of it. St. Paul *advised* virginity but did not *command* it. Without disparaging virginity, the Wife of Bath acknowledges that she is not one who cares to abstain. Not all the vessels in the household of a lord can be of gold. Did Christ, the source of perfection, bid *every* person sell all his goods and give to the poor? Of course not! He meant only those who wanted to live "parfitly":

> "And lordynges, by youre leve, that am nat I.
> I wol bistowe the flour of al myn age
> In the actes and in fruyt of mariage."
> (D, ll. 112–14)

She does not claim that barley bread is as pure as wheat bread:

> "And yet with barly-breed, Mark telle kan,
> Oure Lord Jhesu refresshed many a man."
> (D, ll. 145–46)

Her "instrument," then, she chooses to use in wifehood, "As frely as my Makere hath it sent."

So far, of course, the Wife of Bath is marvelously funny. But when she appeals to her abundant personal experience "To speke of wo that is in mariage," she ceases to be just humorous and begins to acquire pathetic, if not tragic, dimensions. As the "daughter" of Mars and Venus, she is endowed with the physical and emotional characteristics of both gods; she is constantly driven by amorous impulses over which she has no control:

> "For certes, I am al Venerien
> In feelynge, and myn herte is Marcien.
> Venus me yaf [gave] my lust, my likerousnesse,
> And Mars yaf me my sturdy hardynesse;
> Myn ascendent was Taur [Taurus], and Mars therinne.
> Allas! allas! that evere love was synne!
> I folwed ay myn inclinacioun
> By vertu of my constellacioun;
> That made me I koude noght withdrawe
> My chambre of Venus from a good felawe.
> Yet have I Martes mark upon my face,
> And also in another privee place."
>
> (D, ll. 609–20)

Mars being one of her ruling planets, it is inevitable that love, for the Wife of Bath, should resemble a military campaign.

With uncensored candor the Wife of Bath tells how she subjugated each of her five husbands. The first three—"goode men, and riche, and olde"—she took the measure of rather quickly; her chief weapons were a quick attack on their real or fictitious vices, a vivid depiction of the misconduct of which wives are capable should their husbands fail to supply them with gifts, and—particularly pleasant for her to remember—her enormous sexual appetite. No longer young, she nevertheless looks back at the fullness of her youth with pride rather than self-pity. She has lived to the hilt and will continue to do so:

> "But, Lord Crist! whan that it remembreth me
> Upon my yowthe, and on my jolitee,
> It tikleth me aboute myn herte roote.
> Unto this day it dooth myn herte boote [good]
> That I have had my world as in my tyme."
>
> (D, ll. 469–73)

"That I have had my world as in my tyme"—is there not something heroic in this summation of a life? And there are no tears; she will meet the future with the best that she has left:

> "But age, allas! that al wole envenyme [poison],
> Hath me biraft my beautee and my pith.
> Lat go, farewel! the devel go therwith!
> The flour is goon, ther is namoore to telle;
> The bren [bran, husks], as I best kan, now moste I selle;
> But yet to be right myrie wol I fonde.
> Now wol I tellen of my fourthe housbonde."
>
> (D, ll. 474–80)

It is characteristic of the Wife of Bath that she should quickly snap out of her philosophic reverie and get on with the story of her husbands. The fourth husband was a reveler, and it infuriated the good Wife that he should have a mistress. Her remedy in this case was to beat him to the punch and make him fry "in his owene grece" for anger and jealousy. He died, a conquered man, on her return from a pilgrimage to Jerusalem. But she remembers how at the bier of Number Four she was already casting an admiring eye at Number Five, a poor scholar, Jankyn, "Which that I took for love, and no richesse. . . ."

> "As help me God! whan that I saugh hym go
> After the beere, me thoughte he hadde a paire
> Of legges and of feet so clene and faire
> That al myn herte I yaf [gave] unto his hoold."
>
> (D, ll. 596–99)

Jankyn was twenty and she was forty, "But yet I hadde alwey a coltes tooth [a youthful appetite]." Her toughest adversary, this Jankyn spent all his time reading and quoting from his vast library of antifeminist writers, always regaling her with long recitations of historical and literary precedents for men brought to grief by women. Finally, to shut him up, she tore three pages from his book and smacked him so hard that he fell into the fireplace. He retaliated in kind, with a vigorous clout that permanently impaired her hearing in one ear. But, overcome with fear and remorse, he bent over her prostrate form and yielded up to her the management of his house, his land, his tongue, and his hand. Immediately she ordered him to burn his book, and from that moment on Jankyn and the Wife of Bath made a harmonious couple.

The Wife of Bath's Tale, which has analogues in Gower's Tale of Florent in the *Confessio Amantis* and in several ballads, is set in the days of King Arthur, when the land was filled with fairies and elves

—before the days, she says pointedly, when the fairies were crowded off the roads by the begging friars (the pilgrim friar had objected to her long Prologue). It is clear from her Prologue that the Wife of Bath, though valuing the pleasure and profit to be derived from men, actually holds men in contempt. This attitude is reflected in the "hero" of her tale—a brutal and faithless knight of Arthur's court. The knight rapes a maiden and is sentenced to die unless he can find out for the Queen "What thyng is it that wommen moost desiren." Far and wide he investigates, but he cannot discover two people who agree on an answer:

> Somme seyde wommen loven best richesse,
> Somme seyde honour, somme seyde jolynesse [wantonness],
> Somme riche array, somme seyden lust abedde,
> And oftetyme to be wydwe [widow] and wedde.
>
> (D, ll. 925–28)

Some say that women most desire flattery; others, the freedom to do whatever they like without reproof; still others maintain that women want most to have a reputation for wisdom and purity. Despairing of finding the solution, the knight stumbles upon a number of dancing ladies who mysteriously disappear, leaving behind only a wrinkled hag. On condition that he marry her, the hag whispers in his ear the answer. Back at Arthur's court, the knight announces what it is women most desire and wins acquittal:

> "Wommen desiren to have sovereynetee
> As wel over hir housbond as hir love,
> And for to been in maistrie hym above."
>
> (D, ll. 1038–40)

Mastery over the husband—exactly what the Wife of Bath had been preaching and exemplifying in her Prologue. The objectionable knight now tries to get out of his contract with the hag who saved his life; but he is forced to marry her. (Some listeners, the Wife of Bath interposes, may wonder why she omits a description of the wedding feast, that set piece in medieval romance. The Wife has a simple answer: "I say ther nas no joye ne feeste at al"; there was only "hevynesse and muche sorwe.") On their wedding night the hero upbraids his withered bride with her age, her ugliness, and her low birth. After lecturing him on a subject in which he could use some instruction, namely that true "gentillesse" is measured by virtuous living and not by noble birth, she offers him a choice: he may have her ugly and know that she is faithful, or he may have her young and beautiful and take his chances. His answer, from the Wife of Bath's point of view, is perfect:

> "My lady and my love, and wyf so deere,
> I put me in youre wise governance;
> Cheseth [choose] youreself which may be moost plesance,
> And moost honour to yow and me also.
> I do no fors [do not care] the wheither [whichever] of the two;
> For as yow liketh, it suffiseth me."
>
> (D, ll. 1230–35)

The hag has won the mastery over her husband, and, having gained the crucial point, she chooses to be both beautiful *and* good. For her, as for the Wife of Bath, marriage has been the means to security and power.

Because the Wife of Bath, in her Prologue and Tale, introduces the question of the proper relationship between husband and wife, scholars have detected in *The Canterbury Tales* a so-called "Marriage Group," consisting of *The Wife of Bath's Tale, The Clerk's Tale, The Merchant's Tale,* and *The Franklin's Tale.** Theoretically, of course, the "Marriage Group" could be enlarged, for marriage figures just as prominently in some of the tales that are not traditionally included in the group. But inasmuch as the tales in the "Marriage Group" follow more or less in sequence and address themselves specifically to the problem of "maistrye," it is instructive to examine together the different attitudes toward marriage expressed by the Wife of Bath, the Clerk, the Merchant, and the Franklin. Before anyone has a chance to answer the Wife of Bath, however, an argument develops between the Summoner and the Friar.

THE FRIAR'S TALE AND THE SUMMONER'S TALE

The feud between the Friar and the Summoner—the two callings must have had a history of mutual enmity—erupts quite unexpectedly at the end of the Wife of Bath's Prologue. After the Friar interrupts the Wife to comment, "This is a long preamble of a tale!" the Summoner exclaims that it is just like a friar to meddle in every-

---

* See George L. Kittredge, *Chaucer and His Poetry* (Cambridge, Mass.: Harvard University Press, 1915), pp. 185–211. (MEB 216.)

thing; a fly and a friar will fall in every dish. The Friar threatens to tell a story or two about a summoner; the Summoner counters with a threat to tell two or three good ones about friars. Harry Bailey intervenes to calm them down and orders them to let the Wife of Bath proceed with her tale. That formidable woman announces, with cutting politeness, that she is ready—"If I have licence of this worthy Frere." When she has finished, the Friar, who has been glowering at the Summoner, declares that he will tell a "game [joke]" about a summoner, of whom no good may be said:

> "A somonour is a rennere up and doun
> With mandementz [summonses] for fornicacioun,
> And is ybet [beaten] at every townes ende."
> (D, ll. 1283–85)

Again the Host tries to restore civility, but the Summoner says, let the Friar rave on; he will bide his time and get back later at that "flaterynge lymytour."

The Friar begins his tale—not without another interruption from the Summoner and another angry arbitration by the Host—an *exemplum* about a summoner and the Devil who, realizing the similarities of their professions, agree to divide their profits between them. (Both, after all, are out to get wealth no matter how.) When the summoner angers a poor widow by threatening to extort from her a new pan, she goes down upon her knees and consigns both pan and summoner to the Devil. The latter is delighted to bear away his winnings:

> "Now, brother," quod the devel, "be nat wrooth;
> Thy body and this panne been myne by right.
> Thou shalt with me to helle yet to-nyght,
> Where thou shalt knowen of oure privetee [private affairs]
> Moore than a maister of dyvynytee."
> (D, ll. 1634–38)

When the Friar has finished, the Summoner, quaking like an aspen leaf with rage, tells an anecdote about a friar who dreams of being in hell but is surprised at not seeing any friars there. At length they are revealed to him nesting by the thousands under Satan's tail. *The Summoner's Tale* proper is a longer dirty joke about a friar who has bled a poor man and his wife of everything they have. At last the man, ailing in bed, promises to give the friar a gift provided that he divide it equally among his twelve brethren. The gift turns out to be both obscene and indivisible. What gives the story its point is that the friar, who has been portrayed as a hypocrite with vast pretensions to scholarship, is more disturbed at his failure to solve the intellectual problem posed by the undistributable gift than he is by the humiliation entailed in the gift itself. Suffice it to say, a perfect solution *is* found—not by the conceited friar, but by a lowly squire carving meat at the table of the lord of the village. The dialogue in *The Summoner's Tale,* like that in *The Friar's Tale,* pulsates with the fresh rhythms of earthy, colloquial speech. Take the following passage in which the friar tells the sick man that he has just been in church, where he taught the congregation to be charitable:

> "And there I saugh oure dame,—a! where is she?"
> "Yond in the yerd I trowe that she be,"
>   Seyde this man, "and she wol come anon."
> "Ey, maister, welcome be ye, by Seint John!"
>   Seyde this wyf, "how fare ye, hertely?"
>   The frere ariseth up ful curteisly,
>   And hire embraceth in his armes narwe [tightly],
>   And kiste hire sweete, and chirketh as a sparwe
>   With his lyppes: "Dame," quod he, "right weel,
>   As he that is your servant every deel [bit],
>   Thanked be God, that yow yaf soule and lyf!
>   Yet saugh I nat this day so fair a wyf
>   In al the chirche, God so save me!"
> "Ye, God amende defautes [faults], sire," quod she.
> "Algates [by all means], welcome be ye, by my fey!"
> "Graunt mercy, dame, this have I founde alway. . . ."
>   (D, ll. 1797–1812)

Not only does Chaucer hear with a faultless ear, but he makes the dialogue contribute to the revelation of his characters—note the oily charm of the friar and the not entirely masked flirtatiousness of the wife. The whole exchange is conducted with dazzling speed.*

THE CLERK'S TALE

After the Friar and the Summoner have finished heaping abuse upon each other, the Host addresses the Clerk of Oxenford. "Ye

* The passage in question is ably analyzed by Bennett, *op. cit.,* p. 95.

ryde as coy [shy] and stille as dooth a mayde." Let him cheer up, forget his books for a while, and tell the company some merry adventure. But no fancy language!

> "Speketh so pleyn at this tyme, we yow preye,
> That we may understonde what ye seye."
>
> (E, ll. 19–20)

The Clerk obliges. Taking up the theme of marriage introduced by the Wife of Bath, he retells from Petrarch's Latin translation of a tale in Boccaccio's *Decameron* the story of the patient Grisilde, whose behavior runs completely counter to the Wife's notion of "maistrye." The Host need not have worried that the Clerk's learning would get in the way, for in spite of his running moralizing comments the Clerk tells his story (in rhyme royal) with a refined simplicity that would strike a responsive chord in the plainest of men.

The tale itself is far from "realistic." Walter, the Marquis of Saluces, in western Italy, takes in marriage the lovely Grisilde, daughter of a poor shepherd, Janicula. Although Grisilde has pledged complete obedience to her husband, Walter imposes a series of hideously cruel tests: he orders first the removal, and ostensibly the death, of her infant daughter; some seven years later he takes from her an infant son; after about five more years he suddenly announces that the pope has ordered him to discard Grisilde and marry another (he even forges papal bulls to that effect), and he augments the humiliation by calling Grisilde back from the poverty to which he has returned her in order that she might prepare the palace for the new bride (actually Grisilde's daughter, who had been brought up in Bologna by Walter's sister, the Countess of Panico). Even this Grisilde endures, assuring Walter of her infinite capacity to love him and to do his bidding:

> "Nat oonly, lord, that I am glad," quod she,
> "To doon youre lust, but I desire also
> Yow for to serve and plese in my degree
> Withouten feyntyng, and shal everemo;
> Ne nevere, for no wele ne no wo,
> Ne shal the goost [spirit] withinne myn herte stente [stop]
> To love yow best with al my trewe entente."
>
> (E, ll. 967–73)

At last convinced of Grisilde's constancy, Walter reveals that he has been merely testing her. He reunites her with her children, now twelve and seven years old, and takes her back as his wife. Quite touching is that joyous moment when Grisilde, weeping, embraces her children once again:

> "O tendre, o deere, o yonge children myne!
> Youre woful mooder wende [supposed] stedfastly
> That crueel houndes or som foul vermyne
> Hadde eten yow; but God, of his mercy,
> And youre benyngne fader tendrely
> Hath doon yow kept,"—and in that same stounde [moment]
> Al sodeynly she swapte [fell] adoun to grounde.
>
> (E, ll. 1093–99)

The Clerk concludes with the observation that there are few Grisildes in the world nowadays—with all deference to the Wife of Bath and "al hire secte" (may they live a long life "in heigh maistrie")—and, in an ironic Envoy, which he dedicates to the Wife of Bath, he advises present-day wives how they ought to behave toward their husbands:

> Ne dreed hem nat, doth hem no reverence,
> For though thyn housbonde armed be in maille,
> The arwes of thy crabbed eloquence
> Shal perce his brest, and eek [also] his aventaille [front or mouth-
> piece of a helmet].
> In jalousie I rede [advise] eek thou hym bynde,
> And thou shalt make hym couche [cower] as doth a quaille.
>
> (E, ll. 1201–6)

It is important in discussing this fine tale not to regard Walter, or even Grisilde, primarily as individuals. They both stand for a principle of order whereby the wife submits cheerfully to the authority of the husband. Whatever one may think of this principle in the twentieth century, it was sufficiently vital in Chaucer's time to have made Grisilde's conduct not only justifiable but morally obligatory. Walter as a person does not count; of course, as the Clerk implies, he is inhuman. But the principle of fidelity to a vow, such as the pledge of absolute obedience Grisilde had made to Walter, counts for everything. Moreover, as some critics have pointed out, it is not Grisilde's patience that stands out but her *constancy*, which is a positive virtue. One displays constancy to an ideal when he has taken full measure of the cost and made a choice; and Chaucer is very careful to make Grisilde aware of what her original choice and subsequent conduct imply. Only a character endowed with intelligent awareness could say, as she says,

> "I have noght had no part of children tweyne
> But first siknesse, and after, wo and peyne."
>
> (E, ll. 650–51)

And surely a wife possessing only the negative virtue of patience could not muster the strength to address her husband as Grisilde addresses Walter before his supposed second marriage. True enough, she wishes him well; but she also voices a warning and an eloquent plea:

> "O [one] thyng biseke I yow, and warne also,
> That ye ne prikke with no tormentynge
> This tendre mayden, as ye han doon mo [others];
> For she is fostred in hire norissynge [upbringing]
> Moore tendrely, and, to my supposynge,
> She koude nat adversitee endure
> As koude a povre fostred creature."
>
> (E, ll. 1037–43)

The Clerk's (and Chaucer's) attitude is complex. As Walter's social inferior Grisilde feels that she must accept marriage to him on any terms, but no husband should treat a wife the way Walter treats Grisilde. Given a husband like Walter, however, a wife must respect her husband's authority and remain firm to her marriage vows. Moreover, the obligation to respect a vow is not confined to social and domestic relationships. The whole medieval and Renaissance world was founded upon a hierarchy of authority and order—what Shakespeare's Ulysses, in *Troilus and Cressida* (I, iii), calls "degree," or "the specialty of rule." A wife, a sovereign, a subject, a planet, a part of the body—every animate and inanimate object in the universe must act in accordance with carefully defined responsibilities; otherwise, the world becomes chaos.*

THE MERCHANT'S TALE

After the Clerk has finished his tale, the Host remarks that he wishes his wife could have heard the story of Grisilde. At this point

---

* The present discussion of *The Clerk's Tale* is especially indebted to E. Talbot Donaldson's stimulating commentary; see his *Chaucer's Poetry*, pp. 917–20. (MEB 199.)

the Merchant, so adroit—we learned in the *General Prologue*—at concealing his business affairs, explodes in rage against women in general and against his own wife in particular:

> "Wepyng and waylyng, care and oother sorwe
> I knowe ynogh, on even and a-morwe [evening and morning],"
> Quod the Marchant, "and so doon other mo
> That wedded been."   (E, ll. 1213–16)

Only two months married, and already the Merchant is disgusted. Since he cannot possibly express the full extent of his wife's "hye malice," he declines to rehearse his personal misery in any detail. But he proceeds to tell a cynical story that lays bare his own sordid conception of married life.

In *The Merchant's Tale,* which has several analogues in European and Oriental fiction, the knight January, a sixty-year-old bachelor who has devoted his life to lechery, decides to take a young, lusty girl in marriage. Certainly, the Merchant interposes in a long, ironical passage, "To take a wyf it is a glorious thyng":

> . . . For who kan be so buxom [submissive] as a wyf?
> Who is so trewe, and eek [also] so cntentyf
> To kepe hym, syk and hool [healthy], as is his make [mate]?
> For wele or wo she wole hym nat forsake;
> She nys nat wery hym to love and serve,
> Thogh that he lye bedrede, til he sterve [die].
>   (E, ll. 1287–92)

Ignoring the advice of his one honest counselor, Justinus, who warns him of his folly, January proceeds to examine various candidates—eventually selecting May, a young maiden "Fulfild of alle beautee and plesaunce." After January has become blind, May—far from loving and nursing him—arranges to meet an old acquaintance, the young Damyan, in a pear tree for the purpose of enjoying his embraces. January's sight is miraculously restored by Pluto, "kyng of Fayerye," and Proserpyne just in time for him to behold the lovers committing adultery. May succeeds in persuading January that she only did it because she knew she could heal his blindness in that manner; furthermore, she assures him, he must have seen incorrectly. January, spiritually blind, though his physical sight is now unimpaired, accepts the ugly situation, caresses his adulterous wife, and leads her back dotingly to the palace.

The tale is steeped in the unhealthy irony of the Merchant himself, who plays upon the contrast between the romantic ideal and the revolting reality. Although January is carried away by "heigh fantasye" of himself as husband and lover, the picture of him on his wedding night is nothing short of grotesque. Filled with wines and spices calculated to increase his amatory powers, he kisses May frequently and rubs her tender face,

> With thikke brustles of his berd unsofte,
> Lyk to the skyn of hounfyssh [dogfish], sharp as brere [briar]. . . .
>
> (E, ll. 1824–25)

His slack skin meanwhile shakes about his lean neck, and he raises his voice in croaking song. Damyan is the ultimate debasement of the courtly lover. Chaucer has perhaps never been more crushing in his sarcasm than in his comment on the reason for May's physical surrender to this unscrupulous young squire: "Lo, pitee renneth soone in gentil herte!" The line had appeared in *The Knight's Tale* to characterize an act of real "gentillesse" on the part of the noble Theseus. In the context of *The Merchant's Tale,* where nobility suffocates, the line is a colossal mockery.*

Upon hearing this grim but fascinating tale, the Host, as we might expect, deplores May's "sleightes and subtilitees" and hopes fervently that he may be spared such a wife—though his own experience in matrimony would seem to bear out everything the Merchant has said of women. To clear the air he calls upon the romantic Squire to "sey somwhat of love."

THE SQUIRE'S TALE

The Squire starts to tell a long, elaborate romance, full of exotic elements. The tale is set in the court of the Tartar King Cambyuskan (Genghis Khan) and his daughter Canace. As the King entertains at his birthday feast, a stranger rides in with several wonderful gifts —a brass horse that may ride anywhere on earth and even soar through the air, a mirror in which one may discern the future or detect treachery, and a ring which confers upon the wearer the ability to hold discourse with the birds. But either Chaucer deliberately left the tale unfinished, or the final pages of the original manuscript have been lost. In the most extended episode Canace hears a falcon

---

* There have been recent attempts to read *The Merchant's Tale* as a Christian allegory. See MEB 307.

lamenting her experiences with a false-hearted lover and carries the bird home to ease its pain. Spenser treated the story (not too successfully) in Book IV of *The Faerie Queene*. The unfinished tale must have kindled the imagination of Milton, for in *Il Penseroso* he would summon Chaucer back to complete it:

> Or call up him that left half told
> The story of Cambuscan bold,
> Of Camball, and of Algarsife,
> And who had Canace to wife,
> That owned the virtuous ring and glass,
> And of the wondrous horse of brass
> On which the Tartar king did ride.

After some 670 lines, with the end nowhere in sight (according to the summary of future action provided in the tale itself), the Franklin commends the Squire and, a bit enviously, speaks of his own son who plays dice instead of living virtuously. The Franklin praises the Squire in the only language that he, a middle-class businessman, can appreciate: he would rather have a son like the Squire than twenty pounds' worth of land. If only *his* son could acquire "gentillesse." "Straw for youre gentillesse!" interrupts Harry Bailey. Let the Franklin tell his tale without any more words.

THE FRANKLIN'S TALE

The Franklin's Tale is a Breton lay—a short, good-natured romance set in Brittany and gently touched with the atmosphere of the supernatural. In Chaucer's beautifully constructed narrative, a young wife, Dorigen, impatiently wishes that the treacherous rocks on the coast of Brittany be taken away so that her husband Arveragus may come safely home from his knightly sojourn in Britain. Meanwhile, she is solicited by Aurelius, a standard courtly lover who for more than two years has been languishing in illicit, though unrequited, love. Dorigen, a loyal wife, rejects his advances, seeking to forestall him with the half-playful and half-angry promise to give herself to him only if he clears the coast of Brittany of those terrible rocks. The promise boomerangs, however, when a young scholar-magician is engaged by Aurelius to remove the rocks—at any rate, he creates the illusion that the rocks have disappeared. What is the poor girl to do? Just what a respectable middle-class wife (*not* a romantic heroine) would do: she talks it over with her husband. Arveragus, without anger, assures her that a contract is a contract: " 'Trouthe is the hyeste thyng that man may kepe. . . .' " He therefore sends her to Aurelius lest she be guilty of breaking her word. Aurelius takes pity and, inspired by the gentle example of Arveragus, releases Dorigen from the agreement:

> Thus kan a squier doon a gentil dede
> As wel as kan a knyght, withouten drede [doubt].
>
> (F, ll. 1543–44)

The magician, who will not have it said that a scholar is incapable of "a gentil dede," refuses to claim his fee of Aurelius. The Franklin concludes with a nice little puzzle: "Which was the mooste fre [generous], as thynketh yow?" This is the kind of question the courts of love delighted to debate.

In *The Franklin's Tale* the happy marriage has replaced the adulterous code of courtly love, and mutual respect between husband and wife has driven away any notion of sovereignty in marriage. In a union built on love and understanding, such as that of Arveragus and Dorigen, neither party can be master:

> Love wol nat been constreyned by maistrye.
> Whan maistrie comth, the God of Love anon
> Beteth his wynges, and farewel, he is gon!
>
> (F, ll. 764–66)

The Franklin has struck a balance between the one-sided and highly individualized views of marriage expressed by the Wife of Bath, the Clerk, and the Merchant. Whether right or wrong, its essence is compromise, give-and-take—virtues that we are not surprised to find embodying the moral wisdom of a man like the Franklin.

The character of Dorigen has given rise to some pleasant speculation. It has been suggested by several critics that her resentment against the rocks constitutes a dissatisfaction, innocent enough but typically feminine, with the immutable order of things as decreed by God. What right, after all, does *she* have to be annoyed with God for creating "thise grisly feendly rokkes blake" and to think that she could have managed things better had she been the creator of the universe? Be that as it may, we cannot judge Dorigen harshly; she is a thoroughly delightful heroine in one of Chaucer's most enjoyable tales.

THE PHYSICIAN'S TALE

The Physician, whose tale introduces Fragment VI (Group C), retells an old Roman story, found in Livy and utilized both in *Le Roman de la Rose* and in Gower's *Confessio Amantis,* about Virginius and Virginia. Appius, a corrupt judge, perverts his high office in order to satisfy his lust for Virginia, a maiden of unassailable virtue. Virginia's father, Virginius, rather than see his daughter defiled, kills her himself. Subsequently, Appius and his wicked accomplices are punished. This "pitous" tale (not one of Chaucer's best) having been completed, the Host requires either a drink or a "myrie tale" to cheer him up. He accordingly turns to the Pardoner, hoping, no doubt, to hear something mirthful. But other pilgrims, probably expecting the worst of the Pardoner, insist that he tell "no ribaudye." They want to hear "som moral thyng," and the Pardoner will oblige just as soon as he has had a drink.

THE PARDONER'S PROLOGUE AND TALE

Without warning the Pardoner launches into a cynical confession that reveals his depravity even as it holds his listeners (and readers) spellbound. Taking the pilgrims into his confidence, he shamelessly describes, step by step, the techniques he employs in church to extort money from his audience. After showing his credentials, he stirs the congregation to devotion with a few Latin words and then follows up with a parade of relics, some of which he guarantees to cure a husband of jealousy even though the man may know for a fact that his wife has enjoyed the embraces of two or three priests. What a figure he cuts as he stands in the pulpit preparing to cast his spell!

> "I stonde lyk a clerk in my pulpet,
> And whan the lewed peple is doun yset,
> I preche so as ye han herd bifoore,
> And telle an hundred false japes [jokes] moore.
> Thanne peyne I me to strecche forth the nekke,
> And est and west upon the peple I bekke,
> As dooth a dowve sittynge on a berne [barn].
> Myne handes and my tonge goon so yerne [lively]
> That it is joye to se my bisynesse."
>
> (C, ll. 391–99)

He preaches invariably on one theme, *Radix malorum est Cupiditas*
(The root of all evils is Avarice), a pretty sermon issuing from the
lips of one of the most avaricious characters in literature. The Pardoner does not conceal his intentions when he addresses the Canterbury pilgrims; all he cares about, he tells them, is satisfying his own
"coveityse [covetousness]":

> "Of avarice and of swich cursednesse
> Is al my prechyng, for to make hem free [generous]
> To yeven [give] hir pens, and namely unto me.
> For myn entente is nat but for to wynne,
> And nothyng for correccioun of synne.
> I rekke [care] nevere, whan that they been beryed,
> Though that hir soules goon a-blakeberyed [blackberrying, i.e., to
>   hell]!"
>
>   (C. ll. 400–6)

Of course the Pardoner could make baskets or live by some other
honest means, but why should he willfully choose poverty when he
can preach so profitably? He has expensive tastes; he must have
money, wool, cheese, wheat—even if it means bleeding the children
of the poorest widow in a village:

> "Nay, I wol drynke licour of the vyne,
> And have a joly wenche in every toun."
>   (C, ll. 452–53)

Though freely admitting that he is "a ful vicious man," the Pardoner prides himself in his marvelous abilities as a storyteller. To
carry out his frauds successfully, he habitually entertains his listeners with *exempla*—moralized tales devised, in his case, to aid the
sale of pardons and relics. *The Pardoner's Tale*, the sample *exemplum* Chaucer puts into his mouth, is a dramatic story illustrating
the consequences of avarice: *Radix malorum est Cupiditas*. The tale,
set in Flanders, begins in a tavern with a scene of prodigious debauchery—a nightmare of rioting, gambling, swearing, drunkenness,
gluttony, and lechery. After seizing our imaginations with this brief
but lurid tavern scene, Chaucer daringly reverses the usual procedure
by allowing a sermon to grow out of a tale. The Pardoner suspends
his narrative in order to deliver a vivid sermon condemning the vices
he has just described, but, characteristically, he garnishes his sermon with colorful details of the very sins he preaches against.
    When the narrative resumes, the Pardoner focuses upon three

young men in the tavern whose drunken revelry is suddenly cut short by the ominous clinking of a funeral bell. With a furious oath they resolve to find Death and kill him. The search takes them to an old man, all wrapped up except for his face, and the old man tells them, under compulsion, that he has just seen Death under an oak tree. What they find under the tree, however, is a heap of gold florins. To celebrate their good fortune, the youngest of the three is sent into town for bread and wine. When he returns, he is set upon and killed by the other two, greedy for a bigger share of the treasure; they, in turn, toast their still greater fortune with the wine which, in his own greed, the youngest has poisoned. The three men have indeed destroyed themselves through their *cupiditas*.

The Pardoner's Tale is enmeshed in some of Chaucer's most extraordinary ironies. The young men are eager to live and fated to die; the old man is unable to die, yet is sick of life. " 'Why lyvestow so longe in so greet age?' " the proudest of the rioters impudently demands. The old man answers that he has been unable to find in the course of his wanderings anybody willing to exchange youth for age. He is therefore doomed to walk the earth until God chooses to take him:

> "Ne Deeth, allas! ne wol nat han my lyf
> Thus walke I, lyk a restelees kaityf [captive],
> And on the ground, which is my moodres gate,
> I knokke with my staf, bothe erly and late,
> And seye 'Leeve [dear] mooder, leet me in!
> Lo how I vanysshe, flessh, and blood, and skyn!
> Allas! whan shul my bones been at reste?' "
> (C, ll. 727–33)

The very gold that the young men think has been granted them as a sign of life turns out to be the instrument of their death; thus, they meet Death after abandoning their bizarre search for him and resolving to live. Death is frequently personified in medieval literature, but seldom has he been pursued, literally, with such intensity. It is superbly ironic, then, that in *The Pardoner's Tale* Death should turn out to be not a simple personification after all, but the subtle and unlooked-for outcome of man's own avarice.*

---

* This discussion of *The Pardoner's Tale* incorporates some of the perceptive commentary of John Speirs, in *The Age of Chaucer*, ed. Boris Ford (Pelican Guide to English Literature), 1954, I, 109–17. (MEB 2.) On some recent attempts to interpret the Pardoner and his tale against a theological background, see Robinson, 2nd ed., *op. cit.*, p. 729.

When he has finished his haunting story, the Pardoner—acting from force of habit or from sheer brazenness, or else, perhaps, genuinely carried away by the emotions he has generated—tries to do business in relics and pardons with the Canterbury pilgrims. But he makes the tactical error of first approaching the virile Host, a man especially likely to be repelled by the degenerate Pardoner. Harry Bailey recoils with a vulgar allusion to the Pardoner's sexual abnormalities which all the boasting about jolly wenches has been unable to conceal. And the spell is broken. This, perhaps, is the crowning irony: the Pardoner, despite the fact that he has just rendered a great performance, does not collect a penny from the pilgrims. The transition from the elevated horror of the tale to the rude reality of the Pardoner's failure—failure as a swindler and as a man—is managed with incredible brilliance.

THE SHIPMAN'S TALE

Some of the problems posed by *The Shipman's Tale* were raised earlier in connection with *The Man of Law's Epilogue:* Fragment VII (Group B²), which *The Shipman's Tale* introduces, may have been meant to follow *The Man of Law's Tale;* and *The Shipman's Tale* itself seems originally to have been assigned to the Wife of Bath and, later, transferred to the Shipman. The latter theory is based upon the assumption that Chaucer left unrevised some lines near the beginning of the tale that presuppose a feminine speaker. The lines, eleven in all, begin as follows:

The sely [poor, innocent] housbonde, algate [always] he moot [must] paye,
He moot us clothe, and he moot us arraye,
Al for his owene worshipe richely,
In which array we daunce jolily. (B², ll. 1201–4)

The Shipman's Tale, a fabliau, would certainly fit the personality of the Wife of Bath. A merchant's wife, in need of one hundred franks to pay for apparel which she has secured without her husband's knowledge, explains her plight to a young monk, Daun John, a frequent visitor to the house. The monk borrows the hundred franks from the merchant himself and, in the latter's absence, transfers the sum to the wife in exchange for her sexual favors. When the merchant, returning from his profitable business excursion, learns

from the monk that the debt has been paid, he upbraids his wife for
not having informed him of the fact. In a speech which (like much
else in the story) abounds in *double-entendre,* the merchant's wife
insists that she thought the money was a gift for the "beele cheere,"
the good treatment the monk has so often enjoyed in the house—
thanks to the merchant. She promises to repay her husband regularly
in her own way:

> "Ye han [have] mo slakkere [slower] dettours than am I!
> For I wol paye yow wel and redily
> Fro day to day, and if so be I faille,
> I am youre wyf; score it upon my taille [score it on my tally; i.e.,
> charge it to my account]. . . ."
>
> (B², ll. 1603–6)

The merchant, none the wiser, is satisfied. Here, again, is one of the
motifs associated with the Wife of Bath—the equation of marriage
and conjugal love with financial gain.

THE PRIORESS'S TALE

Harry Bailey is delighted with the lusty tale told by the Shipman,
and he voices his approval in his characteristically earthy manner.
Then he turns with inordinate, almost satiric, politeness—"As cur-
teisly as it had been a mayde"—to "My lady Prioresse, by youre
leve," and requests a tale, "if so were that ye wolde." She obliges
with a tale in honor of the Virgin Mary, introduced by a prayer of
exquisite beauty imploring the Virgin to guide her song. *The Prioress's Tale* is about a widow's seven-year-old son, who regularly sings
Alma redemptoris to the Virgin as he passes through the Jewish
section of the city. One day the Jews cut his throat and cast him
into a privy, or "wardrobe," to use the Prioress's own dainty euphe-
mism. The child continues to sing, however, thus enabling Christians
to discover his body and remove it. After honoring the boy with a
great procession, they have the guilty Jews hanged. Only when a
monk removes from the boy's tongue a grain placed there by the
Virgin does the little martyr give up the ghost. The Prioress concludes with a reference to young Hugh of Lincoln, of ballad fame,
who was also said to have been slain by Jews.

It is difficult to know what to make of *The Prioress's Tale.* Unlike
similar medieval miracles of the Virgin, this one does not restore

the boy to life; nor does it even convert the Jews to Christianity (like the miracle in the *Croxton Play of the Sacrament,* discussed in Chapter XV). It accomplishes merely the negative object of destroying the boy's murderers. Even after allowance has been made for the strong anti-Jewish feeling that permeated Christian thought in Chaucer's age—a feeling grounded in religious, not racial, issues— the tale seems surprisingly vindictive. And if one recalls from the *General Prologue* that Madame Eglentyne was all "conscience and tendre herte," a gentle soul "so charitable and so pitous" that she would weep if she saw a mouse caught in a trap or if one of her little dogs died or was beaten—then her attitude toward the Jews seems even less humane. To call *The Prioress's Tale* a satire, as some have done, is probably going too far, though implicit in the tale—and perhaps more so in the *General Prologue*—is a measure of criticism leveled against exaggerated and somewhat misdirected "conscience." On the other hand, there seems to be authentic beauty and pathos in the child's piety and suffering and in the agony of the bereaved mother, "This newe Rachel" weeping at the bier of her son. It has recently been suggested that in his attitude toward the Prioress, Chaucer goes no farther than "understanding pity," that he underscores the huge gulf between her bigotry (*hers,* not the Church's) and her professed devotion (see MEB 289). There may be, after all, something rather pathetic in her inability to comprehend what Christian love, as distinguished from sentimentality, really involves. Her tale is in any case flawlessly constructed, and each reader will probably weight his interpretation according to his basic conception of the Prioress's elusive character.

THE TALE OF SIR THOPAS

About the deliberately absurd *Sir Thopas* there can be no doubts. Setting out in perfect innocence to tell "a rym I lerned longe agoon," Chaucer, impishly assigning the ludicrous story to himself, skillfully burlesques just about every wretched feature of the popular Middle English metrical romances. The rhyme is often forced, the jog-trot rhythm is unbearable to the point of distorting the pronunciation of individual words, and the already meaningless lines—some of them actually taken from extant romances—are padded with even more meaningless literary clichés (e.g., "For sothe, as I yow telle may"; "The briddes [birds] synge, it is no nay"). Further parodying the rhetoric of medieval romance, Chaucer begins the second "fit [canto]" with an absurd mixture of rudeness and politeness:

> Now holde youre mouth, *par charitee,*
> Bothe knyght and lady free. . . .
>
> (B², ll. 2081–82)

The chivalric hero, more excellent than Horn or Bevis or Guy of Warwick, is a Flemish knight, and the Flemings in Chaucer's day were almost exclusively identified with the unchivalric wool trade. Like all the *heroines* of romance, Sir Thopas is "fair and gent," and his waist is small. Chaucer frequently ridicules him through the device of deliberate anticlimax, as in the sublimely inane last line of the following stanza, a line that occurs after the hero has been thoroughly sissified:

> Sire Thopas wax [grew into] a doghty swayn;
> Whit was his face as payndemayn [fine white bread],
> His lippes rede as rose;
> His rode [complexion] is lyk scarlet in grayn,
> And I yow telle in good certayn,
> He hadde a semely nose.   (B², ll. 1914–19)

What labors to bring forth what a mouse! The words have been wrenched out of their natural accentuations (e.g., "His rode is lyk scarlet in grayn"), and the hero has been wrenched out of nearly all resemblance to any knight. Sir Thopas' adventures never amount to much in a forest carpeted with ginger, licorice, and nutmeg and infested with wild beasts, both buck and hare. He does manage to meet a giant, Sir Olifaunt, whom he promises to meet in battle "tomorwe," when he has his armor; and as the knight flees, the giant reverses the David-and-Goliath pattern by throwing stones at *him*. But the hero never finds the elf-queen he loves and dreams about. No doubt Sir Thopas would still be riding on and on and getting nowhere if impatient Harry Bailey had not called a halt to this "drasty [rubbishy] rymyng"—much to the relief of the weary Canterbury pilgrims.

THE TALE OF MELIBEE

Poor Chaucer! His feelings hurt, he now elects to tell "a litel thyng in prose"; only *this* time, he plaintively asks, "lat me tellen

al my tale, I preye." The "litel thyng in prose" turns out to be the
interminable *Tale of Melibee,* a static moral debate (translated from
the French *Le Livre de Mellibee et Prudence*) in which Melibee, a
rich young man, is persuaded by his wife, Dame Prudence, to forego
seeking revenge upon three "olde foes" who invaded his home and
beat his wife and daughter. At the proper time Prudence meets with
the three adversaries, speaks to them of "the grete goodes that comen
of pees,/and the grete harmes and perils that been in werre," and
prevails upon them to repent:

> And whan they herden the goodliche wordes of dame Prudence,/
> they weren so supprised and ravysshed, and hadden so greet joye of
> hire that wonder was to telle./"A, lady," quod they, "ye han shewed
> unto us the blessynge of swetnesse, after the sawe of David the
> prophete;/for the reconsilynge which we been nat worthy to have in
> no manere,/but we oghte requeren it with greet contricioun and
> humylitee,/ye of youre grete goodnesse have presented unto us. . . ."
>
> (B², ll. 2922–27)

They place themselves completely at the disposal of Melibee and
Prudence. No one will pretend that the tale is a masterpiece; the discussions are supported in almost every other line with quotations from
learned authorities or from proverbial lore. But the prose style, as
the foregoing quotation indicates, is lucid and efficient. Moreover,
the subject matter was of real interest to Chaucer's contemporaries
and is not obsolete in any age. In addition to focusing on the
question of private revenge as opposed to organized justice, the
parable also glorifies the Christian principle of forgiveness of one's
enemies.

When the tale is finished, the Host, of course, uses Dame Prudence
as an excuse for a new tirade against his impatient and unforgiving
wife. When he beats his servants, she urges him to kill them and
brings him "grete clobbed staves" with which to break their bones.
She also insists that he fight anyone she thinks has slighted her:

> "Allas!" she seith, "that evere I was shape [made]
> To wedden a milksop, or a coward ape,
> That wol been overlad [browbeaten] with every wight!
> Thou darst nat stonden by thy wyves right!"
>
> (B², ll. 3099–3102)

"But lat us passe away fro this mateere," he resignedly says.

THE MONK'S TALE

Harry Bailey now calls upon the lusty Monk for a contribution to the entertainment, spicing his invitation with good-natured ribaldry. The Monk, perhaps because the Host's vulgar remarks have put him on his best behavior, offers for the edification of his companions a lengthy recitation (in eight-line stanzas rhyming *ababbcbc*) of tragedies patterned mainly after *Le Roman de la Rose* and a work by Boccaccio, *De Casibus Virorum et Feminarum Illustrium* (On the Falls of Illustrious Men and Women). Accepting the medieval concept of tragedy, derived largely from Boethius, he promises tales

"Of hym that stood in greet prosperitee,
And is yfallen out of heigh degree
Into myserie, and endeth wrecchedly."
(B², ll. 3165–67)

The Monk's subjects include notable persons who (not necessarily as a result of their own flaws of character) sit at the top of Fortune's wheel and then are catapulted down. Some he treats very briefly: Lucifer, Adam, King Peter of Cyprus, and Barnabò, Viscount of Milan. Others are more fully developed: Samson, Nero, Alexander, Julius Caesar. Of particular interest and excellence is the account of Hugelyn (Ugolino, the Earl of Pisa), slowly starving to death, with his three children, in a prison tower. Chaucer does not achieve or even attempt anything like the horror and strength of the great Ugolino episode in Dante's *Inferno,* in which the poet finds in the ninth circle of Hell the unfortunate nobleman who is a traitor, gnawing on the skull of his enemy, the Archbishop Ruggeri. But the version in *The Monk's Tale* has its own quality, Chaucer's Hugelyn being a less dramatic but more pitiable figure. The pathos of the children is exploited to the fullest, as in the innocent query of Hugelyn's three-year-old son:

"Fader, why do ye wepe?
Whanne wol the gayler bryngen oure potage?
Is ther no morsel breed that ye do kepe?
I am so hungry that I may nat slepe."
(B², ll. 3622–25)

The boy wishes that he might sleep forever. "Thanne sholde nat hunger in my wombe [stomach] crepe." His wish is granted:

> Thus day by day this child bigan to crye,
> Til in his fadres barm [lap] adoun it lay,
> And seyde, "Farewel, fader, I moot dye!"
> And kiste his fader, and dyde the same day.
>
> (B², ll. 3629–32)

The remaining two children, seeing their father biting his own arms for grief, mistakenly believe that he is doing so out of hunger and beg him to eat their flesh:

> And after that, withinne a day or two,
> They leyde hem in his lappe adoun and deyde.
>
> (B², ll. 3643–44)

As the Host had cut short the "drasty rymyng" of *Sir Thopas,* the Knight—more tactfully—rescues the company from the Monk's grim catalogue of human woe. The Knight approves of the Monk's moralizing tales, but a little "hevynesse," he suggests, goes a long way with most people. The Host agrees enthusiastically: "Swich talkyng is nat worth a boterflye." When the Monk is invited to tell another tale—a story about hunting, his true vocation—he declines. Whereupon the Nun's Priest is boldly asked for "swich thyng as may oure hertes glade [cheer]."

THE NUN'S PRIEST'S TALE

According to the *General Prologue,* the Prioress was accompanied on the pilgrimage by another nun "and preestes thre." To one of these priests, unnamed and undescribed, Chaucer awarded the privilege of telling one of his greatest tales, a hilarious mock-heroic fable about the cock, the fox, and the hen. Chauntecleer, a proud rooster adored by no fewer than seven lovely hens, dreams of impending danger at the hands of the wily fox Daun Russell. But he is persuaded by Pertelote, his favorite wife, to ignore the dream. Consequently, the hero falls easy prey to the fox's flattery (What a fine voice you have!) and is snatched up as he stands on tiptoe, stretches his neck, closes his eyes, and begins to crow. The whole barnyard—human beings included—having been roused to riotous pursuit, Chauntecleer now tricks the fox into opening his mouth to speak and gets away. When the fox apologizes for having frightened him and offers friendship, Chauntecleer, from a safe perch high in a tree, refuses to be taken in a second time. He has learned his lesson, and the fable ends happily.

This tale of the cock who takes the bad advice of a gentle hen finds Chaucer once again ridiculing the literature of romance. The narrative begins, most unromantically, with a bleak picture of a poor old widow living frugally in a "narwe cottage," unable to afford wine, "neither whit ne reed"; then, in ironic contrast, we are transported into her barnyard and given a brilliant description of her resplendent rooster:

> His coomb was redder than the fyn coral,
> And batailled [battlemented] as it were a castel wal;
> His byle [bill] was blak, and as the jeet [jet] it shoon;
> Lyk asure were his legges and his toon [toes];
> His nayles whitter than the lylye flour,
> And lyk the burned [burnished] gold was his colour.
> (B², ll. 4049–54)

Could anyone imagine a more incongruous setting for a romance? Chauntecleer, who struts arrogantly, takes inordinate pride in his crowing; he loves to sing for "faire damoysele Pertelote," as he graciously addresses her, "My lief is faren in londe [My love has gone away]!" At one point Chaucer gives to this fabulous compound of knight and fowl an additional dimension: Chauntecleer stalks about "as it were a grym leoun [lion]." A very learned rooster in the best scholarly tradition, he advances a score of historical and literary precedents in order to prove to Pertelote that dreams ought to be heeded. But although he easily outargues Pertelote, who is capable of only a woman's logic, Chauntecleer is less interested in disputation than in the "solas" of love. He therefore lets Pertelote charm him out of obeying the dictates of his sound judgment. "Now let us speke of myrthe," he says to his lady fair, "and stynte [stop] al this." He knows how to put his superior dialectical powers to romantic use. To feed Pertelote's vanity, he deliberately translates *Mulier est hominis confusio* (Woman is man's ruin) for Pertelote as "Womman is mannes joye and al his blis"! It is only poetic justice that Chauntecleer's own head should be turned by the sweet talk of Daun Russell.

In addition to sounding a warning against permitting a pretty face (or a pretty feather) to obscure one's reason, *The Nun's Priest's Tale* contains some spirited satire of rhetorical excesses. The Nun's Priest—one wonders whether he himself is aware of the humor he achieves—continually employs glorious epic similes appropriate to a

Hector or an Achilles in order to enlarge the scope of his barnyard fable. He intellectualizes the most trivial turns of the plot, as when he raises the immense question of free will versus necessity—with copious references, of course, to St. Augustine, Boethius, and other authorities—to account for Chauntecleer's flight down from the beams to the ground, where the fox can get at him. As if to parody the Monk's somber remarks on Fortune, Chaucer reduces Destiny to absurdity:

> O destinee, that mayst nat been eschewed!
> Allas, that Chauntecleer fleigh fro the bemes!
> Allas, his wyf ne roghte [heeded] nat of dremes!
> And on a Friday fil al this meschaunce.
>   (B², ll. 4528–31)

The Nun's Priest regrets that he does not have the rhetorical skill of Geoffrey of Vinsauf, a poet (notoriously dull) who extravagantly mourned the death of Richard I. "For on a Friday, soothly [truly], slayn was he." Not when Troy fell and not when the Romans burned Carthage had there been such an outpouring of grief as from the hens when their handsome rooster flew down from the beams on that black Friday:

> O woful hennes, right so criden ye,
> As, whan that Nero brende the citee
> Of Rome, cryden senatoures wyves
> For that hir husbondes losten alle hir lyves. . . .
>   (B², ll. 4559–62)

The Nun's Priest's Tale is indeed the work of a virtuoso. Chaucer has created a perfect rooster, hen, and fox and, at the same time, managed to convey the marvelous illusion that they are human. With magnificent art he has sustained through every line the rich, fresh humor of his barnyard characters and their silly situations; yet he has succeeded in producing a poem that can be taken seriously both as a satire on man's romantic pretensions and as a mockery of his ridiculous efforts to adorn his petty triumphs and misfortunes in high-flown poetry and philosophy. A reader searching for the quintessence of Chaucer's comic genius could make no better choice than *The Nun's Priest's Tale.**

---

* As has been the case with other tales, there have been various attempts in recent years to view *The Nun's Priest's Tale* as a Christian allegory. See MEB 313.

THE SECOND NUN'S TALE

If every person "Chaucer the Pilgrim" meets is the best of his kind, every tale "Chaucer the Poet" writes is just about the best in its genre. *The Second Nun's Tale* is a very skillfully told saint's life of St. Cecilia, who—like Katherine, Juliana, and others previously discussed—ends in martyrdom. Cecilia, after converting her husband Valerian and his brother Tiburce to Christianity, holds her ground against the Roman prefect Almachius. When his efforts to make her bow before idols meet with unwavering rejection, Almachius orders Cecilia to be burned. As is generally the case in the saints' legends, the heroine is unharmed by tortures. For a night and a day, instead of perishing of heat, Cecilia "sat al coold." She is then given three strokes in the neck and almost beheaded, but for three days she continues to teach the faith—until she has had time to recommend to Pope Urban the souls of the new Christians she has converted. She is then buried and her memory hallowed. The tale is in all likelihood a translation from a Latin life of St. Cecilia (she appears in *The Golden Legend*), but its exact source has not been found. Introducing the tale proper is a beautiful invocation to the Virgin Mary, woven together out of passages from Dante, various Latin hymns, and other sources.

THE CANON'S YEOMAN'S PROLOGUE AND TALE

Shortly after the Second Nun has finished her tale, two new characters ride briskly onto the scene, a Canon and his Yeoman. For "Chaucer the Pilgrim," always impressed by superior accomplishments in any field, it is a thrill even to behold a man who perspires better than anyone else; of the Canon he records admiringly that "it was joye for to seen hym swete!" The Yeoman begins to answer questions posed by Harry Bailey, and the Canon perceives that his servant is about to expose him as a rogue. " 'Hoold thou thy pees,' " he threatens, " 'and spek no wordes mo. . . .' " When the Host encourages the Yeoman to say more, the Canon rides away as suddenly as he came.

With a mixture of fear and fascination, the Canon's Yeoman proceeds to disclose his experiences as assistant to the Canon, an alchemist. The tale, which bustles with the sordid vitality of London low life, is in two parts. The first part deals with the sincere, though unsuccessful, efforts expended by the Canon to transmute baser metal into gold (the mixture blows up at the crucial moment). The Yeoman, despite his oft-proven suspicion that alchemy is a "racket" that brings more frustration to the alchemist than to the victims he defrauds, seems to be caught up in the excitement of the work, and he manipulates alchemical jargon with obvious relish. In the second part of his tale, the Canon's Yeoman exposes the swindle perpetrated upon a gullible chantry priest by a particularly fiendish canon-alchemist and his disciple (the Yeoman assures us that this was a different canon, but we wonder). The Yeoman cannot speak of this monster without his cheeks beginning "for to glowe"; constant exposure to the fumes of various metals has robbed his face of its redness so that he is unable to blush. He concludes with a Christian moral: Whoever works against the will of God, "never shal he thryve."

It has been suggested on several occasions that Chaucer did not feel himself rigidly bound to the original plan of *The Canterbury Tales*. No doubt he decided that the unexpected arrival of two new characters would enhance the drama of the narrative. For the inspired afterthought that produced *The Canon's Yeoman's Prologue* and *Tale* readers have cause to rejoice.

THE MANCIPLE'S TALE

Ever the dramatist, Chaucer stirs up a new feud—this time between the Cook and the Manciple. After the Host makes a few coarse jokes at the expense of the Cook, who is in a drunken stupor, and invites him to tell a story, the Manciple declares that this "stynkyng swyn" may be excused from offering a tale and proceeds to shower insults upon him. The Cook is furious but unable to speak; he falls off his horse and has to be lifted back on. The Host decides that the Cook is in no condition to tell a tale properly and therefore asks the Manciple for a story. Whatever hard feelings have developed are smoothed over by a bottle of wine which the Manciple produces; and after the Host has praised Bacchus, "That so kanst turnen ernest into game," the Manciple begins. Scholars interpret the episode, together with the fragment already discussed as *The Cook's Tale*, as indication of some change of plan or inconsistency on Chaucer's part with reference to the Cook's role in the pilgrimage.

The Manciple's Tale, probably derived from Ovid's *Metamorphoses,* is the story of the telltale bird who gets punished. The master of a house teaches a crow (a white-feathered, sweet-singing bird) to talk, only to have the bird inform him that his wife has committed adultery. After killing his wife, the master suffers remorse and curses the crow who started it all. He then tears out the crow's white feathers and makes him black, takes away his power of song and speech, and hurls him out the door to the devil—simply because, the Manciple moralizes, he could not keep his mouth shut. The Manciple relays the practical advice given him by his mother:

> "My sone, be war, and be noon auctour [author] newe
> Of tidynges, wheither they been false or trewe.
> Whereso thou come, amonges hye or lowe,
> Kepe wel thy tonge, and thenk upon the crowe."
>
> (H, ll. 359–62)*

THE PARSON'S PROLOGUE AND TALE

The Manciple has ended his tale, the sun is receding into the horizon, and the pilgrims are coming to the edge of a village. Whatever Chaucer's original intention, there is a mysterious air of finality about the journey and the storytelling. The Host turns to the Parson for the one tale still lacking to fulfill the agreement. The serious Parson, who disapproves of "fables and swich wrecchednesse" and does not know how to "rum, ram, ruf" in the fashion of alliterative verse, resolves upon "a myrie tale in prose" that will "knytte up al this feeste, and make an ende":

> "And Jhesu, for his grace, wit me sende
> To shewe yow the wey, in this viage [journey],
> Of thilke [that] parfit glorious pilgrymage
> That highte [is called] Jerusalem celestial."
>
> (I, ll. 48–51)

The pilgrims consider it appropriate to conclude the storytelling with "som vertuous sentence" and urge the Host to encourage the Parson. This Harry Bailey does most cordially. "But hasteth yow," he warns, "the sonne wole adoun."

The long, systematic sermon on the Seven Deadly Sins and Penitence which constitutes the Parson's "myrie tale" may not amuse or excite modern readers, but it is an acceptable conclusion for the entire poem. Many theories have been advanced, none of them completely

---

* R. D. Spector, "Chaucer's 'The Manciple's Tale,' " *Notes and Queries,* New Series, IV (1957), p. 26, shows that the Manciple may be getting back at the Host for encouraging the Canon's Yeoman to tell tales on his master.

satisfactory, as to what *The Canterbury Tales,* unfinished as the work may be, means in its totality. Some have seen the poem as a celebration of Venus, an exploration of various aspects of profane and holy love; others have read it as a discourse on the Seven Deadly Sins; the suggestion has also been made that *The Canterbury Tales* is an inquiry into the nature of illusion and reality. But this much, at least, would seem clear: the pilgrims, representing as they do diverse social backgrounds and literary tastes, are in the first place a cross section of fourteenth-century English society; they are linked together in temporary fellowship by virtue of a common journey to a specific well-known shrine, the grave of St. Thomas à Becket. The Parson reminds them, however, that this pilgrimage does not end in Canterbury or even with a return to the Tabard Inn. He transforms the pilgrimage into a symbol of man's spiritual journey: *all* men become permanent traveling companions, not just on the road to Canterbury but during the long journey from earthly vanity through penitence to the ultimate destination—death and "the endelees blisse of hevene." Recent criticism, as has been indicated, has taken more seriously the religious current in Chaucer, interpreting many of the individual tales in the light of medieval scriptural exegesis.

It does not seem strange, therefore, that Chaucer should have appended to *The Canterbury Tales* a Retraction * in which he asks divine forgiveness for having written *Troilus and Criseyde, The Hous of Fame, The Legend of Good Women, The Book of the Duchesse, The Parlement of Foules, The Canterbury Tales* (at least "thilke [such] that sownen into [tend toward] synne"), the lost "book of the Leoun," and "many another book . . . and many a song and many a leccherous lay." But he is thankful to Christ, the Blessed Mother, and all the heavenly saints for his having produced "the translacion of Boece de Consolacione, and othere bookes of legendes of seintes, and omelies, and moralitee, and devocioun." There is no reason to question the authenticity of the Retraction or to regard it as an empty convention.

*   *   *   *   *   *

How does one summarize the literary achievements of a poet of Chaucer's stature? No one has bettered the appraisal of John Dryden, who was quoted briefly at the beginning of this discussion. Dryden

* Group I, ll. 1081 ff.

calls Chaucer "a perpetual fountain of good sense" and elaborates with eloquence and love upon his infinite variety:

> He must have been a man of a most wonderful comprehensive nature, because, as it has been truly observed of him, he has taken into the compass of his *Canterbury Tales* the various manners and humours (as we now call them) of the whole English nation, in his age. Not a single character has escaped him. All his pilgrims are severally distinguished from each other; and not only in their inclination, but in their very physiognomies and persons. . . . Some of his persons are vicious, and some virtuous; some are unlearn'd or (as Chaucer calls them) lewd, and some are learn'd. Even the ribaldry of the low characters is different: the Reeve, the Miller, and the Cook, are several men, and distinguished from each other as much as the mincing Lady-Prioress and the broad-speaking, gap-toothed Wife of Bath.

"But enough of this," Dryden continues. "There is such a variety of game springing up before me, that I am distracted in my choice, and know not which to follow. 'Tis sufficient to say, according to the proverb, that *here is God's plenty*." *

* John Dryden, "Preface to the Fables," in *Essays of John Dryden* (2 vols.), ed. W. P. Ker (Oxford: Clarendon Press, 1900), II, 257.

XIV: FIFTEENTH–CENTURY CHAUCERIANS

The fifteenth century produced both in England and in Scotland a group of writers who considered themselves, with only partial appropriateness, disciples of Chaucer. In addition to many anonymous Chaucerian works, some of which were attributed to Chaucer (like the allegorical dream-vision *The Flower and the Leaf*), one finds many known poets consciously copying Chaucer's external characteristics, like rhyme royal and the dream convention, without capturing, or even approaching, his more subtle lyric and narrative skills. England offers few Chaucerian poets of value apart from John Lydgate and Thomas Hoccleve, and both of these claim our attention for reasons not chiefly—if at all—poetical. In Scotland, however, there were at least three genuine poets: the author of *The Kingis Quair,* who may have been King James I; Robert Henryson, who wrote a continuation of *Troilus;* and the many-faceted William Dunbar.

JOHN LYDGATE (c. 1370–c. 1450) *

Chaucer's principal English disciple, a monk at the abbey of Bury St. Edmunds, turned out more than 145,000 lines of verse—a feat which makes him one of our most prolific poets. Lydgate's faults are well known: incessant moralizing, padding of lines to fill in the meter, and drastic dislocation of the natural stresses of his words. Most disturbing, perhaps, is the bloodless, mechanical quality of nearly everything he wrote. Nevertheless, Lydgate's poems are not without historical interest. The allegorical *Reason and Sensuality* (c. 1408), one of his most pleasant works, is a translation, in octosyllabic couplets, of a French romance celebrating chastity; most of the ingredients of conventional allegory are there: the spring setting, gardens, and personified abstractions. The *Troy Book* (1412–21), mentioned in Chapter VII, is the most ambitious—30,000 lines or so—treatment of the legend of Troy in English; it is a free translation, in heroic couplets,

---

* Dates in this section are taken from Henry S. Bennett, *Chaucer and the Fifteenth Century* (New York: Oxford University Press, 1947).

of Guido delle Colonne's book in Latin prose. The best-known passage in the *Troy Book,* however, is a tribute to Chaucer. The *Siege of Thebes* (1421–22), perhaps his most readable epic, rehearses the struggle between the two sons of Oedipus for control of Thebes; in the Prologue, by far the most interesting part of the poem, Lydgate joins the Canterbury pilgrims on their homeward journey and offers this story of Thebes as his tale. *The Pilgrimage of the Life of Man,* begun in 1426, is a lengthy (24,000 lines) translation of the first part of Deguilleville's trilogy *Le Pèlerinage de la Vie Humaine*—additional evidence that the symbolism of the pilgrimage was employed frequently by medieval poets. Also worth mentioning is *The Fall of Princes* (1431–38), adapted from Boccaccio's *De Casibus Virorum et Feminarum Illustrium* and therefore resembling *The Monk's Tale.* A catalogue of tragedies in the medieval style, the work looks ahead to the *Mirror for Magistrates,* the famous Tudor collection of tragedies.* Lydgate was very highly regarded by his contemporaries, though he himself entertained no illusions as to his poetic endowments. Today his reputation is in sad and probably irreversible decline. †

THOMAS HOCCLEVE (c.1368–c. 1437?)

Very different from Lydgate's seclusion from the world was the life of the Londoner Thomas Hoccleve, underpaid clerk in the Privy Seal Office by day and gay carouser by night. Hoccleve turned to poetry to supplement his income and conducted a constant search for patronage. His poetic output includes *De Regimine Principum* ("The Regiment [or Regimen] of Princes"; 1411), a conduct book for the future Henry V. But he is primarily interesting for the unabashed glimpses into his personal life that are scattered throughout his poems, especially *La Mâle Règle de T. Hoccleve* (1406?). He was, he confesses, the most prodigious drinker in the office; he loved to cut a handsome figure in his wide-sleeved cloak; and he delighted in the frequent embraces "Of Venus femel lusty children deere." We learn much from Hoccleve about fifteenth-century London. There is something pleasantly unpretentious, though undistinguished, about his down-to-earth poetry; and he seems to have been Chaucer's most devoted and self-effacing pupil. Chaucer, he says, would gladly have taught him, "But I was dul, and lerned lite or naught."

* See Lily Bess Campbell, ed., *The Mirror for Magistrates* (New York: Barnes & Noble, Inc., 1960).

† For good critical commentary on Lydgate, see Bennett, *op. cit.,* pp. 137–46.

THE KINGIS QUAIR (1423)

A Scottish "Chaucerian" poem of unusual charm is *The Kingis Quair* ("King's Book"). Traditionally taken to have been written by King James I of Scotland (not to be confused with James I of England, who reigned in Scotland as James VI), this dream-vision is presumably an autobiographical love poem—in the style of *Le Roman de la Rose*—recounting the poet's capture by the English, his love at first sight from his prison window for Joan Beaufort, his release after eighteen years, and his subsequent marriage to Joan. The story illustrates Fortune, as derived from Boethius, reversing her usual direction: here a turn of the wheel raises one who has been cast down in misery up to the heights of happiness. The poet's rendering of that first glimpse of his beloved is an especially fine specimen of his art:

> And there-with kest [cast] I doune myn eye ageyne,
> Quhare [where] as I sawe, walking under the toure,
> Full secretly, new cummyn hir to pleyne [play],
> The fairest or the freschest yong floure
> That ever I sawe, me-thought, before that houre,
> For quhich [which] sodeyn abate, anone astert
> The blude of all my body to my hert.

The poem is in rhyme royal, the seven-line pentameter stanza rhyming *ababbcc*, used in so many of Chaucer's works. The stanza is, in fact, called "rhyme royal" because it is employed in *The Kingis Quair*.

Authorship of the poem has been assigned to James I on the basis of scribal notations to that effect found in the manuscript. But recent scholarship (see MEB 322–324) disputes the manuscript attribution of the poem to him and vigorously rejects any literal interpretation of the dream-vision.

ROBERT HENRYSON (1429?–1508?)

The schoolmaster Robert Henryson is Scottish through and through in his love for fresh poetic images drawn from his native countryside. He is "Chaucerian" mainly on the basis of his *The Testament of Cresseid* (1460?). In this sequel to Chaucer's masterpiece, Henryson follows the career of the heroine until she has become a leper and is begging alms. Troilus, who is still alive in Henryson's poem, passes by one day and is momentarily touched with a vague memory of his earlier love:

> Than upon him scho [she] kest up baith hir Ene [eyes],
> And with ane blenk [glance] it come into his thocht,
> That he sumtime his face befoir had sene.
> But scho was in sic plye [plight] he knew hir nocht,
> Yit than hir luik into his mynd it brocht
> The sweit visage and amorous blenking
> Of fair Cresseid sumtyme his awin darling. . . .

Without making any definite connection between the fair image in his mind and the miserable beggar now before his eyes, Troilus bestows alms and moves on. It is a "recognition scene" in which full recognition is skillfully averted. When Cresseid later learns that it was Troilus who passed, she condemns herself and dies. "Fy! fals Cresseid! O, trew knight Troilus!" Henryson is perhaps more explicit than Chaucer in his disapproval of Cresseid, but he manages to retain something of the master's ironic sympathy.

Enjoyable as is *The Testament of Cresseid* (to say nothing of Henryson's *Fables,* which includes the lively story of the town mouse and the country mouse), readers will probably cherish most his engaging ballad of *Robin and Makin.* In this early example of the *pastorelle,* the love-tormented shepherdess Makin is cruelly rejected by the shepherd Robin. Later, however, when Robin feels differently inclined, so does Makin. He should have struck, Makin gaily tells him, while the iron was hot:

> The man that will nocht quhen he may
> Sall haif nocht quhen he wald.

He who does not want it when he may have it shall not have it when he wants it.

WILLIAM DUNBAR (c. 1460–1521?)

William Dunbar, the greatest of the "Chaucerians" and perhaps the most accomplished Scottish poet before Robert Burns, lived and wrote well into the sixteenth century. Dunbar's immense range includes lush dream-allegories, like *The Thistle and the Rose* and *The Golden Targe;* jaunty ballads, like *The Ballad of Kind Kittock;* nightmarish descriptive pieces, like *The Dance of the Seven Deadly Sins;* poems of exuberantly obscene comic energy, like *The Two Married Women and the Widow;* and numerous dramatic and reflec-

tive lyrics. Whatever form he essays, Dunbar discloses a robust imagination, a passion for metrical experimentation, and, as one critic has
rightly said, "a voice to lift a roof with." *

Dunbar's wild comic fancy is given fullest play in *The Two Married Women and the Widow*. This ingenious poem is a parody—of
the stylized rhetoric of the literary pastoral, of the debate, and of the
convention of courtly love. Beginning with a lyrical passage invoking
a setting of ideal beauty—a midsummer evening, a garden "full of
gay flouris," the "sugarat sound" of the lovely bird singing her happy
song—the poet hides in order to eavesdrop on a disputation. This
debate involves two lascivious married women and an even more lustful widow, all of them reviewing their experiences with marriage and
placing particular emphasis upon the sexual incapacities of their husbands. The women are depicted in the language of courtliness; the
widow prides herself on her "gentil hert" that understands how to
grant "merci." After listening to the torrent of obscenity issuing from
these women, the poet poses a new kind of courtly "problem." Which
one of these wanton wives, he asks ironically, would *you* take? †

But there is a serious side to Dunbar, and the organ tones which
he sometimes produces invest his serious poems with great power.
Listen to heaven and earth sounding a glorious welcome to Christ at
the Nativity:

> Sing Hevin imperiall most of hicht,
> Regions of air mak armony,
> All fishe in flud and foull of flicht
> Be myrthfull and mak melody;
> All *gloria in excelsis* cry,
> Hevin, erd, se, man, bird and best;—
> He that is crownit abone the sky
> *Pro nobis puer natus est* [for us a child is born].

The third and fourth lines quoted above,

> All fishe in flud and foull of flicht
> Be myrthfull and mak melody. . . .

illustrate Dunbar's fondness for alliteration, one of the ways in which
he achieves his musical effects. The third line, in fact, uses double

* C. S. Lewis, *English Literature in the Sixteenth Century* (Oxford: Clarendon Press, 1958), p. 97.

† This discussion is indebted to Patrick Cruttwell's analysis in *The Age of
Chaucer*, ed. Boris Ford, pp. 176–82. (MEB 2.)

alliteration (*f* and *l*)—a technique also employed in the resounding opening lines of a poem on the Resurrection:

> Done is a battel on the dragon blak,
> Our campioun Chryst confoundithes his force.

Alliteration, rhyme, and repetition combine in *Of the World's Vanity* to make a familiar theme seem fresh:

> Heir nocht abydes, heir standis no thing stabill,
> [For] this fals world ay flittis to and fro;
> Now day up-bricht, now nycht as blak as sabill,
> Now eb, now flude, now freynd, now cruell fo;
> Now glaid, now said, now weill, now in-to wo;
> Now cled in gold, dissolvit now in ass [ashes];
> So dois this world (ay) transitorie go:
> *Vanitas Vanitatum, et omnia Vanitas.*

"Walk furth, pilgrame," the poet urges in lines recalling Chaucer's *Balade de Bon Conseyl*, "quhill thow hes dayis lycht."

One of Dunbar's best-known poems is the *Lament for the Makers,* a reflection upon the mortality of poets. The poem accumulates intensity through its Latin refrain, *Timor mortis conturbat me* (The fear of death disturbs me). In a series of four-line stanzas Dunbar demonstrates that no one escapes death—not the prince, not the knight, not "the lady in bour full of bewte," not even the innocent babe at its mother's breast:

> That strang unmercifull tyrand
> Takis, on the moderis breist sowkand,
> The bab full of benignitee:
> *Timor mortis conturbat me.*

As the poem nears its climax, we are told that even the "makers" are mortal—Chaucer, Gower, Barbour (author of the Scottish *Bruce*), Henryson. For Dunbar, also a maker, death has gained the urgency of a personal threat:

> Sin he has all my brether tane
> He will nocht lat me lif alane;
> On forse [necessarily] I man [must] his nyxt pray be:
> *Timor mortis conturbat me.*

Look not for subtlety and restraint in Dunbar; his art is of a different order. "When you are in the mood for it," writes an eminent literary historian, "his poetry has a sweep and volume of sound and an assured virility which (while the mood lasts) makes most other poets seem a little faint and tentative and half-hearted. If you like half-tones and nuances you will not enjoy Dunbar; he will deafen you." *

* Lewis, *op. cit.*, p. 98.

XV: MEDIEVAL DRAMA IN ENGLAND

The story of the reappearance of the drama during the Middle Ages, after centuries of almost total neglect, comprises one of the most exciting chapters in literary history. From meager and tentative beginnings in the liturgy, at first on the Continent and somewhat later in England, this reactivated art, which had formed a major part of the glory that was Greece and Rome, gradually grew in popularity until it acquired a large and enthusiastic audience. In the course of its later growth (though this phase of the story does not belong to the period here under discussion) the drama enlisted the talents of an army of professional theater people—playwrights, producers, scenic designers, directors, and actors. During the reign of Queen Elizabeth I (1558–1603) and her successor, James I, the English theater was to serve as the home of poets of transcendent gifts, including the dramatist Coleridge referred to as "the greatest man that ever put on and put off mortality." Shakespeare, Ben Jonson, Molière, Ibsen, Chekhov, Shaw—the more one surveys the illustrious list of great playwrights of the Western world, the more irresistibly is he drawn to examine the origins of the modern drama in the tenth and eleventh centuries.

The contribution of the Greek and Roman theater had been tremendous, but long before the fall of Rome (in the fifth century) performances of serious Greek and Roman plays had ceased. Whatever "dramatic" entertainment the Romans enjoyed seems to have been provided by lewd farces and pantomimes or by brutal gladiatorial spectacles in the arena. These debasements of the theater, however, did not last very long. The Church, naturally enough, condemned them as immoral, and the invading barbarians did not find them attractive. For all practical purposes, then, significant acted drama had been dead for hundreds of years prior to its rebirth in the Middle Ages.

The decline of formal drama did not mean that all traces of dramatic representation had been obliterated. For one thing, there was the virtually unbroken tradition of strolling mimes, minstrels, and troubadours who, in the manner of the Germanic *scop*, wandered throughout Europe with a repertoire of recitations from classical and medieval narratives. Second, there was the folk-play, which must have been derived from dances and fertility rites associated with the four seasons.* Near the end of the Middle Ages we find these pagan ceremonies, which were also frowned upon by churchmen, transformed into more "literary" plays about Robin Hood and St. George. (The "mummers' plays" of St. George are still performed in parts of rural England.) Then, too, there was a vigorous pulpit literature in which characters and moral qualities were depicted in realistic, pseudo-dramatic fashion. Finally, the classical drama itself was not un-known. Plays were studied as literature even if they may not have been publicly acted, and a tenth-century German nun, Hrotsvitha, actually wrote didactic works modeled after the Latin comedies of Terence. We cannot determine precisely the extent to which min-strelsy, folk ritual, sermons, and the reading of plays in schools may have influenced the earliest playwrights. But these factors, taken to-gether, would seem to suggest that for most of the people in the Middle Ages, drama could not have been a completely new experience.

As early as the ninth century, a more formal kind of drama began to take shape—under the auspices, surprisingly enough, of the Church, the very institution that had done most to suppress any sort of dramatic representation. From certain *tropes,* simple Latin embel-lishments upon the liturgy, there evolved, as we shall see, practically all of the ingredients necessary for fully developed plays—gesture, action, dialogue, impersonation, and even costumes and stage proper-ties. As a result of the innovations, audiences at church ceremonies grew so large and staging became so bulky that the dramatizations, which had increased considerably in scope, overflowed from the choir stalls to the nave of the church. Later, when the assembly was par-ticularly large and noisy, they moved out into the churchyard.

Meanwhile an important trend toward secularization had started to operate in the drama. In order to edify the laity, who could not understand Latin, clerics tried incorporating translations of the li-turgical embellishments and went on to add bits of dialogue in the vernacular. This concession also proved immensely entertaining; even-tually Latin disappeared from the drama entirely—except for an occa-

---

* There were, in addition, various medieval feasts and revels which may have contributed to the development of comedy in English drama. Among these may be mentioned the Feast of the Ass, the Feast of Fools, the Boy Bishop, and revels associated with the "Lord of Misrule."

sional name of a character or for a stage direction. At the same time, comedy and mimicry had crept into the liturgical plays and lessened the serious objectives which the plays were supposed to fulfill. If the Church by and large approved of the use of drama, there were some who vigorously protested. "No man," argues a fourteenth-century blast against the drama, "can be converted to God but only by the earnestful doing of God, and by no vain playing." Plays, the author continues, are made "more to delight men bodily than to be books to unlearned men, and, therefore, if they be living books, they be living books to wickedness more than to goodness." While this may have been an extreme reaction (the Church itself probably opposed merely the abuses which accompanied the presentation of the religious plays), the attack certainly indicates some degree of dissatisfaction on the part of the clergy with the unexpected direction in which the drama was moving. Small wonder, then, that the drama—with or without the blessing of the churchmen—passed out of the physical control of the Church into the hands of lay authors and producers. Plays literally moved into the streets and, later, into innyards and regular theaters.

Even under the impact of secularization the medieval drama nevertheless continued to draw its nourishment primarily from Christianity. On the basis of their subject matter the religious plays of the Middle Ages have been classified as *mysteries, miracles,* and *moralities.* In the original French usage a *mystery* (mystère) was a play on a scriptural subject and a *miracle* was a dramatization of an episode from the life of a saint—often the Virgin Mary or St. Nicholas. In England both kinds of plays are usually called *miracles.** The *morality* is a dramatized allegory, best exemplified in *Everyman.*

Still another type of play—probably of secular origin—was the *interlude.* This term was very loosely used for all sorts of plays; often it was a comic performance acted between courses of a great feast. Whatever its origin and use, the purpose of the interlude seems primarily to have been entertainment rather than edification. This form of drama reached its perfection in the works of John Heywood, who flourished during the reign of Henry VIII (in the sixteenth century). Although the interlude will not be discussed in the present volume, it should be noted that its form was frequently related to that of the

---

* E. K. Chambers, *English Literature at the Close of the Middle Ages* (New York: Oxford University Press, 1945), p. 16, says that no English play was called a "mystery" until 1744.

morality—especially in its introduction of characters or types from contemporary life and in its occasional use of allegory. Many English miracles (mysteries), for example the *Second Shepherds' Play*, may have been partly inspired by the farcical entertainment that was the staple of many of the interludes.

TROPES AND LITURGICAL PLAYS

It has often been observed that the line dividing religious ritual from pantomime is a very fine one. The Christian liturgy contains many sections that are inherently dramatic—for example, the celebration of the Mass and the "dialogue" that is implicit in the responsive chanting of antiphonal choirs. These rituals, however, lack at least one crucial dramaturgical element: *impersonation,* the process whereby a worshipper would actually pretend to assume the character of somebody else.

The modern drama, much like the drama of ancient Greece, seems to have originated—almost by accident—in religious ritual. During the Easter service certain monastic communities began to protract the last syllable of the Alleluia. For a time this trope remained a wordless musical ornamentation, but before long, words were added to the embellishment. A rudimentary dialogue then developed in the form of an antiphonal chorus between the "angels" presiding over Christ's tomb, whose parts were sung by a choir of monks on one side of the altar, and the "Three Marys" who discover the empty sepulchre, their parts sung by singers on the other side. In the earliest extant trope, dating from the ninth century, the angels ask the Marys, *"Quem quaeritis in sepulchro, O Christicolae?"* Here is the trope in translation:

> *Angels:* Whom do you seek in the sepulchre, O Christian women?
> *Marys:* Jesus of Nazareth, who was crucified, O celestial ones.
> *Angels:* He is not here; he is risen, just as he foretold. Go, announce that he is risen from the sepulchre.

This simple but revolutionary trope played a central role in religious drama for hundreds of years. Complete plays dating from as late as the twelfth century still retain the *Quem quaeritis* trope as their core.

By degrees this trope was elaborated into full-length dialogue, and those impersonating the Marys actually go through the motions of visiting the tomb. The following instructions for Easter matins, composed (*c.* 965–75) by St. Ethelwold of Winchester, prescribe costumes and accompanying gestures that resemble modern stage directions:

> While the third lesson is being chanted, let four brethren vest themselves; of whom let one, vested in an alb, enter as if to take part in the service, and let him without being observed approach the place of the sepulchre, and there, holding a palm in his hand, let him sit down quietly. While the third responsory is being sung, let the remaining three follow, all of them vested in copes, and carrying in their hands censers filled with incense; and slowly, in the manner of seeking something, let them come before the place of the sepulchre. These things are done in imitation of the angel seated in the monument, and of the women coming with spices to anoint the body of Jesus. When therefore that one seated shall see the three, as if straying about and seeking something, approach him, let him begin in a dulcet voice of medium pitch to sing: [*Whom do you seek in the sepulchre, O Christian Women?*] *

After the angel shows them the place where Christ was laid, the Marys lift up the cloth in which a cross was wrapped, and, "as if making known that the Lord had risen and was not now therein wrapped," they sing an anthem and place the cloth upon the altar. In later versions of the *Quem quaeritis* trope the Marys speak Latin and then paraphrase their lines in English. New scenes were added —the appearance of Christ to Mary Magdalene and the race of Peter and John to the tomb.

Dramatizations were not restricted, however, to events surrounding the Resurrection. A similar trope developed during the Christmas service; and by the process of amplification like that of the Easter service, this Christmas trope, too, grew into scenes and plays centering upon the Nativity. The Nativity plays offered a new attraction— a favorite stage character in the person of the colorful King Herod. In a twelfth-century play from France, Herod finds a book prophesying the coming of Christ, hurls it to the floor in a fit of rage, and brandishes his sword menacingly—no doubt at the spectators as well as at the personages in the play. This ranting Herod, a familiar figure in medieval Nativity plays, is an ancestor of the blood-and-thunder characters who roar their way across the Elizabethan stage. Hamlet, drama critic *par excellence*, specifically warns the players who visit

* *Chief Pre-Shakespearean Dramas*, ed. Joseph Quincy Adams (Boston: Houghton Mifflin Company, 1924), p. 9. Reprinted by permission of the publisher. All quotations in this chapter from medieval plays are from the Adams anthology.

Elsinore against tearing a passion to tatters: "It out-herods Herod; pray you, avoid it." (*Hamlet,* III, ii.)

MIRACLE (MYSTERY) PLAYS

Scholars have not been able to piece together the many scattered details of the transitional period during which the liturgical drama of the Middle Ages, in a form much more elaborate than that of the extended Resurrection and Nativity episodes which were just discussed, moved out of the churches and came under the jurisdiction of the laity. In fact, it has been cogently argued in recent years that the Church never relinquished control over the presentation of medieval religious plays and that ecclesiastics freely participated in them as authors and actors until the Reformed Church put an end to the performance of miracle plays in the sixteenth century. At any rate, when we next pick up the story of the growth of medieval drama, somewhere in the fourteenth and fifteenth centuries, the English miracle play has fully bloomed.

The English miracle, or mystery, play was defined above as a play based upon a saint's life or upon a scriptural subject. Miracles were rarely, if ever, performed in England as individual plays, but were combined as long series (cycles). The English cycles were produced frequently on Corpus Christi Day, in late May or early June, when the weather was suitable for open-air performances. Most of the extant English miracles are found in four major cycles, named for the localities where they were acted: the *Chester Cycle* of 25 plays; the *York Cycle* of 48 plays; the *Wakefield Cycle* of 32 plays (sometimes called the *Towneley* plays, after the family that owned the manuscript); and the *Lincoln Cycle* of 42 plays (sometimes called the *Hegge* plays, after the former owner of the manuscript, or the *Ludus Coventriae,* on the now discarded assumption that the plays were acted at Coventry). Many cycles apparently have been lost; miracles are known to have been produced at Beverley, Norwich, Newcastle-upon-Tyne, and other cities. A few single plays (like the Brome *Abraham and Isaac*) have also survived—some of them, perhaps, from complete cycles that have not been preserved in their entirety.

The cycles (according to the traditional scholarly view) were sponsored by the trade guilds, each of which insofar as possible dramatized a story that may have been in line with its particular talent or equipment. The carpenters portrayed the building of Noah's ark, the bakers produced the Last Supper, and the cooks (perhaps because their pots and pans could be counted on for a devilish racket) gave the Harrowing of Hell. The guilds spent lavish sums on costumes and props: gloves for God, a robe for Herod, gunpowder for Judgment Day. Although the actors may not have been professionals in the modern sense, there are records indicating that they were sometimes handsomely rewarded with foodstuffs and other valuable commodities. Plays were generally performed in a procession of horse-drawn floats, called pageants. At appointed stations along the way, the individual wagon with its carefully prepared scene stopped for the guildsmen to act out their play. Spectators could thus stand in one spot and enjoy an unbroken sequence of scriptural history lasting sometimes a full day or even longer. But not all of the cycles were presented in the manner just described. Some were enacted on fixed stages in a large field; indeed, the researches of Dr. Richard Southern (whose reconstruction of a medieval theater is reproduced on p. 282, below) would seem to prove that there were large multiple-stage amphitheaters built for the express purpose of accommodating thousands of spectators. Such theaters would presuppose a fairly elaborate and professionalized theatrical tradition in medieval England.* Other cycles seem to have been taken on tour throughout the countryside and performed in smaller communities that could not afford to mount large cycles of their own. There is evidence that sometime before 1390 the whole *York Cycle* was borrowed and set up at Wakefield; some of the York and Wakefield plays are, in fact, almost identical.

The close links between the *York* and *Wakefield Cycles* give additional emphasis to a point that may be overlooked by the twentieth-century reader who brings to the study of medieval drama his own modern set of theatrical experiences and traditions. The English miracles, it should be observed, were usually composed incrementally by the communities rather than all at once by individual authors. Once the nucleus of a play was established, details could be added or modified according to the tastes of each locale—a procedure that calls to mind the method of composition of the folk ballads. Most of the miracles are variants upon a few familiar themes: the Creation, Noah's flood, Abraham and Isaac, the shepherds' visit to the scene

---

* See Richard Southern, *The Medieval Theatre in the Round* (New York: Theatre Arts Books, 1958). (MEB 348.)

of the Nativity, the Crucifixion, the Resurrection, Doomsday, and others. The plays derive their essential strength from their very artlessness. The tradesmen must have taken authentic pride in creating a beautiful pageant that could express the depth of their religious faith as well as reflect honor upon their crafts, but these amateurs tell their scriptural stories simply and with little conscious striving for dramatic effects. One notable exception, however, is the sophisticated playwright known as "The Wakefield Master," an artist of unique literary gifts who (perhaps in the second quarter of the fifteenth century) made several contributions to the *Wakefield Cycle*—including the superior *Second Shepherds' Play*. Some of these plays will now be examined more closely.

The Croxton Play of the Sacrament

As was mentioned earlier, there is only one complete extant miracle in the French sense of the term that has been preserved in English—*The Croxton Play of the Sacrament*. In addition to occupying this unique place in the annals of English drama, the play (which is of slight literary value) is interesting as a sidelight on what was said in the preceding chapter about the miracle recounted by Chaucer's Prioress. In the *Croxton Play* a Jewish merchant, Jonathas, pays a Christian merchant to bring him the Host from the church, in order to find out whether it is really God. Together with his four servants, Jonathas abuses the Host by piercing it with a dagger. When it starts to bleed, Jonathas tries to throw it into a cauldron full of oil, but it cleaves to his hand. The servants nail the Sacrament to a post and try to pull Jonathas' hand from it, whereupon the arm comes off and leaves the hand still nailed to the post with the Eucharist. Finally, the hand is thrown into the cauldron and the Eucharist into a burning oven. From the midst of the oven the bleeding Christ emerges entreating the Jews to repent. When Jonathas, at Christ's bidding, places his maimed arm in the cauldron, the hand is miraculously restored. Jonathas invites the bishop to his home, informs him of the miracle, and promises to accept baptism. The Jews have had a direct experience of Christ's mercy and are now convinced of His divinity. The play ends on a note of forgiveness. Such was not the case, it will be recalled, in *The Prioress's Tale;* not only is the little Christian boy martyr left unrestored to life, but his Jewish murderers are destroyed with no thought at all of converting them to Christianity through Christ's infinite love.

The Brome Abraham and Isaac

Whether or not medieval dramatists were overtly concerned with the subtleties of their art, they certainly understood instinctively what stories would provide sure-fire theater. There are seven different extant versions of the sacrifice of Isaac; the best is an isolated play found in a manuscript preserved at Brome Manor, Suffolk. Whether the play was acted separately or was at one time part of a larger cycle, now lost, is not known. But the Brome *Abraham and Isaac* achieves a generally successful blend of pathos and humor and would seem to have been quite effective on the medieval stage.

The intention of the author of *Abraham and Isaac* was that of all Christian commentators on the Old Testament before him: the story is used as an analogue of the sacrifice of Christ, the Son of God, with the objections of young Isaac matching those of the Son in the Garden of Gethsemane and with the lengthy explanation of the worth of sacrifice in the eyes of God clearly paralleling the New Testament. The two central characters are developed with simple strokes that point up the all-too-human conflicts they experience. After thanking God for the many blessings granted him, Abraham learns that his most precious blessing, his son, must be forfeited. He receives God's command resolutely, but with a father's anguish; he loves his child as his own life, but he loves his God even more. Isaac's innocent readiness for anything his father might require of him proves almost too much for Abraham to bear:

> A! Lord, my hart brekyth on tweyn,
> Thys chyldes wordes, they be so tender.
> (ll. 127–28)

When Isaac discovers that he himself is to be sacrificed, he expresses his understandable desire to live:

> Now I wold to God my moder were her on this hyll!
> Sche woold knele for me on both hyr kneys
>   To save my lyffe.
> And sythn [since] that my moder ys not here,
> I prey yow, fader, schonge [change] yowr chere [face],
>   And kyll me not with yowyr knyffe.
> (ll. 175–80)

The preparation for the sacrifice is dragged out almost interminably; even after the angel takes the sword from Abraham's uplifted hand

and directs him to the ram who will take Isaac's place on the altar, the kneeling Isaac, his face covered with a cloth, pleads with his father to smite him quickly. Once the crisis is past, however, there is room for a bit of touching humor. Isaac still has to be reassured that Abraham will not kill him when he stoops down to light the fire for the ram. And he does not exactly enjoy the sight of the sword:

> Ya! but I woold that sword wer in a gled [fire],
> For, iwys, fader, yt make me full yll agast.
>
> (ll. 381–82)

Never, he tells his father, has he been so anxious to go home and speak to his dear mother!

After Abraham and Isaac have left the stage, a Doctor enters to point out the moral of the solemn story just re-enacted: we must keep God's commandments, however hard they might seem, "withowt grochyng [grumbling]." The moralizing Doctor is a familiar figure in medieval drama; he appears in countless plays—including *Everyman*—to speak the epilogue which interprets the action of the play. The moral of the Brome *Abraham and Isaac* may occasionally be obscured by the play's somewhat excessive sentimentality, but it manages to emerge with a good deal of charm.

The Chester Deluge

One of the most interesting plays in the *Chester Cycle* (perhaps the earliest of the four great cycles) is *The Deluge*, which deals with the Biblical flood. In this brief and generally sober play God finds the people of the earth "sett fowle in sinne" and accordingly decides to destroy mankind—except, of course, for his righteous servant Noah. After Noah's family has completed the arduous task of building the ark, a complication develops: Noah's wife refuses to take her place in the ark. She cannot, after all, leave her "gossips," or cronies. Noah seizes the opportunity to address the spectators on the subject of the cantankerousness of women:

> Lord, that women be crabbed aye,
> And never are meke, that dare I saye.
> This is well sene by me to daye,
> In witnes of yow each one.
>
> (ll. 105–8)

The "Good Gossips," for their part, enter with a bottle of malmsey; they want to have one more drink before the flood comes in. Noah's wife finally has to be dragged into the ark, but she is not satisfied until she has dealt Noah a lively blow. (Mrs. Noah was bound to become, like Herod, a popular favorite—the perfect embodiment of the stubborn shrew.) After this domestic squabble, the play resumes its serious tone. Noah dispatches the raven and the dove, and God seals a new covenant of peace with mankind. Early though the play may be, the Chester *Deluge* illustrates how easily a grave subject could be seasoned with gaiety. In the Wakefield *Noah*, a later work probably by "The Wakefield Master," the comedy is more fully exploited. Noah and his wife have a resounding free-for-all in which name-calling and good solid clouts are just about equally mixed. Noah, of course, is finally victorious.

The Second Shepherds' Play

To conclude this survey of the English miracle, we turn to what is probably the most distinguished dramatic creation of the Middle Ages—that remarkable work by "The Wakefield Master" known as the *Second Shepherds' Play* (to differentiate it from the *First Shepherds' Play*, by the same author). This astonishing metrical tour de force employs alliteration and is written in an intricate nine-line stanza, rhyming *aaaabcccb*. The first four lines, which are longer, also rhyme together in midline.

The play consists of two episodes, a comic one about sheep-stealing, followed by a serious one about the Nativity. In the longer first part the rascally shepherd Mak pretends to be an enchanter, steals a sheep from his three sleeping comrades, and, with his wife Jill, dresses it as an infant and conceals it in a cradle in his cottage. The trick works for a while, thanks largely to Jill's well-earned reputation for almost unlimited fecundity. But the victimized shepherds, after a fruitless search of the cottage, suddenly remind themselves that they have neglected to bring presents for the supposed baby. When they return to the cottage and discover that the "baby" has an unusually long snout, the indomitable Mak tries desperately to brazen it out; surely, he says, the child has been bewitched. Nevertheless, the shepherds expose the ingenious hoax, toss Mak in a blanket, and return to the fields to sleep. In the very brief second part of the play, the shepherds are awakened by an angel and directed to Bethlehem to see the Christ child.

Despite the apparent differences in mood between the first and second episodes, "The Wakefield Master" has succeeded brilliantly in unifying the farcical and serious elements of the play. The visit of the shepherds to Mak's cottage with gifts for the "baby" nicely anticipates their subsequent visit to the manger. In both episodes the shepherds are roused from a sleep to visit a newborn child. The first birth that they are prepared to honor turns out to be a fraud, an experience that emphasizes in the writer's intention the genuineness of the Nativity. Moreover, the poet does not think of the Nativity primarily as an event of overpowering solemnity—as Milton does in his philosophic poem *On the Morning of Christ's Nativity*. To "The Wakefield Master" Christ's birth is a simple, though momentous, part of the familiar everyday experience of humble shepherds who can frolic one moment and quietly adore the next. A reader comes to feel that the tone of the *Second Shepherds' Play* is just right for expressing the view of the Nativity as something intimate and peaceful—an approach that makes its future impact upon the world seem all the more wonderful.

Perhaps the most memorable quality of the *Second Shepherds' Play* is the vitality of its characters. Each of Mak's victims is crisply differentiated. The first shepherd, shivering with cold, complains about exploitation at the hands of the gentry; no wonder shepherds are poor, he laments, when their taxes are overwhelming and their lands lie fallow. The second shepherd is woefully henpecked; he bewails his private marital troubles, then addresses a warning to the young bachelors in the audience. "Be well war of wedyng," he advises; for it does not help to exclaim belatedly from the depths of matrimonial misfortunes, "Had I wyst [known]." The third shepherd grumbles about how he sweats and toils while his rich master takes it easy. "We ar oft weytt and wery/when mastermen wynkys [sleep]." All three of these characters, merely lumped together as "Shepherds" in the scriptural account, are touchingly humanized; witness, for example, their marvelous simplicity in bringing to the Christ child gifts which they know children appreciate—a bob of cherries, a bird, and a ball! The vivacious Mak, an expertly realized character, blusters and cringes with sparkling comic effect. When he is accused of the theft, he enjoys the daring little joke of protesting his innocence while pointing to the very cradle that contains the stolen sheep:

> As I am true and lele,/to God here I pray
> That this be the fyrst mele/that I shall ete this day.
>   (ll. 521–22)

His wife Jill picks up the amusing irony—assuring the suspicious shepherds that if she is guilty she will gladly eat the child that lies in the cradle. And how splendidly she groans to simulate the pain of a woman who has just given birth! Has she not had ample experience to equip her to put on a realistic act?

In addition to its many intrinsic merits as dramatic art, the *Second Shepherds' Play* crystallizes the development of English drama up to the time of its composition and simultaneously furnishes a preview of what is to come later. For one thing, "The Wakefield Master" freely introduces native English figures into a traditional Biblical plot, just as Elizabethan dramatists will transplant almost everything they write about—whether it be derived from ancient Rome, early Scotland, or Renaissance Verona—to essentially English soil. Then, too, the play, as was suggested before, illustrates the complete ease with which medieval and Elizabethan dramatists can move from farce to high seriousness within the very same work. Moreover, the *Second Shepherds' Play* anticipates one of the structural characteristics of later English plays in which a comic subplot may be employed to parallel, and thereby illuminate, the more solemn business of the main plot.

It may be true, as at least one scholar has recently observed, that the *Second Shepherds' Play,* with its emphasis upon farce, has fostered in the minds of many readers a distorted image of what the typical serious English miracle, or mystery, play was like.* Be that as it may, the artistic excellence of the *Second Shepherds' Play* has made it—deservedly—a delight for the twentieth-century reader. And the fifteenth-century spectator, who had the privilege of actually watching the goodhearted shepherds take their revenge upon the playful Mak and then make their pleasant pilgrimage to the Christ child, must have enjoyed this fine play even more.

MORALITY PLAYS

It is especially difficult to speak with certainty about the origins of the morality play, a relatively late occurrence in medieval drama. The form may have developed, at least in part, out of the lively pulpit literature of the Middle Ages. It is also possible that the morality, together with its companion, the interlude, descended from the fabliau or from the folk play. A somewhat more recent hypothe-

* Hardin Craig, *English Religious Drama of the Middle Ages* (Oxford: Clarendon Press, 1955), p. 234 and *passim.*

sis is that the morality represents the dramatic treatment of the celebrated Dance of Death, a recurring motif of medieval art. We know, in any event, that the Middle Ages had a virtually insatiable capacity to construct and to enjoy moral allegory, and the living stage must have provided a rich outlet for the expression of this deeply ingrained allegorical impulse.

The morality, which was defined earlier as a dramatized allegory, dates from around 1400—the approximate date for *The Pride of Life,* a fragment which comprises the earliest extant English morality play. In this primitive work, the King of Life tries desperately to evade his enemy, Death, only to be inevitably overcome. *The Castle of Perseverance* (*c.* 1425), probably the oldest complete morality to have survived, presents the characteristic theme of the morality play: Man struggles to win salvation as the personified vices and virtues grapple for dominion over his soul. This theme is also treated in *Mankind* (*c.* 1475), but here the action is dominated by the farcical elements that are introduced in order to delineate the moral conflict more realistically. The crowning glory of the English morality is *Everyman* (*c.* 1500), a play so compelling that it has enjoyed commercial success even in twentieth-century revivals. But more of these plays in a moment.

Although the morality play declined in popularity around the middle of the sixteenth century, it left a permanent imprint upon English drama. The allegorical figures of the good and bad angels who appear in medieval plays hover above Marlowe's Faustus and fight for possession of his soul. The Prologue to Shakespeare's *Henry IV, Part Two* is spoken by Rumor, and Time himself bridges the gap between the first and second portions of *The Winter's Tale.* Morality can easily merge into tragedy, as in *Doctor Faustus;* and the tragic hero in Shakespeare usually seems, in a sense, to transcend his own personal agonies and to take on the larger nature of Everyman. In a more direct way, however, the morality (or interlude) may move into chronicle-history—a phenomenon illustrated in John Bale's curious *King John* (written sometime before 1548). Here the unfortunate sovereign, who lost Normandy to France and had the Magna Carta forced from him, suffers at the hands of conspirators named Sedition, Dissimulation, Private Wealth, and so on. These enemies of the state manage to seduce his subjects—Nobility and Clergy. By the end of the play the vice Sedition has become the man Stephen Langton (Archbishop of Canterbury, appointed over the opposition of King John by Pope Innocent III). All is eventually set right when Imperial Majesty, who was apparently a personification of Bale's own sovereign, Henry VIII, assumes the reign. The transition from allegory to history is complete.*

The Castle of Perseverance (c. 1425)

The Castle of Perseverance is a useful play with which to begin a study of the English morality, for it contains nearly all of the themes found in individual plays throughout the genre. This long work of more than 3,600 lines traces the entire life of its hero, *Humanum Genus* (Mankind), as he first wages a continually fluctuating battle with evil forces, and then, at the end, stands before the Lord to be judged. The play is of added interest because appended to the manuscript is a fascinating diagram showing how the elaborate action was staged. The plan calls for five scaffolds—belonging, respectively, to the World, the Flesh, the Devil, Covetousness, and God—to be erected in a circle around an area known as "the place." At the center of "the place" stands the Castle of Perseverance, under which is Mankind's bed. The protagonist remains at the bed "tyl he schal ryse and pleye." From time to time Mankind mounts the various scaffolds to indicate his commitment to one or another of the five forces; and when he himself is not involved in the action, the other figures act out their scenes on whatever scaffold is most appropriate for the particular setting. The staging therefore helps to clarify in visual terms the moral and psychological ordeal through which Mankind must pass.

As the play begins, Mankind ignores the counsel of his Good Angel and allows the Bad Angel to entice him into the service of the World. Mankind ascends the scaffold occupied by the World and his attendants (Lust and Folly), who array the hero in splendid garments and lead him to the scaffold of Covetousness. There he accepts the Seven Deadly Sins. But he is persuaded by Shrift and Penance to confess and is subsequently placed in the Castle of Perseverance ("strenger [stronger] thanne any in Fraunce"), where he will be protected from sin by the Seven Moral Virtues. His enemies (the World, the Flesh, and the Devil) attack the Castle; but they are repulsed by the Virtues, who are armed with roses—emblems of the Passion. All would seem to be in order until Covetousness, still aching from the beating administered him by the other Vices for letting

* See Thomas M. Parrott and R. H. Ball, *A Short View of Elizabethan Drama* (New York: Charles Scribner's Sons, 1943), p. 21.

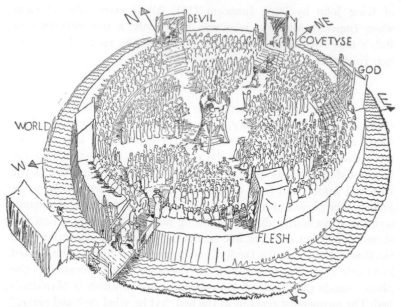

Richard Southern's reconstruction of a medieval theatre. From *The Medieval Theatre in the Round* by Richard Southern. Reproduced by permission of the author and the publisher, Theatre Arts Books, New York. All rights reserved.

Mankind slip away, tempts the now aged hero out of the Castle with promises of wealth. As the Virtues plead with Mankind to remain in the Castle, they are interrupted by the impatient Bad Angel. "Ya! go forthe, and lete the qwenys [harlots] cakle!" Mankind's greed is cut short, however, by Death, who appears without warning and strikes him with a dart. In vain Mankind calls upon the World for help. His entreaties having been spurned, there is nothing for Mankind to do but pray that God may deliver his soul from hell:

> Now my lyfe I have lore [lost].
> Myn hert brekyth. I syhe sore.
> A word may I speke no more.
> I putte me in Godys mercy.
>
> (ll. 3005–8)

The Four Daughters of God are divided as to the destiny of Mankind's soul. Righteousness, supported by Truth, would punish the Soul according to its deserts. "As he hath browyn [brewed], lete hym drynke!" But Mercy and Peace eloquently plead with the Father in Mankind's behalf. Of course God pardons Mankind and admits the

Soul to heavenly bliss. Then the actor impersonating God turns to the spectators and points out the moral:

> Thus endyth oure gamys!
> To save you fro synnynge,
> Evyr at the begynnynge
> Thynke on youre last endynge!
> *Te, Deum, laudamus!*
> (ll. 3046–50)

To be sure, *The Castle of Perseverance* does not move with the swiftness and efficiency of the greater *Everyman,* which is one-fourth its length. Nevertheless, it frequently comes alive with earthy, colloquial dialogue. And no other morality can match its comprehensive treatment of man's spiritual journey.

Mankind (c. 1475)

Perhaps the strangest specimen of medieval religious drama is *Mankind.* Superficially, at least, the play looks like a morality. The hero forgets the sound advice of Mercy and succumbs to the temptations of Mischief, New-Gyse, Now-a-Days, and Nought—all agents of Titivillus, a hideously attired devil armed with a net to ensnare the soul. At the end of the play Mankind departs with Mercy's blessing. Mercy then warns the spectators to "serche your condicyons with dew examinnacion," for "the world ys but a wanite [vanity]. . . ." But the reader will not find in *Mankind* the dignity and edification he has come to expect of the morality. What stands out is the play's almost perpetual emphasis upon low comedy—a fact which underscores the kinship frequently observed between the morality and the interlude. The medieval moralist, quite properly, had to paint a disgusting picture of vice; but it is possible that the author of *Mankind* did not accurately gauge his artistic effects. Titivillus and his grotesque crew simply revel in foul speech and coarse antics, almost to the point of obscuring the moral purpose for which these characters were introduced. The play also indicates the extent to which professionalism had crept into the drama. At one point there is an explosion, followed by the off-stage shouting of the as yet unseen Titivillus (a popular stage name for a devil). "I com, with my leggis undur me!" The spectators, however, are not permitted sight of "hys abhomynabull presens" until the actors have stopped the action and passed among them for a collection.

Everyman (c. 1500)

Outstanding among the moralities is the justly celebrated *Everyman,* which is either an original English work or, as is generally believed, a derivation from a Dutch play of approximately the same date, *Elckerlijk.*

The story was conventional enough in its day, but it is told here with exceptional skill. After a brief Prologue announces the theme of the play, God dispatches his servant Death to get Everyman ready for a pilgrimage "which he in no wyse may escape." Everyman, naturally enough, is initially untroubled by any thought of death. "Full lytell he thynketh on my comynge," Death observes. "His mynde is on flesshely lustes, and his treasure." When Everyman learns the identity of the messenger who has come for him, the change in his attitude is striking:

> O Deth! thou comest whan I had ye leest in mynde!
> In thy power it lyeth me to save;
> Yet of my good [goods] wyl I gyve ye, yf thou wyl be kynde;
> Ye, a thousande pounde shalte thou have,
> And [thou] dyfferre [defer] this mater tyll an other daye.
>
> (ll. 119–23)

Everyman, who is very human, does not realize that Death may be neither bribed nor forestalled. But if Everyman is not granted the twelve years he needs to build up his moral account, he is at least permitted to take any of his lifelong associates with him—provided, of course, that they are willing to make the journey.

Much to his disappointment, Everyman makes the painful discovery that none of his former companions will accompany him. Fellowship, Kindred, Cousin, Goods—each of these figures speaks as an abstraction, but each is a sharply defined individual. Fellowship breezes in ready to follow Everyman anywhere; he would even die for his friend, but when he hears that death literally awaits Everyman, he backs down:

> And yet, yf thou wylte ete, and drynke, and make good chere,
> Or haunt to women the lusty company,
> I wolde not forsake you whyle the daye is clere,
> Truste me, veryly.
>
> (ll. 272–75)

There is delightful irony as Fellowship, with a perfectly straight face, continues to protest his devotion by assuring Everyman that he would be happy to join him in murder. "In that I wyll helpe the with a good wyll." Such is the delusion under which Fellowship labors! Kindred offers Everyman her maid to help in the journey, but she herself must stay behind. Cousin, after pledging eternal loyalty, withdraws on account of a cramp in the toe. Besides, Cousin's own life has to be lived. All of Everyman's friends, of course, wish him well.

Everyman's encounter with Goods is perhaps the most brilliant scene in the play. When he perceives the emptiness of men's promises of love, Everyman turns as a last resort to Goods, whom he has adored more than all else in life. It takes a while for Goods to arrive, for he must work his way out of the corners, chests, and bags into which he has been packed. He may help Everyman to remedy any earthly sorrow, but he follows no man into the grave. It is, in fact, man's devotion to Goods that has most soiled his record. Goods would therefore only jeopardize Everyman's future bliss:

> For, and I wente with the,
> Thou sholdes fare much the worse for me;
> For bycause on me thou dyd set thy mynde,
> Thy rekenynge I have made blotted and blynde,
> That thyne accounte thou can not make truly—
> And that hast thou for the love of me!
>
> (ll. 416–21)

His excuse is blunt and cruel, but correct: "I am to brytell; I may not endure." At Everyman's insistence that he has always loved him deeply, Goods makes a fearful retort:

> That is to thy dampnacyon, without lesynge [lying]!
> For my love is contrary to the love everlastynge.
>
> (ll. 429–30)

Once Everyman is dead, Goods promises to deceive someone else in precisely the same way. The interview with Goods is both sound theology and exciting theater.

From this point on, the play deals with the way in which Everyman can achieve salvation. The only character who can go with him is Good Deeds, who at first lies cold in the ground, too weak to stand or even to speak. But Good Deeds sends Everyman to Knowledge, who leads him to the cleansing river of Confession and, later, guides him to Priesthood—the orthodox way to redemption. At last Good Deeds is strong enough to rise and join Everyman. Gradually Everyman is deserted by the last of his worldly possessions—Beauty, Strength, Discretion, the Five Wits, and, on the very threshold of the grave, even by Knowledge. As the redeemed Everyman enters Paradise, Knowledge announces that he has been saved:

> Now hath he suffred that we all shall endure.
> The Good Dedes shall make all sure.
> Now hath he made endynge.
> Methynketh that I here aungelles synge,
> And make grete joy and melody
> Where Everymannes soule receyved shall be.
>   (ll. 888–93)

An angel receives Everyman's soul. "Thy rekenynge is crystall clere."

Despite a tendency to obvious moralization—a characteristic shared by all the moralities—*Everyman* occupies a distinguished place in English drama. It retains all the universality and grandeur of allegory without surrendering the freshness and immediacy of everyday reality closely observed. The reader is almost always aware of the figures in the play as flesh-and-blood people rather than empty personifications. Moreover, within the brief compass of some nine hundred lines *Everyman* presents a stirring summary of the most deeply felt tenets of medieval faith. It is therefore a fitting work with which to conclude an examination of the literature of the Middle English period.*

* The present discussion of the drama is heavily indebted to several "classic" studies by Edmund K. Chambers, Karl Young, and, more recently, Hardin Craig. There are, in addition, the important "revolutionary" studies by Gardiner, Salter, Southern, and Wickham (see MEB 326, 329, 330, 333). For a clear account of the tangled development of medieval drama, the student or general reader can consult the first chapter of Parrot and Ball, *op. cit.;* or Alan S. Downer, *The British Drama: A Handbook and Brief Chronicle* (New York: Appleton-Century-Crofts, Inc., 1950), pp. 1–48.

PART THREE
BIBLIOGRAPHIES

PREFACE TO OLD AND MIDDLE
ENGLISH BIBLIOGRAPHICAL GUIDES *

The bibliographies in the following chapters are designed to guide the general reader, the college undergraduate, and the graduate student onto the highways, and a few of the byways, leading to a further understanding of the literature and culture of Anglo-Saxon and later medieval England. It is hoped that they will be of service to the teacher and scholar as well. They are planned both to complement and to supplement the text of this *Guide,* and to this end the major divisions are arranged in the same order as the chapters in the text. (Note that although the major divisions are numbered the same as the chapters in the text, individual item numbering starts over again for the Middle English section.)

These are selected bibliographies, with the emphasis on recent studies and on current scholarly thought and controversy. As a general principle, there are no entries of critical or textual notes on individual words, lines, or passages. All works cited are in English.

The following special features may be mentioned: (1) items that may be read pleasurably and profitably by the general reader and undergraduate, as well as items considered indispensable for all readers, have been starred (*); and material that the general reader should examine first has been listed ahead of other items in the same category; (2) the annotations are generally fuller than those in any other bibliography except for the annual *Year's Work in English Studies* (OEB 15), and they attempt in many cases to provide a critical evaluation of the items entered; (3) many sections have introductory paragraphs summarizing critical trends and opinions; (4) items in some categories—e.g., on the structure and unity of *Beowulf*—have been listed chronologically to clarify the direction of scholarly debate and interpretation; and special topical groupings—e.g., on "Reading Medieval Allegory-Symbolism"—have been set up; (5) items that summarize and review critical scholarship, as well as important bibliographical sources, are mentioned prominently;

* Research for these bibliographies has been supported in part by a grant from the Office of Scientific and Scholarly Research of the University of Oregon.

(6) cross references from one title to other sources and to other titles in the two bibliographies appear throughout (e.g., in the citation under 4 [Kennedy, Charles W. . . .], the cross reference [OEB 43, 98, 134, 171] refers to the respective numbers within the Old English Bibliography of the present book).

The following abbreviations have been used:

ABR   *American Benedictine Review*
AS   *American Speech*
CBEL   *Cambridge Bibliography of English Literature*
CE   *College English*
CHEL   *Cambridge History of English Literature*
CL   *Comparative Literature*
CMH   *Cambridge Medieval History*
E & S   *Essays and Studies of the English Association*
EETS   *Early English Text Society*
EETSES   *Early English Text Society, Extra Series*
EIC   *Essays in Criticism*
ELH   *ELH, A Journal of English Literary History*
ES   *English Studies*
JAF   *Journal of American Folklore*
JEGP   *Journal of English and Germanic Philology*
MAE   *Medium Aevum*
MEB   *Middle English Bibliography (of this book)*
MHRA   *Modern Humanities Research Association (Annual Bibliography)*
MLN   *Modern Language Notes*
MLQ   *Modern Language Quarterly*
MLR   *Modern Language Review*
MP   *Modern Philology*
MS   *Mediaeval Studies (Toronto)*
Neophil   *Neophilologus (Gröningen)*
OEB   *Old English Bibliography (of this book)*
PBA   *Proceedings of the British Academy*
PMLA   *Publications of the Modern Language Association of America*
PQ   *Philological Quarterly*
RES   *Review of English Studies*
RSSCW   *Research Studies of the State College of Washington*
SN   *Studia Neophilologica*

SP   *Studies in Philology*
TSE   *Tulane Studies in English*
UTQ   *University of Toronto Quarterly*
YWES   *Year's Work in English Studies*

Note: N.S. after any abbreviation or title means New Series.

CHAPTER XVI: AN OLD ENGLISH BIBLIOGRAPHICAL GUIDE

A large part of the scholarship in this period, and in the Middle English period, has been devoted to establishing texts, provenience (sources and analogues), dialect, date, etc. Since most editions have full critical apparatus and do discuss these features, and since editions of major works have been listed, special articles relating to these matters are not mentioned here. When these features have already been authoritatively dealt with by scholarship, modern criticism has been concerned to elucidate such problems as Christian philosophy and practice as they appear in the literature, the complexities of medieval allegory and symbolism, the structure and unity of individual poems, and matters of style such as the questions of conventionality (formulas) vs. originality and of oral vs. written composition; it is this *literary* criticism to which this bibliography is largely devoted.

A. *General Collections (Editions and Translations)*

1. *The Anglo-Saxon Poetic Records.* Eds. George P. Krapp and Elliott V. K. Dobbie. New York, 1931–53. I. *The Junius Manuscript;* II. *The Vercelli Book;* III. *The Exeter Book;* IV. *Beowulf and Judith;* V. *The Paris Psalter and the Meters of Boethius;* VI. *The Anglo-Saxon Minor Poems.* This uniform edition is primarily for scholars. The object of the series is to establish the texts of the poems. Each volume contains a bibliography, chronologically arranged, within the conventional categories (i.e., Manuscript and Transcripts, Complete Texts, Partial Texts, Translations, General Works, Textual Criticism or Critical Discussions). The bibliographies are extensive but not exhaustive. Notes are mainly textual and linguistic. No glossaries.

2. * *The Exeter Book: Edited from the Manuscript with a Translation.* Part I, poems I–VIII, ed. Israel Gollancz. EETS 104. London, 1895. Part II, poems IX–XXXII, ed. W. S. Mackie. EETS 194. London, 1934. Although outdated, and with no critical apparatus, still of value for its face-to-face text and translation of this important MS, containing, among other poems, *Christ, Guthlac, Phoenix, Juliana,* the elegies, *Widsith,* and the riddles.

3. * Gordon, Robert K. *Anglo-Saxon Poetry.* Rev. ed. Everyman's Library, New York, 1954. Translations in prose. Readily accessible, serviceable, and comprehensive in its coverage.
4. * Kennedy, Charles W. *An Anthology of Old English Poetry.* New York, 1960. A paperback selection from Kennedy's famous translations (see OEB 43, 98, 134, 171).
5. * Whitelock, Dorothy. *English Historical Documents, I, c. 500–1042.* London, 1955. Brings together and translates material from many sources which would be otherwise difficult to come by and to use. Excellent introductions to the various pieces. The extracts are arranged under the headings of Secular Narrative, Charters and Laws, and Ecclesiastical Sources.
6. * Douglas, D. C., and Greenaway, G. W. *English Historical Documents, II, 1042–1189.* London, 1953. Brings together and translates many late Old English texts (especially good for the *Annals* or *Anglo-Saxon Chronicle*) and many important Latin works of the period. Has an excellent discussion of the historical background of the age, valuable introductions to texts, and useful bibliographies. Also has a complete facsimile of the famous Bayeux Tapestry.

Editions and translations of individual poems and of special collections (e.g., elegiac, Cynewulfian) are entered in the appropriate sections below.

B. *General Bibliographies*

Cumulative:

7. *The Cambridge Bibliography of English Literature.* 5 vols. Cambridge, 1941, 1957. See pp. 53–110 of Vol. I and pp. 40–94 of Vol. V (a supplement, to 1954). The most convenient and the fullest cumulative bibliography, covering historical, cultural, and literary material. For a review of *The Supplement* (Vol. V), see *MP,* LVI (Feb. 1959), 197–203.
8. Heusinkveld, Arthur H., and Bashe, E. J. *A Bibliographical Guide to Old English.* University of Iowa Humanistic Series, IV, 5. Iowa City, Iowa, 1931. Selected items, but annotated. Basic, though of course not up to date.
9. Ker, Neil R. *Catalogue of Manuscripts Containing Anglo-Saxon.* Oxford, 1957. Lists all known manuscripts which have any writings in Old English. Indispensable for the advanced student and scholar. For an excellent, detailed review, see R. Willard, *JEGP,* LIX (1960), 129–37.
10. * Renwick, William L., and Orton, H. *The Beginnings of English Literature to Skelton, 1509.* Rev. ed. London, 1952. Extremely useful and readable, with annotated bibliography. Before the bib-

liography of each work, there is a brief summary of subject matter and critical problems. Bibliographical entries give references to pages in *CBEL* (OEB 7) and in Heusinkveld and Bashe (OEB 8) where further bibliography may be found on the particular item. Unfortunately, the bibliography has been only sketchily supplemented since the first edition (1939).

Special cumulative bibliographies will be found in appropriate sections below. They will also be found in many of the other entries, especially *editions.*

Periodic:

11. *Annual Bibliography of English Language and Literature,* edited for the MHRA. Cambridge, 1921——. Essential. Especially good for finding reviews of books and the contents of various Festschriften, Anniversary Studies, Memorial Studies, etc.

12. *PMLA: Annual Bibliography.* Appears in April or May issue. Essential. Since 1956 it has international coverage (prior to that, only American scholars) and is nearly exhaustive. Does *not* contain purely historical or cultural references.

13. *Progress of Medieval and Renaissance Studies in the United States and Canada.* Present ed. S. Harrison Thomson. Boulder, Colorado, 1923——(published annually till 1933, biennially since). Contains bibliographical items produced by United States and Canadian scholars under heading of "List of Active Medieval and Renaissance Scholars." Also lists papers read at meetings of learned societies, books in press, doctoral dissertations, and special articles on a variety of subjects.

14. *Speculum.* A "Bibliography of Periodical Literature" appears in each quarterly issue, covering historical, cultural, linguistic, and literary material published in periodicals. (As of 1959, it deals only with American periodicals.)

15. *The Year's Work in English Studies.* London, 1921——. Contains excellent summaries of chief books and articles of current year. Some evaluation as well as summary from time to time. See chapter on "Old English."

See also OEB 32.

I. HISTORICAL AND LINGUISTIC BACKGROUNDS

A. *Historical and Cultural Backgrounds*

Bibliographies:

16. Bonser, Wilfrid. *An Anglo-Saxon and Celtic Bibliography, 450–1087.* 2 vols. Berkeley and Los Angeles, Calif., 1957. Vol. II con-

sists of an Author Index and a Subject and Topographical Index. Includes only cultural and historical material through 1953. Some items are descriptively annotated. Some main headings: General Culture (includes, among other subheadings: Scholars, Medicine, Music, Science), Archaeology, Numismatics, Epigraphy, Art. Essential.

17. Magoun, Francis P., Jr. "The Sutton-Hoo Ship Burial: A Chronological Bibliography," *Speculum*, XXIX (1954), 116–24. Bessinger, Jess B., Jr. "The Sutton-Hoo Ship Burial: A Chronological Bibliography, Part Two," *Speculum*, XXXIII (1958), 515–22. Together, these bibliographies provide an exhaustive, annotated account of writings about the burial from 1939, the date of its discovery, to 1958.

For later references, see OEB 11, 14, 15.

Studies:

Early historical and cultural studies emphasized Teutonic Antiquities and Germanic Heroic Legend; recent studies stress the cultural roles of the Church, law, economic policy, etc., and explore the revelations afforded by such sciences as numismatics, onomastics, etc. The general reader will find the first two items below an excellent introduction to the scholarship on, and the cultural backgrounds of, the Anglo-Saxon period.

18. * Whitelock, Dorothy. *Changing Currents in Anglo-Saxon Studies: An Inaugural Lecture.* Cambridge, 1958. This 32-page pamphlet gives an excellent sketch of the breadth and scope of recent Anglo-Saxon studies. Emphasis is historical rather than literary.

19. * Whitelock, Dorothy. *The Beginnings of English Society.* Pelican History of England, II. Baltimore, 1952. This paperback volume is especially valuable for its use of literature and history to illuminate each other. Contains a selected, annotated bibliography of works in English.

20. * Blair, Peter H. *An Introduction to Anglo-Saxon England.* Cambridge, 1956. Designed to introduce the general reader to the political, ecclesiastical, social, and economic history of the times. Contains a fuller treatment of literature in the vernacular tongue than is usual in historically oriented books. Plates; selected bibliography.

21. *The Cambridge Medieval History.* 8 vols. 2nd ed. Cambridge, 1924. A comprehensive history of the Middle Ages. For the student of Old English literature, the following volumes and chapters will be especially rewarding: I, 13; II, 15–17; III, 14, 15, 19.

22. Chadwick, Hector M. *The Heroic Age.* Cambridge, 1912. Perhaps

the most important study of the Migration Period on the Continent and of the heroic elements behind the literature of the Old English period.

23. * Duckett, Eleanor S. *Alcuin, Friend of Charlemagne: His World and His Work*. New York, 1951. An illuminating contribution to our knowledge of one of the greatest of English scholars of Anglo-Saxon times (735–804), an important figure in the Carolingian Renaissance.

24. * Duckett, Eleanor S. *Anglo-Saxon Saints and Scholars*. New York and London, 1947. Studies of Aldhelm, Wilfrid, Bede, and Boniface. A thorough, inspirational study.

25. Gummere, Francis B. *Germanic Origins: A Study in Primitive Culture*. Reissued as *Founders of England*, ed. Francis P. Magoun, Jr. New York, 1930. A standard reference work on the subject.

26. * Hodgkin, Robert H. *A History of the Anglo-Saxons*. 2 vols. 3rd ed. London, 1953. Valuable, though it covers the period only to the death of Alfred (899). *The third edition has an important appendix, by R. L. S. Bruce-Mitford, on "The Sutton Hoo Ship-Burial."*

▮ 27. Levison, Wilhelm. *England and the Continent in the Eighth Century*. Oxford, 1946. A monumental work, surveying the culture England took from, as well as that which it gave to, the Continent. For the advanced student and scholar.

28. Schütte, Gottfried. *Our Forefathers: The Gothonic Nations. A Manual of the Ethnography of the Gothic, German, Dutch, Anglo-Saxon, Frisian and Scandinavian Peoples*. Trans. Jean Young. 2 vols. Cambridge, 1929–33. Indispensable reference work for the advanced student and scholar.

29. Stenton, Sir Frank M. *Anglo-Saxon England*. 2nd rev. ed. Oxford, 1947. Undoubtedly the most comprehensive one-volume history of the period. Fundamental for any serious study. Contains a full bibliography.

30. Thompson, A. Hamilton, ed. *Bede: His Life, Times, and Writings*. Oxford, 1935. Contains eleven essays by divers hands on various aspects of Bede and his age; e.g., Northumbrian Monasticism, Bede as Historian, Bede as Exegete and Theologian, Bede's Miracle Stories.

(On Bede, see also OEB 196 and MEB 168; for further references to Anglo-Latin literature, see OEB 7.)

Valuable also is Poole, *Medieval England* (MEB 20), which has much to say on Anglo-Saxon England, and Duckett, *Alfred the Great* (OEB 92). See also Anderson, *The Literature of the Anglo-Saxons* (OEB 44), and the entries under "General" in Section III (*Heroic Poetry*).

B. *Linguistic Background*

Bibliographies:

31. Kennedy, Arthur G. *A Bibliography of Writings on the English Language . . . to 1922.* Cambridge, Mass., 1927. Although not up to date, essential. Over 13,000 items.

32. Dobbie, Elliott V. K. "General and Historical Studies," *AS.* Appears in May and December issues under general heading of "Bibliography." An annotated bibliography of the history of the language. See also OEB 11–15, 34.

33. * Baugh, Albert C. *A History of the English Language.* 2nd ed. New York, 1957. A very readable, basic text with good bibliographies at the end of each chapter. Germanic backgrounds and Old English are treated only briefly. Stresses cultural aspects of history of the language. Cf. OEB 38.

34. Campbell, Alistair. *Old English Grammar.* London, 1959. Uses West-Saxon, Anglian, and Kentish documents as basis of grammar. Has an extensive if selected bibliography. For the specialist.

35. * Jespersen, Otto. *Growth and Structure of the English Language.* 9th ed. New York, 1955. Eminently readable and easily accessible in paperback edition. A classic in its field.

36. Moore, Samuel, and Knott, T. *The Elements of Old English.* 9th ed. Ann Arbor, Mich., 1942. A good introductory grammar, with interesting readings.

37. * Quirk, Randolph, and Wrenn, C. L. *An Old English Grammar.* 2nd ed. London, 1958. Most valuable for its discussion of syntax, an aspect of the grammar slighted in other handbooks.

38. * Robertson, Stuart, *The Development of Modern English,* rev. by F. G. Cassidy. 2nd ed. New York, 1954. Better than Baugh (OEB 33) on purely linguistic matters.

39. Thieme, Paul. "The Indo-European Language," *Scientific American,* CXCIX (Oct. 1958), 63–74. A very readable yet learned spread on the Indo-European background.

40. Wright, Joseph and E. M. *Old English Grammar.* 3rd ed. Oxford, 1925. A standard reference work for the specialist.

The above merely scratch the surface; consult also OEB 7, 11, 12, 31, 32.

Dictionaries:

41. Bosworth, J. *An Anglo-Saxon Dictionary.* With Supplement by T. N. Toller. Oxford, 1882–1920. Commonly referred to as "Bosworth-Toller." The most comprehensive of Old English dictionaries.

42. Hall, J. R. Clark. *A Concise Anglo-Saxon Dictionary.* Cambridge, 1931. More convenient for the student than Bosworth-Toller.

There are also an important dictionary of the poetic vocabulary and an etymological dictionary *in German,* by Grein and Holthausen, respectively.

II. ANGLO–SAXON LITERARY CULTURE

Note: Bede and other Anglo-Latin writers have been considered in the previous section.

A. *Surveys*

43. * Kennedy, Charles W. *The Earliest English Poetry.* London, 1943. Though subtitled "A Critical Survey," it is more significant for its knowledgeable and inspiring enthusiasm and for its communication of the vitality of Old English poetry than for its critical perspectives. Large chunks of the poetry are translated here into fine alliterative verse. (Does not, of course, consider the prose.)

44. Anderson, George K. *The Literature of the Anglo-Saxons.* Princeton, N. J., 1949. The most recent literary history devoted exclusively to Old English literature. Readable and contains a bibliography in notes at the end of each chapter. But the book's generalizations, critical judgments, and even facts must be used with great caution: see K. Malone, *JEGP,* XLIX (1950), 243–45.

45. *The Cambridge History of English Literature.* Vol. I. Cambridge, 1907. Valuable survey, though it does not, of course, take into account recent scholarship and critical approaches.

46. * Malone, Kemp. "The Old English Period, to 1100," in *A Literary History of England,* ed. Albert C. Baugh. New York, 1948. An excellent survey with perceptive critical comments. Numerous footnotes give a selected, useful bibliography.

47. * Wardale, Edith E. *Chapters on Old English Literature.* London, 1935. Despite being dated, a full and lucid account of the literature, with many translations of portions of the poetry.

48. Wilson, Richard M. *The Lost Literature of Medieval England.* London, 1952. Attempts to reconstruct the nature of "lost" material in Old and Middle English literature. Its most important conclusion for Old English is that there was a large body of historical narrative, now lost, and that it was this material, not the romance, which probably supplanted the older heroic poetry.

See also Renwick and Orton (OEB 10).

B. *Studies in Diction, Meter, Style, Themes, etc.*

Two important studies suggest that Anglo-Saxon literature is not cut off, as has often been assumed, from the general line of development of English literature:

49. * Chambers, Raymond W. *On the Continuity of English Prose from Alfred to More and His School.* In N. Harpsfield's *Life of Sir Thomas More.* EETS 186. London, 1932. Reprinted separately, Oxford, 1957. One of the earliest studies to disprove the theory of Anglo-Saxon decadence. A classic.

50. * Wrenn, Charles L. "On the Continuity of English Poetry," *Anglia,* LXXVI (1958), 41–59. Shows that there has been a survival of the Old English syllabic and stress patterns and a continuity in thought and mood and subject matter.

For an understanding of Anglo-Saxon versification:

51. * "Anglo-Saxon Versification," in Bright's *Anglo-Saxon Reader,* rev. and enlarged by James R. Hulbert. New York, 1935. Pp. 229–40. A clear presentation of Sievers' five-type system of scansion.

52. Pope, John C. *The Rhythm of Beowulf.* New Haven, Conn., 1942. For the advanced student and scholar. An important theory on the scansion of Old English poetry. Sees rhythm in musical analogies, with rests being a significant feature. Each half-line has two feet, sung or chanted in 4/8 or 4/4 time, the first foot being heavy or light, the second, regularly heavy. For criticism of Pope's theory, see R. Girvan, *RES,* XIX (1943), 73–77.

53. Bliss, Alan J. *The Metre of Beowulf.* Oxford, 1958. Argues that the Heusler-Pope interpretations of Old English scansion, based on a chronometric assumption, are untenable; that Old English rhythm is more likely based on ordinary prose rhythm (like its musical contemporary, Gregorian chant); that the basic Old English verse rhythm is ⌐ x (x) ⌐ x (underlying 40 per cent of the verses in *Beowulf*); that if the stresses are shifted forwards or backwards only four other patterns are possible; and that these five patterns (the basic and the possible displacements) explain the types of rhythm which actually occur in the verse and no others. These types are those advanced by Sievers, and Bliss's theory is a return to, and an expansion of, Sievers' method of scansion. *An important book,* containing a complete index to the scansion of *Beowulf* and other relevant statistical data. For a detailed review, see W. P. Lehmann, *JEGP,* LIX (1960), 137–42. See also Nist (OEB 103).

For insights into poetic diction, use of formulas, and other stylistic features:

54. Bartlett, Adeline C. *The Larger Rhetorical Patterns in Anglo-Saxon Poetry.* New York, 1935. Studies various larger verse patterns (e.g., "envelope," "incremental") widely used by Old English poets. Bibliography.

55. * Bracher, F. "Understatement in Old English Poetry," *PMLA*, LII (1937), 915–34. An important investigation of the origin, occurrence, and uses of litotes. Finds understatement used for irony, emphasis, humor, moderation—these categories being neither exclusive nor exhaustive.

56. Cross, J. E. " 'Ubi sunt' Passages in Old English—Sources and Relationships," *Vetenskaps-Societetens i Lund Årsbok* (1956), 25–41. Examines the fourteen examples of the *ubi sunt* ("Where are . . . ?") formula in Old English prose and verse, deducing that the formula is of Latin derivation and suggesting a close relationship between homiletic material, the elegies, and the Latin sources.

57. Greenfield, Stanley B. "The Formulaic Expression of the Theme of 'Exile' in Anglo-Saxon Poetry," *Speculum*, XXX (1955), 200–206. Examines various exile figures (Satan, Grendel, elegiac speakers, historical exiles, etc.) appearing in the poetry and finds common formulas used to depict them. Suggests a definition of originality in formulaic poetry and discusses examples of originality in some of the elegies.

58. * Magoun, Francis P., Jr. "Oral-Formulaic Character of Anglo-Saxon Narrative Poetry," *Speculum*, XXVIII (1953), 446–67. An important study. Calls attention to the pervasiveness of formulaic patterns in the narrative poetry, including *Beowulf*, and suggests that such poetry must have been orally composed. This oral-composition theory, though stimulating, has been challenged; see Schaar (OEB 60) and Brodeur (OEB 99).

59. Merwe Scholtz, H. van der. *The Kenning in Anglo-Saxon and Old Norse Poetry.* Utrecht, 1927. While not the best study of the kenning, it is the most thorough on the subject *in English*. But see also Brodeur (OEB 99).

60. Schaar, Claes. "On a New Theory of Old English Poetic Diction," *Neophil*, XL (1956), 301–305. A restrained attack on Magoun's theory of the oral nature of Old English poetry (see OEB 58), in particular on the contention that "lettered poetry is never formulaic."

61. * Stanley, E. G. "Old English Poetic Diction and the Interpretation

of *The Wanderer, The Seafarer* and *The Penitent's Prayer,*" *Anglia*, LXXIII (1956), 413–66. Most important for its survey and analysis of the *figurative use of language* by Old English poets, a study which takes up about two thirds of the article. Also has an illuminating if brief comparison of the three poems mentioned in the title: would place the first two within the penitential tradition.

62. Wyld, Henry C. "Diction and Imagery in Anglo-Saxon Poetry," *E & S*, XI (1925), 49–91. Discusses the problems in understanding shades of meaning in a diction so remote from our own times. (For further remarks on the oral vs. written composition of Old English poetry, see Girvan, Wright, and Brodeur (OEB 71, 74, 99). Bonjour (OEB 119), Schaar (OEB 172), and Oakden (MEB 53) also offer various comments on Old English poetic style.)

On religious thought, Christian and Teutonic, in prose and poetry:

63. * Gerould, Gordon H. *Saints' Legends*. Boston, 1916. Chapter III (The Epic Legend in Old English) and Chapter IV (Prose Legends before the Conquest) will give the beginner a survey of, and some insight into, the cultivation of this genre in Anglo-Saxon England.

64. Huppé, Bernard F. *Doctrine and Poetry: Augustine's Influence on Old English Poetry*. New York, 1959. Suggests that Old English poetry should be examined in the light of the Christian Latin tradition of medieval Biblical exegesis stemming from Augustine's comments in the *De doctrina Christiana* on the literal vs. the underlying meaning. In this light examines Caedmon's *Hymn* and the Caedmonian *Genesis* in detail.

65. Phillpotts, Bertha S. "Wyrd and Providence in Anglo Saxon Thought," *E & S*, XIII (1928), 7–27. An analysis of heroic Northern tales to ascertain the philosophy underlying the pagan attitude toward life.

66. Smithson, George A. *The Old English Christian Epic: A Study of the Plot Technique of the Juliana, the Elene, the Andreas and the Christ in comparison with the Beowulf and with the Latin Literature of the Middle Ages*. Berkeley, Calif., 1910.

67. Timmer, Benno J. "Wyrd in Anglo-Saxon Prose and Poetry," *Neophil*, XXVI (1940), 24–33; XXVI (1941), 213–28. Finds that in both the extant prose and poetry the word *wyrd* has lost any association with the heathen concept of a superhuman, blind, and hostile Fate. Asserts that it means "lot" or "death."

68. * Woolf, R. E. "The Devil in Old English Poetry," *RES*, N.S. IV (1953), 1–12. An interesting article suggesting that the Christian

devil and evil characters in Northern mythology and literature
(e.g., Loki, Bikki) had a certain affinity which helped in assimilat-
ing the concept of the wicked counselor with that of the faithless
retainer and eternal exile in Old English poetry.
See also OEB 57, 109, 116, 117.

Other studies of special interest:

69. Anderson, Lewis F. *The Anglo-Saxon Scop.* University of Toronto
    Studies in Philology, I. Toronto, 1903. A useful if somewhat ro-
    mantic treatment of the role of the poet in Anglo-Saxon society.

✓ 70. * Enkvist, Nils E. *The Seasons of the Year: Chapters on a Motif
    from Beowulf to the Shepherd's Calendar.* Copenhagen, Denmark,
    1957. (Commentationes Humanarum Litterarum, XXII, 4. Hel-
    singfors, Finland, 1957.) Contends that the Old English poets em-
    phasized winter and that passages describing winter are more
    forceful than those on other seasons but that the Christian poets
    in later Anglo-Saxon times were beginning to introduce descrip-
    tions of more pleasant weather, which is most apparent in the
    Phoenix.

71. * Girvan, Ritchie. "The Medieval Poet and His Audience," *English
    Studies Today,* International Conference of University Professors
    of English, ed. Charles L. Wrenn. Oxford, 1951. Pp. 85–97. Sug-
    gests that the poems in the four Old English codices (including
    Beowulf) were of written, not oral, provenience and were designed
    for the entertainment of religious houses. Elaborates on the differ-
    ences between oral and written poetry.

72. Meritt, Herbert D. *Fact and Lore about Old English Words.* Stan-
    ford University Publications, University Series, Language and
    Literature, XIII. Stanford, Calif., 1954. A treasury of lexico-
    graphical lore. Discusses and applies methods of elucidating words
    and word meanings. Invaluable for the scholar; interesting for the
    student.

73. Sisam, Kenneth. *Studies in the History of Old English Literature.*
    Oxford, 1953. An important book for advanced students and schol-
    ars. Collects various articles by Dr. Sisam, most of which concern
    problems of textual transmission. There are, among others, articles
    on "Cynewulf and His Poetry," "The Beowulf Ms.," and "Dialect
    Origins of the Earlier Old English Verse."

74. Wright, Cyril E. *The Cultivation of Saga in Anglo-Saxon England.*
    Edinburgh, 1939. Argues that the Anglo-Saxons had a fairly well-
    developed oral prose literature which had the form of saga. For
    adverse criticism, however, see A. G. Brodeur, *JAF,* LIV (1941),
    88–90.

III. BEOWULF AND THE HEROIC TRADITION

A. *General*

The books listed in this section need little comment; their titles generally indicate their scope. They will provide the general reader and the student with the larger background necessary to a fuller understanding of *Beowulf* and other Germanic heroic poems.

75. Bowra, Cecil M. *Heroic Poetry*. London, 1952. A major examination of written and oral heroic poetry from some thirty countries.
76. Brady, Caroline. *The Legends of Ermanaric.* Berkeley, Calif., 1943. A thorough study of one of the important figures in Germanic heroic legend.
77. * Carpenter, Rhys. *Folk Tale, Fiction and Saga in the Homeric Epics*. Berkeley and Los Angeles, Calif., 1946. Contains references to *Beowulf* throughout; Chapter VII and the "Postscript" especially have interesting comments on the "Bear's Son Tale" and on parallels between *Beowulf* and the Homeric epics.
78. Chadwick, Hector M. and Nora K. *The Growth of Literature*. Vol. I: *The Ancient Literature of Europe*. Cambridge, 1932.
79. Hart, Walter M. *Ballad and Epic*. Harvard Studies and Notes in Philology and Literature, XI. Cambridge, Mass., 1907. Though dated, it remains a classic study.
80. * Ker, William P. *Epic and Romance*. 2nd ed. London, 1908. Reissued, New York, 1958. One of the most famous of earlier studies. Eminently readable and still valuable.
81. Malone, Kemp. *Studies in Heroic Legend and in Current Speech*. Eds. S. Einarsson and N. E. Eliason. Copenhagen, Denmark, 1959. Reprints, with some revisions, many of the author's famous analyses and criticisms.
82. * Olrik, Axel. *The Heroic Legends of Denmark*. Trans. Lee M. Hollander. New York and London, 1919. An important and readable study of legendary material, most of which is relevant to the first part of *Beowulf*.
83. Routh, Harold V. *God, Man, and Epic Poetry*. Vol. II (Medieval). Cambridge, 1927. Has stimulating and original insights. Much on *Beowulf*.

See also Chambers (OEB 91).

For the reader who wishes to examine some of the Scandinavian heroic material for himself, the following translations are recommended: (1) *The Nine Books of the Danish History of Saxo Grammaticus*. Trans. Oliver Elton. 2 vols. Norroena Anglo-Saxon Classics, I and II.

London and Stockholm, 1905. (2) *The Saga of Hrolf Kraki.* Trans. Stella M. Mills. Oxford, 1933. (3) *The Poetic Edda.* Trans. Henry A. Bellows. Princeton, 1936. (4) *The Story of Grettir the Strong.* Trans. E. Magnússon and W. Morris. London and New York, 1900. (5) *The Saga of the Volsungs.* Trans. Margaret Schlauch. Scandinavian Classics, XXXV. 2nd ed. New York and London, 1949.

B. *Early Heroic Poetry: The Finnsburg Fragment, Waldere, and Widsith Editions of The Finnsburg Fragment and of Waldere:*

84. Dickins, Bruce. *Runic and Heroic Poems of the Old Teutonic Peoples.* Cambridge, 1915. Contains texts and translations and full critical apparatus.
   See also OEB 1, 94.
85. Mackie, W. S. "The Fight at Finnsburg," *JEGP,* XVI (1917), 250–73. A separate edition of the poem, with textual notes and introductory comment.
86. Norman, F. *Waldere.* London, 1934. A separate edition of the poem, with full critical apparatus.

Translations of *The Finnsburg Fragment* and of *Waldere* may be found in OEB 3, 5; of the former:

87. Malone, Kemp. *Ten Old English Poems, Put into Modern English Alliterative Verse.* Baltimore, 1941. In addition to *FF,* contains translations of *Dream of the Rood, The Wanderer, The Seafarer, The Wife's Lament, Wulf and Eadwacer, Brunanburh, Maldon, Widsith,* and *Deor.*

Commentaries on these two poems:

88. Carroll, Benjamin H., Jr. "An Essay on the Walther Legend," *Florida State University Studies,* V (1952), 123–79. Considers sources and problems. Reconstructs the original Walther story and discusses the meaning of the *Waldere* fragments.
89. Lawrence, William W. "Beowulf and the Tragedy of Finnsburg," *PMLA,* XXX (1915), 372–431. Pp. 407–14 deal especially with the "fight in the hall," to which the Fragment is devoted.
   See also Klaeber (OEB 94).

The best edition of Widsith:

90. Malone, Kemp. *Widsith.* London, 1935. Full discussion and critical apparatus.
   See also OEB 1, Vol. III, and OEB 2.

For translations, see Gordon (OEB 3) and Malone (OEB 87).

For commentaries on Widsith:

91. * Chambers, Raymond W. *Widsith: A Study in Old English Heroic Legend.* Cambridge, 1912. Essential for any study of the poem. A treasure mine of information.

92. French, Walter H. *"Widsith* and the Scop," *PMLA,* LX (1945), 623–30. Sees a unity in the poem centered on a poet's bid for patronage.

93. Lawrence, William W. "Structure and Interpretation of *Widsith,"* *MP,* IV (1906–07), 329–74. Studies the processes in the poem's evolution, isolating earliest structure of this "composite" poem as the lay of an imaginary scop written on the Continent before the 7th C.

See also Brady (OEB 76).

C. *Beowulf*

Important modern editions:

94. * Klaeber, Fr. *Beowulf and the Fight at Finnsburg.* 3rd ed. Boston, 1936. Supplements, 1941, 1950. *The* edition for a study of the poem. Elaborate critical and textual apparatus, including an extensive introduction (Argument of the Poem; Fabulous Elements; Historical Elements; Christian Coloring; Structure; Time, Style, Meter; Language and Manuscript; Genesis of the Poem), critical and textual notes, glossary, and *an annotated and exhaustive bibliography* (exhaustive to 1936).

95. * Wrenn, Charles L. *Beowulf: With the Finnesburg Fragment.* London, 1953. Rev. and enlarged, 1958. Although Klaeber's edition is fuller in every respect, this edition merits consideration as a sound and useful text, with some interesting interpretative suggestions in its notes. Particularly valuable for its introduction, which is comprehensive without being complicated. The 1958 revision adds little but some selected bibliographical items.

96. Zupitza, Julius. *Beowulf.* 2nd ed. EETS 245. London, 1959 (for 1958). Of great importance to the scholar and of interest to others is this new facsimile of the famous *Beowulf* MS with the transliteration of the text and the notes of Zupitza.

Important also, for the scholar especially, is Vol. IV of *The Anglo-Saxon Poetic Records* (OEB 1).

Translations:

97. * Hall, J. R. Clark. *Beowulf and the Finnsburg Fragment. A Translation into Modern English Prose.* Rev. by Charles L. Wrenn, with prefatory remarks by J. R. R. Tolkien. Rev. ed. London, 1950.

98. * Kennedy, Charles W. *Beowulf, the Oldest English Epic, Translated into Alliterative Verse.* New York, 1940. Undoubtedly the best translation for the student and general reader. Gives the flavor of the original. *Has an excellent introduction* of 65 pages, ranging in subject matter from the historical and legendary backgrounds to the possible influence of Virgil.
See also Gordon (OEB 3).

Commentaries

Important commentaries on *Beowulf* have been divided below into (1) books dealing with the variety of problems posed by the poem; (2) articles on the structure and unity of the poem; (3) miscellaneous works on special features. For the first category, the reader should see, of course, the introductions to Klaeber (OEB 94), Wrenn (OEB 95), Kennedy (OEB 98), and the following important books:

99. * Brodeur, Arthur G. *The Art of Beowulf.* Berkeley, Calif., 1959. An illuminating and systematic study of the poem as a work of art: chapters on Diction, Variation, Structure and Unity, Episodes and Digressions, Christian and Pagan, etc. Assumes a familiarity with the poem and with Old English for discussions of diction, but other chapters may be pleasurably and profitably read by all.

100. * Chambers, Raymond W. *Beowulf: An Introduction to the Study of the Poem with a Discussion of the Stories of Offa and Finn.* 3rd ed., rev. by Charles L. Wrenn. Cambridge, 1959. Indispensable for any advanced work on the poem. One of the great studies with extensive bibliography. The revision includes a significant chapter on Sutton Hoo.

101. Girvan, Ritchie. *Beowulf and the Seventh Century.* London, 1935. Stimulating discussion of the language, background, and legendary and historical material.

102. * Lawrence, William W. *Beowulf and Epic Tradition.* Cambridge, Mass., 1928. An extremely readable and knowledgeable book, not addressed exclusively to scholars. Shows how plot material and social and political background have been woven into the epic structure.

103. Nist, John A. *The Structure and Texture of Beowulf.* São Paulo, Brasil, 1959. A combination of elementary synopsis and critical evaluation. Contains new ideas about Old English metrics as well as remarks on structure and texture.

Some of the important recent articles on *structure and unity,* arranged chronologically, to give an idea of current thought on this central problem:

104. Du Bois, Arthur E. "The Unity of *Beowulf*," *PMLA,* XLIX (1934), 374–405. A compendium of interpretative information on many features of the poem; contains as much material in the footnotes as in the body of the article. Sees the poem as "an elaborate symphony of variations" in which "nations and principles within them, embodied in fabulous creatures [e.g., Grendel and his dam = Dane's liability to punishment for weakness and pride and treachery; the dragon = Geats' internal discord], are controlled by the poem's theme–fate, God."

105. * Tolkien, J. R. R. *Beowulf: The Monsters and the Critics.* London, 1959. (In *PBA,* XXII [1936], 245–95.) An important landmark in critical studies of the poem. Sees a symbolic unity, a rise and fall expressed in youth and age—challenging earlier opinion that the poem was loosely structured and held together only by the person of the hero.

106. Blomfield, Joan. "The Style and Structure of *Beowulf*," *RES,* XIV (1938), 396–403. A brief but perceptive article, suggesting that, as the accretion of "synonyms" in the poem gradually reveals different aspects of the "thing" described, so the structure of the poem itself is not sequential but cumulative, the parts of a situation being given coherence and significance by progressive addition.

107. Malone, Kemp. "Beowulf," *ES,* XXIX (1948), 161–72. Sees unity in the two parts of the poem in terms of the poet's patriotism for "Germania" and in the spiritual quality of the hero.

108. * Bonjour, Adrien. *The Digressions in Beowulf.* Medium Aevum Monographs, V. Oxford, 1950. Convincingly demonstrates that the digressions do not interrupt but rather advance the action of the poem and thus are structurally integral.

109. O'Loughlin, J. L. N. "*Beowulf*—Its Unity and Purpose," *MAE,* XXI (1952), 1–13. Finds unity and purpose in the parallel between Germanic and Christian ethical conflicts. Suggests that in its secular aspect, the poem stresses the conflict between the Germanic ideal of feud-settlement and the refusal of people to abide by this ideal; in the religious aspect, between the Christian ethic and the inhuman evil which cannot by its nature abide by that ethic.

110. Gang, T. M. "Approaches to *Beowulf*," *RES,* N.S. III (1952), 1–12. A bold attack on those who would find a unity in the poem

by being oversubtle; particularly finds Tolkien's symbolic approach invalid.

111. * Bonjour, Adrien. "Monsters Crouching and Critics Rampant: Or the *Beowulf* Dragon Debated," *PMLA,* LXVIII (1953), 304–12. Ably defends Tolkien's theory about the unity of the poem.

112. * Brodeur, Arthur G. "The Structure and Unity of *Beowulf,*" *PMLA,* LXVIII (1953), 1183–95. Sees continuity throughout the poem in subplot: the downfall of the Geatish and Danish kingdoms, the defeat of both ultimately being caused by Hygelac's death in his ill-fated Frankish raid. Beowulf's victories in both parts of the poem are thus counterbalanced by alluded-to defeats of the nations involved.

113. Van Meurs, J. C. "Beowulf and Literary Criticism," *Neophil,* XXXIX (1955), 114–30. Argues that modern criticism (i.e., Tolkien's and Bonjour's work) takes into too little account the historical setting. Suggests, as Gang had done, that perhaps there is not as much structural and artistic unity as the modern critic tends to see.

114. * Rogers, H. L. "Beowulf's Three Great Fights," *RES,* N.S. VI (1955), 339–55. Sees failure of artistic unity in the poem because poet found difficulty in imposing his moral ideas on his source. Examines motifs of weapons, treasure, and society throughout the poem. Finds material of second and third fights less congenial than that of the first fight to the poet's design.

115. Wright, Herbert G. "Good and Evil; Light and Darkness; Joy and Sorrow in *Beowulf,*" *RES,* N.S. VIII (1957), 1–11. Another defense of the unity of the poem (calling into question Gang's conclusions). Sees the poem's fundamental unity in the interrelation throughout of the opposites good-evil, light-darkness, joy-sorrow.

116. Fisher, Peter F. "The Trials of the Epic Hero in *Beowulf,*" *PMLA,* LXXIII (1958), 171–83. Sees unity in the theme of redemption and judgment, skillfully blending the Germanic hero and the Christian saint.

117. Kaske, Robert E. *"Sapientia et Fortitudo* as the Controlling Theme of *Beowulf,*" *SP,* LV (1958), 423–56. A judicious examination of the theme, stressing the fusion of Germanic and Christian concepts.

Articles on miscellaneous topics in connection with Beowulf:

118. Blackburn, F. A. "The Christian Coloring in the *Beowulf,*" *PMLA,* XII (1897), 205–25. An example of the attitude of

earlier criticism, which believed that the Christian element in the poem was an accretion, the work of a redactor, and of no poetic value.

119. Bonjour, Adrien. "On Sea Images in *Beowulf*," *JEGP*, LIV (1955), 111–15. An examination of connotative differences in synonyms for "sea" in the poem.

120. * Du Bois, Arthur E. "The Dragon in *Beowulf*," *PMLA*, LXXII (1957), 819–22. Suggests five ways in which an image acquires meaning: (1) arbitrary assignation by people *before* its use; (2) author's explications; (3) common associations; (4) self-declaration by the image itself; (5) in terms of a poem's context. In the light of (5), especially, sees the *Beowulf* dragon as an image of civil war.

121. Haber, Thomas B. *A Comparative Study of the Beowulf and the Aeneid.* Princeton, N. J., 1931. Suggests the possible debt of the *Beowulf* poet to Virgil.

122. * Hulbert, James R. "The Genesis of *Beowulf*: A Caveat," *PMLA*, LXVI (1951), 1168–76. Provides an interesting summary of various scholarly opinions about the composition of the poem, with a warning that Klaeber, Chambers, and others have not *proved* that the author was a Christian writing in the 8th C.: he *may* have been a pagan and the poem *may* be a "folk epic" which a later Christian redactor added to.

123. * Lumiansky, Robert M. "The Dramatic Audience in *Beowulf*," *JEGP*, LI (1952), 545–50. Maintains that the poet creates suspense in the three fights, despite his anticipating the outcomes, by using a dramatic audience which does *not* know the outcomes: in the Grendel fight, the terror-stricken Danes and bewildered Geats; in the fight with Grendel's dam, the Danes and the Geats by the pool; in the dragon fight, Wiglaf and the cowardly thanes.

124. Malone, Kemp. "Time and Place in the Ingeld Episode of *Beowulf*," *JEGP*, XXXIX (1940), 76–92. A good example of specialized study of one of the "digressions." Attacks the "prophetic" interpretation of Beowulf's report to Hygelac about the political peace between Danes and Heathobards and the ultimate renewal of the feud. Sees the action described by Beowulf's use of the present tense as contemporaneous with Beowulf's visit to Denmark and considers it to have taken place in the Danish court. But see Brodeur (OEB 99), pp. 157–81, for a convincing refutation and an illumination of this whole matter.

125. Peters, Leonard J. "The Relationship of the Old English *Andreas* to *Beowulf*," *PMLA*, LXVI (1951), 844–63. A study of the

verbal parallels between the two poems, coming to the conclusion that the generally accepted theory that the *Andreas* poet
used *Beowulf* as his model and borrowed therefrom is questionable.

126. Robertson, Durant W., Jr. "The Doctrine of Charity in Medieval
Literary Gardens: A Topical Approach Through Symbolism and
Allegory," *Speculum*, XXVI (1951), 24–49. Pp. 32–34 suggest
an allegorical interpretation of Grendel's mere as the "evil garden" of Scripture. By use of Christian parallels, we are supposed,
for example, to see in the hart who would rather give up its life
"than . . . hide its head in the grove surrounding the pool . . .
the faithful Christian who seeks his Lord in the Living Waters."

127. * Sisam, Kenneth. "Beowulf's Fight with the Dragon," *RES*,
N.S. IX (1958), 129–40. A fascinating reconstruction of the details of the dragon fight, with comments on inconsistencies, textual cruxes, etc. Infers that the audience had a special interest
in the fighting, and that it wanted details and wanted them well-
knit.

128. Storms, G. "The Figure of Beowulf in the O. E. Epic," *ES*, XL
(1959), 3–13. Analyzes the poet's synthesis of the "fairy-tale"
Beowulf and the "historic" Beowulf in the poem, concluding
that there could not have been a real historical prototype, as
many critics have suggested there was, behind the figure of this
epic hero.

129. * Whitelock, Dorothy. *The Audience of Beowulf*. Oxford, 1951.
A thoughtful and stimulating discussion of, among other items,
the probable knowledge of the *Beowulf* audience about events
and persons of Christian doctrine. Argues for a late 8th C. date
for the composition of the poem.

See also chapter on *Beowulf* in Chambers' *Man's Unconquerable Mind*
(MEB 168).

D. *The Religious Heroic Tale: Andreas and Judith*

Editions:

130. Krapp, George P. *Andreas and the Fates of the Apostles*. Boston,
1906.

131. Timmer, Benno J. *Judith*. London, 1952.
See also OEB 1, Vols. II and IV.

Translations: see Gordon (OEB 3) and Kennedy (OEB 171), the latter for *Andreas* only.

Commentaries: see Peters (OEB 125) and Schaar (OEB 172): these
discuss *Andreas*.

IV. ELEGIAC, CAEDMONIAN, AND CYNEWULFIAN VERSE

A. *Elegiac Verse: Deor, The Husband's Message, The Ruin, The Seafarer, The Wanderer, The Wife's Lament, and Wulf and Eadwacer*

Editions:

132. * Kershaw, Nora K. *Anglo-Saxon and Norse Poems.* Cambridge, 1922. Contains texts and translations of, and critical comments on, all the above verse except *Deor* and *Wulf and Eadwacer.* Also includes *Brunanburh.*

The elegies have been collectively edited also in OEB 1, Vol. III, and in OEB 2, along with other poems in *The Exeter Book.* Dickins (OEB 84) contains *Deor.* There is also a separate edition of *Deor:*

133. Malone, Kemp. *Deor.* London, 1933.

Translations:

134. * Kennedy, Charles W. *Old English Elegies.* Princeton, N. J., 1936. Contains an introduction to and excellent verse translations of all but *Wulf and Eadwacer.* Has a good selected bibliography.

See also OEB 2, 3, 87, 132.

Commentaries: these have been numerous, especially on *The Wanderer* and *The Seafarer.* Structure and unity and the Christian view of life expressed therein have been focal points of critical attention on these two poems. The comments on *The Wanderer* and *The Seafarer* have been listed chronologically.

Articles on The Wanderer and The Seafarer:

135. Ferrell, C. C. "Old Germanic Life in the Anglo-Saxon *Wanderer* and *Seafarer*," *MLN,* IX (1894), 402–407. An example of the earlier scholarly approach in its search for Teutonic antiquities.

136. * Lawrence, William W. "The Wanderer and The Seafarer," *JEGP,* IV (1902), 460–80. A critical landmark in the scholarship on the poems. Stresses an essential unity in the Christian and pagan elements. Still valuable and interesting.

137. * Anderson (Arngart), O. S. *The Seafarer: An Interpretation.* Lund, Sweden, 1937. (In K. Humanistiska Vetenskapssamfundets i Lund, Årsberättelse [1937–38], 1–50.) Provides a good summary of earlier critical theories, an analysis, a translation, and notes. Finds a unity in the poem by taking the first part (the sea voyage) as an allegory of man's life in this world. Cf. Smithers (OEB 145). Details of this interpretation are open to question, but this is a good place to begin a study of the poem.

138. Huppé, Bernard F. *"The Wanderer:* Theme and Structure," *JEGP*, XLII (1943), 516–38. The first modern "breakthrough" in understanding the thematic and structural unity in terms of the contrast between the mercy and eternality of God and the misfortunes and ephemerality of this life. Sees the structure as consisting of an introduction, a monologue by a wanderer, a bridge passage, a monologue by a wise man, and a conclusion. But see Greenfield (OEB 142) for detailed criticism of Huppé's arguments.

139. * Lumiansky, Robert M. "The Dramatic Structure of the Old English *Wanderer*," *Neophil*, XXXIV (1950), 104–12. Gives a detailed account of previous critical controversy. Sees the poem as a dramatic monologue in which the speaker expresses a "consolation of philosophy" that finds peace in virtuous conduct leading to God instead of in the tribulations of this transitory world.

140. * Whitelock, Dorothy. "The Interpretation of *The Seafarer*," in *The Early Cultures of North-West Europe*, eds. Sir Cyril Fox and Bruce Dickins. Cambridge, 1950. Pp. 261–72. Convincingly demonstrates the unity of the poem by adroit repunctuation between the "seafaring" and homiletic halves and by taking the seafarer as a *peregrinus* seeking salvation by forsaking earthly joys.

141. Robertson, Durant W., Jr. "Historical Criticism," *English Institute Essays, 1950*. New York, 1951. Pp. 3–31. Pp. 17–23 provide a good example of the "modern" allegorical approach to medieval literature, this time of *The Wanderer*. (Cf. OEB 126.)

142. Greenfield, Stanley B. *"The Wanderer:* A Reconsideration of Theme and Structure," *JEGP*, L (1951), 451–65. While subscribing to Huppé's thesis about the poem's unity, finds many flaws in his arguments. Sees the introduction and the conclusion of the poem as contrasting the superiority of the Christian way of life (seeking the mercy of God) to the Stoic way of life exemplified by the fictitious speaker in his growing awareness (from *eardstapa* to *snottor on mode*) of the universality of change and decay.

143. Greenfield, Stanley B. "Attitudes and Values in *The Seafarer*," *SP*, LI (1954), 15–20. Differs from Whitelock's theory (OEB 140) in finding the mind of the *peregrinus* torn between earthly joys he leaves behind and eternal joys he goes to find. Sees a further unity in double meanings (secular and Christian) of key words and phrases used in both parts of the poem.

144. Gordon, Ida L. "Traditional Themes in *The Wanderer* and *The Seafarer*," *RES*, N.S. V (1954), 1–13. While believing in the Christian unity of these poems, the author emphasizes the traditional elegiac material as the basis of poetic inspiration and form.

145. Smithers, George V. "The Meaning of *The Seafarer* and *The Wanderer*," *MAE*, XXVI (1957), 137–53; *MAE*, XXVIII (1959), 1–22. The most elaborate and persuasive attempt to establish an allegorical meaning for the exile-seafaring figures in these poems. Sees typical medieval eschatological sequences of thought, found in homilies and other literature of the period, mirrored, if not explicitly stated, by the poet(s); cites extensively parallels in thought and language. Makes the wider claim, on the basis of his investigation, that Old English poetry can be implicitly allegorical. Has some bold and interesting interpretations of several cruxes in *The Seafarer*.

146. * Rumble, Thomas C. "From *Eardstapa* to *Snottor on mode*: The Structural Principle of 'The Wanderer,' " *MLQ*, XIX (1958), 225–30. Valuable for its summary of recent critical theories.

147. Elliott, Ralph W. V. "The Wanderer's Conscience," *ES*, XXXIX (1958), 193–200. Assuming a *real* situation as the basis of the poem, the author advances the thesis that the wanderer is where he is because of an uneasy conscience, the result of his failure to carry out a boast to fight for his lord unto death and his subsequent exile and humiliation. He seeks comfort in the only source he can find it, the Christian faith; but the religion of the poem, says Elliott, is an ethical compromise.

148. Campbell, Jackson J. "Oral Poetry in *The Seafarer*," *Speculum*, XXXV (1960), 87–96. By analysis of formulas and poetic words, persuasively argues for an older and a later stratum in the poem, though believes that the poet smoothly fused both strata for his pious purposes. Accepts the allegorical interpretation as valid. Cf. OEB 137, 145.

See also OEB 61.

For comment on Deor:

149. Lawrence, William W. "The Song of Deor," *MP*, IX (1911–12), 23–45. As with his *Widsith* study (OEB 93), the author asserts that the poem is not autobiographical, but an imaginary artistic whole. Attempts to explain various allusive difficulties that many later articles (see bibliographies) still find elusive.

See also Brady (OEB 76) and various editions.

For comment on The Husband's Message:

150. * Elliott, Ralph W. V. "The Runes in *The Husband's Message*," *JEGP*, LIV (1955), 1–8. Provides a neat clarification of the difficult runes near the end of the poem in terms of the meaning of the whole poem. Sees the runes as the core of the message sent by the husband to his wife, the rune-names themselves tersely

giving the message carved on the wood: that the wife should go south over the sea to find new joy with her husband.

For comment on The Ruin:

151. Hotchner, Cecelia A. *Wessex and Old English Poetry, with Special Consideration of The Ruin.* Lancaster, Pa., 1939. Attempts to see the elegies as of Wessex provenience, and *The Ruin* as referring to Bath.

152. Dunleavy, Gareth W. "A 'De Excidio' Tradition in the Old English *Ruin?*" *PQ,* XXXVIII (1959), 112–18. Believes that the poet was working in the literary tradition of Gildas and Alcuin and may have drawn on first- or secondhand knowledge of the events and sights of Romano-British Chester, which the author proposes as the city described in the poem.

For comment on The Wife's Lament:

153. * Greenfield, Stanley B. *"The Wife's Lament* Reconsidered," *PMLA,* LXVIII (1953), 907–12. Summarizes earlier theories and finds an emotional unity in the speaker's hatred for, yet love of, her husband, who has used her cruelly.

154. Ward, J. A. *"The Wife's Lament:* An Interpretation," *JEGP,* LIX (1960), 26–33. Suggests that the husband of the wife has himself been exiled when the poem opens and that the speaker (the wife) suffers on account of his exile and their separation rather than on account of his enmity towards her. Sees the situation of the poem as resembling that of *The Husband's Message.*

For comment on Wulf and Eadwacer:

155. Adams, John F. " 'Wulf and Eadwacer': An Interpretation," *MLN,* LXXIII (1958), 1–5. Argues that Eadwacer is not a proper name, as has generally been assumed: that it is a common noun, "property-watcher," used in context ironically; therefore, that there are only two characters in the piece, the speaker and her lover, Wulf, whom she implores to settle down. Provides a translation.

B. *The Caedmonian Poems: Caedmon's Hymn, Christ and Satan, Daniel, Exodus, Genesis*

A *collected edition of the poems* (with the exception of the *Hymn*) may be found in OEB 1, Vol. I. See also:

156. Gollancz, Israel. *The Caedmon Manuscript of Anglo-Saxon Biblical Poetry, Junius XI in the Bodleian Library.* Oxford, 1927. Contains a valuable introduction.

Separate editions:

157. Blackburn, F. A. *Exodus and Daniel.* Boston, 1907.
158. Clubb, Merrill D. *Christ and Satan, an Old English Poem.* New Haven, Conn., 1925.
159. Dobbie, Elliott V. K. *The Manuscripts of Caedmon's Hymn and Bede's Death Song.* New York, 1937.
160. Irving, Edward B., Jr. *The Old English Exodus.* New Haven, Conn., 1953.
161. Klaeber, Fr. *The Later Genesis and other Old English and Old Saxon Texts relating to the Fall of Man.* Heidelberg, 1913, 1931 (with Supplement).
162. Smith, A. H. *Three Northumbrian Poems: Caedmon's Hymn, Bede's Death Song, The Leiden Riddle.* London, 1933.
163. Timmer, Benno J. *The Later Genesis: Edited from MS Junius 11.* Oxford, 1948, 1954 (revised).

Translations of the Caedmonian poems may be found in Gordon (OEB 3) and Kennedy (OEB 171).

For critical comments on the Caedmonian poems, see the various surveys (OEB 43–48), Kennedy (OEB 171), and the editions listed above. In addition:

164. * Wrenn, Charles L. *The Poetry of Caedmon.* London, 1948. (In *PBA,* XXXII [1946], 277–96.) Originally a lecture, this 19-page monograph reviews Caedmon scholarship and devotes attention to the only authentic poetry by Caedmon, his 9-line *Hymn.* Suggests that the "miracle" to the Anglo-Saxons in Caedmon's feat was in Caedmon's overnight mastery of a long and specialized poetic discipline.

See also Huppé (OEB 64) and Woolf (OEB 68).

C. *The Cynewulfian Poems: Christ, Dream of the Rood, Elene, Fates of the Apostles, Guthlac, Juliana, Phoenix, and Physiologus*

Collected editions are in OEB 1, Vol. II (contains *Dream of the Rood, Elene,* and *Fates of the Apostles*), Vol. III (contains *Christ, Guthlac, Juliana, Phoenix, Physiologus*); OEB 2 contains the same poems as OEB 1, Vol. III.

Separate editions:

165. * Campbell, Jackson J. *The Advent Lyrics of the Exeter Book.* Princeton, N. J., 1959. A fine edition of *Christ I,* with translation and text on facing pages. Full bibliography, notes, glossary.
166. Cook, Albert S. *The Christ of Cynewulf: A Poem in Three Parts: the Advent, the Ascension and the Last Judgment.* Boston, 1900.

167. Cook, Albert S. *The Old English Elene, Phoenix and Physiologus.* New Haven, Conn., 1919.
168. Dickins, Bruce, and Ross, A. S. C. *The Dream of the Rood.* 4th ed. London, 1954.
169. Gradon, Pamela O. E. *Cynewulf's Elene.* London, 1958.
170. Woolf, Rosemary. *Juliana.* London, 1955.

Translations:

171. * Kennedy, Charles W. *Early English Christian Poetry.* New York, 1952. Contains an introduction and six chapters with forewords: The Loss of Paradise, The Redeemer, Acts of the Apostles, The Holy Rood, Christian Allegories, The Second Advent. Fine alliterative translations of many entire poems (e.g., *Andreas, Dream of the Rood, Elene, Phoenix*), and of selections (e.g., from the *Physiologus, Christ I, Genesis*).
See also OEB 2, 3; and 165 for *Christ I.*

Commentaries:

172. * Schaar, Claes. *Critical Studies in the Cynewulf Group.* Lund Studies in English, XVII. Lund, Sweden, and Copenhagen, Denmark, 1949. The most thorough and, though in parts technical, exciting examination of these poems as a group. Contains chapters on Background and Subject Matter; Texts, Textual Criticism, and Interpretation; and Style and Manner. Seeks to establish individual stylistic features in Old English poetry.
Of great importance, too, is Kenneth Sisam's "Cynewulf and His Poetry," reprinted in his *Studies* (OEB 73).
The individual poem in this group that has received most critical attention is the *Christ:*

173. Campbell, Jackson J. "Structural Patterns in the Old English Advent Lyrics," *ELH,* XXIII (1956), 239–55. Believes the twelve poems constituting *Christ I* are the nearest approach to *lyric* in Old English poetry (lyric being associated with music and these poems being based on the Church Antiphons). Analyzes four of the lyrics in detail, including the Joseph-Mary dialogue. Concludes that "each poem is organized into a unity on a small scale around some governing impulse or idea. . . ." See also Campbell's edition (OEB 165).
174. Greenfield, Stanley B. "The Theme of Spiritual Exile in *Christ I,*" *PQ,* XXXII (1953), 321–28. Emphasizes a minor theme in the twelve lyrics: man's life on earth as an exile from heaven. Sees in this theme a commentary on the necessity for, and the mean-

ing of, the Incarnation, the major concept of the poem as a whole.

175. Mildenberger, Kenneth. "Unity of Cynewulf's *Christ* in the Light of Iconography," *Speculum*, XXIII (1948), 426–32. Believes that the association of the three themes of Advent (the Virgin Mother), Ascension, and Judgment Day in Christian iconography, and specifically as found on the coffin of St. Cuthbert, argues analogically for the unity of this tripartite poem, despite the Cynewulfian runes at the end of Part II.

176. Philip, Brother A. "The Exeter Scribe and the Unity of the *Christ*," *PMLA*, L (1940), 903–909. Argues that the three parts are separate poems.

See also Elliott (OEB 181).

The Dream of the Rood has also recently received critical attention:

177. Schlauch, Margaret. "The *Dream of the Rood* as Prosopopoeia," in *Essays and Studies in Honor of Carleton Brown*. New York, 1940. Pp. 23–34. Shows the relationship of the central artistic device of the poem (having the Cross itself speak about its part in the Crucifixion) to pagan Latin rhetorical theory and poetic practice.

178. Woolf, Rosemary. "Doctrinal Influences on *The Dream of the Rood*," *MAE*, XXVII (1958), 137–53. Sees a brilliant resolution in the poem of the tensions between the medieval doctrines of the Crucifixion as an heroic triumph (Divinity) and as an intense suffering (humanity), in the poet's description of a warrior Christ willingly ascending the Cross and of the Cross itself as sharing in His agony.

179. Burrow, J. A. "An Approach to the Dream of the Rood," *Neophil*, XLIII (1959), 123–33. Comes to conclusions similar to those of Woolf (above), though emphasis is more literary than doctrinal. Compares the Old English poem with later medieval English poems on the Crucifixion, finding that the early poem is nonnaturalistic compared to later representations—the same contrast that is found between the religious art of the earlier and that of the later Middle Ages. Sees the Cross, in its own narrative, as a surrogate for both Christ and Dreamer; finds poem's unity in "simple emotional sequence" by which Dreamer moves from fear and sorrow to hope.

On the other poems:

180. Cordasco, Francesco. "The Old English *Physiologus:* Its Problems," *MLQ*, X (1949), 351–55. Provides a summary of the

problems and of earlier theories concerning the length and prototype of the Old English Bestiary.

181. Elliott, Ralph W. V. "Cynewulf's Runes in *Christ II* and *Elene*,"
ES, XXXIV (1953), 49–57. Shows that Cynewulf artistically
used the runes—the significance of their *names*—to depict Judgment Day and at the same time to weave his name into the narrative.

182. Elliott, Ralph W. V. "Cynewulf's Runes in *Juliana* and *Fates
of the Apostles*," *ES*, XXXIV (1953), 193–204. Shows that
Cynewulf used the rune-names in these two poems for the same
double purpose as in *Christ II* and *Elene;* but that in *Juliana* he
inserted them in three groups, and in *Fates* he did not use the
proper order.

183. Emerson, Oliver F. "Originality in Old English Poetry," *RES*, II
(1926), 18–31. A study of the *Phoenix* and of the Old English
poet's handling of his source material.

184. Gerould, Gordon H. "The Old English Poems on St. Guthlac and
Their Latin Source," *MLN*, XXXII (1917), 77–89. By comparing *Guthlac A* and *B* with the Latin *Vita* by Felix of Croyland,
Gerould attempts to prove the indebtedness of the Old English
poet(s) to the Latin. Also maintains that the poet of *Guthlac B,*
if not Cynewulf, at any rate was his peer in the writing of poetry.

185. Kurtz, Benjamin P. *From St. Anthony to St. Guthlac: A Study
in Biography.* Berkeley, Calif., 1926. An interesting study in
hagiographic "biography."

See also Gerould (OEB 63) and Enkvist (OEB 70).

V. PROSE AND MISCELLANEOUS POETRY

A. *Prose*

For general commentaries see Chambers (OEB 49) and Wright (OEB
74).

Aelfric: some of his work has been edited for the EETS as follows:

186. *Lives of the Saints.* EETS 76, 82, 94, 114. London, 1881–1900.
187. *Old English Version of the Heptateuch.* EETS 160. London, 1922
(for 1921).
188. *De temporibus anni.* EETS 213. London, 1942 (for 1940).

Also of importance:

189. Garmonsway, George N. *Aelfric's Colloquy.* 2nd ed. London, 1947.

For selected translations, see Whitelock (OEB 5).

Commentary:

190. White, Caroline L. *Aelfric: A New Study of his Life and Writings.* Yale Studies in English, II. Boston, 1898. See also Sisam (OEB 73).

Alfred: biographies of this great king:

191. *Asser's Life of King Alfred.* Ed. W. H. Stevenson. Oxford, 1904. Trans. Albert S. Cook, Boston, 1906; and L. C. Jane, Oxford, 1924. This is the "official" life of the king, by a contemporary.

192. * Duckett, Eleanor S. *Alfred the Great.* Chicago, 1956. A vibrant yet scholarly account of the man and his times. *Also provides a stimulating criticism of the Alfredian prose works.* Available in paperback.

193. Plummer, Charles. *The Life and Times of Alfred the Great.* Oxford, 1902.

Works that Alfred translated or had translated into Old English have been edited as follows:

194. *Gregory's Pastoral Care.* EETS 45, 50. London, 1871. Contains a translation into modern English.

195. *Orosius.* EETS 79. London, 1883. Contains Old English text and Latin original.

196. Bede's *Ecclesiastical History.* EETS 95–96, 110–111. London, 1890–98. Trans. J. Stevenson, rev. L. C. Jane. Everyman's Library, New York, 1954. Also translated under the title of *A History of the English Church and People* by Leo Sherley-Price. Penguin Classics, Baltimore, 1955. Both are excellent translations, and readily accessible.

197. Hargrove, Henry Lee. *King Alfred's OE Version of St. Augustine's Soliloquies.* Yale Studies in English, XIII. New York, 1902. Translated, Yale Studies in English, XXII, 1904.

198. Sedgefield, W. J. *King Alfred's OE Version of Boethius de Consolatione Philosophiae.* Oxford, 1899. Translated, Oxford, 1900.

For commentary on Pastoral Care, see Sisam (OEB 73).

Anglo-Saxon Chronicle: editions:

199. Plummer, Charles. *Two of the Saxon Chronicles Parallel A & F. With Supplementary Extracts from all Others.* 2 vols. Oxford, 1892–99.

200. Rositzke, H. A. *The C-Text of the Old English Chronicles,* Bochum, Germany, 1940.

201. Classen, E., and Harmer, F. E. *An Anglo-Saxon Chronicle from BM Cott. MS. Tiberius B IV.* Manchester, 1926.
202. Smith, A. H. *The Parker Chronicle.* London, 1935.
203. Dickins, Bruce. *The Genealogical Preface to the Anglo-Saxon Chronicle: Four Texts Edited to Supplement Earle-Plummer.* Cambridge, 1952.

For an excellent translation of the Chronicle:

204. * Garmonsway, George N. *The Anglo-Saxon Chronicle.* London, 1953.
See also Whitelock (OEB 5) and Douglas and Greenaway (OEB 6).

For commentaries on the Chronicle, see OEB 19, 26, 29.

Apollonius of Tyre: edition:

205. Goolden, Peter. *The Old English Apollonius of Tyre.* Oxford English Monographs, XXXVI. Oxford, 1958.

Blickling Homilies: edition:

206. EETS 58, 63, 73. London, 1874–80.

Wulfstan: editions:

207. Bethurum, Dorothy. *The Homilies of Wulfstan.* Oxford, 1957. An excellent and extensive introduction covers, among other things, Wulfstan's intellectual stature and his prose style. No glossary.
208. Whitelock, Dorothy. *Sermo Lupi ad Anglos.* London, 1939; rev. 1952. Translated in Whitelock (OEB 5).

B. *Poetry*

Editions of the "Battle Poems":

209. Campbell, Alistair. *The Battle of Brunanburh.* London, 1938.
210. Gordon, Eric V. *The Battle of Maldon.* London, 1937. Reprinted with corrections, 1957.
See also OEB 1, Vol. VI.

Translations of the Battle Poems may be found in Gordon (OEB 3), Malone (OEB 87); of *Brunanburh,* in Kershaw (OEB 132.

Editions of Solomon and Saturn, Charms, Riddles, Gnomic Poetry:

211. Menner, Robert J. *The Poetical Dialogues of Solomon and Saturn.* MLA Monograph Series, XIII. New York, 1941.

212. Storms, Gottfrid. *Anglo-Saxon Magic.* The Hague, 1948. Contains a treatise on Anglo-Saxon magic and furnishes texts and translations of the *Charms.*
See also OEB 1, Vol. VI.

213. Tupper, Frederick. *The Riddles of the Exeter Book.* London, 1910.

214. Williams, Blanche C. *Gnomic Poetry in Anglo-Saxon.* New York, 1914.

For translations, see Gordon (OEB 3).

Of the many interpreters of the *Riddles,* perhaps Erika von Erhardt-Siebold has done the most extensive and the most striking work. See page 74 of the *CBEL* Supplement (Vol. V) and the other bibliographies.

CHAPTER XVII: A MIDDLE ENGLISH BIBLIOGRAPHICAL GUIDE

As in the Old English field, much of the earlier scholarship in Middle English centered on the establishment of texts, dates, etc. (see introduction to Chapter XVI), with an additional search for biographical material, since there was less anonymity in the later period. More recent criticism (as for the earlier period) has been engaged in explicating the religious milieu, the problems of allegory and symbolism, and their significance for particular works, and in examining the *art* of Middle English writings. Because of the limitations of space, the vastness of the literature, and the excellence of already existing bibliographical tools, the MEB following does not have the kind of comprehensiveness that the OEB has. The emphasis here is on major works of literature and major critical *opera*.

A. *General Collections (Anthologies, Editions, and Translations)*

1. Dickins, Bruce, and Wilson, R. M. *Early Middle English Texts.* 2nd ed. Cambridge, 1959. Provides a good selection of material through the 13th C. Excellent introduction to the language. Notes, and glossary. More suitable for linguistic than for literary study.

2. * Ford, Boris. *The Age of Chaucer.* Pelican Guide to English Literature, I. Baltimore, 1954. After a series of essays by divers hands on the literature and background from Chaucer to Spenser, designed to guide the literate modern reader into an appreciation of the literature of this period, there is a 200-page Middle English anthology, including the complete *Sir Orfeo, Sir Gawain and the Green Knight,* and the *First Shepherds' Play.* Explanation of difficult words at foot of each page.

3. Hammond, Eleanor P. *English Verse between Chaucer and Surrey.* Durham, N. C., 1927. An outstanding scholarly edition of secular "formal" verse—narrative, didactic, satiric, amatory, descriptive— especially valuable for its introduction and critical apparatus. *Excludes* romances, ballads, lyrics, and drama. Contains some Hoccleve and Lydgate, among others.

4. * Loomis, Roger S., and Willard, R. *Medieval English Verse and Prose.* New York, 1948. The selections are in *modern English.* Most items are extracts; but the book contains the complete *Pearl*

(Jewett translation), *Gawain* (Banks translation), *St. Erkenwald,* and Henryson's *Testament of Cresseid* (Stearns translation). Excludes Chaucer.

5. Neilson, William A., and Webster, K. G. T. *Chief British Poets of the Fourteenth and Fifteenth Centuries.* Cambridge, Mass., 1916. A fine collection. Verse is in Middle English, with footnote glosses, except for *Piers Plowman* (Prologue and *Passus* i–viii of A-text), *Pearl, and Gawain,* which appear in translation. Good selection of ballads.

6. Robbins, Rossell Hope, ed. *Historical Poems of the XIVth and XVth Centuries.* New York, 1959. Completes the series of modern editions of Middle English lyrics (see under Section IX). Includes a substantial body of political, military, and satiric poems.

7. Sisam, Kenneth. *Fourteenth Century Verse and Prose.* Oxford, 1921. Frequently reprinted. An excellent edition, with fine introduction, discussion of the language, notes, and full glossary. More suitable for linguistic than for literary study.

8. Weston, Jessie L. *The Chief Middle English Poets.* Boston, 1914. Verse translations of histories, legendaries, romances, tales, and of didactic and lyrical pieces.

9. Weston, Jessie L. *Romance, Vision and Satire: English Alliterative Poems of the Fourteenth Century.* Boston, 1912. Good verse translations.

See also Mossé (MEB 44).

For editions and translations of individual works, of collections of works of one genre (e.g., romance, lyric), and of works of individual authors, see below under appropriate sections. For early editions and for editions of works not mentioned in this bibliography, see footnotes in Baugh (MEB 47).

B. *General Bibliographies*

Cumulative:

10. Wells, John E. *A Manual of the Writings in Middle English 1050–1400, and Supplements I–IX.* New Haven, Conn., 1916–52. Indispensable, though one must learn to use its somewhat complicated machinery. Each volume has two major sections: (1) the Text, which summarizes the gist of critical writings on the literature under various topics and subtopics (e.g., Romances, Homilies and Legends, Chaucer, the *Pearl*-Poet); (2) Bibliographical Notes, which lists all published works—bibliographies, editions, critical writings—on Middle English literature down to 1945 (9th Supplement). Cross references. Exhaustive.

11. Brown, Carleton, and Robbins, R. H. *The Index of Middle English Verse.* New York, 1943. Originally Vol. II of Brown's *A Register of Middle English Religious and Didactic Verse.* 2 vols. Oxford, 1916–20. Indispensable for scholars.

12. Farrar, Clarissa P., and Evans, A. P. *Bibliography of English Translations from Medieval Sources.* New York, 1946. Very valuable, indicating the existence and adequacy of translations of medieval writings from the 4th C. to 1500, within an area roughly inclusive of Europe, Northern Africa, and Western Asia.

Other important *general bibliographies:* see *CBEL* (OEB 7) and Renwick and Orton (OEB 10). For *specialized bibliographies* (e.g., on romances, Chaucer, drama), see the appropriate sections below. Surveys, editions, etc. often contain valuable bibliographies; see esp. Bennett (MEB 55) and Chambers (MEB 56).

Periodic: see *MHRA* (OEB 11), *PMLA* (OEB 12), *Progress of Med. and Ren. Studies* (OEB 13), *Speculum* (OEB 14), *YWES* (OEB 15).

VI. GENERAL VIEW: HISTORICAL AND LINGUISTIC STUDIES, LITERARY SURVEYS, AND STUDIES IN PROSODY AND STYLE

A. *Historical and Cultural Backgrounds*

Bibliographies: see especially *CBEL* (OEB 7) for cumulative and *Speculum* (OEB 14) for periodic.

General: the first two items below are highly recommended to the general reader as readable, authoritative, and easily accessible.

13. * Stenton, Doris M. *English Society in the Early Middle Ages (1066–1307).* Pelican History of England, III. Baltimore, 1951. Rev. and annotated, 1952. Uses contemporary sources to show the development of different phases of society: the king, his people, the Church. Has a selected list of essential dates and a good index.

14. * Myers, Alec R. *England in the Late Middle Ages (1307–1536).* Pelican History of England, IV. Baltimore, 1952. Reprinted with revisions, 1956. Continues where Stenton leaves off; same pattern. Has two maps and a genealogical table of Kings of England during the period.

15. * Coulton, George G. *Medieval Panorama: The English Scene from Conquest to Reformation.* New York and Cambridge, 1938, 1947. A vast survey (52 chapters in some 800 pages, with notes and index), under such topics as Nature and Superstition, The Making of a Priest, The Monastery, Home Life, The Ghetto, The Lollards, Sports and Theatre, Marriage and Divorce.

16. Gilson, Etienne. *The Spirit of Mediaeval Philosophy*. New York, 1940. A series of twenty essays (originally lectures) defining medieval Christian philosophy under such aspects as Being and Its Necessity, Christian Providence, The Glory of God, The Object of Love.

17. Huizinga, Johan. *The Waning of the Middle Ages*. London, 1924. While not dealing with English literature, provides excellent material for the *understanding* of English literature of the 14th and 15th centuries by studying, in Continental art and literature of those centuries, such concepts as the Idea of Chivalry, Symbolism and Its Decline, The Vision of Death, Art and Life, Types of Religious Life, The Hierarchic Conception of Society. Available in paperback edition.

18. McKisack, May. *The Fourteenth Century, 1307–1399*. (Oxford History of England.) Oxford, 1959. See especially chap. xvi, "Learning, Lollardy, and Literature."

19. Poole, Austin L. *From Domesday Book to Magna Carta, 1087–1216*. (Oxford History of England.) Oxford, 1951. Contains extensive bibliography of original sources and of secondary works.

20. * Poole, Austin L., ed. *Medieval England*. 2 vols. Oxford, 1958. (This is a revision of H. W. C. Davis's *Medieval England*.) An extremely valuable book, consisting of nineteen essays by divers hands under such titles as The English Landscape, Art of War, Towns and Trade, Heraldry, Learning and Education, Science. It covers almost every conceivable aspect of medieval life. A list of reference works follows each chapter. *Copious photographs and illustrations:* a veritable treasure mine.

21. Powicke, Maurice. *The Thirteenth Century, 1216–1307*. (Oxford History of England.) Oxford, 1953. Imaginative and scholarly. Point of view is primarily political and constitutional. Excellent bibliography.

22. * Rickert, Edith. *Chaucer's World*. Eds. Clair C. Olson and M. M. Crow. New York, 1948. A fairly comprehensive view, powerfully recreating Chaucer's world *through a collection of modern renderings of 14th C. writings*. Chaucer holds stage center, despite the general titles of chapters (e.g., Travel, Death, Religion). For specialist and general reader alike.

23. Taylor, Henry O. *The Mediaeval Mind*. 2 vols. 4th ed. London, 1927. An invaluable survey of the history of medieval thought in its various manifestations.

See also *CMH* (OEB 21): of special interest for Middle English literature are V, 15–17, 22, 23; VI, 7, 8, 17–19, 25; VII, 14–16, 26; VIII, 11, 12, 20, 22–24.

Special Topics:

a) Medieval Allegory: How to read medieval allegory is a subject much under critical discussion at this time. Exposition and application of the fourfold symbolic approach (literal, allegorical, tropological, anagogical) to Middle English literature may be conveniently found in three works by Robertson (OEB 126, 141; MEB 166); for application of this approach to Chaucer's *Nun's Priest's Tale* and *Pardoner's Tale,* see notes to bibliographical entries under those tales below. Arguments against the extensive use of this method in Middle English literature may be conveniently found in the first two items below (MEB 24 and 25), in MEB 165, and in the cited review of MEB 165.*

24. Bloomfield, Morton W. "Symbolism in Medieval Literature," *MP,* LVI (1958), 73–81. An attack on the multiple-level approach. Makes six objections to this approach: (1) it assumes no difference between literary and theological works; (2) its emphasis on the symbolic as opposed to the literal is not characteristic of the later Middle Ages; (3) even in the period of its greatest application, the system was not applied rigorously to Scripture; (4) it makes no distinction between the Bible and the works of man; (5) it provides no adequate check on the correctness of a particular interpretation, since there are so many symbolic interpretations of the same thing; (6) it is essentially "simplistic," forcing "a non-historical order and system on what was in fact disordered and unsystematic."

25. Frank, Robert W., Jr. "The Art of Reading Medieval Personification-Allegory," *ELH,* XX (1953), 237–50. Distinguishes between symbol-allegory and personification-allegory, concentrating on the latter. Suggests how modern reader can overcome difficulties: if the fourfold method is used, that it is used will be obvious, and the reader does not have to look for anagogical meanings everywhere.

26. * Lewis, Clive S. *The Allegory of Love.* London, 1938. New York, 1958 (a paperback reprint). One of the most famous studies of the century. Makes a distinction between allegory (use of personification, the "less real") and symbolism (use of the sensible to define the archetypal), seeing the former as the mode of expression of the Middle Ages. (The distinction is not, perhaps, as valid as Lewis claims.) Does not find the fourfold sense of allegory too important for secular works. Chapters on Courtly Love, Allegory, *The Romance of the Rose,* Chaucer, Gower and Usk, Allegory as the Dominant Form, and Spenser's *Faerie Queene.* A very stimulating

* For the most recent discussion of allegory, see *Critical Approaches to Medieval Literature.* Ed. Dorothy Bethurum. New York, 1960.

and suggestive book, though many of its ideas must be modified in the light of more recent scholarship.

b) Courtly Love: Lewis (MEB 26) is invaluable; Andreas Capellanus, *Art of Courtly Love* (see MEB 227 for translation), codifies the system for the Middle Ages.

27. Denomy, Alexander J. *The Heresy of Courtly Love.* New York, 1947. Discusses the sources (Arabian mystical philosophy) of the antinomy between natural reason and faith in the 12th C. and the reflection of this "double truth" in Andreas Capellanus and Chaucer's *Troilus*. Sees Andreas, Chrétien de Troyes, and Chaucer as clearly choosing, in the last analysis, the viewpoint of Christian faith and rejecting the heresy of courtly love.

28. Silverstein, Theodore. "Andreas, Plato, and the Arabs: Remarks on Some Recent Accounts of Courtly Love," *MP*, XLVII (1949), 117–26. A critical survey of recent discussions (notably of Father Denomy's) of courtly love. General, not dealing with English literature as such. For the scholar: condensed and difficult writing.

Note: See section on Chaucer's *Troilus* for further references; also see introductory remarks in Kreuzer's introduction to *Sir Gawain* (MEB 139); and for special application in two of *Canterbury Tales,* see Holman (MEB 308).

c) Miscellaneous:

29. * Aurner, Nellie S. *Caxton: A Study of the Literature of the First English Press.* London, 1926. Popular treatment. Describes Caxton's life and then examines his printed works as literary material for the illustration of thought, manners, tastes, and interests of the 15th C.

30. Bloomfield, Morton W. *The Seven Deadly Sins.* East Lansing, Mich., 1952. A volume wide in scope, rich in implications; tightly packed, does not make for easy reading. Establishes syncretic nature of concept of the seven deadly sins and finally examines the concept in English literature. Has a 49-page bibliography.

31. Brewer, Derek S. "The Ideal of Feminine Beauty in Medieval Literature, Especially 'Harley Lyrics,' Chaucer, and Some Elizabethans," *MLR*, L (1955), 257–69. An interesting tracing of the medieval ideal of beauty from Maximian (6th C.), with a discussion of it in the literature cited. Finds the heroine of the Middle Ages to have a "childlike innocence, gaiety and helplessness"; she is "above her worshippers and yet, in a sense, because she is passive and needs protection, she is inferior to them."

32. Chaytor, Henry J. *From Script to Print: An Introduction to Medieval Vernacular Literature.* Cambridge, 1945. A stimulating book,

reconstructing the imaginative world of the medieval poet and his audience before the advent of printing changed auditors to readers. *References are mainly to French literature.*

33. Jusserand, Jean J. *English Wayfaring Life in the Middle Ages.* 4th ed. New York, 1950. An important study of the life of the road in the 14th C., revealing much about the background in reality of Chaucer's Canterbury pilgrimage.

34. Owst, Gerald R. *Literature and Pulpit in Medieval England.* Cambridge and New York, 1933. Traces literary motifs in sermons of the period. Believes popular preaching brought about secularization of drama and contributed to the emergence of the Morality Play. Especially valuable for its discussion of the *exemplum.*

35. Patch, Howard R. *The Goddess Fortuna in Medieval Literature.* Cambridge, Mass., 1927. A thorough investigation, including a discussion of the effect of Chaucer's conception of the goddess on the plot of the *Troilus.*

36. * Patch, Howard R. *The Tradition of Boethius: A Study of His Importance in Medieval Culture.* New York, 1935. A scholarly and readable account of the influence of Boethius. Examines the *Consolatio* itself at some length, its use by medieval scholars, its influence, translations, etc. Bibliography and index.

37. Smalley, Beryl. *The Study of the Bible in the Middle Ages.* London, 1941. A valuable if exacting book; treats the study of the Bible in England, northern France, and the Rhineland.

38. Thompson, J. W. *The Medieval Library.* Chicago, 1939. Contains a good deal of miscellaneous information on libraries, scribes, and scriptoria.

39. * Utley, Francis L. *The Crooked Rib: An Analytical Index to the Argument about Women in English and Scots Literature to the End of the Year 1568.* Columbus, Ohio, 1944. Begins with the 13th C. The bibliographical skeleton is fleshed with a perceptively written and enjoyable 90-page introduction, discussing the motives behind medieval satire and defense of women, the genesis of satire and defense, and the history of English satire and defense to 1568.

40. White, Beatrice. "Medieval Animal Lore," *Anglia,* LXXII (1954), 21–30. A delightful study, tracing the history of animal lore from *Physiologus* down to the 17th C. and examining its popularity and decline in favor in relation to religious and scientific purposes and movements.

On the medieval sciences, see Curry (MEB 231); on nature, see Enkvist (OEB 70); on the author and his public, see Bennett (MEB 55) and Bronson (MEB 239).

B. *Linguistic*

Bibliographies: see *PMLA* (OEB 12), Kennedy (OEB 31), and Dobbie (OEB 32).

Dictionaries, Grammars, and Histories of the Language:

41. Jamieson, John. *An Etymological Dictionary of the Scottish Language.* Rev., with supplement, by J. Longmuir and D. Donaldson. Paisley, 1879–82. Useful for reading the Scottish Chaucerians.
42. Kurath, Hans, and Kuhn, S. M. *Middle English Dictionary.* Ann Arbor, Mich., 1952——. Currently being published in fascicles. Exhaustive and authoritative.
43. Moore, Samuel. *Historical Outlines of English Sounds and Inflections.* Rev. by A. H. Marckwardt. Ann Arbor, Mich., 1951. A convenient tabulation.
44. Mossé, Fernand. *A Handbook of Middle English.* Trans. by James A. Walker. Baltimore, 1952. Valuable grammar; selected texts with introductions, notes, glossary, bibliographies.
45. Stratmann, Francis H. *A Middle English Dictionary.* Rev. by Henry Bradley. Oxford, 1891.
46. * Wright, Joseph. *An Elementary Middle English Grammar.* 2nd ed. Oxford, 1928. A standard authority.

See also Baugh (OEB 33), Jespersen (OEB 34), Robertson (OEB 38), and the grammatical sections of Dickins and Wilson (MEB 1), Sisam (MEB 7), and Robinson (MEB 197).

C. *Literary Surveys*

General:

47. * Baugh, Albert C. "The Middle English Period," in *A Literary History of England* (cf. OEB 46). Good survey, although thin on Chaucer, with bibliographical footnotes. Fullest on the lyric.
48. * Ker, William P. *English Literature, Medieval.* London, 1912. Reset 1945, with supplementary note by R. W. Chambers. A small book, but invaluable for its comprehensiveness and its stimulating comments.
49. Schofield, William H. *English Literature from the Norman Conquest to Chaucer.* New York and London, 1906. Still valuable although written early in the century.

Important also is *CHEL* (OEB 45), Vols. I and II, which, in addition to covering subject matter, has valuable information on The Beginnings of English Prose, English Prose in the Fifteenth Century, and the Introduction of Printing into England.

Special Periods and Subjects:

The arrangement in this section is for the most part chronological.

50. Atkins, John W. H. *English Literary Criticism: The Medieval Phase.* Cambridge, 1943. Historical and descriptive. Finds that medieval efforts at literary criticism were limited in scope and un-illuminating and that there were few valuable efforts at speculative criticism dealing with literature in the abstract: chief value of medieval criticism is historical. Topics discussed: Rhetoricians, Allegory, etc. Worthy of note is the fact that the "English" criticism of this period is in Latin!

51. * Wilson, Richard M. *Early Middle English Literature.* 2nd ed. London, 1951. Surveys the literature of 1066–1300. Perhaps the most interesting chapters to the general reader are on the *Ancren Riwle, The Owl and the Nightingale,* Romance, Tales and Fables, and Lyric Poetry.

52. * Kane, George. *Middle English Literature: A Critical Study of the Romances, the Religious Lyrics, 'Piers Plowman.'* London, 1951. A tightly packed book, primarily a literary study, making firm critical judgments as to the value of individual poems and genres.

53. Oakden, James P. *Alliterative Poetry in Middle English: A Survey of the Traditions.* 2 vols. Manchester, 1930–35. Vol. I deals primarily with meter and dialect. Vol. II considers vocabulary, phraseology, style. Describes character of individual works and often summarizes and discusses critical theories. Traces the tradition from Old English to 14th C. revival. Sees distinction in style only in *Gawain. A basic study.*

54. Speirs, John. *Medieval English Poetry: The Non-Chaucerian Tradition.* London, 1957. Finds one of the main sources of power in 13th and 14th century English literature to be the folkloristic or ritual (non-Christian) element. For severe strictures, see G. Kane, *MLR,* LIV (1959), 249–51.

55. * Bennett, Henry S. *Chaucer and the Fifteenth Century.* Oxford, 1947. Extremely readable and valuable. Cont~:ns chapters on Chaucer, His Age, Religion, 15th C. Verse and Prose, the Author and His Public, etc. *Has extensive chronological tables and an extensive annotated bibliography,* the latter especially useful for references to background, library, religion, law, education, architecture, etc. Especially successful in relating Chaucer to his age. Does not say much about structural artistry of Chaucer's poems, however.

56. * Chambers, Edmund K. *English Literature at the Close of the Middle Ages.* Oxford, 1945, 1947 (with corrections). A volume, like the Bennett above, in the Oxford History of English Literature

Series. Has chapters on Drama, Carol and 15th C. Lyric, Popular Narrative Poetry and Ballad, and Malory. *Annotated bibliography.* For some strictures, see review by L. H. Loomis, *MLQ,* VIII (1947), 496–98.

57. Kingsford, Charles L. *English Historical Literature in the Fifteenth Century.* Oxford, 1913. An outstanding work on historical writings, including correspondence (e.g., The Paston Letters).

58. * Lewis, Clive S. *English Literature in the Sixteenth Century.* New York, 1954. A vivid and witty survey of the early Renaissance, though it includes Dunbar, who is discussed in this volume.

See also Wilson, *Lost Literature* (OEB 48): the chapter on Lyric is probably the most valuable for Middle English studies.

Miscellaneous Essay Collections:

59. * Everett, Dorothy. *Essays on Middle English Literature.* Ed. Patricia Kean. Oxford, 1955. Consists partly of reprints and partly of posthumous material. Contains delightful and instructive discussions of, among other things, Chaucer's *Parlement of Foules* and *Troilus and Criseyde,* English Romances, Layamon, the Alliterative Revival. An essay on *Pearl* stresses the human emotion in the poem.

60. * Lowes, John Livingston. *Convention and Revolt in Poetry.* Boston, 1919. A rich, interesting book about poetry *per se,* but including, among other stimulating comments on Middle English poetry, the author's revealing delineation of Chaucer's Prioress against her Romance-prototype (pp. 60–67).

See also Ford, *Age of Chaucer* (MED 2).

D. *Studies in Prosody, Style, etc.*

61. Birney, Earle. "English Irony before Chaucer," *UTQ,* VI (1937), 538–57. Examines pre-Chaucerian irony under the headings of Battle-Irony, Proverb-Irony, Irony of Fate, Dramatic Irony, Irony of the Underdog, Parody and Burlesque, Ironists. Somewhat sketchy.

62. Krapp, George P. *The Rise of English Literary Prose.* New York, 1915. Takes position (challenged by Chambers, OEB 49) that English prose began with Wyclif in late 14th C. Examines prose through Bacon.

63. Russell, J. C. "An Introduction to the Study of Medieval Biography," *MLQ,* IV (1943), 437–53. A "handbook" to guide prospective biographers of medieval subjects through the labyrinthine problems they must face. Suggestive.

64. Saintsbury, George. *A History of English Prosody from the Twelfth Century to the Present Day.* 3 vols. London, 1906–10. The most useful work on meter and verse in English.

65. Waldron, Ronald A. "Oral-Formulaic Technique and Middle English Alliterative Poetry," *Speculum*, XXXII (1957), 792–804. Follows Magoun's method (OEB 58), investigating the first 25 lines of the *Alliterative Morte Arthure* for formulaic diction.

See also Atkins (MEB 50), Chambers, *On Continuity* . . . (OEB 49), Wilson, "Three Middle English Mystics" (MEB 103), the general surveys listed above, and section on Chaucer's Techniques.

Note: On Latin and Anglo-Norman literature in Medieval England, see chapters in Baugh (MEB 47) and the *CBEL* (OEB 7).

VII. ROMANCE

A. *Collections and Translations*

66. French, Walter H., and Hale, C. B. *Middle English Metrical Romances.* New York, 1930. The most extensive collection.
67. Comfort, William W. *Arthurian Romances by Chrétien de Troyes.* Everyman Library, New York, 1913. Translation, notes, bibliography.
68. *Loomis, Roger S. and Laura H. *Medieval Romances.* New York, 1957. A convenient collection of romances in translation, including the English *Havelock, Sir Orfeo, Sir Gawain and the Green Knight,* and *The Book of Balin* (Malory). Contains brief but incisive introductions to each piece.

Note: A translation of Geoffrey of Monmouth's *History of the Kings of Britain* may be found in Everyman 577 (rev., paperback edition, 1958); of Layamon's *Brut,* in Everyman 578 (*Arthurian Chronicles*); of the alliterative and the stanzaic *Morte Arthure,* in Everyman 634.

B. *Bibliography:* See under Bruce (MEB 70).

C. *General Comment*

69. * *Arthurian Literature in the Middle Ages.* Ed. R. S. Loomis. Oxford, 1959. A collaborative history by 30 of the best-known Arthurian scholars. Surveys all the literature in which the figure of Arthur appears: Welsh, Latin, French, German, Dutch, Scandinavian, etc., as well as English. (Actually, the space devoted to English literature is relatively small.) Bibliography in footnotes, the extensiveness varying with the individual contributors.

See also Ker, *Epic and Romance* (OEB 80), Kane (MEB 52), Everett (MEB 59), introduction to Kreuzer-Rosenberg (MEB 139). On nature in the Romances, see Enkvist (OEB 70).

D. *Arthurian Romance before Malory*

70. Bruce, James D. *Evolution of Arthurian Romance from the Beginnings down to the Year 1300.* 2 vols. Baltimore, 1923. Reprinted, with supplement to bibliography by A. Hilka, 1928. An invaluable study. Goes from early traditions, chronicles, lays, and romances to Holy Grail and prose romances. Subsequent bibliography in *Arthurian Bibliography,* Vol. I (1922–29), Vol. II (1930–35), by John J. Parry and M. Schlauch, for MLA, 1931, 1936. Yearly thereafter in *MLQ.*

71. * Chambers, Edmund K. *Arthur of Britain.* London, 1927. A readable, brief introduction to the Arthurian material and its problems. Has chapters on the Early Tradition, Geoffrey of Monmouth and His Sources, the Acceptance of Arthur, The Round Table, The Historicity of Arthur, and Arthur and Mythology. Also reprints documents (Nennius, etc.) containing earliest Arthurian references.

72. Loomis, Roger S. *Arthurian Tradition and Chrétien de Troyes.* New York, 1949. Illustrates that Chrétien was indebted to Celtic material on Arthur but that he also vitalized the pagan traditions he inherited. Covers Chrétien's romances in detail, one by one, after discussing the background.

73. Loomis, Roger S. *Celtic Myth and Arthurian Romance.* London, 1927. Takes the extreme position of the Celticists, who believe in the Celtic provenience of the Arthurian romances, as over against the "inventionists."

74. Tatlock, John S. P. *The Legendary History of Britain: Geoffrey of Monmouth's 'Historia Regum Britanniae' and Its Early Vernacular Versions.* Berkeley and Los Angeles, Calif., 1950. A monumental work. Its purpose is "to discover what was in Geoffrey's mind; the probable background of his book, not only written, but in oral tradition and especially in common knowledge and contemporary life and in his own imagination." Valuable chapter on Layamon's *Brut.* For a judicious appraisal, see J. J. Parry, *JEGP,* L (1951), 111–16.

75. * Vinaver, Eugène. "The Dolorous Stroke," *MAE,* XXV (1956), 175–80. An illuminating "anti-Celticist" article. Suggests, via an examination of the "dolorous stroke" theme as it appears chronologically in medieval texts, that a study of the chronological appearance of Arthurian material, especially in the French romances of the late 12th and early 13th centuries, will reduce the confusion in Arthurian studies and lead to a better understanding of the shaping of medieval narrative art.

76. Weston, Jessie L. *From Ritual to Romance.* Cambridge and Garden City, N. Y., 1920. Reprinted, paperback, 1957. A most influ-

ential volume, not only for its synthesis of so much material on the Grail Legend but for its repercussions in T. S. Eliot's *The Waste Land*. Argues that folklore elements (e.g., vegetation ritual) in the story are sufficient to account for mystic development of Grail tradition.

77. Wyld, Henry C. "Layamon as an English Poet," *RES,* VI (1930), 1–30. Concerned with the literary quality of the *Brut*. Not a mere translation of Wace, argues Wyld: shows a love of nature in its similes, and the subject of war excites the poet to some of his best efforts. The *Brut* reminds us of Old English poetry.

See Everett (MEB 59) on Layamon and the *Alliterative Morte Arthur*. On the latter, see also Kane (MEB 52) and Waldron (MEB 65).

E. *Malory*

Since Vinaver's definitive study (MEB 84), attention has been focused on the unity of Malory's work and on artistic qualities in his narrative.

78. * Lumiansky, Robert M. "The Question of Unity in Malory's *Morte Darthur,*" *TSE,* V (1955), 29–39. Presents a good summary of the reaction (mostly favorable) to Vinaver's theory that Malory produced a series of romances rather than a unified whole. Argues, however, that despite Vinaver's views, "Malory's intention of producing a carefully unified book can be observed through consideration of the *explicit* for Tale I, of the unlikelihood of political allegory in Tale II, and of the internal time-scheme for the book as a whole."

79. * Lumiansky, Robert M. "Malory's Steadfast Bors," *TSE,* VIII (1958), 5–20. Sees Bors as a consistently drawn figure, one whose steadfastness and ability to overcome the one blemish on his character (his begetting of Elaine) afford a thematic contrast to Launcelot's instability. *Footnote 2 gives a valuable list of theses, articles, reviews that offer counterargument to Vinaver's contention that Malory's work is a group of separate tales rather than a unified whole.*

80. Moorman, Charles. "Malory's Treatment of Sankgreall," *PMLA,* LXXI (1956), 496–509. Argues, like Lumiansky, that Vinaver is wrong: sees Malory's changes in his sources—changes in characterization, in religious material, and in the Grail Quest (which Malory intended to mark the beginning of the fall of the Round Table)—as integrating the Grail adventure into the whole romance.

81. Rumble, Thomas C. "Malory's *Works* and Vinaver's Comments: Some Inconsistencies Resolved," *JEGP,* LIX (1960), 59–69. Cau-

tions against overreliance on Vinaver's Commentary in his edition
of the Winchester MS (MEB 84). Footnote 3 directs the reader
to other articles calling attention to Vinaver's inaccuracies.

82. Schofield, William H. *Chivalry in English Literature: Chaucer,
Malory, Spenser and Shakespeare.* Cambridge, Mass., 1912. Examines the four authors for their attitudes toward the ideal of
chivalry; finds Chaucer pragmatic, Malory romantic.

83. * Vinaver, Eugène. *Malory.* Oxford, 1929. The most comprehensive
study of the man, his subject matter, and his technique. Read in
conjunction with next item.

84. * Vinaver, Eugène, ed. *The Works of Sir Thomas Malory.* 3 vols.
Oxford, 1947, 1948 (with corrections). The text itself is reproduced in one volume, 1954, without the introduction, critical apparatus, commentary, index, and bibliography of the three-volume
edition. The design of the text brings out the dramatic pattern of
each of the stories, which, Vinaver argues, Malory wrote as eight
separate romances. Vinaver also believes Malory was not as
moralistic as Caxton's *Preface* has led us to believe.

See also Chambers, *English Literature at the Close of the Middle Ages*
(MEB 56).

F. *Non-Arthurian Romance*

Editions and Translations:

85. Bliss, A. J. *Sir Orfeo.* Oxford, 1954. Prints in full three versions
of the poem. Elaborate introduction, dealing with MSS, sources,
and literary qualities. Palaeographical notes, commentaries, glossary, and index of proper names.

86. Magoun, Francis P., Jr. *The Gests of King Alexander of Macedon.*
Cambridge, Mass., 1929. Contains the texts of the alliterative
Alexander A and *B.* Organizes much previously scattered mate-
rial.

87. Mackenzie, William Mackay. *Bruce: Edited from the Best Texts
with Literary and Historical Introduction, Notes and Appendices,
and a Glossary.* London, 1909.

88. Skeat, Walter W. *The Lay of Havelok the Dane.* 2nd rev. ed. by
K. Sisam. Oxford, 1915. Complete text, introduction, critical apparatus.

89. Smithers, George V. *Kyng Alisaunder.* 2 vols. EETS 227, 237.
London, 1952, 1957. Vol. I contains the text, Vol. II the introduction, commentary, and glossary.

See also Ford (MEB 2) and French and Hale (MEB 66). Translations of *Sir Orfeo, Havelok,* and parts of the *Bruce* may be found in
Loomis and Willard (MEB 4).

Commentaries:

90. French, Walter H. *Essays on King Horn.* Ithaca, N. Y., 1940. A series of essays, with text attached, examining type and quality, meter, and MSS of the tale. Reviews the relation of the poem to courtly and popular literature, finding the poem, because of its rapidity and suppression of narrative elements, to be a good English example of the Breton *lai* rather than of *romance.*

91. Hill, D. M. "An Interpretation of *King Horn,*" *Anglia,* LXXV (1957), 157–72. A critical examination, seeing the unity of the poem in a conflict between the ideals of fighting-avenging and love. The poem illustrates the growth to maturity of a medieval knight.

92. Hibbard, Laura A. *Mediaeval Romance in England: A Study of the Sources and Analogues of the Non-cyclic Metrical Romances.* New York, 1924. New ed., with additional bibliography, 1959. A thorough and authoritative study of 39 noncyclic romances.

93. Smithers, George V. "Story-Patterns in Some Breton Lays," *MAE,* XXII (1953), 61–92. An interesting and penetrating study. Sees three basic patterns: Type I, which involves mortal and fairy; Type II, in which fairy and mortal have a son; Type III, in which lovers are mortal and son brings parents together after fight with his father (Sohrab and Rustum type). Examines *Sir Degare, Sir Gowther,* and *Sir Orfeo* for their grafting of parts of formulas on to other material.

VIII. PROSE

For survey and bibliography, see Wilson (MEB 51) and Bennett (MEB 55), in particular. For selected translations of extracts, see Douglas and Greenaway (OEB 6) and Loomis and Willard (MEB 4).

A. *Religious Prose*

General Commentary: see Chambers, *On Continuity* . . . (OEB 49) and Krapp (MEB 62); also:

94. Zeeman, Elizabeth. "Continuity in Middle English Devotional Prose," *JEGP,* LV (1956), 417–22. Stresses the increasing use of Eastern dialect for vernacular prose in 12th and 13th centuries. Argues that Chambers ignores growth and development in the East and the existence of different traditions of English devotional prose.

Ancrene Riwle:

a) Editions and Translations:

95. Morton, James. *The Ancren Riwle.* Camden Society, 1853. The only complete text to date; but see next item.

96. Baugh, Albert C. *The English Text of the Ancrene Riwle. Edited from British Museum MS. Royal 8 C.I.* EETS 232. London, 1956 (for 1949).
    Day, Mabel. *The English Text of the Ancrene Riwle. Edited from Cotton MS. Nero A XIV.* EETS 225. London, 1952 (for 1946).
    Wilson, Richard M. *The English Text of the Ancrene Riwle. Edited from Gonville and Caius College MS. 234/120,* with an introd. by N. R. Ker. EETS 229. London, 1954 (for 1948).
    Note: There are *eight* Middle English texts of this work.

97. Salu, M. B., trans. *The Ancrene Riwle [The Corpus MS.: Ancrene Wisse].* London, 1955; Notre Dame, Ind., 1956. A skillful translation, with introduction by Dom Gerard Sitwell, which discusses the difference between the 14th C. mystics' emphasis on contemplation and *The Ancrene Riwle's* stress on asceticism.

b) Commentary: Most of the criticism has dealt with origin, author, date: see Baugh (MEB 47). For literary comment, see especially Wilson, *Early Middle English Literature* (MEB 51) and Bloomfield, *Seven Deadly Sins* (MEB 30).

Wyclif:

98. Deanesly, Margaret. *The Lollard Bible, and Other Medieval Biblical Versions.* Cambridge, 1920. A good account of the Middle English Bible, showing Wyclif to have been responsible for the idea of a vernacular Bible and presenting evidence about the genesis of the Bible and about contemporary interest in it. Describes the two versions of the Wyclif Bible and the controversies stemming from its appearance. Appendices, with much documentary matter.

99. Spinka, Matthew, ed. *Advocates of Reform: From Wyclif to Erasmus.* The Library of Christian Classics, XIV. Philadelphia, 1953. Deals with Wyclif, the Conciliarists, Hus, and Erasmus. Consists of a general introduction and introductions to each part, followed by translations. Gives a very good idea of religious thought in the 14th and 15th centuries.

100. Workman, Herbert B. *John Wyclif: A Study of the English Medieval Church.* 2 vols. Oxford, 1926. A sympathetic yet discriminating biography. Studies Wyclif as Schoolman, Politician, and Reformer.

See also *CMH* (OEB 21), Vol. VII.

The Mystics:

a) General:

101. Pepler, Conrad. *The English Religious Heritage.* St. Louis, Mo., 1958. An introduction to the English mystics of the later Middle

Ages, especially Rolle, Julian of Norwich, Hilton, *The Cloud of Unknowing.*

102. Underhill, Evelyn. *Mysticism: A Study in the Nature and Development of Man's Spiritual Consciousness.* 12th ed., rev. London, 1957. The most comprehensive study of the subject.

103. Wilson, Richard M. "Three Middle English Mystics," *E & S,* N.S. IX (1956), 87–112. Examines the writings of Rolle, Julian of Norwich, and Margery Kempe for their revelation of 14th C. prose style rather than for their religious ideas.

See also OEB 49 and MEB 97.

b) Individual Mystics: Editions, Translations, Comments:

104. Allen, Hope E., ed. *The English Writings of Richard Rolle.* Oxford, 1931. Important edition with "meaty" introduction and notes.

105. Meech, Sanford B., and Allen, H. E., eds. *The Book of Margery Kempe.* EETS 212. London, 1940 (for 1939). A definitive edition, with full critical apparatus.

106. Molinari, Paul. *Julian of Norwich: The Teaching of a Fourteenth-Century English Mystic.* London, 1958.

107. Progoff, Ira, ed. and trans. *The Cloud of Unknowing.* New York, 1957. Introduction takes a modern psychological approach to this particular work and to mysticism in general.

108. Sherley-Price, Leo, ed. and trans. *The Ladder of Perfection* [Hilton]. Penguin Books, Baltimore, 1957.

For bibliography of the "Katherine Group," see Baugh (MEB 47), pp. 124–26, and *CBEL.* Comment on these works may be found in Chambers (OEB 49) and Wilson (MEB 51).

B. *Secular Prose*
Mandeville:

109. Hamelius, Paul, ed. *Mandeville's Travels, tr. from the French of Jean d'Outremeuse.* 2 vols. EETS 153, 154. London, 1919–23 (for 1916).

110. Bennett, Josephine W. *The Rediscovery of Sir John Mandeville.* New York, 1954; London, 1955. An extremely valuable scholarly work. The first part gives an excellent account of the literary values: surveys sources and emphasizes artistic use of them and Mandeville's own imaginative additions; the second part deals with the problem of authorship, Bennett arguing cogently for a real Mandeville, who lived at St. Albans; a third part deals with reputation and influence of *Travels.* Valuable appendices.

Paston Letters:

111. Davis, Norman, ed. *Paston Letters.* Oxford, 1958. An attractive selection and presentation in the Clarendon Medieval and Tudor Series. Has "appreciations," introductions, notes, and glossary.
112. *The Paston Letters.* 2 vols. Everyman 752, 753. New York, 1924. Contains most of the letters, with précis of the less important ones.
113. Bennett, Henry S. *The Pastons and Their England.* Cambridge, 1922, 1931. Examines the whole correspondence and its background. Provides a good introduction to 15th C. England through the eyes of some of its letter-writers. (Same material, abbreviated, may be found in Bennett ⌊MEB 55⌋.)

Thomas Usk:

114. Heninger, S. K., Jr. "The Margarite-Pearl Allegory in Thomas Usk's *Testament of Love,*" *Speculum,* XXXII (1957), 92–98. Studies Usk's handling of the Margarite-Pearl symbol. Concludes that he reconciles courtly love worldliness and Boethian *contemptus mundi* through the symbol, illustrating the duality of manna (bodily food—Grace), a pearl (glittering, sensuous gem—pearl of great price), and Margarite (woman to be loved physically—Church)—"each of which exists simultaneously in both the mortal and the eternal worlds . . . yet partakes of an undying oneness. . . ."

See also Lewis, *Allegory of Love* (MEB 26). On historical writings, see Kingsford (MEB 57). Trevisa and other prose writers of the period are discussed in *CHEL,* Bennett (MEB 55), etc.

IX. LYRICS AND FOLK BALLADS

A. *Lyrics: Secular and Religious*

Collections:

115. Brook, George L. *The Harley Lyrics: The Middle English Lyrics of MS. Harley 2253.* 2nd ed. Manchester, Eng., 1956. This volume and the following collections are definitive editions with full critical apparatus, including introduction, notes, and glossary.
116. Brown, Carleton. *English Lyrics of the XIIIth Century.* Oxford, 1932.
117. Brown, Carleton. *Religious Lyrics of the XIVth Century.* Oxford, 1924. Rev. by G. V. Smithers, 1952.
118. Brown, Carleton. *Religious Lyrics of the XVth Century.* Oxford, 1939.
119. Robbins, Rossell H. *Secular Lyrics of the XIVth and XVth Centuries.* 2nd ed. Oxford, 1959.

120. Greene, Richard L. *The Early English Carols*. Oxford, 1935. An important collection, with extensive introductions and full critical apparatus, of a special form of the lyric.

See also Robbins (MEB 6). MEB 121 provides an anthology of Middle English lyrics under the headings Amorous, Divine, Moral, and Trivial.

Studies:

121. * Chambers, Edmund K., and Sidgwick, F. *Early English Lyrics*. London, 1907. Contains an essay by Chambers, "Some Aspects of Mediaeval Lyric," which provides a convenient introduction to the Middle English lyric; also contains a list of the MSS in which Middle English lyrics are found.

122. Jones, W. Powell. *The Pastourelle: A Study of the Origins and Tradition of a Lyric Type*. Cambridge, Mass., 1931. Finds the origins to be popular rather than courtly and literary, though the genre is treated more as a theme: a love adventure between a country girl and a knight or noble, who is repulsed.

123. Moore, Arthur K. *The Secular Lyric in Middle English*. Lexington, Ky., 1951. For the advanced student. A compendium of knowledge, embracing the lyric origins in folklore through the secular lyrics of William Dunbar.

124. Robbins, Rossell H. "The Authors of the Middle English Religious Lyrics," *JEGP*, XXXIX (1940), 230–38. Stresses the importance of the Franciscans as authors of the religious lyrics.

125. Robbins, Rossell H. "Middle English Carols as Processional Hymns," *SP*, LVI (1959), 559–82. Suggests that the traditional theory (expounded by Chambers; see above) of the ring-dance origin of the Middle English carol is in need of reappraisal; that at least 80 per cent of extant Middle English carols were composed by ecclesiastical authors for singing in church processions and that they were patterned on the Latin processional hymns with burden, stanza, and repeated burden.

Kane (MEB 52) has an exciting chapter on the *poetic quality* of the religious lyrics; on the carol and 15th C. lyric, see also Chambers (MEB 56); see further Wilson, *Lost Literature* (OEB 48), and Enkvist (OEB 70), the latter for the use of nature in the lyrics.

B. *Ballads*

Bibliography:

126. Wilgus, D. K. *Anglo-American Folksong Scholarship since 1898*. New Brunswick, N. J., 1959. Provides a history of British and American scholarship on the English ballads.

Collections:

127. Child, Francis J. *The English and Scottish Popular Ballads.* 5 vols. London, 1882–98. Reprinted, New York and London, 5 vols. in 3, 1957. The famous collection of 305 popular ballads, including many variant versions.
128. Graves, Robert. *English and Scottish Ballads.* London and New York, 1957. A convenient selection with introduction and critical notes.
129. * Leach, MacEdward. *The Ballad Book.* New York, 1955. A very large selection: Sec. 1 consists of English and Scottish ballads with American and Danish variants; Sec. 2, of American ballads by origin or adoption. Has a good, readable introduction, glossary, bibliography, and index. Each ballad has a brief, separate introduction.
130. * Sargent, Helen C., and Kittredge, G. L. *English and Scottish Popular Ballads.* Boston, 1904; London, 1905. Based on the famous Child collection, it has a valuable introduction and bibliographical appendix.

See also Wells (MEB 136).

Studies:

131. * Gerould, Gordon H. *The Ballad of Tradition.* Oxford, 1932. A pleasant introduction to the genre, with chapters on the Nature of Ballads, Ballad Stories, Ballad Characterization, the Nature of Ballad Variation, etc. Selected bibliography. Now available in paperback edition.
132. Gummere, Francis B. *The Popular Ballad.* Boston, 1907. A "classic." Argues for the communal theory of ballad origins; says a good deal about ballad form (e.g., incremental repetition).
133. * Hodgart, Matthew J. C. *The Ballads.* London, 1950. A concise survey with perceptive and stimulating comments. Eminently readable and informative. Bibliography, notes, and index.
134. Moore, Arthur K. "The Literary Status of the English Popular Ballad," *CL,* X (1958), 1–20. Offers a survey of ballad scholarship, briefly examining as *art* some of the ballads included in most anthologies, and concluding "that attention to internal form, besides demonstrating the achievement of individual ballads, can lead to the recognition of new and less ambiguous groupings."
135. Pound, Louise. *Poetic Origins and the Ballad.* New York and London, 1921. A famous study, summarizing previous theories and arguing *against* the communal theory of authorship expounded by Gummere and Kittredge.

136. * Wells, Evelyn K. *The Ballad Tree.* New York, 1950. A discriminating study, less technical than Gerould (MEB 131), of ballads, British and American, with comments on development of genre, verse, and music. The chapter on Romantic ballads offers a fine analysis of prominent features of ballad style and method: economy, concreteness, convention, narrative conduct, meter, and refrain. Prints 60 traditional ballads and their tunes.

See also Chambers (MEB 56) and, for Scottish ballads, Kinsley, ed. *Scottish Poetry* (MEB 317), Speirs, *Scots Tradition* (MEB 318), and Wittig (MEB 319).

X. THE ALLITERATIVE REVIVAL

This section of the bibliography is concerned mainly with *Sir Gawain and the Green Knight, Pearl,* and *Piers Plowman,* the three greatest poems in the alliterative revival of the 14th C. For general comment on the revival, see Oakden (MEB 53) and Everett (MEB 59); see Section VII on *Alliterative Morte Arthure;* see below, D, for editions of *Patience, Purity,* and *St. Erkenwald.*

A. *Sir Gawain and the Green Knight*

Editions and Translations:

137. Tolkien, John R. R., and Gordon, E. V. *Sir Gawain and the Green Knight.* Oxford, 1936. A standard edition, with a brief introduction discussing the history of the legend, the poet's use of his sources, language, date, etc., with notes and a glossary.

138. Gollancz, Israel. *Sir Gawain and the Green Knight* (with introductory essays by Mabel Day and Mary S. Serjeantson). EETS 210. London, 1940. Contains a full Introduction describing the MS, its contents and its connection with the *Wars of Alexander,* theories about the author's identity, origins of the story. Serjeantson gives a comprehensive survey of dialect. Extensive bibliography and notes. All in all, a better text and a more satisfactory account than MEB 137.

For a convenient printing of the text itself, see Ford (MEB 2).

There have been numerous *translations* of the poem: by Jessie L. Weston (1898), T. H. Banks (1929), G. H. Gerould (1934), James L. Rosenberg (1959). The last is accessible in paperback; the Banks translation is reproduced in Loomis and Willard (MEB 4).

Studies:

a) General:

139. * *Sir Gawain and the Green Knight,* trans. James L. Rosenberg, ed. and introd. James R. Kreuzer. New York, 1959. Kreuzer's

lengthy introduction, covering the romances in general and courtly love as well as the poem itself, provides solid background with which to begin a study of the poem.

140. Kittredge, George L. *A Study of Gawain and the Green Knight.* Cambridge, Mass., 1916. The most exhaustive and comprehensive study of sources and background of the component parts (the beheading game and the temptation) of the poem.

141. Savage, Henry L. *The Gawain-Poet: Studies in His Personality and Background.* Chapel Hill, N. C., and Oxford, 1956. Although some of the material is pure hypothesis (a suggestion of a French knight as the original of Sir Gawain), and some is mere repetition of older commentary (on the anonymous poet himself), the book has something of interest to say, especially in the dovetailing of the hunting scenes and the scenes in the castle.

See also MEB 73.

b) Recent Articles on Meaning and Style:

142. Ackerman, Robert W. "Gawain's Shield: Penitential Doctrine in *Gawain and the Green Knight,*" *Anglia* LXXVI (1958), 254–65. Finds that the 16-line interpretation of Gawain's pentangle in the poem stresses deeply religious devotion in the language of the confessional. Sees this as an innovation of the English poet, and a deliberate contrast with the girdle, a symbol of Gawain's falling away from truth, for which he must do penance.

143. Burrow, John. "The Two Confession Scenes in *Sir Gawain and the Green Knight.*" *MP,* LVII (1959), 73–79. Compares Gawain's confessions to the priest (ll. 1876–84) and to the Green Knight (ll. 2379 ff.), and finds a delicate equilibrium in the poem's ending between the penitential theme and the traditional Arthurian setting.

144. * Englehardt, George J. "The Predicament of Gawain," *MLQ,* XVI (1955), 218–25. Finds the poem is "a humane and sympathetic presentation designed to reveal how human and imperfect is even a supposedly perfect knight such as the pentagonal Gawain"; for Gawain violates the three main virtues of the medieval knight: valor (in his taking of the girdle), piety (in his breaking of oath *re* the exchange of gifts and in his receiving absolution without confessing this violation), courtesy (in his antifeminist tirade). But the poet blends justice with mercy, and Gawain learns humility.

145. * Friedman, Albert B. "Morgan Le Fay in *Sir Gawain and the Green Knight,*" *Speculum,* XXXV (1960), 260–74. Demonstrates that the poet's recourse to Morgan as his "prime mover" of the plot resulted from his changing the nature of Bercilak from the

folklore creature who needs beheading to be disenchanted to a "shape-shifter," this change being the offshoot of the combination of the Beheading and Temptation motifs. Finds this use of Morgan artistically unconvincing.

146. * Goldhurst, William. "The Green and the Gold: The Major Theme of *Gawain and the Green Knight*," *CE*, XX (1958), 61–65. Sees the major theme as a study in contrast between man's tendencies to be drawn to nature (green) and his "uncertain efforts to maintain a hold on the comforts and codes of civilization" (gold). At best, life is but a truce between the natural and the civilized. The Green Knight himself emphasizes the contrast in his color and in his knightliness, as does the green and gold of the girdle, which Gawain says he will wear not for its "gold" but for its "green" reminder.

147. * Markman, Alan M. "The Meaning of *Sir Gawain and the Green Knight*," *PMLA*, LXXII (1957), 574–86. Sees the poem as primarily a romance, not as a "Christian declaration of man's imperfection," though it has Christianity in it, of course. It makes its appeal to its audience through the demonstration of human capacities for good or bad action by submitting a known character (medieval knight) to an unknown test. All its elements— magic, Christianity, realistic details, overtones—reveal Gawain as primarily a *loyal* man, inculcating the moral lesson that "we must act as our duty to others dictates."

148. * Moorman, Charles. "Myth and Mediaeval Literature: *Sir Gawain and the Green Knight*," *MS*, XVIII (1956), 158–72. Attacks myth-hunters (in particular Zimmer, *The King and the Corpse*, and Speirs, *Scrutiny*, XVI [1949], 274–300) as sterile source-hunters and analoguists who fail to account for the poem's uniqueness. The only relevance of myth here, the author says, is that of the journey from innocence to experience (the *rite de passage*), which in this poem adumbrates the tragedy of the Round Table and of secular society as a whole. Contains many provocative insights into structure and meaning, but does not avoid the very pitfall it sets out to obviate.

149. Pearsall, Derek A. "Rhetorical 'Descriptio' in *Sir Gawain and the Green Knight*," *MLR*, L (1955), 130–34. Finds a relationship between medieval rhetorical precept and the stylistic practice of the *Gawain* poet; e.g., the wild scenery is "functional in the strict rhetorical sense."

See also Kane (MEB 52) and Oakden (MEB 53). For a recent view, suggesting that scenery is progressively magnified and Gawain likewise dwarfed as he becomes more apprehensive of death, see A. Renoir, *Moderne Sprak* (1960), 245–53.

B. *Pearl*

Editions and Translations:

150. Gordon, Eric V. *Pearl*. Oxford, 1953. The fullest edition, with critical apparatus and selected bibliography which includes an annotated section on theme and structure (1904–1950), p. lv. Gordon accepts the elegiac basis for the poem (see under *Studies*, below), claiming that without it and the great sense of personal loss which pervades the poem, *Pearl* would be nothing but a theological treatise. For a thorough, appreciative, yet judicious review, see M. P. Hamilton, *JEGP*, LIV (1955), 123–26.
151. * Hillmann, Sister Mary Vincent. *The Pearl: A New Translation and Interpretation*. New York, 1961. This is an edition with original text and literal translation on facing pages. Contains a brief introduction (not comparable to Gordon's), notes, and glossary. Interprets poem on two levels: literally, the Pearl is a lost jewel, and allegorically, it shows the danger of worship of material wealth. Book is also of value for insights on individual lines.

In addition to the translation of Sister Hillmann, one should note the following translations: G. G. Coulton (1907), C. G. Osgood (1907), Sophie Jewett (1908), Stanley P. Chase (1932). The Jewett translation is conveniently reprinted in Loomis and Willard (MEB 4).

Studies:

The *Pearl* has aroused a great deal of critical controversy: Is it an elegy mourning the loss of a real child, whether the poet's or not; or is it an allegory depicting the loss and the rediscovery of some spiritual value? Earlier critics inclined to the elegiac interpretation; and two recent critics, Gordon (MEB 150) and Everett (MEB 59), have reasserted the importance of an elegiac basis and the sense, if not the reality, of personal loss. Allegorical interpretations were advanced as early as 1904, by W. H. Schofield, but it was not till 1925 that an attempt was made to see the poem as *total allegory* (Sister Madeleva, MEB 152). *For convenient summaries of previous theories*, see Gordon (MEB 150), Conley (MEB 155), and McAndrew (MEB 157). Articles below are arranged chronologically.

152. Madeleva, Sister Mary. *Pearl: A Study in Spiritual Dryness*. New York, 1925. Maintains that the poem is by a religious, that the Pearl itself represents spiritual sweetness, and that the whole experience of the poem expresses the fervor of a religious novice. This interpretation, while valuable and suggestive, does not hold up in its details.
153. Robertson, Durant W., Jr. "The 'Heresy' of *The Pearl*: The Pearl as a Symbol," *MLN*, LXV (1950), 152–61. Suggests that

the dreamer is Everyman, having lost the spotlessness of childhood, and, concomitantly, eternal life in the Eternal City. Literally, the Pearl is a gem; allegorically, perfect innocence; tropologically, the soul that attains innocence through penance; anagogically, the life of innocence in the Celestial City. The poet stresses the tropological, the necessity for regaining the life of innocence.

154. * Johnson, Wendell S. "The Imagery and Diction of *The Pearl:* Toward an Interpretation," *ELH,* XX (1953), 161–80. A thoughtful study, reviewing some previous interpretations. It examines the imagery (the world of growing things [earthly] and the world of light and gems [heavenly], which are united by the water [baptism] and blood of Christ [mercy]), and the double meanings of key words in each stanzaic group; and concludes that the contrast between heaven and earth is made both explicitly and in the sets of images throughout the poem. The Pearl itself is a contrasting symbol: of the righteous person, or of the perfect or potentially perfect soul, or of the kingdom of heaven.

155. Conley, John. *"Pearl* and a Lost Tradition," *JEGP,* LIV (1955), 332–47. Summarizes previous theories. Gives a "rule book" of desiderata for the analysis of the poem, scoring realist and earlier allegorical interpretations. The author then interprets the poem as a Christian *consolatio,* analogous to Boethius' famed work in theme, situation, roles, and treatment: what the dreamer has lost is an earthly good, hence transitory, hence false.

156. Hamilton, Marie P. "The Meaning of the Middle English *Pearl,"* *PMLA,* LXX (1955), 805–24. Finds a consistent allegory in the poem: the Pearl is (1) the maiden soul of man, which was "lost" in the Garden of Eden (the *erbere* of the poem—extensive analysis and documentation provided for this assumption) and which becomes incorporated into the Mystical Body of Christ, the Church, through baptismal regeneration; and (2) the gem of eternal life and beatitude. In a later article, "Notes on *Pearl,"* *JEGP,* LVII (1958), 177–91, Mrs. Hamilton examines specific passages to confirm her allegorical interpretation.

157. McAndrew, Bruno. *"The Pearl,* a Catholic *Paradise Lost,"* *ABR,* VIII (1957), 243–51. Sees the Pearl as a personification of Paradise, embodying purity and innocence: the loss of innocence is really a gain since it leads to a greater good, justification through Christ. *Gives a lucid summary of earlier theories.*

See also Hillmann (MEB 151). For the most recent criticism of allegorical interpretations, and a restatement of the primary concern of the poem with "death, its meaning, and its resolution," see S. de V. Hoffmann, *MP,* LVIII (1960), 73–80.

C. *Piers Plowman*

Editions and Translations:

158. Skeat, Walter W. *The Vision of William concerning Piers the Plowman, in Three Parallel Texts.* 2 vols. Oxford, 1886; London, 1924. The standard edition of all three texts, though more recent scholarship has, of course, added to and made corrections of much of Skeat's material.

159. Knott, Thomas A., and Fowler, D. C. *Piers the Plowman: A Critical Edition of the A-Version.* Baltimore, 1952. London, 1953. Full critical apparatus. *Excellent bibliography.* Textual notes and introductory section on MSS and establishment of text intended for scholars; rest of critical apparatus designed for students of Middle English. Does *not* discuss allegorical structure and literary value.

160. Kane, George. *Piers Plowman: The A Version, Will's Visions of Piers Plowman and Do-Wel.* Oxford, 1960. A monumental new edition, departing from earlier editorial principles of ascertaining original readings of the text. For a detailed review of the editorial principles involved, see *Times Literary Supplement,* May 13, 1960, p. 304. B- and C-text editions to follow.

161. Attwater, Donald and Rachel. *The Book Concerning Piers the Plowman.* Everyman's Library. London and New York, 1957. A *translation* of the B-text into Modern English *in alliterative verse,* keeping as close to the original as possible. Has a short introduction, a few notes, and a brief selected bibliography.

162. * Goodridge, J. F. *Langland: Piers the Ploughman.* Penguin Books. Baltimore, 1959. A fine translation, *in prose,* of the B-text, with a long, lucid, scholarly introduction, appendices, and notes. Selections from the poem, and translations of selections, may be found in just about any anthology of Middle English poetry.

Studies:

Much of the earlier scholarship dealt with the question of unity or multiple authorship and with the identity of Langland; for a summary of this criticism, see Bloomfield (MEB 167) and Hulbert (MEB 170). Recent criticism has been more concerned with the theological background, the allegorical values, and the artistic structure and unity. It should be noted that three recent publications, appearing almost simultaneously (MEB 165, 172, 174), have generally similar conclusions about the triadic progression of Do-Wel, Do-Bet, and Do-Best.

a) Book-length Criticism:

163. Donaldson, E. Talbot. *Piers Plowman, the C-Text and Its Poet.* Yale Studies in English, CXIII. New Haven, Conn., and London,

1949. A major, well-written study. Re-examines the authorship question and reaffirms the unity of the poem. Makes a contribution to our understanding of the whole poem, not alone of the C-text, though it analyzes in detail only this text. Has, among others, chapters on The Art, The Politics, Changes affecting the Interpretation of the Religious Allegory, and The Poet. The author finds the C-text of high poetic quality, though he observes that Langland is more concerned with theological and moral matters in this text than in B and notes a consequent reworking of many images of the B-text into theological statements.

164. Dunning, Thomas P. *Piers Plowman: An Interpretation of the A-Text*. Dublin, 1937. Illuminates the structure of the poem and the intellectual milieu out of which it sprang. Concentrates on the *Visio*, regarding the *Vita* as secondary, and finds that it carefully combines a developing tendency towards realism with the earlier medieval spirituality.

165. * Frank, Robert W., Jr. *Piers Plowman and the Scheme of Salvation: An Interpretation of Dowel, Dobet, and Dobest*. Yale Studies in English, CXXXVI. New Haven, Conn., and London, 1957. Perhaps the best single study of this difficult poem. A chapter on the plan of the poem summarizes traditional views. Has an excellent analysis of the Pardon Scene. Rejects the notion that Dowel, Dobet, and Dobest rest on the Triad of Active, Contemplative, and Mixed Lives or Purgative, Illuminative, Unitive stages; instead, sees them as all part of the same concept (Dowel), the progression being grammatical rather than mystical. Cf. Dunning (MEB 172) and Hussey (MEB 174). An important review, by T. Silverstein, is in *MP*, LVI (1959), 204–205.

166. Robertson, Durant W., Jr., and Huppé, B. F. *Piers Plowman and Scriptural Tradition*. Princeton, N.J., 1951; London, 1952. An exposition of the meanings and associations attached to the texts Langland quotes and, beyond that, an attempt to show similarities *throughout* between the poem and traditional Biblical exegesis. Often scholarly and illuminating, but see reviews by R. Quirk, *JEGP*, LII (1953), 253–55, and M. W. Bloomfield, *Speculum*, XXVII (1952), 245–49.

b) Articles and Monographs, arranged chronologically:

167. * Bloomfield, Morton W. "Present State of *Piers Plowman* Studies," *Speculum*, XIV (1939), 215–32. An indispensable summary of literary and nonliterary (e.g., authorship) controversies.

168. * Chambers, Raymond W. *Man's Unconquerable Mind*. London, 1939. Two chapters on *Piers Plowman* provide an excellent introduction to the poem and to the critical problems connected there-

with. *But see Hulbert* (MEB 170). Chambers is largely identified with the "three lives" theory—see MEB 165 and MEB 174. (The book also contains valuable chapters on Bede and *Beowulf*.)

169. Coghill, Nevill K. *The Pardon of Piers Plowman*. London, 1946. (In *PBA*, XXX [1944], 303–57.) * Beginning with the Pardon Scene in Passus VIII of the A-text, Coghill presents an interpretation of the poem. This 57-page monograph is full of interesting and stimulating comments, breaking ground that was then (1946) relatively new (i.e., suggesting that the B-text employs fully the four senses of allegorical meaning). Cf. MEB 166. For a judicious appraisal, see review by M. W. Bloomfield, *Speculum*, XXII (1947), 461–65.

170. * Hulbert, James R. *"Piers the Plowman* after Forty Years," *MP*, XLV (1948), 215–25. Summarizes views and points out fallacies in the 40-years' arguments for unity of authorship (esp. attacks Chambers). Does not advocate multiple authorship but demands that differences in structure, esp. between A- and B-texts, be recognized and not obscured.

171. Meroney, Howard. "The Life and Death of Longe Wille," *ELH*, XVII (1950), 1–35. Reviews the evidence for the existence of William Langland. Sees the B-text as the original poem composed before 1376, the A-text being an abridgment for a nonclerical audience. Controverting the triadic theory of Active, Contemplative, and Mixed Lives, suggests that the *Visio* and *Do-Wel* represent a Purgative Stage, *Do-Bet* an Illuminative Stage, and *Do-Best* a Unitive Stage.

172. Dunning, Thomas P. "The Structure of the B-Text of *Piers Plowman*," *RES*, N S VII (1956), 225–37. Believes that critics have not fully understood the connotations of the terms Dowel, Dobet, and Dobest in Langland's time. Proceeds to explain. Concludes that "the beginning of Dowel is love; . . . the perfection of love . . . Dobet; while Dobest is superabundant love, overflowing into the works of the apostolate. . . ." Cf. Frank (MEB 165) and Hussey (MEB 174).

173. Mitchell, Alexander G. *Lady Meed and the Art of Piers Plowman*. London, 1956. This Chambers Memorial Lecture reviews earlier views about Lady Meed, and then argues that the meaning of this allegorical figure is revealed through the poem's action, character, and motive. Sees the revelation—reward is unnecessary in the reign of Reason—as dramatically worked out with great subtlety.

---

* All references I have seen to this item get either the date or volume number (or both) wrong. The paper was delivered on 28 February 1945, but printed in volume of the preceding year.

174. Hussey, S. S. "Langland, Hilton, and the Three Lives," *RES,* N.S. VII (1956), 132–50. Denies an exact equation between Dowel, Dobet, and Dobest and either the triad Active, Contemplative, and Mixed Lives or the triad Purgative, Illuminative, and Unitive states. Sees the ideas as simple ones, which may have undergone modification from A- to B- to C-text, but which remained basically the same: Dowel represents the good life in any state to which man is called, and Dobet and Dobest simply are different degrees of the same thing. Cf. Frank (MEB 165) and Dunning (MEB 172).

175. Lawlor, John. "The Imaginative Unity of *Piers Plowman,*" *RES,* N.S. VIII (1957), 113–26. Accepts Father Dunning's doctrinal exposition of the B-text. Proceeds to examine the poem *qua* poem, seeing the "truly imaginative appeal of the poem" as in "the very failure of inquiry so long as the initiative is with the Dreamer," who, in the end, not only has "knowledge" but "realization."

176. Bloomfield, Morton W. "*Piers Plowman* and the Three Grades of Chastity," *Anglia,* LXXVI (1958), 227–53. An extensive examination of Langland's reworking of a traditional concept, examining the ramifications of the concept, esp. for B XII, 31–52, and the image of the tree in B XVI and C XIX.

177. * Zeeman, Elizabeth. "*Piers Plowman* and the Pilgrimage to Truth," *E & S,* N.S. XI (1958), 1–16. A lucid exposition of the poem (B-text), arguing that the major theme is "the exploration of the journey to God through Christ," a theme uniting "the two concepts of the going out towards God, and the ultimate finding of God within"—personified in Piers-Christ, presented humanly and dramatically and at the same time signifying moral and mystical values.

See also Ford (MEB 2), Owst (MEB 34), and Kane (MEB 52).

D. *Editions and Translations of Purity (Cleanness), Patience, and St. Erkenwald:*

Translations of parts of *Purity* and *Patience* may be found in Weston, *Romance* . . . (MEB 9); and translation of the whole *St. Erkenwald* in Loomis and Willard (MEB 4). Among other editions may be noted the following:

178. Bateson, Hartley. *Patience.* 2nd ed. Manchester, 1918.
179. Gollancz, Israel. *Patience.* London, 1913.
180. Gollancz, Israel. *St. Erkenwald.* London, 1922.
181. Menner, Robert J. *Purity.* Yale Studies in English, LXI. New Haven, Conn., 1920.

182. Savage, Henry L. *St. Erkenwald.* Yale Studies in English LXXII. New Haven, Conn., 1926.

XI. DEBATES, DIDACTIC POEMS, SATIRE; MANNYNG AND GOWER

Of the debates and didactic poetry of the Middle English period, apart from Mannyng, Gower, and metrical saints' lives, this bibliography gives data only on *The Owl and the Nightingale,* the most distinguished piece of literature in this group. A collection of 14th and 15th C. satiric and historic poems may be found in Robbins (MEB 6). For commentary and bibliography on the *Ormulum, The Debate of Body and Soul, The Cuckoo and the Nightingale, The Proverbs of Alfred,* John Audelay's poems, etc., see the various surveys and bibliographies. On *Bestiary,* see White (MEB 40) and Lowes (MEB 60).

A. *The Owl and the Nightingale*

Editions and Translations:

183. Atkins, John W. H. *The Owl and the Nightingale.* Cambridge, 1922. Contains *text* (of both MSS) and *translation.* 90-page introduction; notes and glossary.

184. Grattan, John H. G., and Sykes, G. F. H. *The Owl and the Nightingale.* EETSES 119. London, 1935 (for 1915). Reprinted, 1959. Valuable edition of the two extant MSS (diplomatic text), with bibliography, supplementing Atkins.

185. Stanley, Eric Gerald. *The Owl and the Nightingale.* London, Edinburgh and New York (Barnes & Noble, Inc.), 1960. An attractive new edition with a vigorously written and appreciative 38-page introduction, an extensive though not exhaustive bibliography, copious notes, an appendix of comparative materials, and a glossary.

Studies:

186. Huganir, Kathryn. *The Owl and the Nightingale: Sources, Date, Author.* Philadelphia, 1931. Considers the subject of date (limiting it to 1182–83, instead of early 13th C. as previously conjectured), some of the poem's literary features (e.g., the Owl and the Nightingale as literary conventions, rather than direct observations of nature), and the identity of Nicholas of Guildford.

187. Donovan, Mortimer J. "The Owl as Religious Altruist in *The Owl and the Nightingale,*" *MS,* XVIII (1956), 207–14. Argues that Owl's mission is to rescue backsliding Christians. Traces the origin of this altruism to a Biblical tradition. Claims that neither bird has advantage in the debate, both partaking of divinity.

188. * Lumiansky, Robert M. "Concerning *The Owl and the Nightingale*," *PQ*, XXXII (1953), 411–17. Sums up conflicting theories; agrees with Huganir that poem is plea for preferment by author, Nicholas of Guildford himself, whose skill in poetry and humane attitude are reflected in the poem. Argues for dating between 1184 and 1194.

189. Peterson, Douglas E. *"The Owl and the Nightingale* and Christian Dialectic," *JEGP*, LV (1956), 13–26. Sees the poem as more than a simple story: it is a dialectical exercise in which "the traditional and Christian struggle against the sensual and heretical"; these points of view are "represented respectively by a logician in quest of truth (Owl) and a rhetorician in quest of sophisticated victory (Nightingale)." The reader is to judge for himself the victory, foreordained of course by the poet.

See also chapter on poem in Wilson, *Early Middle English Literature* (MEB 51), Owst (MEB 34), and Utley (MEB 39).

B. *Mannyng (Robert of Brunne), Gower, Metrical Saints' Lives*
Editions and Translations:

190. D'Evelyn, Charlotte, and Mill, Anna J. *The South English Legendary.* 3 vols. EETS 235, 236, 244. London, 1956 (for 1951–52) and 1959 (for 1957). A fine new edition of these metrical saints' lives, probably composed by a friar-preacher. The stories range from the days of Christ to the near-contemporary period of St. Thomas à Becket. Vol. III contains the introduction and glossary.

191. Furnivall, Frederick J., ed. *Robert of Brunne's "Handlyng Synne,"* *A.D. 1303.* 2 vols. EETS 119, 123. London, 1901–03. Contains only the text, along with William of Wadington's *Manuel des Pechiez.*

192. Macaulay, George C. *The Works of John Gower.* 4 vols. Oxford, 1899–1902.

Selections from *Handlyng Synne* may be found in MEB 5, and 7. Selections from or translations of selected extracts from Mannyng and Gower will be found in most anthologies.

Studies:

193. Coffman, George R. "John Gower in His Most Significant Role," *University of Colorado Studies,* Ser. B, Vol. II (1945), 52–61 (*Elizabethan Studies and Other Essays in Honor of G. F. Reynolds*). Feels Gower has not received his due. An examination of Gower's whole corpus (not presented in this brief essay), argues Coffman, reveals that Gower is an advocate of moral order, which he sees as preserved by reason. The *Confessio Amantis* is his *summa moralis.* Gower's "most significant role is his explanation

and illustration of the ethical basis of God's universe for this little world of man."

194. Crosby, Ruth. "Robert Mannyng of Brunne: A New Biography," *PMLA*, LVII (1942), 15–28. By examining autobiographical references in Mannyng's poems, attempts to "fill in" data about the life and works of "one of Chaucer's most interesting predecessors in the art of storytelling."

195. Fison, Peter. "The Poet in John Gower," *EIC*, VIII (1958), 16–26. Attempts to rescue Gower from the limbo of noncriticism, to assert Gower's command of language and poetic technique and the universality of the *Confessio Amantis*. Compares him with Dryden.

196. Robertson, D. W., Jr. "The Cultural Tradition of *Handlyng Synne*," *Speculum*, XXII (1947), 162–85. Believes that Mannyng's work is in the tradition of medieval penitential literature, that it is, indeed, in the literary genre of the confessional manual.

On Gower, see also Dodd (MEB 232) and Enkvist (OEB 70).

XII. CHAUCER: GENERAL REFERENCES, THE MINOR WORKS AND TROILUS

Chaucer has, properly, received most critical attention from Middle English scholars, making the problem of selection for bibliography a particularly ticklish one. Since there are excellent bibliographical sources (see below) on Chaucer, and since the Robinson edition (see below) summarizes much material in its introductory notes to each work and to each of *The Canterbury Tales*, this bibliography concentrates on the most significant books and articles, and on the most recent, in general not re-covering ground that Robinson covers in his notes. The user of this bibliography is therefore advised to use it in conjunction with Robinson and the bibliographies listed below.

A. *Editions and Translations*

Complete Editions:

197. * Robinson, Fred N. *The Works of Geoffrey Chaucer*. 2nd rev. ed. Boston, 1957. Contains the entire accepted Chaucer canon. The introduction discusses Chaucer's life, canon and chronology, language and meter, and the text. Commentary includes an extensive section of explanatory notes (over 200 pages) and a section of textual notes. Glossary and selected bibliography. Much annotated bibliography in explanatory notes, though the coverage, esp. the annotations, on recent scholarship (i.e., since the first edition, 1933) is nowhere near exhaustive.

198. Skeat, Walter W. *The Complete Works of Geoffrey Chaucer.* 7 vols. Oxford, 1894–97. Still valuable for its notes and glossary. Vol. VII contains many pieces of Chauceriana, poems at the time ascribed to Chaucer but now excluded from his canon: *Plowman's Tale, Tale of Beryn, The Flower and the Leaf, The Assembly of Ladies, The Cuckoo and the Nightingale.*

Selected Edition:

199. * Donaldson, E. Talbot. *Chaucer's Poetry: An Anthology for the Modern Reader.* New York, 1958. This selected edition is designed to make Chaucer in the original Middle English easier for the modern reader by giving internal consistency to the spelling and by other eye-devices, without sacrificing either the phonological values or the general appearance of Middle English orthography. To this end, in addition to a glossary, it has definitions at the bottom of each page. There is a brief but informative section on Chaucer's language, prosody, and life, and a brief but stimulating critical commentary on each of the poems anthologized.

Editions of Major Works:

200. Manly, John M., and Rickert, E. *The Text of the Canterbury Tales.* 8 vols. Chicago, 1940. A monumental collation of the extant MSS. A standard reference work for advanced scholarship. For extensive reviews, appreciations, criticism, see D. Everett, *RES,* XVIII (1942), 93–109; R. K. Root, *SP,* XXXVIII (1941), 1–13; and G. Dempster, *PMLA,* LXI (1946), 379–415.

201. Root, R. K. *The Book of Troilus and Criseyde by Geoffrey Chaucer.* Princeton, N. J., 1926, 1930. Important edition, with extensive introduction and notes. Introduction contains, among other things, description of the 16 MSS in which this poem is found.

Translations:

202. * Coghill, Nevill. *Geoffrey Chaucer: The Canterbury Tales Translated into Modern English.* Penguin Books, Baltimore. 1952. An exhilarating translation, readily accessible. Translates all but the *Parson's Tale* and *Melibeus.* For some discussion of its merits and deficiencies, see review by C. H. Llewellyn, *Speculum,* XXVII (1952), 538–40.

203. Krapp, George P. *Geoffrey Chaucer, Troilus and Cressida: Rendered into Modern English Verse.* New York, 1932. Readable and idiomatic.

204. * Lumiansky, Robert M. *The Canterbury Tales of Geoffrey Chaucer: A New Modern English Prose Translation, Published Together with the Original Middle English Text of the General Prologue and the Nun's Priest's Tale.* Preface by Mark Van Doren. Illus. by H. Lawrence Hoffman. New York, 1948. A revised version (*Geoffrey Chaucer: The Canterbury Tales*) appeared in 1954 in paperback.

205. * Lumiansky, Robert M. *Geoffrey Chaucer's Troilus and Criseyde: Rendered into Modern English Prose.* Illus. by H. L. Hoffman. Columbia, S. C., 1952.

206. Tatlock, John S. P., and Mackaye, P. *The Modern Reader's Chaucer.* Rev. ed. New York, 1938. Has the virtue of translating the complete Chaucer canon.

B. *Bibliographies*

Surveys of Scholarship:

207. * Baugh, Albert C. "Fifty Years of Chaucer Scholarship," *Speculum*, XXVI (1951), 659–72. A stimulating critical survey of major contributions to the study of Chaucer's major works from 1900 to 1950. Most general, in terms of bibliography, on *The Canterbury Tales* and the *Troilus;* most specific on the *Hous of Fame* and the *Parlement of Fowles.*

208. * Purdy, Rob Roy. "Chaucer Scholarship in England and America: A Review of Recent Trends," *Anglia*, LXX (1952), 345–81. A very convenient review of trends since 1933 (1st ed. of Robinson's *Chaucer*), and esp. from 1945 to 1951. Summarizes important studies under headings of The Chaucer Text, Language and Meter, Sources and Analogues, Chaucer Biography, The Chaucer Milieu, Toward Literary Criticism, and New Direction. Sees the new direction in terms of "concern for close textual analysis as a means of discovering the nature of the literary entity," based on sound scholarship, but with a consideration of such elements as structure, texture, and poetic devices. Sees Shelley's *Chaucer* (MEB 219) as stimulating this trend. (This trend has continued, we may add, but with it has come the allegorical-symbolistic approach and reactions to it.)

Cumulative Bibliographies:

209. Griffith, Dudley D. *Bibliography of Chaucer 1908–1953.* Seattle, 1955. An exhaustive bibliography, supplementing Hammond (MEB 210) and Spurgeon (MEB 211). *Esp. valuable for its notice of reviews and listing of theses.*

210. Hammond, Eleanor P. *Chaucer: A Bibliographical Manual.* New York, 1908. Reprinted, 1933.

211. Spurgeon, Caroline F. E. *Five Hundred Years of Chaucer Criticism and Allusions: 1357–1900.* 3 vols. London and New York, 1925.

C. *Concordance*

212. Tatlock, John S. P., and Kennedy, A. G. *A Concordance to the Complete Works of Geoffrey Chaucer and to the Romaunt of the Rose.* Washington, D. C., 1927. Extremely important reference work for the occurrences of words in Chaucer, the study of word meanings in context, and the study of rhyme.

D. *Background and Biography*

213. * Chute, Marchette. *Geoffrey Chaucer of England.* New York, 1946. Reprinted, 1958 (paperback). A "popular" biography, but with a useful bibliography.
214. * Coulton, George G. *Chaucer and His England.* 8th ed. London, 1950. An excellent introduction to the social life of the 14th C. Skillfully uses history and literature to illuminate each other.
215. * French, Robert D. *A Chaucer Handbook.* 2nd ed. New York, 1947. An indispensable grounding for the undergraduate and graduate student. Offers no aesthetic judgments; gathers materials "to give the mature student . . . some knowledge of the world in which [Chaucer] lived, of the way his life shaped itself in that world, of the language which he spoke and wrote, of the dates, the sources, and the special significance of his works. . . ." The kind of information one can find here: a 37-page canto-by-canto summary of *Il Filostrato,* a summary of the *Roman de Renart,* an analogue of *The Prioress's Tale,* as well, of course, as comments on Chaucer's use of his material and various scholarly contributions thereto. Contains an index and a 19-page bibliography.

See also Rickert (MEB 22) and Bennett (MEB 55).

E. *General Studies and Appreciations, book-length*

The following items are arranged chronologically; they have been selected for their special qualities and/or freshness of contribution to our understanding. For a more complete listing, see Robinson (MEB 197).

216. * Kittredge, George L. *Chaucer and His Poetry.* Cambridge, Mass., 1915. Although Kittredge idolatry has recently come under attack in some scholarly quarters, the essays herein (originally lectures) remain fresh, charming, and stimulating. Contains the famous suggestion for the "Marriage Group" among *The*

Canterbury Tales (the original Kittredge article setting forth this suggestion [*MP, IX* (1911–12), 435–67] is reprinted in MEB 245).

217. * Root, Robert K. *The Poetry of Chaucer.* Rev. ed. New York, 1922. Reissued, Gloucester, Mass., 1957. A standard treatment, rich in critical estimates.

218. * Patch, Howard R. *On Rereading Chaucer.* Cambridge, Mass., 1939. A collection of essays "strung together on the theme of Chaucer's humor." Comments on irony in the *Troilus,* on the relation of the love-visions to contemporary events, and on Chaucer's poetic method in *The Canterbury Tales.*

219. Shelley, Percy V. D. *The Living Chaucer.* Philadelphia, 1940. A vigorously written step-by-step tracing of the development of Chaucer's art. Perhaps of most interest to the general reader is the discussion of the *Troilus* (in which the qualities of Troilus, Criseyde, and Pandarus and the poem's structural excellence are appreciatively analyzed) and the brief discussion of the *Legend of Good Women,* which concentrates on the legends rather than on the *Prologue.*

220. * Coghill, Nevill. *The Poet Chaucer.* London, 1949. A brief appreciation of Chaucer's development as a poet. Major share of attention given to the earlier poems: the love-visions and the *Troilus.* Good survey of *Roman de la Rose.*

221. Madeleva, Sister M. *A Lost Language and Other Essays on Chaucer.* New York, 1951. Of interest as an appreciation of the poet by a religious. Contains, among other items, a very sympathetic chapter on Chaucer's Nuns (a reprint of an earlier article), in which the author cites the Rule of St. Benedict, among other arguments, to show that the Prioress was behaving properly and should not be judged harshly by the modern reader—and was not so judged by Chaucer. But cf. Schoeck (MEB 289).

222. Malone, Kemp. *Chapters on Chaucer.* Baltimore and London, 1951. A combination of elementary facts and perceptive critical remarks. Most illuminating in the analysis of passages in detail, such as the analysis of the two versions of the *Prologue to the Legend of Good Women.*

223. * Preston, Raymond. *Chaucer.* London and New York, 1952. Although not always felicitously written, this is a stimulating and original book which tries to interpret Chaucer for the modern reader. Sees Chaucer as "our medieval poet of serenity," and suggests his "balance" forcefully and richly. Excellent index.

224. * Brewer, Derek D. *Chaucer.* 2nd ed. London, 1958. A thorough, workmanlike job, making an excellent beginning for the undergraduate.

See also Muscatine (MEB 235).

The reader's attention is also called to Dryden's classic Preface to the *Fables,* where, despite his misunderstanding of Chaucer's metrics and pronunciation, Dryden offers a perennially rich and inspiring tribute to his fellow poet. This essay is frequently anthologized, and it may also be found in W. P. Ker's *Essays of John Dryden,* II, Oxford, 1900. For studies of individual works and of special topics, see below.

F. *Influences on Chaucer*

Translations of Influential Works:

225. Ellis, Frederick S. *The Romance of the Rose by W. Lorris and J. Clopinel.* 3 vols. London, 1900. Though somewhat Victorian, the only full (or almost full) translation.

226. Griffin, Nathaniel E., and Myrick, A. B. *The Filostrato of Giovanni Boccaccio: A Translation with Parallel Text.* Philadelphia and London, 1929.

227. Parry, John J. *The Art of Courtly Love by Andreas Capellanus.* New York, 1941. Complete text of Andreas, with long and illuminating introduction on origins and development of courtly love.

228. Stewart, H. F. *Boethius: The Theological Tractates and The Consolation of Philosophy.* New York, 1918. *The Consolation* is a revision of the "I. T." translation of 1609, with Latin and English on facing pages.

Note: A new translation of *The Consolation of Philosophy,* by Richard H. Green, for the Liberal Arts Press, New York, is in progress.

Studies on Influences:

229. Braddy, Haldeen. *Chaucer and the French Poet Graunson.* Baton Rouge, La., 1947. Throws light on Chaucer's courtly poetry.

230. Cummings, Hubertis M. *The Indebtedness of Chaucer's Works to the Italian Works of Boccaccio.* University of Cincinnati Studies, X. Cincinnati, Ohio, 1916.

231. * Curry, Walter C. *Chaucer and the Mediaeval Sciences.* Rev. ed. New York, Barnes & Noble, Inc., 1960. An oft-cited study, especially for the relation between the physical characteristics of Chaucer's Canterbury Pilgrims and their temperaments in the light of medieval alchemy, astrology, physiognomy. Studies Chaucer's transmutation of scientific material into art. The rev. ed. contains chapters on the *Troilus* and *The Knight's Tale,* viewing the pure sciences as part of Divine Providence. Selected bibliography indicates trends in recent scholarship and criticism.

232. Dodd, William G. *Courtly Love in Chaucer and Gower.* Boston, 1913. Reprinted, Gloucester, Mass., 1958. A basic study on the subject.

233. Fansler, Dean S. *Chaucer and the Roman de la Rose.* New York, 1914. Studies influence on Chaucer's reading, his style, his philosophical discussions, his situations and descriptions, etc.

234. Jefferson, Bernard L. *Chaucer and the Consolation of Philosophy of Boethius.* An important study, tracing Boethian influence and Chaucer's artistic use of the *Consolatio.*

235. Muscatine, Charles. *Chaucer and the French Tradition: A Study in Style and Meaning.* Berkeley and Los Angeles, Calif., 1957. Sees Chaucer's style and meaning as springing from his fusion of the courtly and the bourgeois traditions of the 12th and 13th centuries in France. Examines Chaucer's major and minor works in this light. Concludes that Chaucer is definitely "medieval" but with a difference: he sees from a new perspective (one which has inherent in it the break-up of medieval values) the relationship of the various and even antithetical values of medieval civilization. Bibliography in notes.

236. * Pratt, Robert A. "Chaucer's Use of the *Teseida,*" *PMLA,* LXII (1947), 598–621. Traces the maturation of Chaucer's artistic use of the *Teseida* from the *Hous of Fame* through the *Troilus* to the *Knight's Tale.*

237. Shannon, Edgar F. *Chaucer and the Roman Poets.* Harvard Studies in Comparative Literature, VII. Cambridge, Mass., 1929. Primarily a study of the influence of Ovid, whom, Shannon feels, Chaucer loved more dearly and knew more in detail, than he did any other writer.

See also Patch, *The Tradition of Boethius* (MEB 36).

G. Chaucer's Techniques

238. Baum, Paull F. "Chaucer's Puns," *PMLA,* LXXI (1956), 225–46; "Chaucer's Puns: A Supplementary List," *PMLA,* LXXIII (1958), 167–70. Provide some sound, some questionable (as Baum himself admits) illustrations of *double-entendre* in Chaucer's diction.

239. * Bronson, Bertrand H. "Chaucer's Art in Relation to His Audience," *University of California Publications in English,* VIII (1940), 1–53 (*Five Studies in Literature*). Shows that Chaucer was constantly aware of a *listening* audience and that this awareness was a primary condition of his writing, contributing to the liveliness of his style, his use of sly allusion, and even his idealization of the Canterbury Pilgrims.

240. * Dempster, Germaine. *Dramatic Irony in Chaucer.* Stanford University Publications, Univ. Ser., Lang. and Lit., IV, No. 3. Stanford University, Calif., 1932. Examines Chaucer's use of dramatic irony in various works. Among other conclusions, finds that the

two main influences on his development of dramatic irony were the *Filostrato* and the fabliaux.

241. Kökeritz, Helge. "Rhetorical Word-Play in Chaucer," *PMLA*, LXIX (1954), 937–52. Reviews previous literature on the subject and then examines Chaucer's use of rhetorical devices. Finds that these devices are more common in Chaucer's earlier works, which were influenced by French models using them.

242. Schaar, Claes. *The Golden Mirror: Studies in Chaucer's Descriptive Technique and Its Literary Background.* Lund, Sweden, 1955. Assesses Chaucer's descriptive technique in terms of emotions, portraits, and landscapes. To this end, compares passages with some from Chaucer's contemporaries and his predecessors. Thorough, specialized study.

243. Schaar, Claes. *Some Types of Narrative in Chaucer's Poetry.* Lund, Sweden, 1954. By judicious comparison with corresponding passages in Chaucer's sources, Schaar assesses Chaucer's originality in use of narrative in three main categories: Summary, Close Chronological, Loose Chronological. Concludes that the earlier poems are, in respect to narrative art, more original and unconventional than later ones: a conclusion that follows the trend of current critical opinion.

244. Schlauch, Margaret. "Chaucer's Prose Rhythms," *PMLA*, LXV (1950), 568–89. Shows that Chaucer's prose was influenced by the tradition of cadenced medieval Latin prose. Examines the Retraction, parts of *Boethius, Melibeus,* the *Astrolabe,* and the *Parson's Tale,* finding the incidence of cadence greatest in the first two. Article provides a good summary of classical and medieval teaching about prose rhythm.

On Chaucer's use of nature, see Enkvist (OEB 70).

H. *Studies of Individual Works* (see introductory remarks to Sec. XII)

Highly recommended is a collection of articles on individual works:

245. * Wagenknecht, Edward. *Chaucer: Modern Essays in Criticism.* New York, 1959. A paperback edition, reprinting some of the important Chaucerian criticisms of modern times. It contains several articles not mentioned in this bibliography; those which are mentioned in this bibliography have been cross-referenced.

Book of the Duchess:

246. Baker, Donald C. "Imagery and Structure in Chaucer's *Book of the Duchess,*" *SN*, XXX (1958), 17–26. A fresh attempt to elucidate the poem, ignoring the relationship between the dreamer and the Black Knight. Sees the external organization of the three parts of the poem (the narrator's love-grief, the Ceyx-Halcyone

grief, and the Black Knight's loss) furnishing structural parallelism, matched by parallel life-death (clothed-naked) imagery. Suggestive.

247. * French, Walter H. "The Man in Black's Lyric," *JEGP*, LVI (1957), 231–41. *Provides an excellent summary of the virtues and limitations of earlier theories about the dreamer's naïveté or sophistication.* Argues that the dreamer does not know until the end that the knight has lost his wife because he takes the lyric in which the knight laments her death as simply the fashionable exaggeration of the courtly love lyric.

248. Lawlor, John. "The Pattern of Consolation in *The Book of the Duchess*," *Speculum*, XXXI (1956), 626–48. Traces the working out of the dreamer's consolation in terms of courtly love and sees the humor of the poem as part of the pattern of consolation.

249. Manning, Stephen. "Chaucer's Good Fair White: Woman and Symbol," *CL*, X (1958), 97–105. Discusses at length the symbolic meaning of *white* for the Middle Ages (beauty, purity, joy), concluding that Chaucer is following tradition in personifying Blanche. But also feels that Chaucer, again in accordance with tradition, is "not only eulogizing Blanche by presenting her as a symbol of the ideals of courtly love, but is also lamenting the departure of such ideals"—so that love is debased and its consequent virtues are no longer practiced.

See also MEB 216–224, 235.

Note: One of the most sensitive and delightful explications of the *Book of the Duchess*, B. H. Bronson's "The *Book of the Duchess* Re-Opened" (which is summarized and attacked in MEB 247) is reprinted in MEB 245 (originally in *PMLA*, LXVII [1952], 863–81).

The Hous of Fame:

250. Allen, Robert J. "A Recurring Motif in Chaucer's *House of Fame*," *JEGP*, LV (1956), 393–405. Finds that the poem "preserves a sustained interest in the nature of literary art" and that this motif, while not structurally unifying the poem, does give it some semblance of order.

251. Ruggiers, Paul G. "The Unity of Chaucer's *House of Fame*," *SP* (1953), 16–29. Finds a unity in a combination of love-vision and quest, and suggests that the announcement of the man of great authority may have been to provide an answer "to the common consideration of the Middle Ages, the relationship of men to the mutable world through the agency of Fame." Hence, the author suggests, Boethius may be the man of great authority. (Reprinted in MEB 245.)

252. Stillwell, Gardiner. "Chaucer's 'O Sentence' in the *Hous of Fame,*" *ES*, XXXVII (1956), 149–57. Considers the underlying theme of the poem to be a Boethian distrust of worldly felicity. See also MEB 216–224, 235.

The Parlement of Foules:

253. Bennett, Jack A. W. *The Parlement of Foules: An Interpretation.* Oxford, 1957. An important book, though more for the advanced student and scholar in its far-ranging erudition, correlating ideas in Chaucer's sources and Chaucer's times with the poet's transmutation of them in this poem. Ignoring as incidental any topical or allusive significance the poem may have, Bennett finds that Chaucer is examining in this poem the ambiguous, paradoxical nature of human love and the relation of this love to human weal. For a detailed review article, suggesting the book's limitations, see T. Silverstein, *MP*, LVI (May 1959), 270–76.

254. Frank, Robert W., Jr. "Structure and Meaning in the *Parlement of Foules,*" *PMLA*, LXXI (1956), 530–39. Sees a unity in the three parts of the poem, with their different attitudes toward love (moral, literary, realistic) which, when set side by side, make each other appear slightly ridiculous. Suggests that the poem reveals love's complex power.

255. Lumiansky, Robert M. "Chaucer's *Parlement of Foules:* A Philosophical Interpretation," *RES*, XXIV (1948), 81–89. *Of value for its convenient summary of earlier theories* more than for its own interpretation.

256. Stillwell, Gardiner. "Unity and Comedy in Chaucer's *Parlement of Foules,*" *JEGP*, XLIX (1950), 470–95. A lengthy article arguing that the poem is "a comedy of medieval manners and ideas adapted to the framework of the love-vision."

257. Stillwell, Gardiner. "Chaucer's Eagles and Their Choice on February 14," *JEGP*, LIII (1954), 546–61. A continuation of his previous article, arguing that though the three eagles affect courtly idiom, they are not as humble as they ought or pretend to be. Concludes that Chaucer is treating the attitude of courtly lovers "with a shrewd and rather lighthearted irony."

258. Seaton, Ethel. *"The Parlement of Foules* and Lionel of Clarence," *MAE*, XXV (1956), 168–74. The most recent attempt to find topical allusion in the poem; uses anagrammatic method to this end, finding the poem to celebrate the marriage of Lionel of Clarence to Violanta of Milan in 1368. See next two articles.

259. Emerson, Katherine T. *"The Parlement of Foules* and Lionel of Clarence: A Reply," *MAE*, XXVI (1957), 107–109; with re-

joinder by E. Seaton, 109–11. Argues against the identification, but does not basically reject the anagrammatic method.

_60. * Friedman, William F. and Elizabeth S. "Acrostics, Anagrams, and Chaucer," *PQ*, XXXVIII (1959), 1–20. The immediate purpose of this essay by these famed cryptographers is to refute Seaton's article, but there is a wider implication against *all* misguided efforts to find anagrams and acrostics in literature.
See also MEB 216–224, 235.

The Legend of Good Women:

261. Estrich, Robert M. "Chaucer's Maturing Art in the Prologues to the *Legend of Good Women*," *JEGP*, XXXVI (1937), 326–37. Discusses Chaucer's revisions of the G-Prologue, showing how he toned down the adoration of the daisy and eliminated a good deal of other conventional courtly love material, thereby heightening the amusement and the irony.
See also Shelley (MEB 219) and Malone (MEB 222).

Troilus and Criseyde:

Earlier studies of this masterpiece were concerned with the acceptance or rejection of the palinode; with attacks on and defenses of the character of Criseyde; with the use Chaucer made of Boethius in the poem; with the relation of the poem to *Il Filostrato* and to other medieval developments of the Troilus story. More recent criticism, involved less directly with these problems, has been concerned with defining more precisely Chaucer's attitude toward the love affair (courtly love, human love in general); with the aesthetic effect of the poem; and with the more pervasive Boethian influence on it. The most exhaustive study is that of Meech, below.

a) Book-length Studies:

262. Kirby, Thomas A. *Chaucer's Troilus: A Study in Courtly Love.* Baton Rouge, La., 1940. Reissued, 1958. A detailed study, with minute comparison with Boccaccio.

263. * Meech, Sanford B. *Design in Chaucer's Troilus.* Syracuse, N. Y., 1959. An extensive, illuminating examination of the poem, with detailed comparison with *Il Filostrato,* revealing the complex transformation Chaucer achieved. Has large chapters on The Action in its Course, Physical Particulars and Time and the Supernatural, Figurative Associations . . . , and Composites. In commenting on the totality of meaning, Meech steers a course between that of C. S. Lewis (MEB 26), who sees the poem as praising courtly love, and that of Father Denomy (MEB 266), who believes the poem completely rejects and disapproves of it.

Meech holds that the poet shows the illusoriness of courtly love, which is one of the specious goods of this transient world, but that he maintains to the very end a sympathetic if critical interest in it. *The book contains much annotated bibliographical material* in notes on each chapter. Primarily, in style and content, for advanced students and scholars; but the final section on The Totality should also interest the general reader.

264. Young, Karl. *The Origin and Development of the Story of Troilus and Criseyde.* Chaucer Society, Second Series, XL. London, 1908 (for 1904). The standard reference work on the backgrounds of the story.

See also introduction to Root's edition of the poem (MEB 201).

b) Articles:

265. Bloomfield, Morton W. "Distance and Predestination in *Troilus and Criseyde,*" *PMLA,* LXXII (1957), 14–26. Argues that Chaucer's portrayal of himself as a narrator of history sets a distance between himself and the events of the story—a distance which Bloomfield examines as temporal, spatial, aesthetic, and religious. Shows that in the end Chaucer finds his peace, leaving behind Troilus' grief, the agony of Criseyde's betrayal, "the perplexities of time and space," and "the tyranny of history and predestination."

266. Denomy, Alexander J. "The Two Moralities of Chaucer's *Troilus and Criseyde,*" *Transactions of the Royal Society of Canada, Ser. III, Sec. 2,* XLIV (1950), 35–46. Sees two moralities in the poem: that of Chaucer and his world and that of courtly love in which the lovers move and act out their drama. Argues that the code of courtly love had been condemned as heretical and that Chaucer knew it; that Chaucer, in the *Troilus,* "not only rejects, disapproves of, and condemns, he repudiates Courtly Love as vain, ephemeral, and fallacious, the blind effect of passion," not only in the palinode, but throughout.

267. * Green, Marion N. "Christian Implications of Knighthood and Courtly Love in Chaucer's *Troilus,*" *Delaware Notes,* XXX (1957), 57–92. This long article traces, detail by detail, Christian echoes and implications in the poem. *It provides en route a convenient summary and bibliography of scholarly points of view.* Concludes that throughout the poem there is overlapping and dovetailing of the principles and virtues jointly upheld by courtly love and medieval Christianity.

268. Jordan, Robert M. "The Narrator in Chaucer's *Troilus,*" *ELH,* XXV (1958), 237–57. Argues that the poem embodies several

distinct perspectives which can be properly understood only in reference to the mediatory role of the narrator.

269. Lumiansky, Robert M. "The Function of the Proverbial Monitory Elements in Chaucer's *Troilus and Criseyde*," *TSE*, II (1950), 5–48. A lengthy examination of proverbial material in relation to its possible literary uses, and a close analysis of the use of such material in each of the books of the *Troilus*. Shows that Chaucer uses this material to differentiate characters and to heighten dramatic structure.

270. Pratt, Robert A. "Chaucer and *Le Roman de Troyle et de Criseida*," *SP*, LIII (1956), 509–39. Tentatively challenges the long-held belief that *Il Filostrato* is the main source of the *Troilus*. Makes a detailed comparison of this French prose translation by Beauvau of Boccaccio's work and the two other poems, concluding that Chaucer's indebtedness to *Le Roman* was apparently greater than to its original, not only in verbal closeness but also in tone and structure. Important study.

271. Robertson, Durant W., Jr. "Chaucerian Tragedy," *ELH*, XIX (1952), 1–37. Derives Chaucer's conception of tragedy from the *Monk's Prologue* and *Tale*, and examines the *Troilus* in this light. Sees in the *Troilus* a tragedy firmly rooted in Christian doctrine and Boethian philosophy, the tragedy of every mortal sinner. In contrast to Slaughter (MEB 273), finds the religious linkage with earthly love censorious: "religious imagery is intended to suggest the values from which the hero departs . . . and to furnish opportunity for ironic humor." Details of argument are open to question.

272. * Sharrock, Roger. "Second Thoughts: C. S. Lewis on Chaucer's *Troilus*," *EIC*, VIII (1958), 123–37. A very readable and lucid appraisal of Lewis' shortcomings in his study of the *Troilus* in *The Allegory of Love* (MEB 26): his overemphasis on the courtly love code and his omission of serious consideration of the concluding stanzas. Sharrock concludes that the total effect is the result of "a bizarre counter-pointing of fleeting human love, the contingency of material life and divine consolation." Article does not say much new, but is urbane and judicious in what it says.

273. Slaughter, Eugene E. "Love and Grace in Chaucer's *Troilus*," in *Essays in Honor of Walter Clyde Curry*. Nashville, Tenn., 1954. Pp. 61–76. Finds that the imitation of Christian grace and its associated notions in the poem contribute to an extenuation of earthly love, making it seem more virtuous, though there are, of course, varying degrees of irony attached to this idea. *For a good*

bibliography of the palinode, se note 4, pp. 61–62. Cf. Robertson (MEB 271).

See also Lewis (MEB 26), Patch (MEB 35), Everett (MEB 59), the general studies (MEB 216–224, 235), and Farnham (MEB 341).

XIII. CHAUCER: THE CANTERBURY TALES

See introductory remarks to XII. The advanced student and scholar will wish to consult the Manly-Rickert edition (MEB 200).

A large part of the scholarship on this work has been devoted to a study of the background of the pilgrimage, the order of the tales and their over-all unity, the characterization of the pilgrims and the dramatic appropriateness of their tales, the dramatic interplay between pilgrims, sources and analogues of the framework and of the tales themselves. More recent criticism has also been concerned with Chaucer's literary handling of his sources, the artistry of individual tales, and the relation of the description of the pilgrims and their tales to Biblical exegetical tradition.

A. *Studies on the Prologue, Framework, Order of Tales*

274. Baldwin, Ralph. *The Unity of the Canterbury Tales.* Anglistica, V. Copenhagen, 1955. Studies the beginning and end of the *Tales,* finding an architectonic unity in them despite their incompleteness. This unity resides in the concept of the Pilgrimage (passing from the City of Man to the City of God) and the call to repentance in *The Parson's Tale,* moving Chaucer the Poet-Pilgrim to his *Retraction.* Contains some interesting detailed comments on the Prologue, its relation to medieval rhetorical conventions and Chaucer's originality therein.

275. * Bowden, Muriel. *A Commentary on the General Prologue to the Canterbury Tales.* New York, 1949. Brings together much material of a literary and historic nature on the portraits in the Prologue. Has a separate chapter for almost every pilgrim; plenty of notes. A very valuable compendium and a good starting point for the inexperienced reader, though for adverse criticism, see *YWES,* XXIX (1950 [for 1948]), pp. 77–8.

276. * Cunningham, James V. "The Literary Form of the Prologue to the *Canterbury Tales," MP,* XLIX (1952), 172–81. Maintains that the search for realistic models for the Prologue is misdirected: the source is, rather, literary, and none other than the *Romance of the Rose* and the dream-vision tradition. Should be studied together with Manly (MEB 286), who seeks realistic prototypes; with Curry (MEB 231) and Kittredge (MEB 216),

who see portraits as typical; with Malone (MEB 222), who sees portraits as idealizing.

277. * Donaldson, E. Talbot. "Chaucer the Pilgrim," *PMLA*, LXIX (1954), 928–36. An entertaining and suggestive article, arguing that the fallible "I" of the *Canterbury Tales* must not be confused with Chaucer and that Chaucer gets a lot of mileage in humor out of the distinction as well as gaining a moral end. But see Major (MEB 285).

278. Duncan, Edgar H. "Narrator's Points of View in the Portrait-sketches, Prologue to the *Canterbury Tales*," in *Essays in Honor of Walter Clyde Curry*. Nashville, Tenn., 1954. Pp. 77–101. Examines Chaucer's device, in the successive portraits of the Prologue, of freely shifting from "a strictly limited point of view of personal observation and deduction . . . to one of omniscience." Concludes that though the device itself was traditional and literary, Chaucer used it originally on "the chaotic elements of actuality: his reading, his observation, his experience. . . ."

279. * Hoffman, Arthur W. "Chaucer's Prologue to Pilgrimage: The Two Voices," *ELH*, XXI (1954), 1–16. *An extremely stimulating article*. Finds a unity in relationships between characters, but primarily in the double theme of love: that generated by nature which impels and the supernatural force which draws all to the shrine. Among other keen observations on the Prologue is a fascinating analysis of the opening 18 lines, showing the combination of natural and supernatural love, and the parallel between the fructification of nature in springtime and the "healing" that the pilgrims have found in the martyred Saint whose shrine they seek for spiritual fructification. (Reprinted in MEB 245.)

280. * Kaske, Robert E. "The Knight's Interruption of the *Monk's Tale*," *ELH*, XXIV (1957), 249–68. A detailed examination that carries more weight than the title would indicate. Sees the Monk and the Knight as contrasts in the scheme of the *Tales*, and their tales as contrasts, pointed up by the Knight's interruption of the Monk, within the Boethian frame of reference (both the tales relying heavily on the *De Consolatione*).

281. * Lawrence, William W. *Chaucer and the Canterbury Tales*. London, 1950. An extremely readable presentation of some of the most significant research on the *Tales*, esp. in connection with structure and unity of the whole work. Lawrence has many original ideas of his own to contribute. In five essays, he discusses Realism and Artifice, The Fabliaux, The Sequence of the Tales, The Marriage Group (to which he would add The *Nun's Priest's Tale* and *Melibeus*), and the ending of the *Tales* (seeing the retraction as genuine, the result of a religious crisis experienced by

Chaucer). The virtues of the book proceed from Lawrence's common sense and his power of reducing a complicated problem to simplest terms.

282. *Lumiansky, Robert M. "Benoit's Portraits and Chaucer's General Prologue," *JEGP*, LV (1956), 431–38. Argues that there is originality in Benoit's portraits of Trojan War heroes and heroines, likewise in Chaucer's portraits in the Prologues; but that there are many points of resemblance between the portraitures in the two, including the combination of physical and temperamental traits and the narrator's personal comments.

283. Lumiansky, Robert M. "Chaucer's Retraction and the Degree of Completeness of the *Canterbury Tales*," *TSE*, VI (1956), 5–13. Believes that Chaucer modified his intention as to the extent of the *Tales* and that what we have may represent almost the complete work. Sees the Retraction as referring only to the *Parson's Tale;* concludes that there is an inevitable propriety in having this tale last.

284. *Lumiansky, Robert M. *Of Sondry Folk: The Dramatic Principle in the Canterbury Tales*. Austin, Texas, 1955. An enthusiastic book, but it presses its case of the suitability of tale to teller and of dramatic appropriateness somewhat far into the realm of conjecture. Sees three stages of dramatic development: simple suiting of tale and teller (e.g., Prioress, Squire); simple suiting plus external motivation (e.g., Miller and Reeve, Summoner and Friar); these two, plus internal motivation, producing a dramatic revelation of pilgrim's character (e.g., Pardoner, Wife of Bath). *Contains a convenient summary of previous theories about suitability, a selected bibliography, and an index.*

285. *Major, John M. "The Personality of Chaucer the Pilgrim," *PMLA*, LXXV (1960), 160–62. Takes exception to Donaldson's view (MEB 277), arguing with some cogency that Chaucer the Pilgrim, like Chaucer the Poet, is the "alert, ironic, and facetious master of every situation."

286. *Manly, John M. *Some New Light on Chaucer*. New York, 1926. Reissued, 1951. Suggests real-life prototypes for many of the Canterbury pilgrims.

287. Owen, Charles A., Jr. "The Development of the *Canterbury Tales*," *JEGP*, LVII (1958), 449–76. Examines some of the contradictions and discrepancies in the *Canterbury Tales* to gain insight into the change and growth of Chaucer's conception of the *Tales*. Challenges some of the ideas of Pratt and Dempster (see MEB 288).

288. Pratt, Robert A. "The Order of *The Canterbury Tales*," *PMLA*, LXVI (1951), 1141–67. This extensive, thorough, specialized

article deserves mention here as virtually assuring that Chaucer's ultimate decision on the order of the tales was that of the "Bradshaw" Shift. (Germaine Dempster, it should be noted, has had several articles on the development of the order of the tales; these are for the scholar, but deserve mention here.) Cf. MEB 287.

289. Schoeck, Richard J. "Chaucer's Prioress: Mercy and Tender Heart," in *The Bridge: A Yearbook of Judaeo-Christian Studies*, II (1956), 239–55. An examination of the Prioress and her tale, showing the gulf between that lady's professed devotion and her bigotry. Claims that her attitude was contradictory to the "mind of the Church" and that Chaucer's attitude toward her is one of understanding pity. Cf. Madeleva (MEB 221) and Steadman (MEB 290).

290. Steadman, John M. "The Prioress' Dogs and Benedictine Discipline," *MP*, LIV (1956), 1–6. Argues that the Prioress' attitude toward her dogs shows a violation of the Benedictine discipline: dogs were not permitted by that order; the Prioress' pity and charity were therefore misdirected. Cf. above article.

See also Lowes (MEB 60), Bowden (MEB 275), and Bradley (MEB 301).

B. *Individual Tales* (in the order presented in Robinson's *Chaucer*)

Many, many articles have appeared on these; in the main, only recent significant articles have been cited in this bibliography: see Robinson's notes and the various bibliographies for further material, esp. for data on tales not listed at all in this bibliography (i.e., Cook's, Summoner's, Squire's, Physician's *Tales; Sir Thopas; Second Nun's,* Manciple's, and Parson's *Tales*).

291. * Bryan, William F., and Dempster, G., eds. *Sources and Analogues of Chaucer's Canterbury Tales.* Chicago, 1941. Reprinted, New York, 1958. An indispensable work for the Chaucer student. Gathers possible sources and analogues to the Prologue and the tales in separate chapters (with a special chapter on *The Wife of Bath's Prologue*), with introductory essays by the divers hands who have collected the material. Comprehensive and reliable.

292. * Owen, Charles A., Jr. "The Crucial Passages in Five of the *Canterbury Tales:* A Study in Irony and Symbol," *JEGP*, LII (1953), 294–311. Has illuminating remarks on the symbolism of the rocks in *The Franklin's Tale;* on the linked images of the garden, the blindness, and the tree in *The Merchant's Tale;* on the gold symbolic of death in *The Pardoner's Tale;* and on the *hominis confusio* of *The Nun's Priest's Tale.* Also comments on

the relation of the tales' meanings to their tellers. (Reprinted in MEB 245.)

Knight's Tale:

293. * Frost, William. "An Interpretation of Chaucer's *Knight's Tale*," *RES*, XXV (1949), 289–304. Demonstrates that the tale as a whole has "three widening concentric circles of interest," the human, the ethical, and the theological. Holds that the emotional focus of the story lies in the conflict between love and comradeship, but that the final meaning lies in an ultimate pattern provided by Providence, into which "the very vicissitudes of life fall. . . ."

294. Ham, Edward B. *"Knight's Tale* 38," *ELH*, XVII (1950), 252–61. Contains a brief, convenient run-down of previous theories. In opposition to Frost and Muscatine, Ham pleads for a return to simplicity in our reading of the tale.

295. * Muscatine, Charles. "Form, Texture, and Meaning in Chaucer's *Knight's Tale*," *PMLA*, LXV (1950), 911–29. Summarizes previous theories. Stresses the poem's complexity, its symmetry, the absence of subtle characterization or thrilling plot. Sees poem as a poetic pageant demonstrating the pursuit of the noble life (Theseus is the central figure in the design), which is a bulwark against the chaos and disorder frequently suggested throughout the poem. (Reprinted in MEB 245.)

296. Underwood, Dale. "The First of *The Canterbury Tales*," *ELH*, XXVI (1959), 455–69. Believes that the theme of the tale reveals divine order through apparent disorder, but that this Boethian meaning is not fully perceived by any of the poem's characters, not even by Theseus.

See also Kaske (MEB 280).

Miller's Tale:

297. Harder, Kelsie B. "Chaucer's Use of the Mystery Plays in the *Miller's Tale*," *MLQ*, XVII (1956), 193–98. Sees a parallel between Chaucer's parody of romances in *Sir Thopas* and what Harder considers his parody of the mystery plays, esp. of the play of the Flood, in this tale.

298. Siegel, Paul N. "Comic Irony in the *Miller's Tale*." *Boston University Studies in English*, IV (1960), 114–20. Suggests that the characters in the fabliau act out of keeping with their avowed religious beliefs, but that their "punishments" are for violations of good sense rather than for moral transgressions. Sees the comedy set against a religious backdrop (of which the teller of the tale is unaware), which lends the tale ironic perspective.

Reeve's Tale:

299. Kaske, Robert E. "An Aube in the *Reeve's Tale,*" *ELH*, XXVI (1959), 295–310. Sees in the parting speech of Aleyn and the miller's daughter a deliberate parody by Chaucer of the conventional aube (aubade or dawn-song) and a possibility that the climactic bedlam burlesques the aube situation itself, with the "watchman," for example (John), "instead of voicing traditional lofty reflections on love, *mesure,* and his own selfless concern for the lover's safety," merely grumbling over *his* being left out of the bed.

Man of Law's Tale:

300. Block, E. A. "Originality, Controlling Purpose, and Craftsmanship in Chaucer's *Man of Law's Tale,*" *PMLA*, LXVIII (1953), 572–616. An exhaustive study, comparing Chaucer's *Tale* with its source (Trivet's *Chronicle*), seeking to determine Chaucer's uniqueness. Considers changes Chaucer made in sequence of events, omissions of details, additions, and passages in which he follows Trivet closely.

Wife of Bath's Tale:

301. * Bradley, C. H. M. (Sister Ritamary). "The *Wife of Bath's Tale* and the Mirror Tradition," *JEGP*, LV (1956), 624–30. Stimulating brief article. Suggests that the Wife's Prologue (the title of this article is misleading) "represents Chaucer's method of comic and ironic characterization . . . built . . . on a contrast between exemplary or mirror values and realistic details," and that the wisdom-folly antithesis of the mirror tradition may be a unifying motif for the whole *Canterbury Tales.*

302. Eisner, Sigmund. *A Tale of Wonder: A Source Study of The Wife of Bath's Tale.* Wexford, Ireland, 1957. A re-examination of the channels of transmission of the "loathly lady" theme in medieval literature, 169-item bibliography.

See also Utley (MEB 39) and Owen (MEB 292).

Friar's Tale:

303. * Cawley, A. C. "Chaucer's Summoner, the Friar's Summoner, and the *Friar's Tale,*" *Proceedings of the Leeds Philosophical and Literary Society* (Literary and Historical Section), VIII (1957), 173–80. Emphasizes the ironies involved. Conveniently summarizes scholarship on subject.

Clerk's Tale:

304. Heninger, S. K., Jr. "The Concept of Order in Chaucer's *Clerk's Tale,*" *JEGP*, LVI (1957), 382–95. Sees the Clerk as a serious

student of medieval theosophy who "naturally accepts the tenets of divinely ordained order"; his tale stresses that this order should be preserved, thus refuting the seductive heresies of the Wife of Bath.

305. Morse, J. Mitchell. "The Philosophy of the Clerk of Oxenford," *MLQ,* XIX (1958), 3–20. Discourses on realist-nominalist controversy, in particular on the influence of Duns Scotus and Ockham, which formed the intellectual milieu of Chaucer's clerk. Finds that the clerk subsumes the dilemmas of his time, that his tale carries realistic authoritarianism to an antisocial extreme to offset the antisocial nominalistic individualism of the Wife of Bath, but that the effect of the tale was to question a set of values then debated in the universities rather than to inculcate an obvious medieval moral.

306. Sledd, James. "The *Clerk's Tale:* The Monsters and the Critics," *MP,* LI (1953), 73–82. Finds the story palatable to a medieval audience and shows Chaucer's skill in presenting it; sees the perspective of the story in terms of Christian implications. (Reprinted in MEB 245.)

Merchant's Tale:

307. * Burrow, J. A. "Irony in the *Merchant's Tale,*" *Anglia,* LXXV (1957), 199–208. Well-presented, illuminating. Finds the tale more solid than the other fabliaux, having more in common, in fact, with the *Pardoner's Tale.* Sees the center of the tale as the ironic contrast between January's dream and the reality. But more than this, Burrow explores sanely and without rigidity allegorical implications and allusions (the earthly paradise, the garden of the *Roman,* the Song of Songs). Suggests that the poem has a dual impulse: a generalizing one (characteristic of allegory) and an ironic or satiric one (characteristic of fabliau) which tends to particularize.

308. Holman, C. Hugh. "Courtly Love in the *Merchant's* and the *Franklin's Tales,*" *ELH,* XVIII (1951), 241–52. Discusses similarities and differences in reference to courtly love. (Reprinted in MEB 245.)

See also Owen (MEB 292).

Franklin's Tale:

309. Benjamin, Edwin B. "The Concept of Order in the *Franklin's Tale,*" *PQ,* XXXVIII (1959), 119–24. Sees the tale as one of harmony disrupted and then restored on a somewhat different basis: Dorigen, a little too frail, traffics with a devil who would

upset cosmic order, but this order is reasserted through Arveragus's honesty and self-sacrifice.
See also Owen (MEB 292) and Holman (MEB 308).

Pardoner's Tale:

310. Sedgewick, G. G. "The Progress of Chaucer's Pardoner, 1880–
1940," *MLQ*, I (1940), 431–58. A convenient review of sixty
years of scholarship. Concludes that Chaucer is not being a sat-
irist: he neither hates nor pities the Pardoner, but presents him
"fully-rounded and without reservation" so that he may "sharpen
our senses against the scourge and blight of Charlatanism." (Reprinted in MEB 245.)
Note: Robinson's summary of the most recent scholarship on the
Pardoner's Tale (e.g., R. P. Miller's allegorical interpretation of the
old man as the *vetus homo, Speculum,* XXX [1955], 180–99) is more
complete than most of his introductory summaries. See also Curry
(MEB 231).

Shipman's Tale:

311. Lawrence, William W. "Chaucer's *Shipman's Tale*," *Speculum,*
XXXIII (1958), 56–68. Argues strongly that the tale was
originally meant for the Wife of Bath and that Chaucer imper-
fectly adapted it to the Shipman: that the tale itself, of all
Chaucer's fabliaux, is closest to the French type and not im-
peded by digressions, *exempla,* and learned citations.

Prioress's Tale:

See Schoeck (MEB 289).

Tale of Melibee:

312. Lawrence, William W. "The Tale of Melibeus," in *Essays and
Studies in Honor of Carleton Brown.* New York, 1940. Pp.
100–10. Finds the tale suited to the taste of a medieval audience,
which liked didacticism and moral allegory. See also Lawrence
(MEB 281).

Monk's Tale:

See Robertson (MEB 271), Kaske (MEB 280), and Farnham (MEB
341).

Nun's Priest's Tale:

313. Severs, J. B. "Chaucer's Originality in the *Nun's Priest's Tale*,"
SP, XLIII (1946), 22–41. Compares the tale with the *Roman de
Renart.* Sees the change in the direction of the tale as demon-

strating antifeminist moral, which is appropriate in the mouth of a priest. Cf. Lawrence (MEB 281).

See also Ford (MEB 2) and Owen (MEB 292). Robinson's introductory notes to this Tale summarize recent allegorical interpretations (e.g., C. A. Dahlberg's interpretation of the cock as Clergy, widow as Church, etc., *JEGP,* LIII [1954], 277–90).

Canon's Yeoman's Tale:

See Muscatine (MEB 235).

XIV. FIFTEENTH-CENTURY CHAUCERIANS

A. *Lydgate*

314. MacCracken, Henry N., ed. *The Minor Poems of John Lydgate.* 2 vols. EETSES 107 and EETS 192. London, 1911–34. For EETS editions of *The Troy Book, Siege of Thebes,* etc., see pp. 295–96 of Baugh (MEB 47) or *CBEL.*

315. Ayers, Robert W. "Medieval History, Moral Purpose, and the Structure of Lydgate's *Siege of Thebes," PMLA,* LXXIII (1958), 463–74. Argues that structure of this 4,716-line work (which Lydgate presented as a supplement to *The Canterbury Tales*) is integral if we understand that Lydgate was writing to inculcate "moral and political lessons by reference to what he regarded as ancient historical example"—he was not writing narrative fiction, as has been assumed by critics. Philosophical framework of poem is Boethian; and despite the obvious social tone of the poem, moral unity becomes of central importance in the final juxtaposition of the changing earthly and the unchanging eternal values.

See also Farnham (MEB 341).

B. *Hoccleve*

316. Furnivall, F. J., and Gollancz, I., eds., *Hoccleve's Works.* 3 vols. EETS 61, 72, 73. London, 1892–1925.

On Lydgate and Hoccleve, see also Hammond (MEB 3) and Bennett (MEB 55).

C. *Scottish Chaucerians*

General Studies:

317. *Kinsley, James. "The Medieval Makars," in *Scottish Poetry: A Critical Survey,* ed. J. Kinsley. London, 1955. Pp. 1–32. An excellent history of this group. The whole volume, ten essays in

all, makes excellent reading. Sir James Fergusson has a refreshing essay on "The Ballads."

318. Speirs, John. *The Scots Literary Tradition: An Essay in Criticism*. London, 1940. A series of essays including studies of the *Kingis Quair*, Henryson, Dunbar, etc., the fullest being on Henryson.

319. Wittig, Kurt. *The Scottish Tradition in Literature*. Edinburgh and London, 1958. More an exposition of moral, aesthetic, and intellectual values in Scottish literature than a history of that literature. Part I, Spring Tide, treats Barbour, Henryson, Dunbar, Douglas, Lyndsay, minor Middle Scots poets, and the Scottish ballads. Some bibliographical references in footnotes.

Henryson:

320. Wood, H. Harvey, ed. *The Poems and Fables of Robert Henryson*. 2nd ed., rev. Edinburgh and London, 1958.

321. Stearns, Marshall. *Robert Henryson*. New York and London, 1949. A full-length study, setting Henryson against the background of his age and providing some critical examination of his poetry, with special reference to the *Testament of Cresseid* and its relation to Chaucer.

See also Ford (MEB 2), and Moore, *The Secular Lyric* (MEB 123).

Kingis Quair:

322. MacKenzie, W. Mackay, ed. *The Kingis Quair*. London, 1939. Introduction spends much time on authorship, demolishing the tradition of its autobiographical nature and attribution to James I of Scotland.

323. Markland, Murray F. "The Structure of *The Kingis Quair*," *RSSCW*, XXV (1957), 273–86. Rejecting the autobiographical interpretation, author sees Fortune as the subject of the poem. Poem reverses *De Casibus* tradition in showing rise in Fortune's wheel as virtuous love and wisdom help man to influence Fortune. Poem asserts a measure of responsibility for man to live virtuously within the Providence of God.

324. Preston, John. "Fortunys Exiltree: A Study of *The Kingis Quair*," *RES*, N.S. VII (1956), 339–47. Argues that the poem is not "the first modern book of love" but a dream-vision in the medieval allegorical tradition, with its possibilities of organizing and even of synthesizing diverse experiences. Holds that the poem's distinction lies in its developed meaning, not in its romantic core.

Dunbar:

325. Kinsley, James, ed. *Dunbar's Poems.* Oxford, 1958. A very attractive selection, with some appreciations, an introduction, notes, and glossary.

326. Baxter, J. W. *William Dunbar: A Biographical Study.* Edinburgh, 1952. A useful biography, with some commentary on the poems interspersed. Bibliography and index.

327. Fox, Denton, "Dunbar's *The Golden Targe,*" *ELH,* XXVI (1959), 311–34. Attempts to rescue this poem from scholarly and critical neglect or disparagement by reappraising the aureate style in which it is written.

328. Hyde, Isabel. "Primary Sources and Associations of Dunbar's Aureate Imagery," *MLR,* LI (1956), 481–92. Concludes that Dunbar used conventional material but that he used it with originality and poetic vitality.

329. * Morgan, Edwin. "Dunbar and the Language of Poetry," *EIC,* II (1952), 138–58. A very good introduction to the Middle Scots tradition and to Dunbar in particular. Finds four forms in Middle Scots poetry: the simple aureate style; the antiaureate; a lyrical run or lilt, the fusion of native alliteration and French-based verse-form; satirical invective and "flyting." Then examines Dunbar at some length, concluding that his main interest in poetry was formal rather than contentual.

See also Ford (MEB 2), Lewis (MEB 26) and Moore (MEB 123). On Barbour's *Bruce,* see MEB 87.

XV. DRAMA

A. *Collections and Editions*

330. Adams, Joseph Q., ed. *Chief Pre-Shakespearean Dramas.* Boston, 1924. A convenient and generous anthology, beginning with "Sources of the Liturgical Drama" and running through the Craft Cycles and Non-Cycle Plays into the 16th C. Latin is translated; Middle English texts have good notes for difficult words. Some running critical commentary.

331. Furnivall, F. J., and Pollard, A. W., eds. *The Macro Plays: Mankind, Wisdom, The Castle of Perseverance.* EETSES 91. London, 1904.

332. Hussey, Maurice, ed. *The Chester Mystery Plays: Sixteen Pageant Plays from the Chester Craft Cycle, Adapted into Modern English.* London, 1957. Contains a brief introduction and an appendix on "Hints on Production."

333. * Pollard, Alfred W. *English Miracle Plays, Moralities and Interludes.* 8th ed. London, 1927. Contains the texts of the more important medieval plays, including *The Second Shepherds' Play* and *Everyman* (with some omission of lines). Valuable introduction.

334. Purvis, John S. *The York Cycle of Mystery Plays, A Complete Version.* New York, 1957. Contains only the text in a "compromised" modern version and a very brief foreword.

B. *Bibliographies*

335. Stratman, Carl L. *Bibliography of Medieval Drama.* Berkeley and Los Angeles, Calif., 1954. Stars important and authoritative items. Includes dissertations and some reviews of major books. For some strictures on its usefulness, see T. W. Baldwin, *JEGP,* LIV (1955), 405–407.

336. * Henshaw, Millett. "A Survey of Studies in Medieval Drama: 1933–1950," *Progress of Medieval and Renaissance Studies in the United States and Canada,* Bulletin No. 21, 1951. Extremely useful, scholarly, annotated survey.

See also Chambers, *English Literature at the Close of the Middle Ages* (MEB 56).

C. *Studies*

Recent scholarship on medieval drama has challenged the traditional view of the "natural evolution" of the mystery cycles, a view identified primarily with E. K. Chambers (MEB 339) and reinforced by H. Craig (MEB 340). Among the iconoclasts may be noted Gardiner, Salter, Southern, and Wickham (MEB 342, 347, 348, 349).

General Studies:

The first two items below give brief historical surveys.

337. * Nicoll, Allardyce. *British Drama: An Historical Survey from the Beginning to the Present.* 4th ed. London, 1946. Reprinted by Barnes & Noble, Inc., 1957. A standard "short view" of the drama. Has some 100 pages devoted to the Middle Ages. Sees medieval plays as created by the common people, with attendant vices and virtues: naïveté, crudeness, lack of artistic sense on the one hand; simple humor, freshness, etc., on the other. The views presented here have been challenged by later critics: see this section, *passim.*

338. * Parrott, Thomas M., and Ball, R. H. *A Short View of Elizabethan Drama.* New York, 1943, 1958. Chapter I, on the Medieval Background: Cycles, Morals, and Interludes, provides a brief, clear account of medieval drama. In paperback edition now with revised (1958) bibliography.

339. * Chambers, Edmund K. *The Medieval Stage.* 2 vols. Oxford, 1903. Reprinted, 1954. A fundamental work. Has sections on Minstrelsy, Folk-Drama, Religious Drama, Interlude. Traces history from Graeco-Roman theatrical breakdown: first two sections deal with secular, third with religious, fourth with transformation of medieval stage under the impact of humanism. More concerned with organization and local distribution of miracle plays than with dramatic and literary qualities.

340. Craig, Hardin. *English Religious Drama of the Middle Ages.* Oxford, 1955. Valuable book, supplementing Chambers (MEB 339) and Young (MEB 351), though parts are quite specialized and hence difficult for general reader and undergraduate. Sees medieval drama as primarily religious, secondarily aesthetic. Plays grew and varied according to locality of production. Argues for theory that York and Wakefield Plays were originally identical, the latter having borrowed the entire cycle from the former, prior to 1390. Second half of book examines individual plays in some detail, though the *Second Shepherds' Play* gets short shrift.

341. * Farnham, Willard. *The Medieval Heritage of Elizabethan Tragedy.* Berkeley, Calif., 1936. Reprinted by Barnes & Noble, Inc., 1957. Traces tragedy from the nondramatic *De Casibus Illustrium Virorum* of Boccaccio, and its statement of the medieval concept of tragedy, through Chaucer (*Monk's Tale* and *Troilus*) and Lydgate, etc. Then discusses the combination of this heritage with neoclassic elements derived from Senecan tragedy in the Elizabethan theater.

342. Gardiner, Harold C. *Mysteries' End: An Investigation of the Last Days of the Medieval Religious Stage.* Yale Studies in English, CIII. New Haven, Conn., and Oxford, 1946. Challenges the traditional view of the "natural" evolution of drama (its secularization) from church to churchyard, to street and market place, to hall, to inn yard, to theater. Also ascribes the disappearance of the mystery plays not to financial difficulties of guilds and growth of new literary interests, as is often maintained, but to a return by the Church to the hostile attitude of the Fathers toward drama and its imposition of this view "from the top."

343. Gayley, Charles M. *Plays of Our Forefathers.* New York, 1907. Studies the traditions behind medieval drama; especially helpful on the tradition of humor.

344. Greg, Walter W. *Bibliographical and Textual Problems of the English Miracle Cycles.* London, 1914. Four essays, originally lectures, examining the cycles. Shows relationship of bibliography to literary criticism and then demonstrates this twofold approach on the Chester cycle, the interrelationship of the York and Wakefield cycles, and the Ludus Coventriae.

345. Nicoll, Allardyce. *Masks, Mimes, and Miracles.* New York and London, 1931. A survey of popular drama from early Greek comedy to the *commedia dell' arte.* Nicoll suggests that early liturgical plays were simplifications of religious themes already existing in Byzantium and transmitted to west via medieval mimes. *Book contains 226 illustrations, bibliography.*

346. Rossiter, A. P. *English Drama from Early Times to the Elizabethans.* London, 1950. Reprinted by Barnes & Noble, Inc., 1958. A compendious literary history, packed into 176 pages, going back beyond liturgical drama to pagan rituals, mimes, etc. Especially good on the craft plays and on the rise and significance of allegory. Challenges opinion about creation of medieval plays by common people.

347. * Salter, Frederick M. *Medieval Drama in Chester.* Toronto, 1955. A pleasant series of essays, originally lectures, on the growth of drama in production and performance in Chester. Treats the plays as art and relates them to origins of Elizabethan drama. Good notes, especially valuable because in them Salter carries on his argument against the traditional view associated with Chambers. For some strictures, see E. Colledge, *RES,* N.S. VIII (1957), 183–84.

348. Southern, Richard. *The Medieval Theatre in the Round: A Study of the Staging of the Castle of Perseverance and Related Matters.* London, 1957; New York, 1958. An important account of the staging of this morality. Argues cogently that the method of presentation was not "crude, occasional, primitive," but one which reflected an elaborate *professional* tradition. Argues that the *place* where the action chiefly occurred corresponds to the *pit* (this did *not* evolve into the Elizabethan platform stage, as Chambers, Nicoll, *et al.,* have claimed), though the action also took place on scaffolds linked to the central "round." Study implies a closed theater (an amphitheater) and tends to confirm the anti-Chambers movement. Fascinating illustrations.

349. Wickham, Glynne. *Early English Stages: 1300 to 1660.* Vol. I: 1300 to 1576. London and New York, 1959. An important book, upholding the Gardiner-Salter view of medieval drama. Bk. I of this volume discusses open-air entertainments (tournaments, pageants, miracles); Bk. II discusses indoor entertainments (minstrelsy, mummings, masks, moralities, interludes); Bk. III deals with medieval dramatic theory and practice. Argues that the cycles were civic events in which the Church gladly participated and which the Church supervised (miracle plays *never* passed from hands of clergy to laity). Patient did not die a natural death (see Gardiner MEB 342) but was put to death by the

Reformed Church. For adverse review, see *Renaissance News*, XIII (Summer 1960), 157–62.

350. Williams, Arnold. *The Characterization of Pilate in the Towneley Plays.* East Lansing, Mich., and Oxford, 1950. A scholarly and stimulating study of the artistry involved in the Towneley Pilate, who is consistently villainous and tragic. (The medieval Pilate was both "good" and "bad," and other cycles represent him as a mixture.) Studies the character from points of view of literary heritage, dramatic structure, social satire, and textual problems.

351. Young, Karl. *The Drama of the Medieval Church.* 2 vols. Oxford, 1933. A basic collection of Latin Church drama with a running commentary on the Latin texts. Sees these liturgical plays "as a spontaneous new birth and growth within the confines of Christian worship." No translation. Bibliography.

Studies of Individual Plays:

a) Everyman:

352. * Ryan, Lawrence V. "Doctrine and Dramatic Structure in *Everyman*," *Speculum*, XXXII (1957), 722–35. Through an analysis of structure and doctrine, shows that the success of the play is dependent on "the representation of an action which brings into harmony the natural, dramatic, and theological elements of Everyman's experience." Finds crucial to an understanding of the play's doctrine the recognition that the character Knowledge means "acknowledgement of sins."

353. de Vocht, Henry. *Everyman: A Comparative Study of Texts and Sources.* Materials for the Study of the Old English Drama, N.S. XX. Louvain, Belgium, 1947. Finds the English play superior to the Dutch in its content if not in its form, and gives priority in time of composition to the former. See review by Zandvoort, *RES*, XXV (1949), 66–8, for devastating criticism.

354. Zandvoort, R. W. "Elckerlijc—Everyman," *ES*, XXIII (1941), 1–9. Presents a summary of the controversy over the relationship between the Dutch and English plays, concluding, after an analysis, that the correspondences between the plays preclude the theory that they are both translations of a French or Latin original; argues that the English play must be a translation of the Dutch, and not vice versa, and that the English play, while inferior to the Dutch, is still good.

b) The Shepherds' Plays:

355. * Watt, Homer A. "The Dramatic Unity of the 'Secunda Pastorum'," in *Essays in Honor of Carleton Brown.* New York, 1940. Pp. 158–66. A very pleasant little essay, pointing out the parallels

contributing to the unity of the Mak episode and the Nativity scene, and maintaining that the theme of childbirth, comic in the first part and serious in the second, dominates the play.

356. Zumwalt, Eugene E. "Irony in the Towneley *Shepherds' Plays*," *RSSCW*, XXVI (1958), 37–53. Suggests that the plays "provide materials that suggest skepticism about the Being of Christ and the efficacy of providential order, and thus a vision of a disordered and potentially tragic cosmos" antedating the Elizabethan tragic vision—though the plays are complex syntheses of hope and despair, held in ironic counterbalance.

See also Bloomfield, *Seven Deadly Sins* (MEB 30), Owst, *Literature and Pulpit* (MEB 34), and Chambers, *English Literature at the Close of the Middle Ages* (MEB 56).

INDEX

A number followed by an asterisk (*) indicates that the reference is to the bibliographical section of the book. All references are to pages.

Teseide (Boccaccio), 221
Testament of Cresseid, The (Henryson), 262–63, 375 *
Testament of Love, The (Usk), 136
allegory in, 339 *
Teutonic (language), 13
Theobaldus, 179
Theodore of Tarsus, Archbishop of Canterbury, 10
Theophrastus, "characters" in *Ancrene Riwle,* 123
Thistle and the Rose, The (Dunbar), 263
Thomas (Anglo-Norman Poet), 110
Thomas of Hales, Friar, 144–45
Thomson, Virgil, 148
Thor, 4
To The Nightingale (Milton), 177
Towneley Plays. See Wakefield Cycle
Tragedy, in Chaucer, 205, 251, 364 *
medieval concept of, 109, 203–4, 261, 341 *, 365 *
Senecan, 378 *
Travels of Sir John Mandeville, The, 133–35
authorship, 133, 338 *
Treatise on the Astrolabe (Chaucer), 202, 360 *
Trevisa, John, 137, 339 *
Tristan and Isolde (Wagner), 97, 102, 107
Trivet, Nicholas, 227, 371 *
Troilus and Cressida (Shakespeare), 206, 238
Troilus and Criseyde (Chaucer), 94, 136, 193, 198, 199, 200, 201, 202–8, 258, 331 *, 358 *, 359 *, 363–66 *
artistry and structure, 202–3, 205–8, 357 *, 365 *
Christianity and, 204–5, 207–8
and Henryson, 263
and *Knight's Tale,* 223
narrator in, 206–7
as romance, 119
sources, 193, 202, 364 *, 365 *
texts and translations, 354 *, 355 *
and tragedy, 109, 203–4, 328 *, 365 *, 378 *
Tropes, 268, 270–72
Troubadours, 91, 140, 267–68
Troy Book (Lydgate), 117, 260–61, 374 *
Troy Legend, 116–17

Truth: Balade de Bon Conseyl (Chaucer), 94, 201, 265
Truth Is Unpopular, 189
Twa Sisters, The, 149
Two Gentlemen of Verona, The, friendship in, 108
Two Married Women and the Widow, The (Dunbar), 263, 264

Ubi Sunt, literary theme, 47, 144–45, 300 *
Ubi Sunt Qui Ante Nos Fuerunt (Middle English lyric), 144
Ugolino, Earl of Pisa, in Chaucer and Dante, 251
Understatement. *See* Litotes
Universal History (Orosius), 69–70
Usk, Thomas, 136, 339 *

Variation, rhetorical device in Old English poetry, 20
Vaughan Williams, Ralph, 148
Velisurmaaja (Swedish ballad) and *Edward,* 149
Vercelli Book, 21, 292 *
Vercelli Book Homilies, 72
Vikings, 11, 82
Villon, François, 145
Vinaver, Eugène, edition of Malory, 104, 105, 334–35 *
Violanta of Milan, 362 *
Virgil, 35n, 96, 306 *, 309 *
and *Beowulf* poet, 35n, 306 *, 309 *
Virgin Mary, 145, 146–47
in ballads, 150
in lyrics, 139–40
miracles of, 247–48
Vision of the Cross. See Dream of the Rood
Vision of Willliam Concerning Piers the Plowman. See Piers Plowman
Vita, of Guthlac (Felix of Croyland's), 61, 318 *
Volsunga Saga, 304 *
Vox Clamantis (Gower), 182–83

Wace, 99–100
Wagner, Richard, 31, 97, 102, 107
Wakefield Cycle, 272, 380 *, 381 *
and *York Cycle,* 273, 378 *
"Wakefield Master, The," 274, 277
Waldere, 24, 25–26, 304 *
Walküre, Die, 31

NELSON'S MEDIEVAL AND RENAISSANCE LIBRARY

BARNES & NOBLE, INC., *American Publishers*
C. S. LEWIS, *General Editor*

OTHER RELATED BOOKS PUBLISHED BY BARNES & NOBLE